I0884767

Radical Origins

Radical Origins

Early Mormon Converts and Their Colonial Ancestors

VAL D. RUST

University of Illinois Press
URBANA AND CHICAGO

© 2004 by the Board of Trustees
of the University of Illinois
All rights reserved

♾ This book is printed on acid-free paper.

Library of Congress Cataloging-in-Publication Data
Rust, Val Dean.
Radical origins : early Mormon converts and their colonial ancestors /
Val D. Rust.
p. cm.
Includes bibliographical references and index.
ISBN 0-252-02910-0 (cloth : alk. paper)
1. Mormon converts—Biography. 2. Mormons—Genealogy. 3. Church
of Jesus Christ of Latter day Saints—Genealogy. 4. Mormon Church—
Genealogy. 5. United States—Biography. 6. United States—History—
Colonial period, ca. 1600–1775. I. Title.
BX8693.R87 2004
289.3'09'034—dc22 2003019683

For Tyler and Stephanie,
who will carry on the tradition

Contents

Preface

Mormons speak about the importance of forerunners who prepared the way for the restoration of the church of Jesus Christ in these latter days. This book is about a special set of forerunners, the ancestors of the early converts to the Mormon church. My involvement in studying these Mormon converts began as a personal quest, but it soon expanded to an analysis of the place of the Church of Jesus Christ of Latter-day Saints (LDS) in American history. Among the early LDS converts were several of my own great-great-grandparents. When I was a child, my parents often told me that the ancestors of these great-great-grandparent converts were among the first to settle colonial America, some two hundred years prior to the founding of the LDS Church. In addition, they told me that these early American ancestors were known as nonconformists and that there was spiritual significance in the fact that they were religious radicals. However, those connections were never entirely clear to me.

As a historian, I was curious to see if the family histories of those first converts in my family were similar to the histories of others baptized into the church in the 1830s, and so I have spent several years tracing the genealogical records of 583 early LDS converts baptized between 1830, when the church was organized, and 1835 (about 40 percent of the early membership). What I discovered about the ancestors of these converts was surprising.

First, I found that they were a distinctive population in New York and in Ohio, where the Mormon church was first organized. Most people living in New York State in the early 1800s were born there and were from families that had been in the state for one or more generations. At that same time, the state of Ohio, in contrast, was being settled by migrants, who were more likely to have come from the Middle Atlantic and southern states than from New England. Early Mormon converts deviated from both these groups in that they had usually been born in New England and had migrated to New York or Ohio.

Second, I found that almost all early LDS converts were descended from forebears who had lived in New England for six or seven generations. In fact, I was able to identify more than 10,000 fifth-generation progenitors of these 583 early converts (see appendix), representing at least 20 percent of the population of New England in the middle of the 1600s. Almost all of them were among the first generation of Europeans to live in New England.

Third, these ancestors lived mostly in the more religiously radical towns of New England. Of course, they were found in most settlements because they constituted such a large portion of the population, but they were greatly overrepresented in towns known for unusual religious beliefs and practices. Many of them had been ostracized and expelled from Massachusetts Bay Colony, and some had been whipped, mutilated, and hanged for their religious beliefs. Others lived in New Hampshire and Rhode Island, regions of New England that were known for their unorthodox religious orientations. Some of them belonged to religious groups representing the radical segment of the Protestant Reformation, including Antinomians, Seekers, Anabaptists, Quakers, and the Family of Love.

This is the story of the religious experiences and orientations of these early ancestors of LDS converts. Did the religious beliefs of these ancestors dispose their descendants to embrace the radical message of Joseph Smith Jr. and to contribute to the formation of a new ("American") religion? Historians have drawn attention to the place of the Mormons in American frontier history. In this book, I extend the place of Mormons beyond their recent historical role and argue that the Mormon story has implications for understanding the larger context of American colonial history. It is my hope that this book will contribute to a better understanding of the LDS Church and its place in American culture and history.

There is some disagreement among historians as to the historical source of the so-called American religion, of which Mormonism is considered a prime example. Conventional historical tradition holds that the American religion is deeply rooted in early New England's Puritan experience. More recently, scholars have argued that the American religion sprang from the First Great Awakening during the eighteenth century. While arguments for both positions are persuasive and complementary, I present evidence for a third point of view. Insofar as Mormonism is one expression of the American religion, it is grounded in the early colonial period but springs more from the tradition of radical religious content than from mainstream Puritanism.

I also raise time and space questions concerning the continuity of attitudes and values of a people. The early Mormon converts were part of a community of believers sharing a historical background and radical spiritual orientation that had been cultivated and honed over a number of generations. They came from families whose community histories may have predisposed them to resonate with the message that the gospel of Jesus Christ had been restored on earth in these latter days. It is not clear whether such a predisposition can be attributed to geography, to genes, to psychology, or to God, but it suggests a strong sense of continuity across the generations of families. Indeed, the religious orientation and values of the fathers are visited upon the children unto the fifth and sixth generations.

Acknowledgments

My deepest thanks go to my colleague Marijana Benesh Weiner, who participated in the development of the ideas presented herein and who was my personal editor. My son Joshua kept the computer alive and working as I struggled with the software, figures, and maps. The libraries of the University of California at Los Angeles and Irvine are wonderful repositories of primary and secondary sources. Appreciation also must be expressed to the Mormon church, which has created the largest genealogical database in the world. These records are now available on-line through FamilySearch at <http://familysearch.org>.

Radical Origins

1. Early Mormons: A Peculiar People

An American Religion

The Church of Jesus Christ of Latter-day Saints has a special place in American culture. Founded by Joseph Smith Jr. in 1830, in the "burned-over district" of upstate New York,[1] the Mormon church began as an American religion and remains so today, embodying such optimistic notions as material and social progress, the unlimited potential of each individual, and the capacity for free moral choice. Its moral code of loyalty, trustworthiness, obedience, discipline, cheerfulness, thriftiness, and cleanliness reads like the Boy Scout Law. Its nineteenth-century communitarian ethos has jelled smoothly with free-market principles of capitalism, melding into an orientation that is both liberal and conservative and uniquely characteristic of America.[2]

Even though the Mormon church has been described as "very American, sometimes super American,"[3] the Church of Jesus Christ of Latter-day Saints is so peculiar that many feel it isn't even Christian. Mormons speak freely of angels, visitations, visions, dreams, and revelations. They believe the president of their church is a literal prophet, seer, and revelator. They have assurance that anyone with the desire can directly know God and his divine plan. Mormons believe Christ took his original church away from the earth because its people fell into a state of apostasy; however, Mormons maintain, he restored his gospel in its celestial purity in these latter days through divine intervention. They accept the Bible to be the word of God but also rely on other ancient and modern scripture. They take for granted that "gifts of the Spirit" are as present today as in ancient times, including the power and capacity to heal the sick, prophesy, work miracles, discern diverse spirits, speak in tongues, and interpret the words of those who speak in tongues.[4] They believe not only in contemporary social and material progress but in Eternal Progress. They believe that everyone, literally, "was in the beginning with God."[5] They hold the assurance that every single person, whether good or bad, possesses a spark of the divine, and that those who endure will one day become gods, ruling as husbands and wives over their own worlds and civilizations. They believe their mission is to prepare for the second coming of Jesus Christ.

Mormonism holds a special place in its doctrine for the New World. Mormons claim the Garden of Eden was located in what is now Missouri. According to Mormon scripture, Christ visited America after his resurrection and there established his gospel; the Savior will reside in America in a New Jerusalem at the time of his second coming. The Book of Mormon gives a historical accounting of the ancient Americas and testifies that this is a land of promise, "choice above all other lands" and "consecrated" for the restoration of the gospel.[6]

Incredible as these beliefs may seem to the typical American, Harold Bloom believes they are the logical conclusion of the American belief that each person is a child of God, who loves each one directly and intimately. Mormons believe they can attain the Godhood that their father in heaven enjoys. Bloom calls Mormonism the "American Religion."[7]

The Church of Jesus Christ of Latter-day Saints was established in 1830 at the time a general religious revival was taking place in America. This revival has often been called the Second Great Awakening; the First Great Awakening took place the century before, peaking between 1739 and 1742.[8] The Mormon church was but one of many new religious groups that came into being at the time, particularly in western New York. Whereas most of these religious groups were short-lived, by the mid-1840s the Mormon church was well on its way to becoming one of the permanent manifestations of the spiritual and social ferment of the time.

The LDS Church experienced hostility and persecution in its early years, and many Americans continue to think of Mormons as alien and different from the American mainstream. However, Mormon doctrines reflect almost every facet of the Second Great Awakening. Mormons were evangelists, proclaiming the good news of Jesus Christ as ardently as did Charles G. Finney and Dwight L. Moody, the preachers best known for the fervent evangelism of the time. Mormons were universalists, announcing Christ's sacrifice was valid for all of God's children. Mormons were adventists, proclaiming the imminent return of Jesus Christ. Mormons were millennialists, believing the reappearance of Christ would be accompanied by catastrophic signs and wonders, destroying the wicked and allowing Christ to set up the New Jerusalem in Jackson County, Missouri, where he would dwell with the Saints for a thousand years. Mormons were communalists, dedicated to establishing an ideal collective economic community, banding together in a cooperative enterprise to form Christ's perfect religious and social order. Mormons were spiritualists, emphasizing a tangible spirit world accessible to those in the mortal world.

The Second Great Awakening was directed toward more than spiritual doctrines and religious change. It also translated into social reconstruction, and early Mormons espoused almost every aspect of this reform movement. Mormons advocated temperance and even abstinence in the use of alcohol, tobacco, tea, and coffee. They emphasized universal education to unleash the unlimited potential of all. They were abolitionists, dedicating themselves to freeing all slaves and helping them find honorable labor. They advocated prison reform and the positive rehabilitation of criminals. And they advocated a reformed national government that would rid itself of factions, patronage, and tangled alliances and would work in harmony with the simple ideas of representative democracy to help create a more perfect union.[9]

Another aspect of the Second Great Awakening was its populist and egalitarian focus. Mormons also believed the common person had the right to shape his or her own religious destiny. The Book of Mormon is, according to historian Nathan O. Hatch, "a document of profound social protest, an impassioned manifesto against the smug complacency of those in power and the reality of social distinction based on wealth, class, and education."[10] The early LDS Church exemplified populist themes and rejected the pride and arrogance that comes with economic success and worldly learning.

The American aspects of Mormonism cannot be located solely in the doctrinal and social reconstruction elements of the First or Second Great Awakenings. It remains in what Harold Bloom describes as the "inner and formless forms of our national faith," in the "perpetual shock of the individual discovering . . . that God loves her and him on an absolutely personal and indeed intimate basis." The American aspects of Mormonism are located in a form of gnosis, an implicit knowing, that God speaks to us not only through the Bible but also through "replacement scriptures" such as the Book of Mormon, Pearl of Great Price, and Doctrine and Covenants. Such documents are found not only in the LDS Church but also in other "American" churches that honor their own texts, such as *Science and Health, Spiritual Gifts, Spirit of Prophecy,* and the *Watchtower.*[11] According to Bloom, these scriptures are not found in traditional Christianity but among Mormons, Seventh-day Adventists, Christian Scientists, and other "peculiarly American varieties of spiritual experience."[12]

Mormonism and Forerunners

Mormons maintain that America played a special role in preparing for the restoration of the gospel of Jesus Christ. With the assistance of God, they believe, Columbus discovered the "promised land" and opened the way for its settlement. God stirred the leaders of the American colonies to rebel against the British in order to build the foundation for a land of freedom. Thomas Jefferson joined with others in crafting a divinely inspired American constitution, which enabled the gospel of Jesus Christ to take root and thrive.[13]

It is a central doctrine of the Mormon church that God prepared the way for the restoration of the gospel of Jesus Christ in these latter days. Even though all individuals make free, personal choices, God participates with them in these decisions. According to this view, the leaders of the Renaissance, the Reformation, and the Enlightenment can be seen as joining with God in fulfilling a grand design.[14] Mormons believe that God moved Erasmus to challenge the formalistic piety of the Catholic Church and to emphasize a return to the simple, moral principles of Christian life. He inspired Martin Luther and other reformers to defy religious evils of their day and make the Bible available to all. He helped Copernicus to conceive a new vision of the universe and stimulated Isaac Newton to discover the basic rules that God had applied in organizing (creating) that universe.

But pathfinders or forerunners are not only outstanding historical figures; they may also be ordinary people. Unfortunately, we rarely learn much about such people because little documentary evidence about them is available. In this book, I undertake the difficult task to describe and analyze a special set of forerunners of the Mormon church, the colonial ancestors of those who responded directly to the radical religious message of Joseph Smith Jr. (1805–44) and made it their own.

I am exploring an innovative way of doing history. In the late 1960s and early 1970s, American historians began studying the colonial beginnings of the nation by using census data and other "silent" records to reconstruct the history of New England towns. From those reconstructions, it was thought, it should be possible to look at what happened to the descendants of the populations of various towns in order to grasp the American social order, economic elites, and all sorts of other communities. In this study, I have turned that method on its head by starting with members of a particular religious group and then tracing their ancestors. In this way, records that initially appear to be silent begin to reveal valuable information.

At its founding, the message of the LDS Church was so revolutionary that it demanded a certain spiritual predisposition on the part of those who were attracted to it. I am certainly not the first to make this claim. John Brooke, in his important study of the roots of Mormonism, also contends that Mormon cosmology did not arise in a vacuum but had deep roots in the American colonial experience.[15] My claim, that those who were drawn to the message of Joseph Smith Jr., especially in the earliest years, likely had family and community histories that predisposed them to resonate with that message, is consistent with Brooke's analysis. The early converts to the LDS Church shared a historical background and radical spiritual orientation that had been cultivated and honed over a number of generations.

Brooke and I both argue that the Mormon story goes back beyond American history since the 1830s and has implications for an understanding of the larger context of American colonial history. But Brooke and I differ importantly in our understanding of both the nature as well as the historical roots of Mormon beliefs and spiritual expression. He connects Mormonism with "restorationism and paradisial universalism" and a whole range of practices that he labels "hermeticism," including Freemasonry, Rosicrucianism, and other manifestations of the occult.[16] He reminds us that there were two broad movements of migrants from England across the Atlantic Ocean to the colonies. The first took place with the founding of the Plymouth and Massachusetts Bay Colonies in the 1620s and early 1630s; the second took place after the 1660s with the restoration of the crown to the Stuarts. The Acts of Uniformity, passed at this time, required everyone in England to conform to the Church of England. Some of them refused and set up their own churches, and many of these so-called nonconformists left for the colonies.

Brooke claims that hermeticism had little to do with the early Puritans coming to New England; rather, it arrived with the migration of the second wave of immigrants coming to America, particularly to the Middle Atlantic region. He therefore concludes that the roots of Mormonism originated with the second migration, taking place after 1660.

However, my data clearly indicate that almost all of the thousands of ancestors of early LDS converts had settled New England during the first migration and were already established before the second wave of migrants arrived and dispersed throughout New York and the Middle Atlantic colonies. Brooke agrees that Mormonism is connected with early New England, and he observes that this presents a "paradox" for his analysis in that the occult phenomena he connects with Mormons "must have taken a different route than that through Puritan culture in orthodox New England."[17]

I argue that there was a different type of religious radicalism among the LDS ancestors than that identified by Brooke as hermeticism and occultism. These ancestors had indeed settled in New England, but they constituted a radical fringe element in a Puritan landscape. And they came to live in parts of New England where they might escape Puritan influence and give expression to a more radical spirit, one characterized by a belief that miracles and direct spiritual communication with God were open to all, rather than only to those who possessed specialized "hermetic" knowledge of magic practices and specialized occult ritual.

Early LDS Church Membership

The Mormon church began on 6 April 1830 with 6 members. About two months after the church was organized, the minutes of the first general conference, held on 9 June 1830 in Fayette, New York, reported 27 members; the minutes of the second general conference, held about four months later on 26–28 September 1830, again in Fayette, reported 62 members.[18] Church membership was first centered in the small towns of Manchester, Fayette, and Colesville, New York, as well as in Harmony, Pennsylvania, towns that were at the time being settled by recent migrants. The names of approximately 140 individuals have been identified who were baptized during the so-called New York–Pennsylvania period, which lasted until the early winter of 1830–31, at which time most of these Saints moved down the Erie Canal and along Lake Erie to Kirtland, Ohio (see figure 1).[19]

A first surge in LDS Church membership began in the fall of 1830, a few months before the Saints left the New York and Pennsylvania region. Parley P. Pratt, Ziba Peterson, Oliver Cowdery, and Peter Whitmer Jr. were on their way to the "wilderness" to declare the gospel to the Indians, and they passed

Figure 1. New York and Ohio about 1830

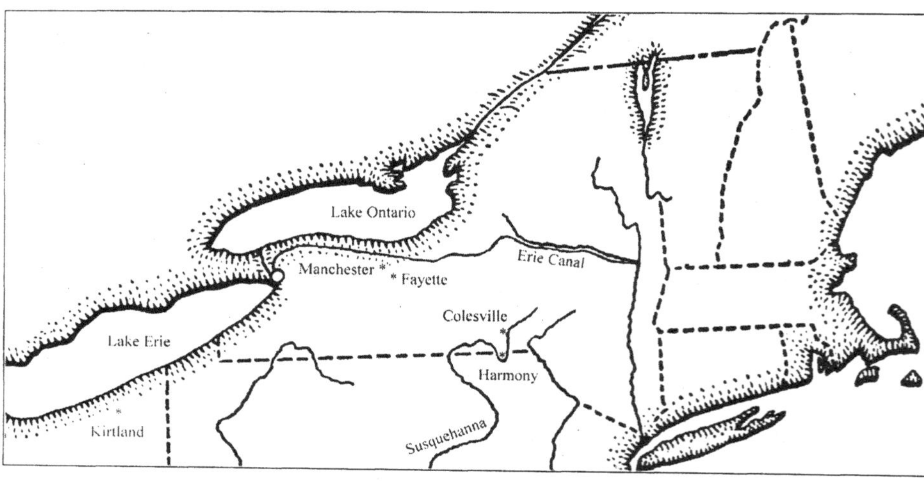

through Ohio, where Pratt had lived for a time.[20] The visit in Ohio was fortuitous; they sought out a local leader of the so-called Campbellites whom Pratt had known, Sidney Rigdon (1793–1876), who had become dissatisfied with many of Alexander Campbell's doctrines and was seeking other means to restore "the ancient order of things," including "supernatural gifts and miracles."[21]

During that first visit, Pratt reported that the missionaries baptized 127 people.[22] About three months later, on 6 January 1831, Lucy Mack Smith, the mother of the prophet Joseph Smith Jr., wrote to her father that 300 had been baptized in Ohio, which increased total church membership three-fold, to about 450 people.[23]

Over the next several years a steady flow of converts came into the church. By 1835, membership had grown to approximately 1,500 and the church's organizational structure and government had stabilized.[24] On 28 March 1835, the first Quorum of Twelve Apostles was appointed, and they were sent out as missionaries and gospel witnesses in an ambitious effort to proselytize in the British Isles.[25]

Membership peaked in 1837 at about 2,500, when most Mormons were still located in Kirtland, Ohio, and then fell again because of economic and spiritual crises.[26] There is some evidence that total membership may have been cut in half, and by the end of the decade, Ohio membership was only about 1,000. This decline in Ohio can be attributed not only to apostasy but also to Mormon migrations to Missouri, where the church leaders were attempting to relocate the main body of the church.[27]

As early as 1831, shortly after the Saints from the New York and Pennsylvania area had moved to Ohio, efforts had been under way to establish a church center in Independence, Jackson County, Missouri, where the Mormons were told the New Jerusalem would be located at the second coming of Christ. However, these efforts were met with strong resistance from the locals, and Mormons were tarred and feathered, jailed, and even murdered, and their property was destroyed or confiscated. In spite of this suffering, most of the LDS members continued moving to Missouri. By the end of the decade, further persecutions at last forced them to leave the state and settle in Nauvoo, Illinois.[28]

By that time, the missionary program was functioning, and the church grew rapidly not only in America but in England. In Great Britain, within the first five-year period of missionary activity, more than 8,000 converts joined the church. By 1841, at least 1,177 British members had sailed to the United States; in 1842, another 1,614 emigrated; and in 1843, another 749.[29] By 1844, at the time Joseph Smith Jr. was martyred, the church had grown to approximately 15,000 members, with about 11,000 living in Nauvoo. More than 7,000 were Americans, but almost 4,000 were English immigrants. The remaining 4,000 members were new converts still living in England.[30]

Early Mormon Converts

As I mentioned in the preface, the writing of this book began informally. My intention had been to trace the spiritual roots of my own family. I was aware that at least 4 of the 8 direct-line great-great-grandparents on my father's side had converted to the Mormon church in the 1830s, and many of his family lines extended back to colonial America.[31] As I proceeded to trace my ancestry, I was surprised to find that 337 of the 384 fifth- and sixth-generation direct-line progenitors of these 4 converts (81 percent) were already in New England by 1639, less than two decades after the Pilgrims had arrived on the *Mayflower.* Further, our ancestors had settled in areas of early colonial New England that today are regarded by historians as havens for the radical religious activity of the time, including Rhode Island, New Hampshire, New London County in Connecticut, and Essex County in Massachusetts. Among my ancestors were names familiar to anyone even casually interested in religious radicalism: Roger Williams, Anne Marbury Hutchinson, Samuell Gorton, John Wheelwright, Stephen Bachiler, and many others. I was astonished by this discovery and wondered whether my family was peculiar or whether the families of other early LDS converts might have had a similar background. That is, did other early Mormons have roots stretching back to New England, to the earliest settlements where religious radicalism was rampant? And so I began the task of identifying early Mormon converts and tracing their family histories.

It was relatively easy to find information on the parents and grandparents of converts, but the task became much more difficult reaching back to early colonial times. Reasoning that early church leaders were well enough known and researched that I could quickly identify them and trace most of their family lines, I located the genealogies of thirty-eight so-called general authorities of the time and found extended genealogical data on thirty-one of them.[32] The profiles of their ancestors were similar to that of my own family. That is, almost all of their family lines went back to the earliest period of colonial New England, and many of these ancestors had been located in areas known for religious radicalism.

I worried that early church leaders might represent a peculiar group of people among the early Mormons, so I then collected some readily available names of more than one hundred ordinary early Mormon converts whose genealogical lines also went back several generations. The collective profiles of their ancestry were also similar to the profiles of the ancestors of my family and of the early LDS Church leaders. That is, most ancestors of this group of ordinary early Mormon converts were also among the first settlers in colonial New England, and they too were heavily concentrated in areas of religious radicalism.

The findings suggested a striking phenomenon in the family histories of the early LDS converts, and so I began identifying and tracing the family histories of as many early Mormon converts as I could. From the beginning, that search focused on converts who were baptized at a time when the church was first being formed and defined. I was curious about the kind of people who were attracted to a new religion that was not yet established and that provided little more than a promise of some future paradise on earth.

Because documentary evidence on ordinary people tends to be scarce, it was a difficult task to engage in a serious study of the religious heritage of all early Mormon church members. Where direct documentary evidence was not available, it was often necessary to draw conclusions from contextual data, such as church affiliation, community profiles, and family ties. I decided to follow what leads I could find. I selected only those early converts who were old enough to have made a mature, deliberate decision to be baptized, rather than children or youth, who may have simply followed the advice and direction of their parents. Finally, because my inquiry would be meaningful only if I were able to trace family histories back several generations, I decided to focus on those early adult converts whose available genealogical records covered at least six generations.

Fortunately, the traditions of the LDS Church make such an inquiry possible, because Mormon doctrine motivates its members to engage in extensive genealogical research. The data collected by millions of researchers are readily available in family history centers and through the Internet. Technology is now on hand to trace many family lines, and that has opened the way for an innovative type of historiography of American religion, a new method of studying the past.[33] Because Mormons are ardent genealogists, my approach to collecting evidence proved to be productive. However, genealogy has become such a widespread avocation that it would be possible to use this approach to study other groups of people as well.

Applying my criteria, it became necessary to eliminate a number of the converts I had already researched, but I was then able to set clear and precise boundaries around those converts on whom I would focus. First, the convert had to be someone baptized between 1830 and the end of 1834. Second, the convert had to be at least fifteen years old when baptized. Third, at least one line of the convert's ancestry had to be traceable back five generations.

Tracing the genealogies of approximately 1,500 members baptized prior to 1835, I was able to identify 583 of these early adult converts who had genealogical records traceable back five generations. That is, about 40 percent of the earliest membership of the church satisfied all three of my criteria.[34] Of course, this number may well increase as others gather further genealogical data.[35]

The Search for Convert Records

I confirmed the year of baptism for 490 of these 583 Saints and found strong contextual information concerning 93 others. The number of converts was distributed relatively evenly across the first five years, except for 1834. In that year, Zion's Camp took more than 200 leaders of the church from Ohio to Missouri to challenge the growing persecution of Saints in that region. Thus, church leaders were not in a position to proselytize new members. This information is shown in table 1.[36]

There is no single source that provides a complete list of early LDS converts.[37] Since the end of the 1970s, researchers at Brigham Young University have been attempting to identify all members who joined the church prior to its exodus from Illinois to the Rocky Mountains in 1847. Under the direction of Susan Easton Black, a catalog of church membership from 1830 to 1848 has recently become available. It is based on primary and secondary sources, including minute books, journals, autobiographies, biographies, periodicals, and genealogical materials. From these materials, Black has compiled a fifty-volume list of information, including dates of baptism, concerning all

Table 1. LDS Converts in This Study and in General

Year	Number of Converts	Church Baptisms[a]
1829–30	104	260
1831	98	245
1832	110	275
1833	144	360
1834	41	103
Date disputed	86	215
Total	583	1,458

Source: Rust Genealogical Data File, 2003.

a. Based on the estimate that the number of converts in this study is about 40 percent of the church converts each year.

known church membership prior to 1848.[38] It has been estimated that approximately 30,000 people, including British converts, had joined the church by the time of the exodus to the West.[39]

Unfortunately, these materials do not provide the time of baptism for several thousand of these earliest converts, including many of those who joined the church before 1835. In an effort to identify those baptism dates, I did my own analysis, using a number of valuable secondary and primary sources. For instance, Larry Porter's doctoral dissertation on the New York–Pennsylvania period is a valuable source. Another source I turned to was the *Far West Record,* a compilation of the minutes of church-related meetings between 1830 and 1844. The appendix of that record lists biographical notes on approximately 375 people noted in the minutes, including several baptism dates.[40] At least 154 of these were people baptized before 1835. There is also the seven-volume *History of the Church,* a compilation of historical materials dictated by Joseph Smith Jr. that provides a chronology of church events during his life, and in the text the prophet names more than 200 people as members before 1835.[41]

Zion's Camp was a group of prominent church members who traveled from Ohio to Missouri and back again to Ohio in 1834. All 218 known adult members of Zion's Camp may be assumed to have been baptized by the time of the Missouri military campaign organized to protect the Saints.[42]

Milton V. Backman provides a detailed analysis of the members of the Kirtland branch in Ohio, where the Saints lived from the fall of 1830 until the main body of the church relocated to Missouri in the latter half of the 1830s. He identifies more than 800 male members, their spouses, and their parents, the most complete list of church membership for the time period.[43] Unfortunately, Backman does not indicate the baptism dates of these members, and so I attempted to ascertain when male members and their spouses were baptized by researching vital statistics sources.

I compiled a catalog of the names of all possible members who had converted prior to 1835 that I located in secondary sources, in part to avoid duplication of names. In addition to sources noted above, I examined other secondary materials, including listings of the members of the Danites,[44] marriages in Kirtland and Nauvoo, and death notices in Nauvoo.[45] Not surprisingly, the secondary sources focus mainly on male members. Whereas I identified 803 adult male members, I was able to identify only 369 adult female members, for a total of 1,172 individuals. Clearly, all the general sources gave excessive weight to the male members, but these sources are not likely to be exhaustive for either males or females.[46]

In an attempt to find who else had been baptized by 1835, I undertook a search through primary sources. The major depository of ordinance information available to the public, including baptisms and marriage dates, is the *LDS Ancestral File.* These data are organized into two primary forms: the family group record and the pedigree chart. A family group record lists a person's parents, spouse, and children, along with vital statistics, such as birth, marriage, and death dates and places, as well as ordinance data, including baptism dates. A pedigree chart shows direct-line ancestry of people through several generations, providing birth, marriage, and death dates and places for each person on the chart.

The LDS Church has always been a record-keeping institution, but its dedication to baptism records is two-edged: on the one hand, tremendous energy is committed to recording ordinance data; on the other hand, because so many baptism dates of early members were lost, these members were often rebaptized, either personally or through proxy. The formal date of baptism appearing on their records is the most recent, rather than the original date.

In spite of this obstacle, by checking with primary sources I was able to confirm that a large number of these nearly 1,200 previously identified converts were recorded as having been baptized prior to 1835. In addition, I checked the family group record for each of the known converts to determine whether their parents, spouses, siblings, and children had also been baptized prior to 1835. This effort yielded more than 200 additional convert names. In other words, my search yielded more than 1,400 names of people who were probably baptized by 1835.

The final task was to identify those early adult converts whose ancestry could be traced back five generations. I chose to focus on fifth-generation ancestors because they would represent the first generation that could have been born in colonial New England, even though reference is often made to other ancestors. It is striking that the pedigree of a convert in the *LDS Ancestral File* is usually either fairly complete or stops with the convert, parents, or grandparents.[47] In spite of the value of the *LDS Ancestral File,* it does not do justice to a number of early converts, particularly women. Pedigrees are incomplete even for many men who played a crucial role in the formative stages of the church; these include William E. McLellin, Ziba Peterson, Hazen Aldrich, Charles C. Rich, Sidney Rigdon, and the Whitmer family (Christian, David, Jacob, Peter, Jr., and John). For illustrative purposes, I have included the pedigree chart of Sidney Rigdon (figure 2), which has known family lines going back only four generations.

The Early LDS Converts

Whitney Cross notes that the early LDS Church members were not "frontier people" in the usual sense of the term; rather, they were recent migrants

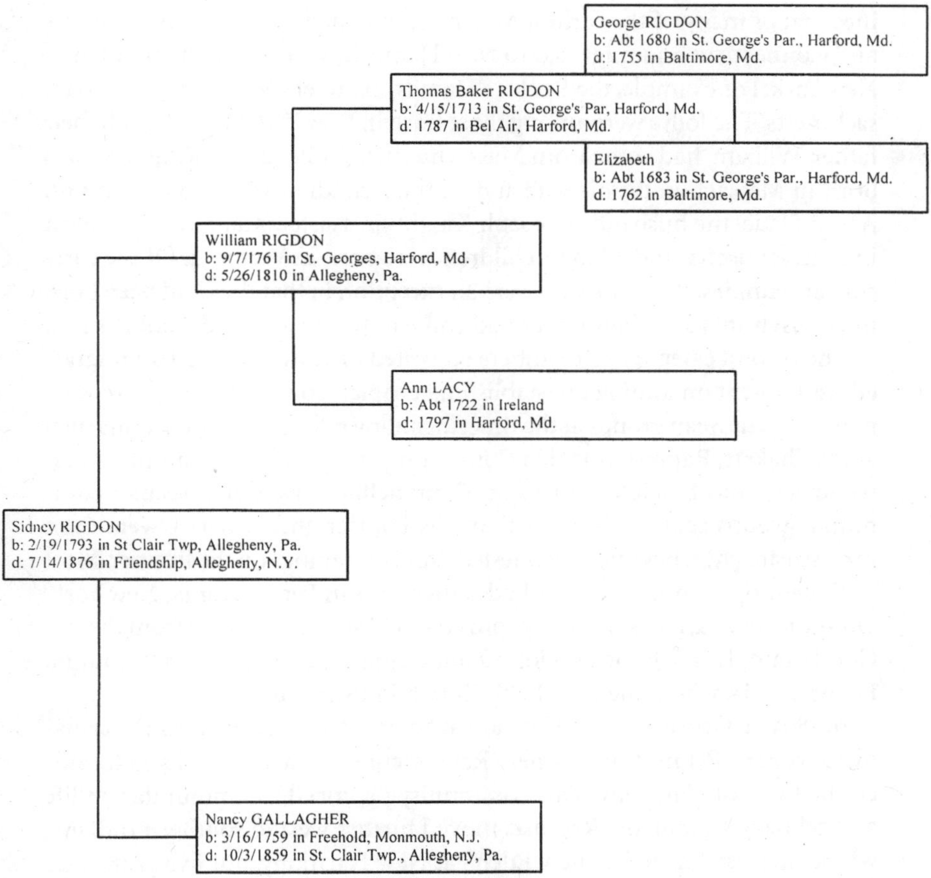

Figure 2. The Known Ancestors of Sidney Rigdon

to western upstate New York, Pennsylvania, and Ohio who felt more comfortable in stable, settled communities and yearned for a life comparable to that on the "civilized" east coast.[48] I have identified three groups of early Mormon converts. The first were members who converted during the New York–Pennsylvania period. The second were members who had initially been part of utopian societies and were living in Pennsylvania, New York, or Ohio. The third group were members who converted while still living in New England.

The first category of early members had migrated to western New York and northeastern Pennsylvania prior to the establishment of the LDS Church, mainly because of economic difficulties where they had lived in New England.[49] These were approximately 140 of the first converts. Their story typifies that of many of the earliest Mormons who had roots in Massachusetts and Connecticut and migrated to New Hampshire or Vermont and then to New York. For example, the Rockwell family members were all born in Massachusetts. The Jollys were among those born in New York State, though their father, William, had come from Massachusetts. While Joseph Knight Sr. was born in Massachusetts, his wife and all their children were from Vermont. Aaron Slade, the husband of Joseph Knight Sr.'s sister, Mary, was also born in Massachusetts, and all their children were born in Vermont. Of the early convert families, the Whitmers were an exception in that they had been born in Pennsylvania and their father had come to the New World from Prussia.

The second category of members consisted of converts who had migrated west, intent on joining or establishing utopian communities. There were many such utopian groups at the time, including religious organizations such as the Shakers, Rappists, Oneida Community, Hopedale Community, Amana Society, and Disciples of Christ (Campbellites), as well as secular communal groups such as those of François Fourier and Robert Owen. Even mainstream churches often manifested utopian leanings on the frontier. Most of these utopian organizations had settlements in Pennsylvania, New York, Ohio, or Indiana, and some early converts to Mormonism came from them.[50] Good examples are Jacob and John Zundel, Rappists living in Phillipsburgh, Pennsylvania, who joined the LDS Church in the 1830s.

In 1803–4, George Rapp's Harmonist Society had migrated from Germany to western Pennsylvania, where Rapp secured a tract of land and founded the town of Harmony. This community practiced a communitarian life and celibacy. In 1819, the Rappists moved further west to southern Indiana, where they established a "new Eden" at New Harmony, but five years later they sold New Harmony to Robert Owen, who wished to establish a village of "unity and cooperation" in Indiana, and the Harmonists returned to their Pennsylvania home. At the time, the Rappists were one of the most economically successful communitarian enterprises in America. Jacob Zundel was a devoted Harmonist until, in 1836, he met a Mormon missionary at Philippsburgh;[51] he and his family accepted Elder Evert's message as true, sold their share of the Harmonist property, and joined the Saints in Ohio.[52] In 1841, his brother Johannes also joined the Mormon church.[53] Both brothers endured the trials of persecution in Nauvoo and the difficulties of pioneer life in Utah.

The most important communitarian group among the early Mormons was the Campbellites, who called themselves Disciples of Christ. They took their informal name from their founders, Thomas and Alexander Campbell. Thomas was a Scotch-Irish Presbyterian minister who migrated to Pennsylvania in 1807, where he was censured by his church for engaging in the practice of open communion and for challenging some other Calvinist doctrines. In 1809, he decided to break away from the Presbyterian Church and form his own Christian Association.

Thomas Campbell's son Alexander emigrated to America in 1809 and joined his father, and in 1811 they set up the Brush Run Church, whose aim, as expressed by the title of a series of thirty-two essays by Alexander Campbell published in 1824, was *A Restoration of the Ancient Order of Things.* Alexander became an itinerant preacher, traveling through Ohio, Indiana, Kentucky, and other places, making converts.

One leader of the Campbellites in northeastern Ohio was Sidney Rigdon, a man famed for his dynamic preaching, first as a Baptist and then as a Campbellite minister. Throughout Rigdon's life, however, he had remained a seeker, searching for the true church that practiced the laying on of hands and possessed gifts of the Holy Spirit.[54] While living in Pittsburgh, Pennsylvania, Rigdon became attracted to communalism and explored the possibility of joining the Harmonists as well as the Shakers.[55] The Shakers were particularly appealing because they were not only communalists but claimed to enjoy visions, healings, and revelations from God, as well as speaking in tongues.[56] However, Rigdon eventually chose to associate himself with the Campbellites. Then, in 1830, he broke away from Campbell and established his own communal congregation near Mendon, Ohio. In the fall of that year, he and many others from his congregation joined the Mormon church, declaring they had finally found the restored church of Jesus Christ.

The geographic origins of Ohio Campbellite converts were similar to those of the New-York–Pennsylvania LDS converts, in that almost all of them were recent migrants to Ohio from New England.[57] The Campbellite leader, Sidney Rigdon, differed somewhat from the other converts because he had been born in Pennsylvania and his father came from Maryland. Edward Partridge Sr., who became the first bishop in the LDS Church, was more typical of those Campbellite converts, having been born in Massachusetts.

Two names stand out among the former Disciples of Christ supporting Rigdon in his fight with Campbell over communalist doctrines: Isaac Morley and Lyman Wight. Morley owned a farm at Kirtland, and he provided the land that would be dedicated to the Mormon community. Several of Morley's family members joined the LDS Church and gave their lives for its cause. Morley was baptized in 1830 and became a counselor in what is today called the Presiding Bishopric. His father was from Hartford County, Connecticut, and his mother from Montague, Hampshire County, Massachusetts. Isaac, his brother Horace, and Diantha were all born in Montague.[58] Isaac Morley's namesake family had not arrived in America until later in the 1600s, but other direct-line ancestors had come to Connecticut when it was first settled.

Lyman Wight was a gospel preacher working with Rigdon when he converted to Mormonism in 1830. He also converted five families at Mayfield, Ohio, a few miles southwest of Mendon, and all of these families dedicated their property to the communal enterprise. The highest office he held in the church was that of apostle. Wight was born in Fairfield, Herkimer County, New York, though his parents had come from Windham County, Connecticut, and the Wights had been in the colonies since the 1630s.

The third category of the earliest Mormon converts were in the majority; they came into the church while still living in upstate eastern New York or New England. After they joined the LDS Church, they migrated west to join the main body of the Saints, which had moved to Ohio. Brigham Young's family is a good example of this third category. The Young family had resided in New England for many generations, but in 1832, after they were baptized, they too migrated to Ohio.

John Young was the first direct-line Young ancestor to arrive in America. He had been born in England, and it is not clear when he emigrated, but a brother was born in Boston in 1632, so we can assume John had arrived soon after the Massachusetts Bay Company migrations began. The Young family remained in Massachusetts for four generations, becoming established and well-to-do residents of Suffolk County.[59] In 1769, Brigham Young's grandfather, a physician, died, leaving a widow, ten children, and a stack of unpaid bills. The estate was sold to pay off the debts. Brigham Young's father, John, was six years old at the time; he was bound over to a wealthy landowner, Colonel John Jones, with whom he remained until 1780, when he enlisted as a soldier in the War of Independence.

The war left a lasting effect on many young people, who became restless and went looking for new adventures. In 1788, with his wife and two daughters, John Young packed up and moved to the Catskills in New York. The family found farming in the wild frontier region to be very difficult, so after two years they returned to their home in Massachusetts. There they remained for ten years before striking out again in 1801, moving this time to Whitingham, Vermont, where six months later Brigham was born. Life continued to be difficult, so in 1804 the family migrated 130 miles west to the community of Smyrna in upstate New York. Even though economic conditions did not improve, the family settled in the area, and it was there in 1830 that Brigham first heard of the LDS Church.

Samuel Smith, the prophet's brother, had passed through upstate New York on a mission and had given Brigham's brother, Phineas, and his brother-in-law, John P. Greene, a copy of the Book of Mormon. After reading it, Phineas passed it around among his family members, most of whom were greatly attracted to its message. Brigham, however, was more cautious, and almost two years passed before he came in contact with other Mormon missionaries and finally embraced the church. Many other members of the Young family soon joined as well; they all subsequently migrated to Ohio.[60]

Even though we have identified three distinct categories of early Saints, members of all three groups had deep roots in New England in common. At first it might appear that their histories were not unusual for people living in western New York and Ohio. However, this turns out not to have been the case.

Populations of Western New York and Ohio

A generations-old westward movement had been under way since early colonial days, but the residents of western New York and Ohio were generally recent arrivals. The western boom taking place at the time the LDS Church was organized was stimulated by the development of highways and land routes to the Ohio Valley, the Erie Canal linking the Great Lakes region with the Hudson River, and the growing number of steamboats on western waters.

Recent historical work indicates that the migrations out of New England at that time were selective. Alan Taylor suggests four sources of upstate New York culture at the time the LDS Church was organized: "first, the centrifugal legacies of the First Great Awakening during the mid-eighteenth century; second, a selective migration that concentrated the most restless seekers in new towns; third, frontier hardships which discouraged institutional regularity; and, fourth, the creative power of dreams and visions."[61] Taylor reminds us that although revivalism affected New England generally, only a minority of the people fully embraced it. Often they were people ostracized and marginalized in their local communities, who found an outlet by migrating west. In other words, migration out of New England from 1790 to 1835 consisted mainly of those who had embraced "the spiritual power of dreams, visions, and inner voices."[62]

Even though the migrations from New England were composed of people who would likely be attracted to the message of Joseph Smith Jr., data indicate additional complexities in settlement patterns. The American Local History Network, for example, has begun gathering data collected by local historians and genealogists about migrations of people within and into various states. These preliminary data are growing rapidly and are now large enough to suggest some general patterns.[63]

Migration data shown in table 2 suggest that early LDS converts differed dramatically from the general population of New York and Ohio. The population of New York State was relatively stable at the time the LDS Church was organized. That is, most of the residents of New York had been born in the state (57 percent), and only 20 percent of the population were migrants from New England. But only 27 percent of LDS converts were native to New York, and 59 percent had migrated from New England.

In contrast to the residents of New York, most Ohio residents, including the LDS converts, had been born outside Ohio and had recently migrated to the state. But LDS converts again differed from the rest of the population. Ohio residents were more likely to have come from the Middle Atlantic (30 percent) and South (16 percent) than from New England (9 percent). Although few Ohio residents were born in New England, most converts (61 percent) were. Ohio settlers outran organized churches in moving west, but "many were earnest and some were zealous in religious matters."[64] Those from the Middle Atlantic and South identified themselves mainly as Baptist, Presbyterian, and Methodist. Many had been infused with the spirit of the First Great Awakening. Methodist evangelists, for example, in their frontier camp meetings encouraged extreme outpourings of "physical display and emotional release" and manifestations of "heavenly fire."[65]

In addition, European-born immigrants were well represented in both New York (20 percent) and Ohio (18 percent). The New York foreign immigrants came largely from continental Europe, and the Ohio immigrants, from

Table 2. General Population Born between 1750 and 1830 and Living in New York and Ohio Compared with Early LDS Converts

Birthplace	New York	Ohio	Converts Born in New York and Ohio
Ohio	0 (0%)	136 (18%)	0 (0%)
New York	376 (57%)	64 (8%)	161 (28%)
New England	131 (20%)	65 (9%)	343 (59%)
Europe	129 (20%)	137 (18%)	1 (0.2%)
Middle Atlantic	17 (3%)	226 (30%)	23 (4%)
South	1 (0.2%)	124 (16%)	27 (5%)
Other	1 (0.2%)	2 (0.2%)	28 (5%)
Total	655 (100.4%)	754 (99.2%)	583 (101.2%)

Note: General population information for New York and Ohio refers only to residents for whom data were available on the respective Web sites.

Sources: See <http://scioto.org/OhioMigrations/> and <http://scioto.org/NewYorkMigrations/>; Rust Genealogical Data File, 2003.

the United Kingdom. In contrast, almost no early LDS converts were foreign-born (2 percent), and those few born out of the country were almost all from Canada.

These demographic data relate to the states of New York and Ohio as a whole, and it is important to determine if the LDS members differed from the general populations in Wayne County, New York, where the church originated, and Geauga County, Ohio, where Kirtland was located. Several dozen non-Mormon residents of these two counties, whose names appear in the 1830 United States census, have ancestors in the *LDS Ancestral File* going back five generations.[66] Ancestors of non-Mormons came from a broader geographical cross-section of America than did the ancestors of LDS converts. Non-Mormon residents of these counties were as likely to have family roots in the Middle Atlantic and southern regions of the country as from New England. In other words, the LDS converts appear to differ not only in regard to state populations but also in regard to Wayne and Geauga Counties. In summary, early LDS converts were a distinctive population in both New York and Ohio.

2. Ancestors of Early LDS Converts

LDS Ancestors

As discussed in the last chapter, the early Mormon converts were a distinctive group among New York and Ohio residents. Their ancestors also were distinctive among the early colonial population. Almost all the progenitors of the 583 early LDS converts for whom genealogical records have been found to date can be traced back to the earliest days of America's colonial period; these ancestors originated in England and Scotland and migrated to New England; the birthplace of almost all the first ancestors born in America was New England.

I have been able to locate records for 10,415, or 56 percent, of all 18,656 possible fifth-generation ancestors for the 583 adult LDS converts. This is a remarkable trove of information and has been possible only because of the dedicated genealogical work of large numbers of Latter-day Saints.

The Theory: Predisposition Explanations

The message of the early LDS Church was so radical that it demanded a certain spiritual predisposition to resonate with it. This study shows that those who converted to the LDS Church in the first years after it was established possessed a shared historical background and a radical spiritual orientation, cultivated and honed from the beginnings of colonial New England. Early converts to the Mormon church, I am proposing, were predisposed to resonate with the message of Joseph Smith Jr. because they had received a spiritual orientation passed down from their ancestors that enabled them to undergo a conversion, moving them to embrace this new faith and to help build the foundations of the restored church.

In this context, the term "conversion" may overstate what happened to early Mormon "converts," because it suggests, in the words of Rodney Stark and William Bainbridge, "a radical, perhaps supernatural transformation in the nature of a person who is converted. The notion of conversion assumes that an individual really changes in some basic sense when he joins a new religious group."[1] Even though a conversion of sorts probably occurred, in that the early LDS convert was "touched by the Spirit," the convert was already radically different before affiliating with the LDS Church.

According to my predisposition explanation, early Mormons might have said, "Who we are is who we were." They felt an attachment that was as much cultural and emotional as it was rational.[2] The early LDS converts, whether they joined as extended family groups or as individuals, had family histories corresponding with the revolutionary orientation of Joseph Smith Jr. and his immediate disciples. Such a religious orientation may not have been directly experiential but perhaps almost archetypal in nature. That is, the unusual personal and family life histories of the converts had been imprinted in their bones and souls. This strange spiritual outlook was, if my theory is correct, part of a collective identity of a group of people, distinguishing them in a special way.

An early convert to the church, having heard the message proclaimed by Joseph Smith and his followers, would probably feel a kinship that was as much familial and social as it was ideological. The new convert had likely grown up hearing tales tying his or her family into a web of experience extending back for generations. These tales were filled with accounts of miracles, spiritual experiences, privations, and persecutions that distinguished the family as religious radicals.

This account of religious affiliation does not correspond with the conventional explanation of conversion. Social scientists have usually stressed the "subconscious deprivations and fears said to afflict the converts," while religionists have stressed the role of reason and the "theoretical virtues of one doctrine over another."[3] However, the predisposition explanation does have much in common with subconscious or rational choice theories, emphasizing instead kinship links between converts, which disposes individuals and groups to join the religions that their family, friends, and neighbors attend.

Kinship theory suggests converts usually are drawn to religions that fit with their preconversion frame of reference. This comes via two major avenues. First, the convert belongs to a "huge, interlocking, kinship network" consisting of extended families, friendship circles, and neighborhoods. Second, converts respond to the message of a religion because it resonates with their life orientation and does not require them to reject what Stark and Bainbridge call their "religious capital."[4] Rather, conversion to a new faith is easier when that new faith "maximizes their conservation of religious capital."[5]

The social pattern of conversion was particularly true in the first year the LDS Church was organized. Those who first joined the church belonged, by and large, to a closely knit set of family relationships. The Smith family set the pattern for such relationships. On 6 April 1830, the day the LDS Church was organized, three of the first six members to join were brothers: Joseph, Jr., Hyrum, and Samuel Smith. Other siblings soon joined, including William, Don Carlos, and Catherine Smith. Their parents, Joseph, Sr., and Lucy Mack Smith, also joined. Also baptized were Joseph Smith Jr.'s wife, Emma Hale; Hyrum Smith's wife, Jerusha Barden; Samuel Smith's wife, Mary Bailey; and William Smith's wife, Carolina Amanda Grant. Carolina's brothers, George Davidson, Jedediah Morgan, and Joshua Grant, also came into the church, as did Joseph Smith Jr.'s uncles, Asahel and Silas Smith.

Others of the earliest converts also usually came into the church via family lines—spouses, brothers and sisters, cousins, in-laws, aunts, and uncles. Richard Bushman describes the conversions in the first months after the church was organized as follows:

> Five Whitmer children and three of their spouses were baptized . . . besides the parents. Eleven Smiths, six Jollys, and five Rockwells joined. . . . The most remarkable collection of kin was the offspring and relatives of Joseph Knight Sr., and his wife Polly Peck Knight. . . . Two of Polly Knight's brothers and a sister, their spouses, and a sister-in-law . . . were baptized. Five of the Knight children, four of them with spouses, joined, plus Joseph Knight's sister, Mary Knight Slade, and five of her children.[6]

While the initial converts to Mormonism exemplify the kinship theory of conversion, it becomes increasingly difficult to explain the further conversions to the LDS Church strictly through immediate kinship and friendship associations. Though obvious clusters of people joined the church, something more is required to explain why these clusters, though quite diverse in origin and geographically distant from each other and having no immediate kinship connections, identified themselves as Mormons.

If those who joined the LDS Church in its first years were infused with family traditions resonating with the proclamation that the church of Jesus Christ was to be restored through divine intervention, they had already been prepared to accept Joseph Smith's basic message. Almost all of them could claim a heritage of shared, radical, spiritual experiences largely in harmony with that message. All the converts were part of a long family and community history that bound them together in a shared life experience of intense spiritual outpourings, spiritual gifts, and divine connections. In addition, the early LDS converts' distinct religious orientation was so strong that it can be validated empirically over several generations.

Five Generations of Ancestors in America

To calculate the number of possible ancestors of each individual, one doubles the number for each preceding generation. Consequently, two first-generation ancestors would multiply to four in the second, eight in the third, sixteen in the fourth, and thirty-two in the fifth generation. While I identified 56 percent of all possible fifth-generation ancestors, I was able to identify, as indicated in table 3, an increasing percentage in the fourth (63 percent), third (76 percent), second (89 percent), and first (99 percent) generations.

Table 3 also provides a general profile of the birthplaces of all six generations, based on the total number of ancestors identified and ignoring, for the moment, the duplication of names among ancestors. Almost all of them, from the first through the fifth generation, were born in America. Fifty-nine percent (343) of the converts were born in New England, as were 76 percent of their known parents, 81 percent of their grandparents, 85 percent of their great-grandparents, and 88 percent of their great-great-grandparents (fourth-generation ancestors). From the beginning, a small and relatively constant number of ancestors (between 238 and 531 for each generation) were born outside New England, and this number becomes less significant as we travel back in time because of the growing number of ancestors in each generation. The percentage of ancestors born in New England then drops off to only 63 percent of the fifth generation, because 29 percent of that generation were

Table 3. Birthplaces of Six Generations: Early LDS Converts and Their Ancestors

		Ancestor Generations				
Birthplace	Converts	First	Second	Third	Fourth	Fifth
Europe	1	6	27	113	226	3,067
Outside New England	238	274	361	417	458	531
New England	343	870	1,686	3,037	5,238	6,548
(percentage)	(59)	(76)	(81)	(85)	(88)	(63)
Total	583[a]	1,150	2,074	3,567	5,922	10,415[b]
(percentage)	(100)	(99)	(89)	(76)	(63)	(59)

Source: Rust Genealogical Data File, 2003.

a. One of these is an unknown birthplace.

b. Two hundred sixty-nine of these are unknown birthplaces.

born in Britain, although almost all of these British-born ancestors immigrated to America. If table 3 were extended to the sixth generation, it would show that few in that generation were born in America, although a large percentage of them died here.

In order to lend substance to these data, let us examine the pedigree chart of Lucy Mack (1775–1856), mother of Joseph Smith Jr., shown in figure 3. There are four generations represented, the equivalent of five generations of

Figure 3. The Ancestors of Lucy Mack Smith

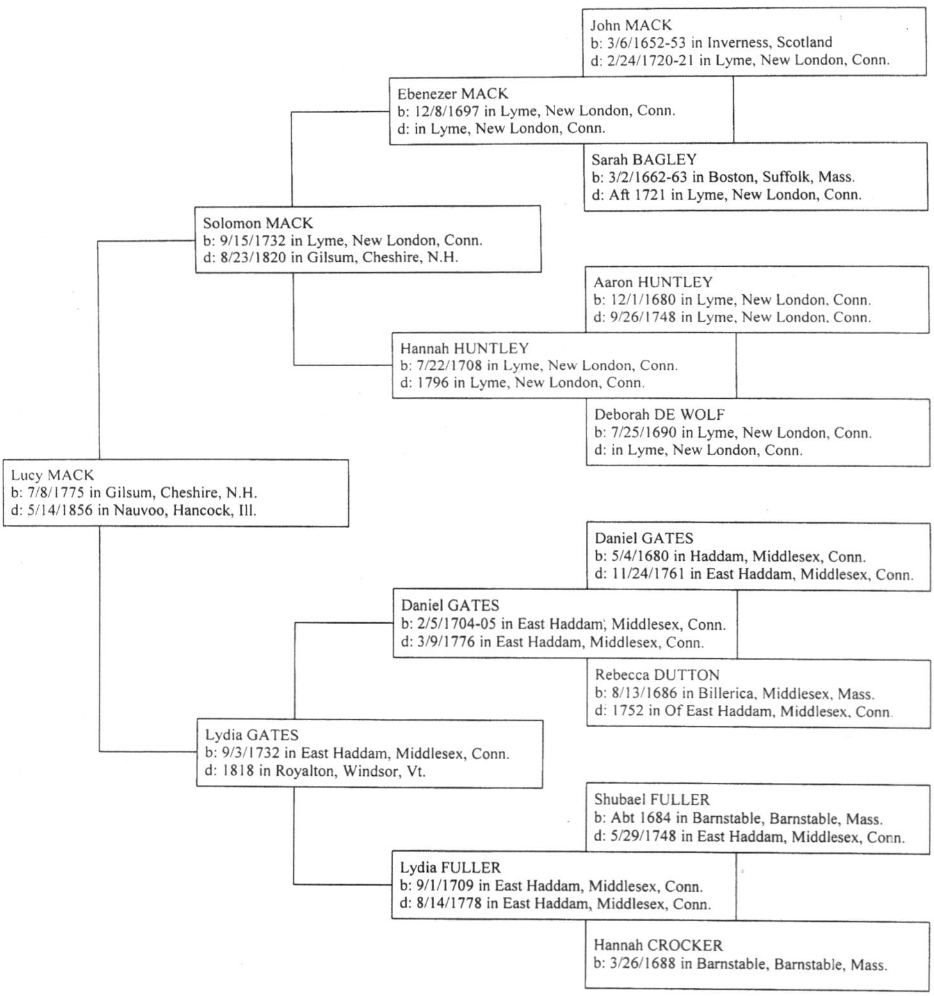

Joseph Smith Jr. on his mother's side. Her pedigree chart has a complete set of ancestors through the first four generations, including names as well as nearly all birth and death dates. While Lucy Mack was born in New Hampshire, all her first-, second-, and third-generation ancestors were born in Massachusetts or Connecticut, except John Mack, who was born in Scotland and died in Lyme, Connecticut. In other words, as far as can be determined, all Lucy Mack's ancestors, through three generations, died in New England.

The fourth generation of her ancestors, though not shown here because of space limitations, becomes a bit more complicated. Among the sixteen fourth-generation ancestors, two birth dates and three death dates are not known. The dates for the remaining fourth-generation ancestors are known, but only one (Orlando Bagley) was born in England, while the rest were born in New England; all of them died there.

Her fifth-generation profile (Joseph Smith Jr.'s sixth) is similar to her fourth. Of thirty-two possible fifth-generation ancestors, seven were known to have been born in England and seventeen in New England; however, all twenty-four of them died in New England. This represents the generation of the Mack family that completed the migration from England and Scotland to America.

Among Lucy Mack's known fifth-generation ancestors, three special and sometimes overlapping clusters are noteworthy. First, some of them were children and grandchildren of Pilgrims who came to America on the *Mayflower,* such as John Howland Jr., who was the son of passengers John Howland and Elizabeth Tillie. John Howland Sr. (1602–72/73) was a servant of John Carver, first governor of Plymouth; Elizabeth accompanied her parents, John Tillie and Joan Hurst, on the initial Pilgrim voyage. Her parents died that winter in Plymouth. Samuel Fuller, another ancestor, was the son of *Mayflower* passenger Edward Fuller.

The second cluster of Mack ancestors belonged to the congregation of John Lathrop (1584–1653), the Separatist minister who settled Barnstable, in Plymouth Colony, with his congregation in 1638–39. Lathrop and his congregation had languished for two years in prison in London before being released on condition that they leave England. The daughter of John Lathrop, Jane, married Samuel, the son of *Mayflower* passenger Edward Fuller. Other Mack forebears in Lathrop's congregation include John Crocker and Mary Lee.

The third cluster of ancestors, Henry Champion, Lewis Jones, and Balthazar de Wolf, were members of a congregation that traveled together to Connecticut to settle Wethersfield, one of the first communities in the colony. They were among a large number of LDS forerunners who belonged to that religiously radical congregation.

The First American LDS Ancestors

The first LDS ancestors in America arrived in 1620, in the earliest days of the colonial period. Table 4 provides information about the total number of fifth-generation ancestors. Overlooking for the moment the duplication of names in these records, we find that about 6 percent (644) were born and died in Europe, 23 percent (2,423) were born in Europe and migrated to America, 68 percent (7,079) were born in America, and 3 percent (269) were of unknown origin. Of those born in America, 92 percent (6,548) were born in New England, and a total of 8 percent (531) were born in other American colonies, 385 in New York, 97 in the Middle Atlantic region, and 49 in the South. Thus, almost all known fifth-generation ancestors of early converts were either born in New England or moved to New England from Europe. And as table 3 shows, these ancestors largely remained in New England through the fourth, third, second, and first generations.

New England in 1650

Early New England had quite different social and religious orientations than either the Middle Atlantic region or the South. On the one hand, it was populated almost entirely by people who had come to America for deeply religious purposes. They settled mainly in small towns throughout the colonies where, many believe, America's democratic tradition originated.[7] On the other hand, the Middle Atlantic region was more diverse. Religious refugees populated part of the region, but their concerns were generally different from those of settlers in New England; these immigrants arrived in America after 1660, and they often came from continental Europe, particularly Dutch- and German-speaking areas. The South was settled for economic reasons, and its population was located on plantations and farms rather than in towns.

Table 4. Birthplaces of Fifth-Generation Ancestors of Early LDS Converts

Birthplace	Number of Ancestors	Percentage of Total
Europe	644	6.2
Europe but migrated	2,423	23.3
New England	6,548	62.8
New York	385	3.7
Middle Atlantic	97	0.9
South	49	0.5
Unknown	269	2.6
Total	10,415	100.0

Source: Rust Genealogical Data File, 2003.

New England was never dominant in population; only about 30 percent of the people of colonial America lived in New England; Virginia contained more inhabitants than all New England colonies combined. But few early Mormons and their ancestors came from the Middle Atlantic region and the South, and those who came from New York generally lived in the northeastern part of the state and shared New England's cultural history.

Birthplace of New England Ancestors

When placed in the context of the general New England population, the raw number of fifth-generation ancestors from that region is striking. In order to show how the ancestors of early Mormons were similar to or different from other early settlers in New England, a measuring rod must be established for comparison. I use the year 1650 in many of my comparisons, choosing this date because it is close to the mean, mode, and median dates of birth of that fifth generation.[8]

The U.S. Bureau of the Census estimates that approximately 22,800 English were in New England by 1650.[9] One might be tempted to conclude, on the basis of the records I have uncovered, that the 8,971 fifth-generation LDS ancestors who lived and died in New England constituted 39 percent of the entire population of the time. However, this would be faulty reasoning, because one finds significant overlap in names. That is, many early LDS converts shared ancestors with other early converts. However, there are no less than 4,532 different, or unique, names found among fifth-generation ancestors, and of these, 3,185 who were ancestors of only one of the 583 individuals among the Latter-day Saints in this study. This means that approximately 20 percent of the 1650 population of New England were direct-line ancestors of LDS converts, though this percentage could rise substantially as additional ancestors are identified and more subtle analysis is done. For example, when determining that percentage, I conservatively counted people with the same name only once, though there were many different ancestors who shared the same name, including such common names as John Clark, Mary Davis, John Cole, Hannah Jones, Richard Moore, and Elizabeth Rogers.[10]

In table 5 we find the distribution of fifth-generation LDS ancestors in New England. Strikingly, they were overrepresented in Plymouth Colony, Connecticut, and Rhode Island and underrepresented in Massachusetts Bay Colony. However, 15.2 percent of the Massachusetts population, 28.9 percent of the Connecticut population, 39.3 percent of the Rhode Island population, and an astounding 43.6 percent of the Plymouth Colony population were

Table 5. New England Population in 1650 and the Total Number of Ancestors Who Were Born in New England or Emigrated and Died in New England

	Plymouth	Massa-chusetts	Connecticut	Rhode Island	New Hampshire	Maine	Total
New England population	1,500	14,100	4,100	800	1,300	1,000	22,800
Fifth-generation LDS ancestors	1,340	4,395	2,203	680	189	169	8,971
Unique names of ancestors	654	2,139	1,226	314	120	79	4,532
Colonial population as percentage of total population	6.6	61.8	18.0	3.5	5.7	4.4	100.0
Unique names as percentage of total population	14.4	47.2	27.1	6.9	2.6	1.7	99.8
Unique names as percentage of state population	43.6	15.2	28.9	39.3	9.2	7.9	n.a.

Sources: Rust Genealogical Data File, 2003; *World Almanac and Book of Facts,* 1997, "United States Population."

fifth-generation ancestors of LDS converts. But it is the individual New England towns that provide the most revealing account of the progenitors.

The New England Town

New England had a unique culture, distinct from that of the rest of the early American colonies. And each colony in New England differed from the others. Every county in each colony crafted its own style and cultural orientation. But the town was the core of New England culture. Writing of Massachusetts, Sumner Chilton Powell notes that "each town was, in a real sense, a little commonwealth."[11] The residents determined who would live in the town and who would not. They established its laws and regulations. The town's church was the heart of religious expression and observance. Congregationalism was the dominant form of church allegiance, and it proclaimed that each community of believers (congregation) should organize itself and select its own pastor and officers through a democratic vote. The towns protected and cultivated the deepest religious feelings of their inhabitants.

The values reflected in the town and its congregation defined in many ways how these people saw the world. The prescribed standards applied to everyone, including ministers, merchants, farmers, sailors, youth, and the elderly. No perfect equality has ever been possible, but a high degree of conformity was expected of a town's residents. While in Europe a great gulf separated leaders from peasants and the poor, no similar gulf was to be found in New England. All worked together and saw each other on a daily basis. They were all subject to the same moral code. Town life was a totality, apparently without seams. All aspects of life—work, religion, recreation, and play—were woven together.[12] Family life itself was bound up with community life. The typical New England town was a product of its English culture but also expressed the core of what was emerging as the American way of life, particularly its democratic traditions.

By the mid-seventeenth century, almost three hundred towns were to be found in New England. They ranged from small hamlets of a few families to Boston, which was at least five times larger than any other town in New England, counting 14,300 souls by 1664.[13] At midcentury, most were still located along the seacoast, though some movement inland was beginning to take place.

In my exploration of the roots of early Mormon converts, the individual New England town became a focal point. Even though LDS ancestors constituted such a large portion of the New England population, they were not evenly distributed across the New England colonies. Among the hundreds of towns, approximately 29 percent (2,555) of all fifth-generation ancestors were born in only ten towns, with almost half (3,991) born in only 20, and more than 57 percent (5,100) born in 30 towns.

Rowley

One such town was Rowley, Massachusetts. Rowley was settled in 1639 by families from Yorkshire, who set sail on the *John,* under the leadership of the Reverend Ezekiel Rogers, formerly pastor of the church at Rowley, Yorkshire, near Hull. In 1620, he had been suspended from the parish he had overseen because he objected to certain of the religious traditions of the day, including sports on God's Holy Sabbath. However, he had covertly continued to function as pastor, and in the fall of 1638, he and his community of followers disembarked at Salem harbor.[14]

At the time, a company was being formed for the purpose of settling a new colony next to Connecticut, to be known as New Haven. Rogers considered joining that group, but after consulting with Puritan ministers he requested and was granted by the general court a tract of land between Ipswich and Newbury. The settlement was begun the spring after Rogers and his congregation arrived in America. The tract extended eight miles in every direction, and it was necessary to purchase some property from the surrounding settlements to achieve this end.

The initial settlement consisted of fifty-nine families, representing an increase of thirty-nine families over the original twenty that had arrived in Salem with the Reverend Mr. Rogers. Many of the added members, including William Bellingham, Jane Grant, Thomas Mighill, and William Stickney, had lived in the Rowley parish in England but had preceded Rogers to America. Most of the fifty-nine original heads of household were freemen, which meant they were members of the Puritan Church, had taken the freeman's oath, and were thereby entitled to vote.

The first church was organized in the settlement on 3 December 1639, and Ezekiel Rogers was named the pastor. That same year, the first meeting house was built on the commons, though a larger building was constructed soon thereafter. Rogers was reportedly "a man of eminent piety, zeal and abilities. His strains of oratory were delightful."[15] Because he left no issue, he was not an ancestor of any LDS convert.

A Rowley town government was set up, probably in the early 1640s, although a fire destroyed early town records so no account of town affairs before August 1647 exists. It is assumed that theocracy was the governmental ideal, though it was never instituted in its full form, because there was accommodation to practical realities and the gifts of leadership manifested by the settlers.

Rowley was, at least formally, a conventional Puritan town and congregation, and the affairs of the town could be duplicated in any one of the fifteen congregations that preceded Rowley in the colony. Its town covenant began with a declaration that the community gave itself up to God the Father, Son, and Holy Ghost. The settlers promised to give up their sins and walk in the path of brotherly love. They submitted themselves to the holy rule of the church in fellowship and meekness. Their economy was based on the principle of Holy Communion. That is, it was based on a communitarian dream, a utopian ideal, a spiritual covenant to act according to God's will.

These settlers of Rowley had suffered the trauma of persecution in England and had been forced to travel across the Atlantic Ocean. Settling in a wilderness that taxed them with physical hardships, most of the first Rowley families became permanent residents of Essex County. Of Rowley's fifty-nine original heads of household, no less than twenty-five were ancestors of early LDS converts. Consider the single convert Lewis Abbott, who was baptized a member of the LDS Church in 1830.[16] His fifth-generation ancestor and family namesake is George Abbott, who, though he had not traveled to New England with the Reverend Mr. Rogers, was among the first settlers in Rowley.

George Abbott was granted a lot along the edge of the commons on which to build his home. Little is known about his life, though an inventory of his estate listed thirty books at the time of his death in 1647. This alone would indicate that he was a man of some education and standing.[17] In this regard, Abbott was like certain other LDS ancestors. For example, William Boynton, progenitor of the Boynton and Draper families, was the first schoolmaster of Rowley and served in that capacity for many years; he was also the ringer of the church bell and the janitor of the meetinghouse.[18]

The Abbott family remained in New England for two centuries, and in fact, Lewis Abbott was baptized a Mormon in 1830 in Wayland, Middlesex County, Massachusetts, where he had been born. Rowley families were typically stable and orderly, in that few moved beyond the town or surrounding communities.

I have identified all children born to those first settlers in Rowley who were direct-line ancestors of LDS converts. Not only were they all born in Rowley but 87 percent of the direct-line grandchildren were also born in Rowley and another 11 percent in the neighboring towns of Essex County, for a total of 98 percent. Finally, 55 percent of the direct-line great-grandchildren were also born in Rowley, 28 percent in neighboring towns, and another 6 percent in neighboring New Hampshire and Maine, for a total of 89 percent.

Rowley clearly resembled the old villages in England where family lands and names passed from generation to generation in an environment characterized by familial and social continuity. Most of the families of Rowley quickly established roots that defined their identities, occupations, and lifestyles in their new homeland.[19] Their communal identity was set by their common experience of being compelled to pull up roots in England, come to a new land, and settle a new town. The lives of Rowley inhabitants were tightly intertwined. Their children married each other. They assisted each other on the farms and in the workshops. They attended church together and formed a close kinship group that lasted, in many instances, for several generations.

The 1650 map of Rowley township (figure 4) shows approximately seventy households. Besides the twenty-four town inhabitants who were in the original group, other LDS ancestors later moved to the town, including Richard Swain, John Smith, John Pearson, James Bailey, Thomas Harris, Humphrey Reyner, Constance Crosby, Richard Wicom, Jane Grant, and Maximilian Jewett. More than half of the heads of household in Rowley at midcentury were ancestors to LDS converts. John Farnum Boynton could claim as his ancestors William Boynton, Jane Brocklebank, William Stickney, Robert Haseltine, and others appearing on the Rowley's household map.

From town to New England town, the level of religious radicalism differed. Some were conventional by New England standards. Others manifested var-

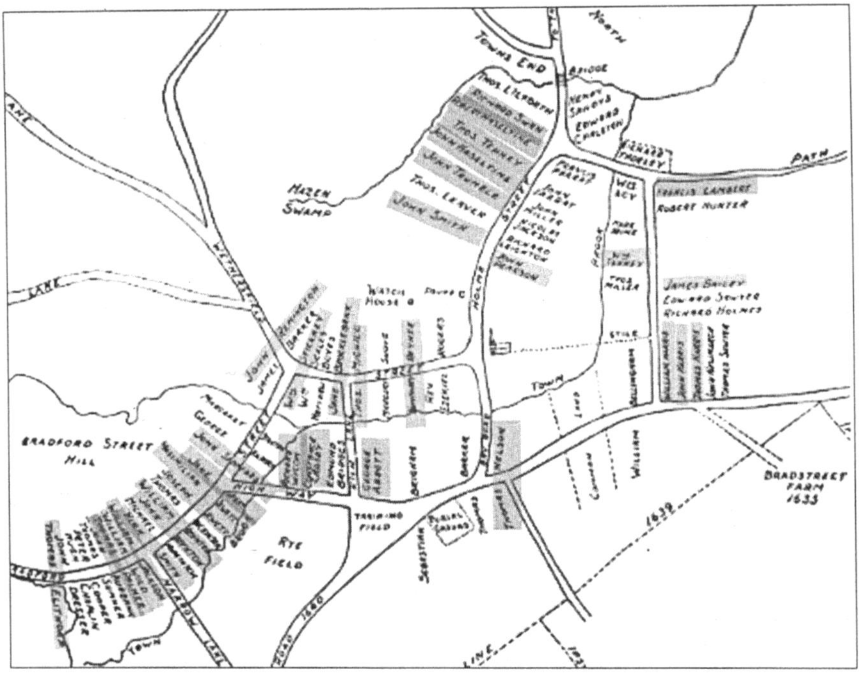

Figure 4. Rowley, Massachusetts, about 1650, with Ancestors Shaded (*Sources:* A. E. Jewett and E. M. Adams, *Rowley, Massachusetts: Mr. Ezechi Roger's Plantation, 1639-1850* [Rowley: Jewett Family of America, 1946], n.p.; Rust Genealogical Data File, 2003)

ious types of extremism. Some had been settled by individuals cast out of Massachusetts Bay Colony. Others, such as Exeter and Hampton in New Hampshire, consisted not only of disenfranchised individuals but of whole congregations that had followed their expelled leaders. Other towns were made up of radical religious groups that had sailed as a body across the Atlantic. Rowley was just such a town.

New England Religious Radicals and Their Early LDS Convert Connections

A number of indicators provide evidence that early LDS converts possessed a "radical" spiritual orientation. One was the fact that almost all of these converts shared a heritage taking them back two hundred years to the earliest years of America's New England colonial history. This indicator suggests that the forerunners of early converts shared a two-century heritage in a country Latter-day Saints believe to be a land of promise, a land of destiny.[20]

Contemporary sociological analysis almost inevitably connects radicalism with socialist thought;[21] however, earlier radicalism was associated with attempts to break away from various sorts of constraining traditions, including religion. To be radical in the framework of this study is to be associated with a view that history promises innovative possibilities, that humankind can and will break away from its constraining past. The more defining feature of political radicalism is to be seized with the idea that fundamental change and transformation are possible, that history is there to be seized, to be molded, to be developed and organized in such a way that the human spiritual condition would be made better.

To provide a glimpse of the spiritual orientation I have in mind, I turn briefly to the more radical aspects of the Protestant Reformation. While we typically identify the Reformation with the theology of Luther, Calvin, and Knox, there were also extreme movements reflecting social, economic, and political struggles. There were mystical-spiritual attempts by fringe groups to overcome the worldly order that adherents felt had infected Christianity.[22] Radical reformers anticipated the imminent return of Jesus Christ and wished to prepare for God's kingdom on earth.

Radical fringe groups shared certain qualities. They all expressed "a strong and ardent element of enthusiasm and fanaticism," and they claimed a special divine illumination and guidance in the form of "private revelations."[23] However, they also differed one from the other in many respects. The less radical were committed to being a "covenant people" and to building a church-state theocracy, while the more radical held additional beliefs that the original gospel of Jesus Christ was going to be restored through divine intervention and that each individual possessed a spark of the divine, could gain a personal knowledge of God, and was able to exercise gifts of the Holy Spirit.

Restoring the Gospel of Jesus Christ

A fundamental assumption of all the radical fringe groups was that the church of Jesus Christ had gone astray but that God would restore it. Restitutionism, or restorationism, became a declaration of faith among Reformation radicals and served as a guide to action.[24] In this respect, the restitutionists went beyond mainstream Reformationists in that they wished to participate in the rebirth of the gospel of Jesus Christ. Of course, there were differing interpretations of restitution. The aim of certain mainstream reformers, such as John Calvin, was modest compared with most restorationists, despite a common rejection of "scholasticized, commercialized, and politicized Catholicism."[25] Puritanism was more akin to the Reformation than it was to restoration, because Puritans were inclined to defend their links with conventional Christianity; otherwise, their claims of possessing divine authority would be groundless. However, Separatists were adamant about making a clean break from their church past, and many radical spiritualists went far beyond the Separatists, claiming to have received direct divine commandment to restore the original gospel of Jesus Christ.

A Personal Knowledge of God and His Works

The radical religious groups were committed to the belief that each individual could have a personal knowledge of God and his works. They shared with Puritans and Separatists the conviction of a genuine conversion of life and the sanctifying power of the Holy Spirit. However, they went far beyond conventional Calvinist Puritans in their claim of personal knowledge. The conversion process for the Puritan was an acknowledgment that God had worked upon one's soul and through the Holy Spirit had given testimony of sinfulness and of the necessity of repentance. Calvin had taught that God is sovereign, and as a sovereign he not only created everything but maintains his creation every moment of every day through time. Calvin insisted that since the fall of Adam all human beings are born depraved and are neither aware of God nor his workings. God is, however, aware of human beings' depravity and their destiny in perdition; he is cognizant of humanity's condition but has taken special measures to save those of humanity whom he will.[26] Through God's mercy, Calvin argued, he has given human beings the spiritual insight to know if they have or have not been saved. Only to this extent does humanity have divine insight; however, of God, men and women know and can know nothing.

In contrast, the radical religious groups emphasized the workings of the Holy Spirit on them such that they could come to know God personally, to love him, and to be an instrument in his hands. Anyone desiring to know God and his gospel plan, they maintained, needed only to ask with an open heart, and through God's Holy Spirit that person would know the simple and everlasting truths of the gospel.

Possessing a Spark of the Divine

The radical religious groups deviated fundamentally from Catholicism and conventional Protestantism about human origins. Conventional Christians assumed we are creations of God and not only entirely subject to his will but entirely different from him in form and substance, having been created ex nihilo. And Calvin, though he was not certain what conditions prevailed prior to Adam's fall, put forward the notion of the total perversity of fallen man, who could have no connection with anything divine and was simply too low and mean to be considered in the same framework as God.[27]

But certain radical groups denounced Calvinistic claims and saw divinity and spirit in all the world and the universe. Hermetics, for example, claimed that matter is cosmologically related to the primal matter from which it sprang. They saw Adam as originally equal with God, having cosmic, supernatural power. Indeed, they claimed, each human being possesses an eternal, everlasting spark of the divine.[28]

Expressing Gifts of the Spirit

Puritans and Separatists recognized that Christ had endowed some in the original church with various spiritual gifts, namely "miracles," "gifts of healings," "helps," "governments," and "diversities of tongues." However, Congregationalists in early colonial America believed these gifts had existed only at the time of the original church, but that these gifts had been withdrawn from the church in later times.[29] This did not stop many Puritans and Separatists from engaging in spiritual expression and demonstrating that they possessed such gifts. However, radical religious groups almost uniformly were more comfortable with the expression of gifts of the Holy Spirit, and certain groups, as we shall see, based their power on the kinds of spiritual gifts manifest in their congregations.

These traits of radicalism were very similar to those that set Mormons apart from their fellow Americans in mainstream religions some two hundred years later. Mormons also believed the gospel of Jesus Christ would be restored through divine intervention, that each person could gain a personal knowledge of God, possess a spark of the divine, and receive and exercise gifts of the Spirit.

3. The Pilgrims of Plymouth Colony

British Origins

English religious refugees on pilgrimage across the Atlantic to New England believed they were participants in God's plan to restore his pure church. While most reformers had resolved to change the Church of England from within, they had met such inflexibility and resistance that many had already given up, and the Reformation in England faltered. But by the early seventeenth century, reformers found a way to revive their commitments. They could emigrate to the New World, where they would be free of the constraints of archbishops and government officials. There they could create a true church of England, a simple, pure church, a church of Jesus Christ on earth.

British reformers had been active since the fourteenth century, since the time of John Wycliff, but the English Reformation was realized only by the middle of the sixteenth century, though as a result of political rather than spiritual intentions. Henry VIII rejected Pope Clement's refusal to grant him a divorce, and in 1534 he repudiated papal authority and established the Anglican Church. Even though Henry introduced a few changes in religious practice, such as the suppression of monasteries, he wished the Church of England to remain Catholic, though independent of the pope in Rome.[1]

After Henry VIII's death in 1547, the advisers of his only legitimate son, ten-year-old King Edward VI, initiated a rapid shift toward Protestantism by introducing a new prayer book and attacking the rituals and ornaments of the old church. However, in 1553 Edward VI's reign, which had lasted less than six years, ended abruptly with his premature death. His successor, Mary, the first queen to rule England, declared that the church was to return to the original Catholic fold. For her executions of Protestant reformers, she was given the title "Bloody Mary," and these executions became a source for John Foxe's influential *Book of Martyrs* (published in 1563). Her reign also was cut short when she died in 1558. That same year, Elizabeth I became queen; she restored Protestantism as the state church and suppressed discontented Catholics.

No one, from the reign of Henry VIII through Elizabeth I, attempted to bring about schism in the church. Religious reformers assumed the church in England would remain a unified body. Clearly, the church's international ties had been broken, but there was almost complete unanimity of belief that there was but one Christian faith that ought to be expressed in a single, unified church. The main struggle was to define the nature of that single faith and church. Even early reformers as outspoken and critical as Thomas Cartwright (1535–1603), twice forced into exile on the Continent because of his attacks on the church, never wanted to break away or establish a new institution. Royalty was intent on maintaining a single church in England that would support the state. Elizabeth, for example, wished to retain state control over the church and suppressed all doctrine that suggested otherwise.[2]

Highly educated scholars, particularly from Cambridge University, wished to draw the church toward the humanistic tradition of the Renaissance. They, too, expressed no desire to see the Anglican Church break apart. They would have agreed with Foxe that though the "Church should mightily be impugned, . . . the same Church, notwithstanding the uttermost of the devil and all his malice, should continue."[3]

Those calling for religious reform of the Church of England were labeled "Puritans." The term was initially pejorative and was applied to anyone wanting to "purify" the church. Mainstream Puritans asked only that the church rid itself of certain corruptions and provide Sunday services in simple, understandable English. Initially, their demands were tempered, and a judicious response might have quickly dissipated the protests.

Unfortunately, even though Queen Elizabeth was flexible in her handling of the economy and governance, she refused to compromise with the demands of the religious reformers; she decided they posed a threat to the power of the state. Many reformers took temporary flight to Europe, where they were radicalized by their discovery of the doctrines of reformers John Calvin, Ægidius Gutmann, Jacob Böhme, and Johann Valentin Andreä; when they returned to England, they demanded more than simple reform. They now claimed the Anglican Church was no better than that run by the "great Antichrist of Europe, or Pope of Rome."[4] The church had become "adulterated and defiled with so many filthy inventions and dark errors of bishops and monks" that it must undergo fundamental reform.[5]

Some priests and their communities began demanding an authority structure quite different from that found in the traditional church. The next logical step was separation and a more radical Puritanism that deemed the church too corrupt to purify. These more radical religious reformers "wanted divorce; they wanted to set up their own congregations, subject to no bishop, no royal 'Defender of the Faith,' subject only to Christ."[6]

The critical year in the development of religious separatism was 1604.[7] The newly crowned King James I had spent his childhood in Presbyterian Scotland, which had a reputation for religious extremism, and the Puritans were hopeful that he would be receptive to their reform proposals. However, James I rejected the Puritan plans and dashed all hopes of genuine reform. This led to more outspoken campaigns for separation, resulting in increased levels of persecution. These more radical reformers identified themselves as Independents or Separatists, outside the boundaries of the Church of England. They renounced their church membership and assumed a posture of hostility.[8] Separatists advocated an egalitarian form of church governance, particularly the notion that each congregation possessed autonomous authority. These Separatist groups initiated the Congregational Church, which would eventually have a major impact on all churches in colonial America.

Separatists in England

Scholars generally consider Separatists to have been "the most radical, unpopular Puritan faction of their age."[9] In England, Separatist and non-Separatist Puritans held strong differences, though they shared important common features. For example, both relied heavily on Calvinist doctrine. However, Separatists were convinced that the Church of England was a false church that could never be reformed; it was "so tainted with Romanism that no true Christian could remain part of it."[10]

Robert Browne (1550–1633) was the first English clergyman to preach separation. He was educated at Corpus Christi College, Cambridge University, where a number of Separatists would study. Considered to be the "most creative religious thinker of his day," his brief leadership had such impact "that all of the religious radicals, regardless of creed, were soon known as Brownists." In 1580, Browne began the Separatist movement in Norwich, and in the first two years of his preaching the local bishop had thrown him in jail thirty-two times for holding private meetings with a "vulgar sort of people."

Consequently, Browne and many of his followers fled to Holland, where he published a number of tracts outlining basic principles for a "revolutionary independent movement."[11]

Browne expected each believer to demonstrate personal piety and an inner spiritual experience with Christ. The believer was required to separate from the Church of England and work to introduce the kingdom of God by forsaking and denying "all ungodliness and wicked fellowship." Browne claimed the Scriptures warranted taking such drastic action.[12] He rejected Calvin's claim that the state constituted the foundation of a new reformed church, and he advocated that believers make a covenant only with God rather than with a church or a state. However, believers could freely join together in an "independent" church.[13]

Browne set the stage for Congregationalism by proclaiming that each community of believers organize itself and select its own pastor and officers in a democratic vote. Soon, the movement for separation numbered at least twenty thousand Brownists.[14] In 1593, the British banished all Separatists from England and decreed that exiled Brownists would be put to death if they returned.

In 1607, John Smyth, an ardent Anabaptist and a bold theorist who gloried in the label "Brownist," took his full congregation to Holland.[15] That community was the first of many that went into exile for disputing attempts of the Church of England to retain the old conformity of faith, ordinances, ceremonies, and practices.

The Separatists from Scrooby

The best known of the banished congregations, the Pilgrims, were Separatists who originated in the village of Scrooby in Nottinghamshire. They have the distinction of being the first exiled group to leave Holland and travel to New England. In 1586, Richard Clyston, a local parson in Babworth, England, attracted a number of villagers from nearby Scrooby, including William Brewster and a young orphan living with Brewster named William Bradford, to journey to Clyston's parish each Sabbath and participate in worship services. When Clyston fell into difficulties with his local church authorities, Brewster offered him and his family refuge. Clyston and Brewster formed a Separatist church in Scrooby and began holding meetings in the Brewster home. John Robinson, a fellow student with Clyston at Corpus Christi College, moved from Norwich to become the teacher of the congregation. He had already tried to develop a Separatist following in Norwich where Robert Browne had begun the movement, but Robinson had experienced little success, so he willingly moved to Scrooby.

In 1607, the local civil authorities formally charged Brewster with Brownism and summoned him to appear before the court. Knowing that such summonses to others had resulted in imprisonment and the gallows, Brewster and his friends refused to appear to answer the charges.[16] This resistance led to increased persecution, and the situation became so intolerable that the Scrooby congregation decided to go into exile and become part of the Ancient Brethren, an Anabaptist congregation from London that had earlier settled in Amsterdam.[17]

The Scrooby villagers were uncomfortable living in the large city of Amsterdam, so many members soon departed for Leyden, taking with them certain of the Ancient Brethren, including Samuel Fuller and Isaac Allerton, as well as Henry May and his daughter Dorothy. Other members of the Scrooby congregation, including the original pastor, Richard Clyston, remained in Amsterdam as members of the Ancient Brethren.[18] The melding of these two groups, the Scrooby congregation and the Ancient Brethren, signaled a further radicalization of many Pilgrims.

On 5 August 1620, members of the Scrooby congregation living in Leyden joined with some adventurers seeking commercial opportunities, and together they set sail on the *Mayflower* for the new colonies in America. William Bradford, the first governor of Plymouth Colony, in his *History of Plymouth Plantation* suggests four reasons why the group migrated. First, "they desired to injoye the ordinances of God in their puritie, and the libertie of the gospell with them." Second, "old age began to steale on many of them" and necessities [were] pressing on them." Third, their children, being exposed to "the manifold temptations of the place, were drawne away by evill examples into extravaagante and dangerous courses, getting the raines off their neks, and departing from their parents." They saw "their posteritie would be in danger to degenerate and be corrupted." Finally, they entertained "a great hope and inward zeal . . . of laying some good foundation, or at least to make some way therunto, for the propagating and advancing the gospell of the kingdom of Christ in those remote parts of the world."[19]

The *Mayflower* landed in what became known as Plymouth, and in the following years more members of the congregation came on the *Fortune* and the *Anne.* The Plymouth Colony quickly expanded its territory until it covered not only what is now the county of Plymouth, Massachusetts, but also Barnstable and Bristol Counties.

Though the Plymouth Separatists failed to flourish in numbers, they established a framework for Congregationalism that took hold in New England with both Separatist and non-Separatist bodies.[20] The foundation of Congregationalism was that each individual freely chose submission to the local church community. The Pilgrims claimed every church was a separate unit, independent of all outside control, including the hierarchical officials of the church. Thus, when the *Mayflower* arrived at Cape Cod, the Pilgrim leaders concluded a compact, based on the Scrooby church covenant, wherein they declared: "We . . . solemnly and mutually . . . covenant and combine ourselves together into a civil body politic for our better ordering and preservation . . . for the general good of the colony, unto which we promise all due subjection and obedience."[21]

That covenant formed the basis of government for the small group; it established the congregation as the ruling body over church members, and it set the pattern for Congregationalism in the colonies, Separatist and non-Separatist alike.[22] Even the Puritans adopted the Congregational framework of a special covenant and the assumption of divine inspiration.[23] While a covenant was based on the premise that God would inspire the covenanters in their decisions, practical application was at times rocky as the congregation worked out practical solutions to the problems they encountered.

The Pilgrims believed America held a providential place in God's design. Most English of the seventeenth century assumed their country was an "elect nation," chosen by God to play a great role in human destiny, and the Separatists were firmer adherents of this belief than most. However, as conditions worsened in England, Separatists easily transferred this conviction to "New" England as the place of destiny. They proclaimed America to be God's promised land; it became the land of a covenant people, living under a theocracy dedicated to building a community of God's chosen.[24]

When the Puritans began to settle in America, the brutal, isolated lands fostered the development of commonalities between Separatists and Puritans, blurring the religious and secular distinctions that had been so sharp in England.[25] For example, the Pilgrims established a communal tradition of land distribution, which had practical as well as idealist implications; the Pilgrims recognized they would perish if they did not work as a common unit for the common good.[26]

LDS Roots with Separatism

Some connection between Separatism and the LDS Church has already been established. For example, in 1920 LDS scholar B. Roland Lewis wrote an article in the *Improvement Era* at the time of the tercentenary celebration of the *Mayflower* voyage extolling the kinship of Pilgrim and LDS beliefs.[27] Lewis correctly suggested that Pilgrim thought had more in common with LDS orientations than did Puritanism, and indeed many early LDS family lines turn out to be directly tied to the Pilgrims.

Significant numbers of ancestors of early LDS converts are tied to those very first English refugees who migrated to New England. At least 62 of the 583 converts in this study have direct-line ancestors who arrived on the *Mayflower.* The large number is especially significant because more than half of the 102 *Mayflower* passengers died that first winter, and several other "adventurers" returned to England within a short time. John Landis has determined that there are only 22 heads of household from the *Mayflower* from whom all subsequent descent can be traced without duplication,[28] and early LDS convert lines can be traced back to at least 15 of these 22 heads of household.[29] Of the 62 LDS converts connected with *Mayflower* ancestors, only 15 were related to the "strangers," or adventurers, while the other 47 were related to the Pilgrim Saints.[30] The number of early Pilgrim ancestors of LDS converts would multiply if we were to engage in a similar analysis of those who arrived on the *Fortune* and *Anne* in the years following.

Many early LDS converts could claim multiple *Mayflower* ancestors. Mary Ann Kennedy had five; and each of the 14 converts who had links with John Howland, including the Pratt brothers and the Joseph Smith family through Lucy Mack, would automatically be connected not only with Howland but with Howland's wife, Elizabeth Tillie (often spelled Tilley), and with her parents, John Tillie and Joan Hurst, who died that first winter.

Even though the population of Plymouth Colony was only about 1,500 at midcentury (see table 5, p. 28), an astounding 654 unique names of ancestors among 1,340 total fifth-generation ancestors so far have been recorded. In other words, even though our calculations are conservative because we relied on unique names—remember that different people sometimes shared the same name—we may conclude that approximately 44 percent of all Plymouth Colony inhabitants around 1650 were fifth-generation, direct-line ancestors of LDS converts. From another perspective, at least 248 (43 percent) of the 583 early LDS converts in our study could claim direct-line connections with fifth-generation ancestors residing in Plymouth Colony.

The ratio of LDS ancestors to inhabitants was higher in Plymouth than in any other colony of New England. While less than 7 percent of the people of New England were living in Plymouth Colony, more than 14 percent of the fifth-generation ancestors were from that colony.[31]

Plymouth Colony had but ten townships by midcentury. There is no specific count of any town populations for that time, but there are estimates from a 1675 survey of the number of houses for eight of the towns in the colony, and it is generally possible to extrapolate the relative size of most of the towns from these data.[32] Table 6 indicates that at least 85 percent of the 1,340 ancestors were born in the ten towns of Plymouth colony or had migrated to them from Europe. In fact, 64 percent came from six towns, and a disproportionately large number were located in Plymouth, Barnstable, Yarmouth, and Rehoboth. Relatively few LDS ancestors were found in towns such as Duxbury, Eastham, and Marshfield, and very few lived in what today would be called unincorporated settlements, such as Norton, Freetown, Hull, or Berry Pomery.

Plymouth Colony consisted of a collection of small villages or hamlets spread across the landscape. Plymouth, for example, began as a small, compact set of houses but by midcentury consisted of a number of hamlets or neighborhoods that embraced an area sixteen miles long and nine miles wide.[33] In contrast, Massachusetts and Connecticut towns consisted of close groupings of houses around a common, or town green, where the meetinghouse was almost always situated. In spite of the distinctive organizational structure of Plymouth Colony, the town of Plymouth remained its most important religious, social, and political entity.

Plymouth Township

A total of 135 names of fifth-generation LDS ancestors have so far been identified in Plymouth Township; 86 names were unique.[34] The population was

Table 6. Houses in the Towns and LDS Ancestors in Plymouth Colony

		County Ancestors		Town Ancestors	
Counties and Towns	Houses in 1675	Total Ancestors	Unique Names	Total Ancestors	Unique Names
Barnstable County		378	184		
Barnstable	100			119	65
Eastham				27	17
Sandwich	100			82	42
Yarmouth	150			127	48
Bristol County		551	193		
Rehoboth				297	98
Taunton	150			110	57
Plymouth County		398	264		
Duxbury	100			36	28
Marshfield				14	12
Plymouth	105			135	86
Scituate	300			71	46
Other Counties		13	13		
Total		1,340	654		

Sources: G. D. Scull, "Historical Notes and Letters Relating to New England," *New England Historical and Genealogical Register* 38 (1884): 378–81; Rust Genealogical Data File, 2003.

approximately 200 at that time, so slightly less than half of the residents so far have been identified as fifth-generation ancestors, and the real number is probably more. At least 83 of the 583 early LDS converts (14 percent) could claim fifth-generation ancestors residing in the town of Plymouth.[35]

Plymouth set the tone for many religious developments in the New World. After arriving in Plymouth, the Pilgrims soon found that the merchant adventurers who had paid the expenses for the initial trip were unwilling to comply with their agreement to continue financial support. In 1625, Miles Standish was sent to London to negotiate with the merchants to purchase all rights for the colony, and Isaac Allerton soon followed to conclude arrangements for paying back the original investment of £1,800. The Pilgrims agreed that they would communally assume responsibility for repayment so that the young colony would become independent of its stockholding company. It was agreed that all heads of families, single young men, and freemen would be admitted to equal partnership.[36] This set New England on a course toward independence, something not enjoyed by other colonies of England.

Circumstance played a role in Plymouth's unusual development. For example, after the Pilgrims arrived in the New World, they went several years without a minister. John Robinson, their minister in Leyden, had remained in Holland with the main body of the congregation. Even though William Brewster assumed the role of spiritual leader, he was not ordained and could not perform the sacraments. This circumstance made it necessary to adjust the way the church was run, and the congregation developed a capacity to work without a professional ministry. In 1624, the financial partners in London sent a minister, but the Pilgrims soon discovered he was unworthy, and he was brought to trial and expelled from the colony.[37] By the time a new minister arrived in 1629, church leadership had evolved, and it would never again return to the hierarchical relationships that had existed in Europe between the congregation and the religious leadership. Also, Plymouth Colony, while the center of the Separatist movement in America, was never able to thrive economically. The situation was so bad that the town was often not able to support a permanent minister. When Plymouth lost its minister in 1654, for example, the congregation again went without one for fifteen years.[38]

Plymouth sheltered many people who did not feel comfortable with the Puritans of Massachusetts. Roger Williams, for example, spent some time in Plymouth prior to his expulsion from Massachusetts, and Governor William Bradford's assessment of him at the time suggests the extent to which the Pilgrim Separatists sided with such radicals. Bradford extolled Williams's work with the Pilgrims, exclaiming that he "exercised his gifts amongst them, and after some time was admitted a member of the church; and his teaching well approoved, for the benefite wherof I still blese God, and am thankful to him, even for his sharpest admonitions and reproufs, so farr as they agreed with truth."[39] However, in his further discussion of Williams, Bradford also reveals the middle ground of radicalism the Separatists occupied: "He this year begane to fall into some strange opinions, and from opinion to practice; which caused some controversie betweene the church and him."[40]

Not only did radicals come into Plymouth from afar but Pilgrims from within began to assert their more radical beliefs. The Reverend Charles Chauncey, for example, was adamant that baptism by immersion was necessary, and in 1641 the conflict over the proper mode of baptism led to such dispute with the Reverend John Reyner and others in the congregation that Chauncey left Plymouth and settled in Scituate.[41] John Howland, who had arrived on the *Mayflower* and was an early leader of civic affairs, was released from the general court for two years because it was feared he was sympathetic with Quakers and would not act as harshly toward them as the law required. Such suspicions had some foundation. John's brothers, Arthur and Henry Howland, had become active Quakers in the Plymouth area.[42]

Barnstable

A total of 119 fifth-generation progenitors have been identified who were born in Barnstable; 65 names are unique.[43] In the middle of the seventeenth century, Barnstable was a relatively small village, and a majority of the residents were LDS ancestors. This means that the ratio of ancestors to residents was higher in Barnstable than in Plymouth Colony in general, which itself was the highest among the colonies in New England. From another perspective, at least 71 of the 583 early LDS converts (12 percent) could claim fifth-generation ancestors from the town of Barnstable.

The spiritual leader of the Barnstable congregation, John Lathrop, has been identified as an ancestor of a host of early LDS leaders, including Frederick G. Williams, Oliver Cowdery, Wilford Woodruff, Joseph Smith Jr. and his brothers and sisters (through Lucy Mack), as well as Orson and Parley Parker Pratt.[44] Lathrop was also an ancestor of a significant number of other converts.[45]

Lathrop's family had firm roots in Yorkshire. As a minister in England, he had established a clear public record of protest against the prevailing religious orientation. After serving as minister in Kent, he came to believe that the Church of England had lost its way; in 1623, he renounced his religious orders and declared that he would henceforth espouse the cause of the religious "Independents." He removed the next year to London, where he succeeded

Henry Jacob as pastor of the First Independent Church, also known as the Southwark Church because it was located on that street. The term "Independent" did not at first signify separation from the Church of England but referred to congregations that were independent from one another and not ruled by the bishops. However, it was soon connected with the term "Separatist."[46]

In 1624, the Southwark Church was formally banned by the government, and for eight years the congregation gathered in secret worship. Then the congregation split over the issue of baptism, and part of Lathrop's flock left, forming an Anabaptist church in London. In 1632, Archbishop Laud arrested Lathrop and forty-three members of his parish on the improbable charge of practicing the teachings of the New Testament.[47] After being thrown into prison, Lathrop was convicted of schismatic behavior and sentenced to Newgate Prison, which Helene Holt describes as "an imposing dark, granite structure. Having been in use for nearly five hundred years, its grim, foul smelling, hellish interior was of infamous renown."[48]

Lathrop's first wife died while he was in prison, and he was released after two long years, on condition he and his followers would leave the country. Lathrop, his family, and many of his parishioners sailed for New England on the same ship as Anne Marbury Hutchinson, arriving in Boston on 18 September 1634. At least nine members of his former congregation had already located in Scituate, where in 1633 a merchant adventurer Timothy Hatherly had begun a settlement. Lathrop and other members of his congregation moved to Scituate, where he organized a church for his flock.[49]

Because Scituate was closer to the Boston area than to Plymouth, there was a good deal of tension between Scituate Separatists and mainstream Puritans. Nearby churches in the Massachusetts Bay Colony spoke out, opposing the way Lathrop conducted his religious duties.[50] In addition, there was tension among the church members in Scituate itself. The newcomers were mainly from Kent, while the other residents were Pilgrims, and they often disagreed on doctrinal issues. The attacks on the part of the Massachusetts Bay churches and internal dissension contributed to Lathrop's decision to remove his group from Scituate and to settle, in October 1639, in what became known as Barnstable.[51] Baptism, a major issue that divided the Puritans, Separatists, and radical spiritualists, contributed to Lathrop's decision to leave Scituate,[52] but controversy over baptism continued in the town even after his congregation had departed.[53]

The world of the Separatists is well represented by the congregation of John Lathrop. He was clearly radical in many of his doctrinal positions, but sometimes members of his congregation were more doctrinaire than he was himself. His was a tempered radicalism, particularly the way he tolerated differences of opinion and accepted every applicant to membership in his congregation without demanding a signature of creed or confession of faith. The only requirements were that the applicant "endeavor to keep His commandments, to live a pure life, and to walk in love with the brethren."[54]

Barnstable, situated on Cape Cod, was isolated from the rest of New England, and its location allowed Lathrop, who was a man of "deep piety, great zeal and large ability," to stabilize his congregation and build the foundations of a spiritual communal utopia.[55] He died in Barnstable in 1653, but the town's isolation allowed it to retain its spiritual orientation for generations.

Rehoboth

At least 89 of the 583 early LDS converts (15 percent) could claim fifth-generation ancestors from the town of Rehoboth—a remarkable number because Rehoboth was a small community. Accounts of the population are so meager as to be almost nonexistent, but estimates range from 130 to 300. For example, Bowen estimates that in 1653 the town had approximately 250 residents.[56]

From a different vantage point, 98 unique names from a total of 297 names of fifth-generation LDS ancestors have been identified.[57] Among the hundreds of towns in New England, Rehoboth is only one of three towns in the study where almost 300 fifth-generation names have been identified.[58] Of course, it is impossible for 297 LDS ancestors to have come from a town of approximately 250 residents, but we can account for most of this discrepancy from the modest number of unique names (98), representing a large overlap in ancestors' names.

Much of the overlap in names can be accounted for by the fact that several whole families descending from Rehoboth ancestors joined the church. Of course, siblings have identical ancestors. Joseph Peck, ancestor of early LDS converts Joseph Peck and his children, Esther, Nicholas, Berthena, Ezekiel, Polly, and Hezekiah, was a founding member of Rehoboth. Polly Peck married Joseph Knight Sr., the most visible name in the Colesville, New York, branch, one of the three earliest branches of the church. The Knight children, Hyruna Nahaum, Esther, Newell, Anna, Joseph, Jr., Polly, and Elizabeth, all of them 1830 converts, also counted Joseph Peck Sr. as their progenitor.

The family of Royal Barney Sr. also illustrates family connections with Rehoboth. Not only were Royal, Sr., and his wife, Rachel Marsh Barney, baptized about one year after the church was organized but their children, Philania, Aramel, Royal, Jr., and Edson were also baptized.[59] All genealogical lines of these early Barney converts go directly back to Rehoboth, where the family had resided since the town was settled.[60] The seven children of Ezekiel Johnson were all baptized in 1831: Joel Hills, Nancy Maria, Seth Garnzey, Susan Ellen, Delcena, Julia Ann, David, and Almera Woodard Johnson.

A small hamlet within the formal town boundaries of Rehoboth was Swansea, situated on the border of Rhode Island. The names Sowams, Sowamsett, and Sowames appear in early records, in obvious reference to Swansea,[61] which began to take on the characteristics of a settlement when dissidents in Rehoboth became unhappy with what they regarded as failings in the spiritual dedication of the Congregational Church to the gospel of Jesus Christ. They withdrew to the area along what is now known as the Swansea River, and under the leadership of John Myles they set up their own small Anabaptist community.[62]

A total of 79 fifth-generation LDS ancestors, 25 with unique names, have so far been identified from the little hamlet of Swansea.[63] Some early Swansea residents were ancestors of prominent LDS Church figures. Reynolds Cahoon, a member of the LDS paramilitary Danites, was a descendant of William Cahoon, who came to America in 1650–51 as an indentured servant. In the civil war between the English and the Scots, England captured more than three hundred Scottish soldiers, who were then shipped to the colonies. They were required to work as indentured servants for six to eight years to pay ship passage.[64] Cahoon was among those Scots, and he was bound to an employer in Swansea; he was surely influenced by the hamlet's Anabaptist religious radicalism.

Another early LDS Church leader, Amasa Lyman, had strong family roots in both Rehoboth and Swansea. Lyman served as an apostle from 1842 until 1867, before he was excommunicated for his unorthodox religious beliefs. His grandfather had been born in Swansea and his grandmother in Rehoboth, and the family had been in those towns through the fifth, fourth, third, and second generations of ancestors. Other early Swansea residents included ancestors of the Peck, Snow, and Barney families, as well as those of Isaac Washington Pierce Sr., Rhoda Walker, and Sarah Webber.

Rehoboth was unusual in that it was one of the few inland towns in the colonies having no direct water access to the sea. Little is known of its early history, though it was originally called Seekonk. In 1643, the settlement was incorporated by the Massachusetts Bay Colony, but Plymouth quickly asserted its claim over the territory, and the matter was eventually settled by the commissioners of the United Colonies in 1644, who handed the township over to Plymouth Colony. The dispute was not resolved without struggle between the two colonies, but when it was finally settled, Plymouth authorities gave the township its permanent name of Rehoboth.[65]

It was a remarkable town, like no other in the Plymouth or Massachusetts Bay Colonies; rather, it was much more akin to the town of Providence, less than ten miles to the west. Its residents were fiercely independent and were regularly engaged in radical religious activities. Its leaders included men such as Richard Wright, who wrote a concordance to the Bible while in Rehoboth. His brother, George, was known as a seducer of women in four colonies.[66] John Browne of Rehoboth echoed Roger Williams's beliefs in professing "liberty of conscience" and a new mode of baptism.[67]

Anabaptism gained an early foothold in the town. In 1648, within a few weeks, no less than fourteen Rehoboth residents were rebaptized. Plymouth had no law against rebaptism, as was the case in Massachusetts, but Boston became so agitated over the prospect that this "disease" would spread to them that they pressed Plymouth to curb the growth of Anabaptists.[68] Consequently, even though a number of residents adopted the new faith, no formal congregation was established until the end of the 1660s, and this was in Swansea. With continued pressure coming from Boston, almost all the original Anabaptist leaders left this little hamlet and moved across the border into Rhode Island, where they became leaders in the Anabaptist congregations of Providence and Newport.[69]

Through the next century, Rehoboth retained many of its Anabaptist roots. As Elhanan Winchester, who was the Baptist minister of the Rehoboth congregation in the early 1770s, became progressively more Calvinistic in his theology, the congregation eventually forced his dismissal, and he had to settle elsewhere.[70] Interestingly, Winchester later converted to Universalism and is today identified as a founding father of that movement.[71] Joseph Smith Jr.'s grandfather, Asael Smith, embraced Universalism at the early stages of the movement, and this had a significant influence on the religious views of his family.[72]

4. Puritan Ancestors in Massachusetts and Maine

Massachusetts Bay Colony

In 1630, hundreds of colonists arrived on the eleven ships of the so-called Winthrop fleet to open the Massachusetts Bay Colony.[1] The fleet had been preceded in 1628 by a group of forty Puritans who landed at Salem under the leadership of John Endecott, but the colony became a reality two years later when John Winthrop came to the New World with about one thousand colonists and founded the Puritan capital of Boston. About one-third of the initial group settled in Boston proper, while the others moved to smaller villages springing up around it, including Charlestown, Newtown (Cambridge), Roxbury, Dorchester, Lynn, and Watertown.

The Massachusetts Bay Company had been incorporated as a commercial venture in 1629 by a group of wealthy Puritans, but its character changed when some members decided to remove themselves from the persecutions of Charles I. They persuaded the government to allow them to take the commercial charter with them and then systematically bought out the investors who remained in Britain; thus, they were able to ensure that those in Massachusetts would retain control of the colony. Most of the people arriving in the Winthrop fleet were of the yeoman class, largely tenants living on land owned by the nobility and gentry. Surely, their motive for coming was as much economic as religious. The downtrodden yeomen sensed an opportunity to gain material freedom and to profit from their own labors. Of course, the control of the Massachusetts Bay Company remained in the hands of the wealthy, but the colony was established on Puritan values and religious principles.

LDS Roots in Puritanism

There are clear parallels between Puritan and Mormon beliefs.[2] The doctrines of both reflect inherent tensions between communalism and individualism. On the one hand, their beliefs are those of a covenant people who dedicate themselves and their community to God and are expected to conform to community and spiritual norms. On the other hand, essential to both Puritan and Mormon beliefs is the idea that human beings should exercise their natural powers and their capacity for logic and personal judgment in deciding how to do the will of God. Both doctrines hold that each person has an innate sense of right and wrong and that no civil law should be obeyed if it violates an individual's own conscience concerning the higher divine law.

Both Puritan and Mormon doctrines declare that the family constitutes the main sacred and secular institution on earth, according to which the father heads the family, conducting religious observances and instructing the children in the ways of God. Civil and ecclesiastical government is conceived of as an extension of the family, and both forms of governing are intertwined with each other. Like heads of the family, theocratic leaders are privileged to be "inspired" by God in their civic and religious duties.

To both Puritans and Mormons, America was a place of destiny, and as long as its people in America exercised their faith in God, they believed they would be blessed, but that if their hearts turned to worldly pursuits, God's blessings would be withdrawn from them. Religious and civic behavior, they insisted, should be guided by a strong inner commitment to self-discipline, industriousness, and frugality. Finally, their doctrines encouraged some dancing, celebrating, and use of ornamentation, while discouraging excess in food, drink, and recreation.[3]

Although Puritans failed to attain the level of radicalism Mormons later manifested, the beliefs of both Puritans and Mormons set them apart as religious radicals. Caution must be exercised when suggesting that Puritans were only moderately radical, because profound distinctions were found within the Puritan population. Massachusetts Puritans differed from Connecticut Puritans, and Puritans living in Suffolk County, where Boston is located, differed from those living in surrounding counties. Such distinctions become crucial when one determines where fifth-generation Puritan ancestors of early Mormon converts were located.

LDS Ancestors in Massachusetts Counties

Generally, LDS ancestors in Massachusetts were Puritans, and some LDS converts were descended from Puritan leaders.[4] However, while 62 percent of the population of New England lived in Massachusetts in the mid-seventeenth century, only 48 percent of the New England ancestors of LDS converts lived there, and few of these lived in the Boston area. Thus, these ancestors were unevenly distributed throughout Massachusetts. Table 7 shows that most of them lived in Essex and Middlesex Counties and only a small percentage (15 percent) in the most populous and politically dominant Suffolk County.

The town was at the heart of New England Puritan culture; it is where the level of religious radicalism can best be determined. Most of the LDS ancestors on whom I focus were simple, ordinary people who left almost no record about themselves beyond birth, marriage, and death dates and places. We must extrapolate from the nature of the town where they lived and the congregation where they worshiped in making judgments about them. If they lived in Hartford and belonged to Thomas Hooker's congregation, I would be inclined to make a different judgment about their religious orientation than if they lived in Providence and associated themselves with Roger Williams and the Anabaptists.

By 1650, there were thirty-one incorporated towns in Massachusetts. The colony was growing so rapidly that in 1643 the general court had decided to divide the region into four counties: Suffolk, Essex, Middlesex, and Norfolk. Later, Franklin and Worcester Counties, noted in table 7, were created.

Suffolk County

By far the most populous county in Massachusetts was Suffolk, with a population estimated to have been 14,600 in 1650, thus accounting for almost three-fourths of the entire Massachusetts population. By midcentury, there were eight towns in Suffolk County: Boston, Dorchester, and Roxbury (in-

Table 7. The Fifth Generation and Unique Names of LDS Ancestors Born in or Emigrating to Massachusetts

Counties	Total Number of Ancestors	Unique Names
Essex	1,541	849
Franklin	10	5
Middlesex	1,355	583
Norfolk	365	179
Suffolk	848	424
Worcester	70	32
Unknown	206	67
Total	4,395	2,139

Source: Rust Genealogical Data File, 2003.

corporated in 1630); Hingham, Nantasket, and Weymouth (1635); Dedham (1636); and Braintree (1640). In 1650, the population of Boston was greater than all the other towns in Suffolk County put together, accounting for more than 7,000 people.[5]

While most Massachusetts Bay Company residents lived in Suffolk County, only 14 percent of the Massachusetts LDS ancestors were born there, and less than 5 percent were born in Boston itself. Clearly, the ancestors of early converts were not concentrated in the theocratic center of Puritan Massachusetts. Of the 583 early LDS converts identified in this study, only 13 have fifth-generation ancestors known to have been born in Boston.[6]

Although LDS progenitors were found in every town of Suffolk County, except Nantasket, relatively few unique names were found in the towns immediately outside of Boston. No Suffolk County town, except Boston, was among the twenty most populous towns in New England, accounting for about half of all LDS ancestors in New England. Because of this, it may be instructive to give some sense of the character of the Suffolk County towns (see table 8).

Even in the heart of Massachusetts Puritanism, there was great variation among towns.[7] Boston was the center of the Puritan commonwealth. It was, for a time, the location of centralized political power; and the colony's charter dictated that the governor, assistant governor, and eighteen assistants chosen annually to rule would be Boston freemen. In 1631, church membership was made a condition for participation in civil government. A fundamental assumption of the colony was that ministers would provide guidance and advice. They constituted a separate body of spiritual peers in the parliamentary process.[8] In other words, Massachusetts set the course toward theo-

Table 8. Houses and LDS Ancestors in the Towns of Suffolk County

Towns	Houses in 1675	Total Number of Ancestors	Unique Names
Boston	2,500	208	101
Braintree	250	144	56
Dedham	250	157	58
Dorchester	350	102	60
Hingham	250	60	41
Nantasket	n.a.	0	0
Roxbury	250	95	54
Weymouth	250	82	54
Total	4,100	848	424

Sources: G. D. Scull, "Historical Notes and Letters Relating to New England," *New England Historical and Genealogical Register* 38 (1884): 378–81; Rust Genealogical Data File, 2003.

cratic rule. Soon, the general court of the colony decided that each town would provide two representatives to the court. Such decisions were not made without considerable expression of concern; freemen argued they should participate at some level in all decisions being made, but those in authority inevitably ruled in favor of retaining authority among the representatives.

Boston was an anomaly among early New England towns. It was the only community with the beginnings of a metropolis, which would inevitably result in religious diversity and instability. It was the center of shipping and was therefore where merchants and adventurers congregated. It became a sumptuous city with beautiful buildings of brick, tile, stone, and slate, with wide and active streets.

The very dynamic nature of Boston dictated that it could not retain its radical religious nature. Metropolitan cities are less likely than smaller towns to be the repository of values and beliefs passed from family to family over the generations, and so Boston would play almost no role in the revolutionary spiritual declarations of later centuries, including those of Joseph Smith Jr.

Boston was not the only Suffolk County community to defy the stereotype of the colonial Massachusetts town. Hingham, where few LDS ancestors were located, deviated as well. Its settlers came from quite diverse regions of England; this led to severe social, economic, and religious tensions. Conflicts subsided only when a class oligarchy emerged that wielded enough power to unify the various groups into a working community. However, in the process Hingham developed into an independent and self-directed community. In other words, it neither sought nor achieved the kind of Puritan utopia that is usually portrayed of Massachusetts towns.

Dedham, on the other hand, where a somewhat larger number of Suffolk County LDS ancestors lived, exemplifies the kind of stereotype that comes to mind for mainstream Puritan towns. Puritans settled Dedham in 1636, aiming to achieve a communal, spiritual utopia.[9] The church was the centerpiece of the town, and early Puritans expected it to help them satisfy their thirst for perfection in spiritual and secular life.

In some respects, the first generation of settlers of Dedham realized their utopian ideals. This was possible because most of the townspeople had been small farmers in England and had extended their perception of an ideal village to America, one that included the notion of a more equitable distribution of land. This had never been possible in England; however, in America land was abundant, and this simple ideal was easily attained. But the communal ideal went beyond land distribution. The covenant under which Dedham residents lived demanded that persons applying to reside in the town undergo a public inquisition about their past that would help determine moral eligibility to live in Dedham. The covenant demanded that all residents live according to the laws of "love, forbearance, cooperation, and peace," with love standing higher than all other laws.[10]

Dedham was not a theocracy in the strict sense of the term. The local clergy were not eligible to serve as civil officers, and an occasional nonmember of the congregation was elected to public office. However, the Scriptures were taken as the basis of the town's ordinances and laws and served as the foundation of the original town covenant.

But there was a flaw in the Puritan design. Salvation was reserved only for God's elect, those who had undergone the gradual process of conversion and were inspired to know they had received God's divine grace. Some residents claimed they had not received that grace or it had not been given to them, and there was a natural tension between those who were and those who were not among the elect.[11] Townspeople recognized this source of dissonance and attempted to compensate through community unity. The town meeting was designed to allow everyone to participate in decisions affecting community welfare. Everyone was expected to accept the importance of Christian order based on love and respect. One factor contributing to initial success in building a communal unity was an increase in the number of the elect. By 1648, at least 70 percent of the adult men and women in town were church members, and 80 percent of the newborn children were baptized.[12]

The church community was especially sensitive to the difficulties some potential members encountered in meeting the town's standards and therefore assisted them with special care. A particular source of stress was the so-called conversion narrative, in which potential members were required to explain why they were among the elect. Robert Hinsdale's wife, Ann Woodward, an ancestor of LDS convert Lyman Wight, became fearful that she would "faint away" while giving her conversion narrative. The church fathers responded to her fear by allowing her to make the narrative in private. Such anxiety was apparently widespread. The account of Jonathan Fairbanks, an ancestor of LDS convert Julia Hills, is especially illuminating: "Jonathan Fairbanke, notwithstanding he had long stood off from the church upon some scruples about public profession of faith and the covenant, yet after divers loving conferences . . . , he made such a declaration of his faith and conversion to God and profession of subjection to the ordinances of Christ in this church that he was readily and gladly received by the whole church."[13]

These are instances of psychological differences within the community, and there is evidence that church fathers made allowances for these differences in an effort to contribute to unity and harmony. At town meetings and church services, members of the community often called on God to shed his spirit and grace upon them so that they could stand fast in one spirit and one mind for generations to come.

The story of Dedham is but a variation on the theme of Puritanism as it played itself out in Massachusetts towns. In the seventeenth century, a typical New England town might have 500 inhabitants. At midcentury, Dedham was not a large town, claiming approximately 400 inhabitants.[14] There were only 58 unique names among the 157 identified fifth-generation LDS ancestors, more names than most other towns in Suffolk County but rather modest when compared with many towns in counties elsewhere in the colony. The overlap in ancestors' names suggests that several LDS converts shared ancestors, including the Knight, Peck, Chadwick, Marsh, Cheney, and Hale families, all well-known families in Mormon history.[15]

In spite of dedicated effort, the utopian perfectionism of Dedham did not last. In fact, by the end of the seventeenth century internal and external forces came to redefine the town. The original settlers eventually died, and the town's new leaders failed to hold to the same standard as their parents. The restrictive rules, applied to those asking permission to move to Dedham, began to break down. Love gave way to greed and self-interest in the use of common properties and communal obligations. Problems with the Indians became acute, particularly in connection with land claims.[16] However, even though the practices of everyday life began to shift, the internalized norms and values of those early years continued to be verbalized. They were challenged, they withered, but they did not die. It is, therefore, no accident that the norms and values of many of the LDS descendants of early Dedham settlers would resonate two hundred years later with assertions that the gospel of Jesus Christ was once again on the earth.

Essex County

By midcentury, Essex County was beginning to rival Suffolk County in terms of population. Its main town, Salem, had been the first in New England, and other towns were soon added. Marblehead was incorporated in 1633, followed by Ipswich (1634), Newbury (1635), Lynn (1637), Rowley (1639), Salisbury (1640), Haverhill (1641), and Andover (1646).

Essex County is particularly relevant because its towns are among those having the greatest number of fifth-generation LDS ancestors in Massachusetts. Table 9 indicates that a total of 1,541 ancestors (35 percent of all Massachusetts ancestors) have been identified in Essex County, with 849 unique names among them (40 percent of all unique names of ancestors in Massachusetts).[17] Some Essex County towns had large numbers of identified LDS ancestors. Ipswich, with a total of 332 ancestors (150 with unique names), had more than any other town in New England. Salem, with a total of 243 (147 with unique names), and Rowley, with a total of 244 (109 with unique names), were among the ten towns in all New England with the largest number of ancestors. Lynn, with a total of 120 (61 with unique names), and Newbury, with a total of 161 (108 with unique names), are also counted among the towns with the largest number. These numbers can be explained in part by the fact that Salem and Ipswich were the largest settlements in Essex County, but it is surprising to find so many ancestors in small towns such as Rowley. In fact, 208 (36 percent) of all early LDS converts so far identified could claim to have at least one fifth-generation ancestor from Essex County.

Essex County deviated in tone and practice from mainstream Puritanism. A number of factors explain this deviance. Politically, the early administrative boundaries of Essex County included religiously radical New Hampshire, which had been formally a part of Massachusetts from 1641 to 1679.[18] This meant that New Hampshire and Essex County shared the same legislative and administrative representatives.[19] Essex County inhabitants also shared a cultural affinity with New Hampshire, in that its people were fiercely independent and tolerated little interference from Boston, Puritanism's theocratic center.

Economically, Essex County was subjected to constant competition between the Massachusetts Bay Company and the Plymouth Company, both of which made claims to the coastal territories where the towns were located. Many Essex County towns had been settled by adventurers before the

Table 9. Houses and LDS Ancestors in the Towns of Essex County

Towns	Houses in 1675	Total Number of Ancestors	Unique Names
Andover	50	49	31
Gloucester		44	30
Haverhill		66	37
Ipswich	400	332	150
Lynn		120	61
Newbury	300	161	108
Rowley		244	109
Salem	500	243	147
Salisbury		92	74
Topsfield		49	21
Other		141	81
Total		1,541	849

Sources: G. D. Scull, "Historical Notes and Letters Relating to New England," *New England Historical and Genealogical Register* 38 (1884): 378–81; Rust Genealogical Data File, 2003.

Massachusetts Bay Company arrived in the New World in 1630. Gloucester, Marblehead, and Newbury, for example, were already small hamlets in 1623. Their settlers came for commercial purposes, particularly related to fishing, from Wales and the West Country of England. These towns did not have the stable, communal characteristics of a typical New England community. Rather, they experienced turbulent beginnings and were characterized by relatively large in- and out-migration, diverse populations, and little religious cohesion.

From the beginning of the colony, Salem, the major town, was quite outspoken in its tendency toward Separatism rather than mainstream Puritanism. Further, in the 1630s Essex County harbored a large number of Antinomians, and in the 1640s and 1650s, many Gortonists and Anabaptists.[20] By the 1660s, internal divisions in communities were accentuated by the successful introduction of Quakerism. Finally, the infamous "Salem" witch trials of 1692 took place in Essex County. Although this occurred at a time later than the focus of this book, they are another indication of the spiritual agitation that cut through these communities. Thus, although Essex County was in Massachusetts and was formally part of the administration of the Massachusetts Bay Company, one finds all levels of radicalism within its borders.

Maine

Puritanism was also a part of the Maine culture. A number of English settlements were established along the Maine coast in the early 1600s. In fact, the Plymouth Company established its first settlement at Popham, Maine, the same year it settled Jamestown, Virginia. The town was named after Captain George Popham, but after he died in 1608, the harsh Maine winter forced the small group to abandon the settlement, so Jamestown is regarded as America's first permanent colony.

Maine's rugged climate, deprivations, and Indian attacks wiped out many of the first settlements, and only a half dozen survived the first century. These included York and Kittery (incorporated in 1647), just above the Piscataqua River separating Maine from New Hampshire. In 1636, Ferdinand Gorges, a firm Episcopalian and royalist, established the first government in Maine, and it assumed an ecclesiastical character following the Episcopal faith. Massachusetts quickly bought up most of the land claims in this wilderness territory, and by 1658 Maine was annexed, an arrangement that lasted until 1820, when Maine became a separate state.

Because of its close contact with Massachusetts, Maine differed markedly from New Hampshire, in that it cultivated mainstream Puritan sentiments and practices, including a spirit against the "wild fanaticism" of those who did not bow to its authority.[21] The first known dissenting group to establish itself in Maine were the Anabaptists, who set up a separate congregation in 1682 under the leadership of William Screven, but the religious and political authorities in Kittery so slandered the group that its members withdrew and moved to South Carolina.[22]

There is relatively little evidence of the presence of LDS ancestors in Maine. Only 79 unique names of fifth-generation LDS ancestors, 7.9 percent of the 1650 estimate of Maine's population, are found to have been born there. None of these have identifiable connections with either the earliest settlers of Maine nor any radical religious activities, so they are presumed to have been largely mainline Puritans.

5. Puritan Ancestors in Connecticut

From Massachusetts to Connecticut

Puritans who fled the problems plaguing Massachusetts moved to Connecticut and New Haven Colonies, where they set up small, tightly knit theocratic polities.[1] A "small, inconspicuous agricultural colony," Connecticut was isolated from the main currents of New England's religious and political activity.[2] It did not fit the general Massachusetts profile of sharp class distinctions, and each small congregation was left to its own devices to form its individual community and character. Connecticut Puritans took pride in their independence, and their norms and politics reflected a strong sense of individualism.

Historians of Connecticut claim the colony, with its strong heritage of Congregationalism, was the birthplace of constitutional government.[3] As early as 1637, a year after Thomas Hooker and his group settled Hartford, Hooker began formulating a constitution for the inhabitants of Windsor, Hartford, and Wethersfield. On 14 January 1639, residents agreed to a written constitution specifying representative government. Although Hooker is credited with having anticipated America's democratic form of government, the more important issue for him was to ensure that all political decisions be made according to "the blessed will and law of God." The written constitution defined for magistrates and officers the "bounds and limitations" that the law of God placed on them.[4]

Connecticut Puritans expressed a religious fervor exceeding that of many other Puritans, leading to a "staunch determination to worship in purity and simplicity."[5] They strove to behave like saints and to lead lives as godly as possible. The first towns of Connecticut exemplify the Congregational wing of the broader Puritan movement. Even though Congregationalism had found a certain resonance in England, especially after Oliver Cromwell aligned himself with its cause, it was in the New England colonies that the so-called Congregational Way took permanent form.

Even though the Connecticut congregations remained formally within the framework of nonseparation, by the middle of the century they had become Separatist in almost every other way.[6] To begin with, the form of governance in Connecticut was very similar to that of Pilgrim Separatists. The *Mayflower* Pilgrims were a covenant people, which meant they had made a compact with the Lord to bind themselves to him and to each other. Further, because Plymouth was without a minister for almost ten years, the local congregation learned to manage its affairs without dependence on the hierarchical English episcopal tradition. Finally, the Pilgrims cast off pomp and ceremony in favor of simplicity of worship.[7] All Puritan congregations incorporated some features of Pilgrim life, but they were particularly evident in Puritan Connecticut.

Because of the manner in which it was colonized, Connecticut escaped the problems racking Massachusetts. Small groups located far from Boston for the specific purpose of establishing autonomous theocratic communities and avoiding the dictates of the hierarchically oriented Puritan leaders of Massachusetts. These communities were theocratic, in that the church and its religious leaders instituted civil authority to secure "the purity and peace of the ordinances to themselves and their posterity."[8]

In their quest to establish some communal utopias, Congregational leaders rejected all divisive behaviors and feared schismatic doctrines. Consequently, they suppressed the development of dissenting sects or any form of religious liberty. In 1656, for example, when the first Quaker women arrived seeking proselytes, the Connecticut general court quickly forbade Quakers, Ranters, Adamites, or "such like notorious heritiques" from remaining in any town for more than fourteen days.[9]

In spite of attempts to suppress religious liberty, certain internal developments in most congregations led to crises.[10] The major leverage for conformity a congregation exercised was dismissal or even excommunication, but that option only contributed to divisions, which the congregations wished to avoid. Another internal problem was caused by "withdrawers," who voluntarily removed themselves from the congregation in one town to join a congregation in another, to the dismay of those just abandoned. Ministers met regularly to resolve these difficulties and to develop policies on which all could agree, but this approach was met with suspicion because it implied the development of centralization, which congregations resisted.[11]

Just as in mainstream Massachusetts, there was no single Puritan way in Connecticut. For instance, Hampden County was originally settled by a company of people led by William Pynchon, who was later charged with heresy for his radical doctrines. Settlers of New London, located on the western border of Rhode Island, felt a kinship with that colony, where inhabitants were generally identified as religious radicals.

LDS Ancestors in Connecticut

A high concentration of fifth-generation ancestors of the early LDS converts was to be found in Puritan Connecticut. While the ratio of LDS ancestors to general inhabitants was not as high as in Plymouth Colony, it was substantial. In 1650, there were only some 4,100 inhabitants in Connecticut, about 18 percent of the New England population, but at least 27 percent of the LDS ancestors so far identified were from that colony.[12]

From another perspective, almost one-third of the Connecticut population at that time were fifth-generation ancestors of early LDS converts, more than our overall finding that one-fifth of the New England population were ancestors. From yet another perspective, at least 309 (53 percent) LDS converts in this study could claim at least one fifth-generation ancestor from Connecticut.

Estimates of the population of various Connecticut towns in 1650 can be extrapolated from the 1675 survey of New England, which counted houses rather than people. Names of ancestors appear to be dispersed throughout the towns and countryside and reflect in large measure the demographic profile of Connecticut (see table 10). For instance, 37 percent of fifth-generation LDS ancestors with unique names in Connecticut were born in Hartford County, where approximately 45 percent of the population lived. Most of the ancestors were to be found in the towns with the largest number of inhabitants: Hartford (250 ancestors, 137 with unique names), New Haven (291 ancestors, 162 with unique names), and Windsor (245 ancestors, 160 with unique names). However, LDS ancestors were to be found everywhere in Connecticut, including small hamlets having only a few households.

Even though LDS ancestors were dispersed throughout Connecticut, a disproportionately large number of them were found in the smaller towns of Stamford, Lyme, and Norwich, and in some of these towns in 1650, a majority of the inhabitants might have been LDS ancestors. And substantial

Table 10. Houses and LDS Ancestors in Connecticut Counties and Selected Towns

		County Ancestors		Town Ancestors	
Counties and Towns	Houses in 1675	Total Ancestors	Unique Names	Total Ancestors	Unique Names
Fairfield County		241	148		
Fairfield	300			51	30
Stratford	200			80	50
Middlesex County		208	101		
Saybrook	100			67	26
Hartford County		819	444		
Hartford	500			250	137
Wethersfield	150			154	87
Windsor	400			245	160
New Haven County		554	310		
New Haven	500			291	162
Stamford	100			81	38
New London County		306	190		
Lyme	60			60	38
New London	200			114	67
Norwich	40			63	41
Other		75	33		
Total	2,550	2,203	1,226		

Sources: G. D. Scull, "Historical Notes and Letters Relating to New England," *New England Historical and Genealogical Register* 38 (1884): 378–81; Rust Genealogical Data File, 2003.

numbers of the inhabitants of Killingworth, Saybrook, and Wethersfield were ancestors as well. But in some small towns, such as Stratford, there were relatively few; however, that town was interesting enough that we will give some attention to it.

The population of Stratford, like most Puritans, came mainly from the eastern part of England and were largely craftsmen, including weavers, masons, joiners, smiths, and husbandmen.[13] But Stratford had the distinction of being the first community in Connecticut that was not under the rule of strict Puritanism, and so it served as a place of refuge for certain settlers. For example, one couple, Milford ancestors of early LDS convert Mary Lovisa Parker, named Birdseye, had been caught kissing on the Sabbath. The couple was condemned to the stocks but broke free and escaped to Stratford.[14]

The town was settled in 1639 by the Reverend Adam Blakeman, who had converted to Calvinism and had joined Thomas Hooker's congregation. He had been among those who arrived with Hooker in Hartford, but eventually he decided to settle in Stratford with a small band of followers. The first settlers in Stratford numbered seventeen families, and by 1649 that number had increased to more than forty households. As noted, a relatively small number of ancestors of early LDS converts were among these people. Of the forty-two heads of families noted on the town records of 1649, only eight have been found to be LDS ancestors. In contrast to Stratford, the towns of Hartford, Windsor, and New Haven each had well over one hundred LDS ancestors.[15]

Hartford

Hartford, Windsor, and Wethersfield were the earliest permanent settlements in Connecticut. In 1635, Thomas Hooker and his congregation had removed from Newtown in Massachusetts and traveled over land to the Connecticut Valley, where they settled Hartford.[16]

Hooker's life in England parallels that of other Puritan divines. He graduated from Emmanuel College, Cambridge University, known for its reformist Puritan orientation. After serving as rector of St. George's in Esher, Surrey, he was assigned to be minister at Chelmsford, a town that was noted for its "intemperance and the profanation of the Sabbath," where a multitude of public houses were maintained and shops opened on the Sabbath. His ministry was so successful there that "these vices were banished from the place."[17]

In 1629, Anglican Bishop Laud threatened to arraign Hooker before the High Commission. Having been "silenced for non-conformity," he escaped to Holland where he spent three years before emigrating to New England, arriving in September 1633. Hooker joined his Chelmsford flock, most of whom had preceded him, and settled at Newtown (later Cambridge), Massachusetts.[18]

When Hooker arrived in New England he was one of only thirteen or fourteen ministers in the colony, so his arrival was cause for some rejoicing. However, he soon found himself involved in the controversies surrounding Roger Williams and other heretics. He was disturbed by the turmoil in Massachusetts and in 1635 decided to remove his flock from the Boston area to the Connecticut Valley, so that they might practice their religion in the way they considered necessary.[19] Accompanying Hooker in that initial overland trip were approximately 60 men, women, and children.[20] Over the next year a number of others from New Town followed, bringing the total of Hartford households to 155.

In Boston, the major crisis of the time was Antinomianism, which rejected civil law in favor of spiritual law (see chapter 7), and even though those moving to Hartford did so in an attempt to escape the turmoil, Hooker nevertheless became a central figure in the controversy. In 1637 he wrote Governor Winthrop a letter about Anne Marbury Hutchinson, who was at the center of the crisis: "I did rejoice from the root of my heart that the Lord did and hath graciously kept you from the taint of those new-coined conceits."[21] Later that year, Hooker was chosen to be a moderator in the debates surrounding Hutchinson. Eventually a judicial council ruled that she was guilty of eighty-two dangerous opinions and nine unwholesome expressions.

In the middle of the 1600s, the largest town in Connecticut was Hartford, and it also had the greatest number of LDS ancestors.[22] Many of them had been together as part of the community of Saints at Chelmsford, England, and as they moved to New Town and then on to Hartford, they solidified their sense of community. Their feelings of kinship must have been intense and served as a bond and a comfort as they suffered trials and tribulations.

Because the congregation had been together as a single religious unit for many years, Hartford settlers gave less thought to theological issues than to physical survival in the wilderness. Their leaders also focused more on civic administration than on doctrine and theology. Hooker gave his energies to holding disparate social forces together and melding a communal utopia. Because he had worked so long with his insular congregation of the faithful, they were his people, and they followed his lead. However, Hooker was also a declared evangelist who wished to convert the wayward and the "unregenerates of the necessity of seeking Christ." In other words, the congregation was not to be considered overly restrictive in its permanent membership but was to be open to those outsiders who also wished to gain salvation.[23] Hooker was successful in holding his congregation together until his death on 7 July 1647 during an epidemic. After he died, divisive factions began to assert themselves, and the Hartford utopian quest faltered. On the one hand, there were many who wished to perpetuate Hooker's emphasis on clerical authority and conformity to the standards laid down by the church covenant. On the other hand, others attempted to mold Hartford into "an agent for consensus and social control in the community by deemphasizing spirituality and demanding, instead, conformity to congregationally determined standards of behavior."[24]

At least twenty-eight of the fifty-five original heads of household who arrived in Hartford in 1635 were ancestors of LDS converts, including such early leaders of the LDS Church as members of the first Quorum of Apostles, Orson and Parley Parker Pratt, the first bishop, Edward Partridge Sr., and the apostle and eventual LDS president, Wilford Woodruff. As dissension developed in the Hartford congregation, the ancestors were not all aligned with any particular faction. The major furor that arose after the death of Hooker was around Samuel Stone, who became the Connecticut Valley's leading clerical voice. Stone wished to modify Hooker's evangelical Congregationalism, and the community had divided over the issue. William Goodwin, an ancestor of Edward Partridge Sr. and others, was an ardent supporter of Stone.[25] On the other side were people such as magistrate John Talcott, ancestor of early LDS convert John Gould; Governor John Webster, ancestor of Editha Marsh and Horace, Isaac, and Lucy Diantha Morley; as well as Deputy Governor Thomas Wells, ancestor of Lucy Gunn and David Johnson, as well as Horace, Isaac, and Diantha Morley.

Windsor

In October 1635, the same year Hooker settled in Hartford, the Reverend John Warham brought a flock of about sixty souls to establish a town just north of Hartford, which they named Windsor. Warham had graduated from Oxford in 1614 and went immediately into church service at Exeter, where he became an "eminent minister."[26] In 1627 he was relieved of his duties for his strong Puritan leanings, and when John Winthrop formed the Massachusetts Bay Company, Warham and many of his congregation were among the first to sign on.

The *Mary and John,* which set sail in March of 1630, was the first of the ships in the Winthrop fleet to land in Massachusetts.[27] About 60 of the 140 passengers were from Warham's Exeter parish. It was still winter when the ship arrived and the passengers survived mainly through the generosity of Indians who brought them corn, clothing, and knives. The members of the parish founded the town of Dorchester, just south of Boston, and they remained there until 1635, when Warham's congregation, seeking more fertile lands and a less hectic political environment, migrated to Connecticut.[28]

Of the twenty-three heads of household who traveled with Warham from Dorchester to Windsor, seventeen, an astounding 74 percent, were forebears of at least forty-three LDS converts, which means that many were ancestors of several converts. Warham himself was an ancestor of several converts.

At midcentury, fifteen years after Warham arrived in Connecticut, the town of Windsor was smaller than Hartford but had almost an equal number of fifth-generation LDS ancestors. Thus, more LDS ancestors were born in Windsor than in Hartford. No less than 81 of the 583 LDS converts in our study had fifth-generation relatives born there. Among the converts who could claim ancestors from Windsor were some well-known leaders of the LDS Church, including Apostles W. W. Phelps, Luke Johnson, and Orson Hyde; Lucy Mack, the mother of the prophet Joseph Smith Jr.; Polly Peck; Bishop Edward Partridge Sr.; the apostle and eventual church president, Lorenzo Snow; and many others.

In spite of tensions and difficulties, the community was relatively cohesive, living in religious and social harmony.[29] The main reason for this was the position John Warham took regarding membership. He refused admission to the congregation to few applicants, baptizing all who requested it.[30] It is therefore not surprising that the ancestors and their families usually remained in Windsor for several generations.

Wethersfield

Wethersfield, located just south of Hartford, was another Hartford County town. Settlers arrived about the same time as the Windsor congregation, but their story is different because some in the group were not seeking a spiritual utopia. Rather, among Wethersfield's first settlers were individuals who left Boston because they were seeking new stimulation and adventure. They were "a high-spirited and very excitable people, impatient of control, delighting in the most daring enterprise."[31] There was also little church leadership to hold the adventurers in check and maintain cohesion. Soon the town fell into a state of instability and confusion, and some people moved on to other areas of Connecticut. In 1641, for example, because of differences with other planters in the settlement, about twenty residents moved as a body to Stamford in the New Haven Colony, including direct-line ancestors of Parley P. Pratt, Orson Pratt, and Joseph Coe.

Wethersfield was a relatively small town at midcentury, claiming about a third as many residents as Hartford or Windsor. However, at least 154 fifth-generation ancestors were born in the settlement, indicating that a high proportion of the town population were LDS ancestors. Some of them were ancestors of well-known LDS converts, including Apostle Orson Hyde, Bishop Edward Partridge Sr., Counselor to the President Frederick G. Williams, apostle and eventual president Wilford Woodruff, and the Joseph Smith Jr. and Brigham Young families.

So many fifth-generation ancestors were born in Hartford County that it might be instructive to elaborate on one individual LDS convert: Parley Parker Pratt. Both Parley and his brother Orson were important theologians of the LDS Church and were among its first apostles. Hymns composed by Parley Parker Pratt are still sung in Mormon services.

The first American Pratt carrying the family name was Lieutenant William Pratt Jr., who accompanied Thomas Hooker to Hartford in 1635. William was the son of the Reverend William Pratt Sr. of Stevenage, England, and had attended Emmanuel College, Cambridge University, at the same time as Thomas Hooker. The two undoubtedly knew each other, and both left Cambridge University with a deep commitment to Puritanism, the theological orientation of Emmanuel College. The Reverend Mr. Pratt never left England, but he sent his two sons, fifteen-year-old William, Jr., and twin brother John to accompany Hooker to America and Hartford.

A year after the group arrived in the Connecticut Valley, William Pratt Jr. married Elizabeth Clarke. She was the sixteen-year-old daughter of John Clarke, a member of the group that traveled with Hooker to the Connecticut Valley. John Clarke and his family had come to Massachusetts from Hertfordshire, England, in 1632. His home had been only a few miles away from Chelmsford, England, where Hooker had lived, and he had been a member of Hooker's Newtown, Massachusetts, congregation.

Yet another member of the group arriving with Hooker was William Parker. His daughter Margaret would eventually marry William Joseph Pratt, the son of William Pratt Jr. and Elizabeth Clarke. The Pratt family would later tie in to other Hartford families who had arrived with Hooker, including Stephen Post, the first town constable.

Even though the LDS Pratt family line is tightly bound up with many of those first settlers of the original Hartford community, this line also extends to communities around Hartford. John Coggins was a member of the original group of settlers of Windsor, and his son would marry Ruth Parker, another daughter of William Parker of Hartford. Thus, two of William Parker's daughters became direct-line ancestors of Parley Parker Pratt; that is, the Parkers are connected to the LDS Pratts through more than one line. The Pratt example illustrates the close kinship ties among the ancestors of LDS converts who abandoned Massachusetts Bay Colony and settled the first towns of the Connecticut Colony.

Even though most of the Parley Parker Pratt family lines connect with other early settlers of Hartford County, a small number extend even beyond Connecticut. One line runs to the family of John Howland, one of the *Mayflower* ancestors. Another line runs to the John Greene family of Rhode Island, who were early Anabaptist and political leaders of that colony. Still another line runs to William Hutchinson and his wife Anne Marbury, who were expelled from Massachusetts during the Antinomian controversy.

Saybrook

The Clarke, Parker, Post, and Pratt names are also associated with the little town of Saybrook, located at the mouth of the Connecticut River, which runs through Hartford south to the Atlantic.[32] Under the leadership of Colonel George Fenwick, members of his household and other "gentlemen of high respectability" arrived in Saybrook in the midsummer of 1639.[33] Their intent was to create a major seaport, but the waters proved too shallow for development, so Saybrook remained a small village. Originally outside the boundaries of the Connecticut Colony, Saybrook joined with Connecticut in 1644. In the 1640s, most of the original adventurers migrated away from Saybrook, but other families took their place, including those of ancestors John Clarke, William Parker, Stephen Post, and William Pratt Jr. These family lines eventually joined with other settlers, so that almost all early Saybrook residents who took up permanent residence have direct-line connections with early LDS converts.[34]

New Haven

The largest Connecticut town outside Hartford County was New Haven. It was established through the efforts of Theophilus Eaton, his brother the Reverend Samuel Eaton, and the Reverend John Davenport. Davenport's saga is typical of those Puritans who set out to form their own utopian colonial community in New England. After graduating from Oxford in 1615, he served for a year as a chaplain before becoming a preacher in London. In 1624 he was "elected by almost unanimous vote of the parishioners . . . to the vicarage of St. Stephen's," a large, wealthy, middle-class parish, which had a clear Congregational orientation.[35]

For Davenport, the Bible held the key to understanding what God expected of his children; it contained everything God had said and all he would say. In addition, the Bible dictated the rules of conduct for all people.[36] With the accession of anti-Puritan Archbishop Laud in 1633, Davenport fled to the Netherlands, where he remained for three years. One of his London parishioners, Theophilus Eaton, a boyhood schoolmate, had become a prominent businessman. Under cover, Davenport returned to London where he and Eaton organized a company mainly of his old wealthy parish, and in April 1637 they set sail for America on the ship *Hector*.

Arriving in June, the group determined to remain in Boston through the next winter. Because of John Davenport's stature, Massachusetts Puritans quickly made his group welcome. Davenport aligned himself with the Puritan hierarchy and played a central role in the Antinomian court decision. He once stated, "There are certain opinions which always come forth, under one form or another, in times of great religious excitement. . . . These opinions, essentially the same under many modifications, have been known in various ages by various names, as Antinomianism, Familism, and—in our day—Perfectionism."[37]

The turbulence surrounding the Antinomian crisis reinforced a decision on the part of Davenport and his friends to leave Boston for a distant location and to establish their own civil and ecclesiastical rule. Davenport and Eaton envisioned setting up God's kingdom on earth and dreamed of establishing the most rigorous theocracy of the New England colonies.[38] After picking up additional followers, the group sailed to New Haven the following spring, and by the end of 1638 approximately five hundred settlers had arrived there. They consisted of original St. Stephen's congregation members plus many people from Boston who were looking for a new spiritual beginning. The churches that were established in the New Haven Colony all followed the Congregational way, signaling that they rejected any central control from Boston or British interference; rather they desired "absolute independency of churches."[39]

In spite of the specific mission of the group, some religious divisions remained relating to Puritan and Separatist sympathies. Also, the New Haven Puritans differed from their Massachusetts counterparts in allowing every freedom of conscience, as long as people refrained from promulgating their views in public. For example, the wife of Theophilus Eaton professed Anabaptism, but no measures were taken against her because she exercised discretion in her beliefs and made no attempt to proselytize others to her faith.[40]

Within the next six years, the colony grew to approximately eight hundred souls, and members of the group established a number of plantations along the coast in the direction of New Amsterdam, including Guilford, Stamford, Southold (on Long Island), Milford, and Branford.[41]

The New Haven Colony began with a substantial amount of hard money, but a series of catastrophes and unwise investments soon depleted these resources, and the colony eventually opted to join Connecticut in 1665. The congregations of New Haven were quite similar to others in the Connecticut Colony, in that both Puritans and Separatists were found among them, and there was great debate about whether the colony should go in one direction or another. John Davenport, the minister, had never been a Separatist and wrote a treatise arguing that the Scriptures demanded the Puritan point of view. Davenport's argument ultimately prevailed; nevertheless, the various congregations practiced a strict Congregationalism that was more akin to Separatism than to Massachusetts reformism.[42]

Even though the population of the New Haven Colony barely exceeded 800 by midcentury and no more than 1,000 prior to annexation with Connecticut in 1665, the colony could claim 554 fifth-generation ancestors of early LDS converts. Of course, many converts had the same ancestors, but at present 310 unique names have been identified among the ancestors.

Looking at the situation from another perspective, we find that at least thirty-seven LDS converts have identified ancestors among the original fifty-four founders of the New Haven Colony.[43] Some LDS converts, of course, had multiple ancestors who settled New Haven. For example, twenty-one of Algernon Sidney Gilbert's twenty-seven known fifth-generation ancestors were born in New Haven of parents who were among the first settlers.[44]

There were other counties in Connecticut, including New London, in which LDS ancestors played a prominent role, but we shall consider New London when we discuss dissidents who gathered in Rhode Island.

6. Schismatic New England

Accord and Discord

"Order, harmony, religiosity, sublimation of the individual to the good of the whole, patriarchalism, zeal for communal perfection," writes Paul Lucas, "have too often characterized Puritan New England."[1] More recently, scholars have recognized that Puritan societies were racked with dissension and conflict. While almost everyone who migrated to early New England agreed that God and his church would be the foundation of their fledgling societies, there was great disagreement among them as to how such objectives would be accomplished and who would participate. Intense and personal spiritual commitments brought them into conflict with each other and led to crises. Lucas has even described the Connecticut Valley, where entire congregations had fled the conflictual atmosphere of Boston, as the "valley of discord."[2] Thus, they escaped one area of conflict only to find themselves in another.

While the Pilgrims saw themselves as a small group of the disenfranchised, attempting merely to survive in the hostile lands of New England, the Massachusetts Bay Colony was well organized and quickly transformed Massachusetts into an intolerant and militant commonwealth. Colony leaders were determined to maintain unity at any cost and often dealt harshly with differences of opinion. This rigidity came about not only because the founders strove to establish a Christian community but also because Puritans felt their civilization to be endangered by the recurrent fights with Indians, the French presence in the north, and especially by the wild frontier before them.

However, from New England's beginnings, theological opinion varied.

"*Heterogeneity*, not unanimity, . . . characterized the colony's religious life," writes Philip Gura. There was no single "Puritan way," no confluence of religious belief, no unanimity even in the voices of religious leadership.[3] Pilgrims, the first group to arrive on the New England shores, were Separatists; they set a tone for opposition not consistent with the aims of the Puritan fathers who later founded the Massachusetts Bay Colony.

Radical spiritualists so threatened the status quo that they were persecuted, ostracized, and often expelled, not only from England but from Massachusetts Bay Colony as well. Some of those barred from Massachusetts were people such as Roger Williams, Anne Marbury Hutchinson, and Samuell Gorton, who gained the spotlight when others in the colonies rallied around them in defense of their ideas and actions. Whole congregations sought refuge outside the boundaries of Massachusetts, such as those led by John Wheelwright and Stephen Bachiler, who had come to America because they identified with a radical cause but were further radicalized when Puritan leaders took action against them. Others were committed Puritans who struck out for new territory in search of a place where they could build their own spiritual utopia on earth, away from the Massachusetts Bay Company's control. Almost all of Connecticut was settled by those uneasy with the ruling gentry of Boston.

Even the more evenhanded Pilgrims found deviant behavior alarming. As early as 1624, two people were banished from Plymouth Colony. John Lyford and John Oldham had arrived in Plymouth in 1623; however, they were soon expelled because the Pilgrims thought their beliefs were too close to those of the Church of England.[4] Lyford eventually settled in Virginia, but Oldham was allowed to return within the year, though he was "forced to run the gauntlet with Pilgrims hitting him on his buttocks with their muskets to punish him for his alien religious beliefs."[5] There were other conservatives among those shunned, such as the Brown brothers, who also were expelled from the colony for supporting Anglicanism.[6]

And there were others who were simply disputatious. Thomas Morton, who had arrived in New England in 1622 with thirty servants, was seen to be so riotous by both whites and Indians that they repeatedly remonstrated with him, to little effect. In 1630, when he was living in Braintree, the Massachusetts Bay Company banished him.[7] In 1631, Phillip Ratcliffe of Salem was whipped, his ears were cut off, and finally he was banished for "malicious and scandalous speeches" against the Massachusetts Bay Company.[8]

For the most part, those being expelled held radical religious views. They were not satisfied with mere purification or even separation. They were usually seekers of the true light of Christ; they often saw themselves as keepers of sacred knowledge received through divine inspiration. Unfortunately, little is known about the earliest heretical radicals, mainly because the Massachusetts clergy and other leaders who upheld the Massachusetts religious and political establishment rarely allowed them a public forum, and they were soon forgotten. Samuel Skelton of Salem, Essex County, was typical in that "little has come down to us concerning him, owing, it is said, to the fact that he differed about clerical associations and other subjects from most of the principal persons in Massachusetts."[9]

The threat of banishment continued for several decades. William Pynchon is a prime case in point, though he is rarely noted among those known for their extreme views, mainly because he chose to return to his homeland when problems began to occur.[10] Pynchon arrived in America in 1630; five years later he and twelve heads of household settled Springfield, in the Connecticut Valley.[11]

By the middle of the century, even though Springfield was distant from the sea, it maintained a thriving and growing population. The distance from Boston allowed Pynchon and others to chart their own religious course, but in 1650 Pynchon published a book entitled *Meritorious Price of Our Redemption,* which brought the full extent of his heresies to light. In his book, Pynchon opposed the prevailing view of the atonement, the trinity, and other doctrines and echoed Socinian doctrines coming out of Poland that emphasized the human, more than the divine, aspect of Jesus.

Boston magistrates immediately condemned Pynchon and arraigned him to Boston to account for his views. He refused to recant and was so disgusted with his treatment that he soon left and returned to England; however, many of his followers in Springfield continued to propagate his teachings.[12] Included among these followers were 297 fifth-generation LDS ancestors (166 with unique names) in Hampden County and most of the population of Springfield, where a total of 123 fifth-generation LDS ancestors (68 with unique names) were located.[13]

Destination of Exiles

Before Roger Williams was expelled from Massachusetts in 1635, at least nineteen people had been thrown out of New England towns. Rhode Island and New Hampshire became the two most likely places of refuge. Significantly, a high concentration of LDS ancestors lived in the areas where the extreme radicals settled. At least 39 percent of the estimated population of Rhode Island at midcentury has been identified so far as direct-line, fifth-generation ancestors of LDS converts. From another vantage point, more than 40 percent of the early LDS converts in this study have ancestors from the small colony of Rhode Island. We find that 38 percent of the population living in New Hampshire (if we include Essex County, Massachusetts, which directly borders New Hampshire and which shared such political and cultural affinity) were direct-line, fifth-generation ancestors.

When Roger Williams and his friends were banished from Massachusetts Bay and Plymouth Colonies, they moved to a territory known by its Indian name of Aquidneck and there established the first settlement at Providence in 1636. Soon other religious dissenters came to Rhode Island and established the settlements of Newport and Portsmouth.[14] In contrast to the other New England colonies, Rhode Island was not established on the basis of a formal written covenant defining the relationship settlers would maintain between themselves and God, but it was dedicated to freedom of conscience and religious toleration.

In 1644 the name Aquidneck was changed to Rhode Island, and in 1647 a confederacy was established, although a royal colonial charter was not granted until 1663. Rhode Island retains to this day a unique place in terms of American individualism.

Rhode Island and Roger Williams

Roger Williams (1603–83) was the first English immigrant to gain historical renown for being expelled from Massachusetts. When he first arrived in Massachusetts on 5 February 1629, he was quickly recognized as a gifted young minister.[15] His father, James, a textile retailer in St. Albans, England, had married Alice Pemberton on 2 January 1597. Roger was the third of four children, who were reared within the confines of the Church of England. In 1621, his father sent him to Charterhouse Grammar School, and after three years he was admitted to Pembroke College, Cambridge University. Though not much is known about his early training, he studied to be a cleric, but by the time he finished his training he had opted for Separatism. He chose to forego receiving his master's degree, which would have brought permanent employment and security, because the rite obliged him to take a vow of obedience to the church and the crown.[16]

In 1629, before coming to America, Williams was hired as a chaplain at the manor of William Masham, a member of Parliament who had been jailed in 1626 for his opposition to a special tax to pay for military conflicts with France. Many household chaplains had been known to organize secret meetings of dissenters anxious to find an isolated location for religious activities, and Williams made arrangements for such meetings at the Masham mansion.

Williams was closely associated with John Cotton and Thomas Hooker, who were prominent Puritans in England. However, it was conversations with John Winthrop that led him to entertain the prospect of coming to the American colonies. Winthrop, the first permanent governor of Massachusetts, was then organizing the Winthrop fleet of thirteen ships filled with dissenters, who emigrated to Massachusetts in 1630. He enticed the young Williams to come with him in order to enter into a state of "primitive purity, lost since the days of early Christianity."[17]

Williams had established a reputation for being "wholly free of guile, open, sincere, and of the most generous disposition, with traits of childlike simplicity and tenderness."[18] In spite of being forbearing and magnanimous in his interpersonal dealings, he was also a man of resolute conviction and beliefs. Upon arriving in Boston he was invited to become a teacher in the Boston church, but he shocked the magistrates by declining the invitation and condemning the congregation because it was not Separatist. He argued that the keys of the kingdom of Christ and the apostles had been lost through the long, corrupt reign of the Antichrist, embodied in the Catholic Church, and that the Church of England was illegitimate because it was able to trace its authority only through the Catholic Church.

In April 1631, Williams accepted an invitation from church leaders in Salem to serve as a minister. However, some Boston officials went immediately to Salem to warn them that Williams was not suitable for such an appointment. As a result, even though many in the Salem congregation sympathized with Williams's Separatist views, the offer to him was withdrawn.

Subsequently, he moved on to the Separatist congregation at Plymouth, which still had no means to support a pastor, so he received no official appointment. In spite of this, the Williams family remained in Plymouth for two years, his wife giving birth in 1633 to a daughter, Mary. Williams had an aptitude for languages and soon learned the language and culture of the Indians of the area. This led to his next encounter with authorities, when he sided with Indians in their complaints that the English were infringing on the Indian hunting grounds. Publicly pronouncing that the land belonged to the Indians and not the king, he branded the king's land patents immoral and fraudulent.

Puritans in Boston became alarmed at his charges against their charter and the insults this represented to the crown. Williams's charges placed the Puritans in a dilemma. While they were resolute in their allegiance to the king, they believed the Indians were the lost tribes of Israel, and they held great, if somewhat abstract, respect for them.[19] These favorable attitudes toward the Indians tempered their response to Williams. He was reprimanded but forgiven after signing a statement that he had intended no disloyalty to the king.

In 1634, Williams joined a debate that raged over whether women ought to wear veils in church, taking the affirmative position. That same year, he challenged the right of the English flag to display a cross, pointing out that the cross had at one time received the blessing of the pope. Subsequently, John Endecott, the first provisional governor of Massachusetts Bay Colony, demonstrated his sympathy for Williams by personally removing the cross, ripping it from the flag.

In 1635, the general court mandated that all adult male inhabitants must take an oath of loyalty to the governor and all other elected officials. The oath included the phrase "so help me God." Williams suggested such an oath was appropriate for believers but pointed out that unregenerate men would be taking the Lord's name in vain if they took the oath in the name of God. The general court expressed alarm at Williams's position and accused him of making a direct attack on the order of government.

Conditions between the supporters and detractors of Williams hardened, and by the fall of 1635, he was called before the Massachusetts bar. They found that he "hath broached & divulged diverse new & dangerous opinions" to the point that he was instructed to depart the jurisdiction of Massachusetts within six weeks.[20]

Shortly thereafter, Williams and his major protagonist, John Cotton, exchanged letters about the charges leading to his expulsion.[21] While they both claimed respect for one another and based their arguments on the Scriptures, each blamed the other for the events that had sent Williams into exile. Cotton agreed with at least one of Williams's complaints. He admitted that New England land did not come from the king, rather "the Natives are the true owners of it, and . . . we ought to repent of . . . receiving it by Patent." However, Cotton admonished Williams for going beyond reason and the Scriptures with regard to the other complaints. He rejected Williams's stubborn insistence that "a wicked person" should not be called upon to take an oath or to join in a prayer since these were "actions of God's Worship." Cotton also rejected Williams's plea that Puritans not participate in Anglican worship services. He further argued against Williams's claim "that the Civil Magistrate's power extends only to the Bodies and Goods, and outward state of men."[22]

Cotton claimed Williams was disputing God's truth and finding fault with everyone but himself. In fact, Cotton insisted that Williams had not been banished by the general court but by himself. Williams, he claimed, had deluded himself and had become so misguided by the devil that he had allowed the evil one to "transform himself into an Angel of light, and to cheer the soul with false peace, and with flashes of counterfeit consolation."[23] Cotton explained that Williams's problem was his "holier than thou" attitude. He wanted to be purer than anyone else, his church more separate, his principles more precise than anyone since the early apostles. In response, Williams agreed that Cotton had identified the right issues; however, his perspective was quite different. Cotton's problem, according to Williams, was that he was only half pure, half separated, and moderately perfect.

There was no way for these two men to find a common ground. The one argued for moderation, the other for awakening those slumbering amid the "prostitution of the Ordinances of Christ," sleeping with "a spirit and disposition of spiritual drunkenness and whoredom."[24] Williams concluded there was no other option than for believers in Christ to separate themselves from the Antichrist found in the Church of England and to separate from the secular government that only invaded and corrupted the believers.

While the hierarchy of Massachusetts expected Williams to go back to England, he chose instead to travel into the wilderness, camping next to the Seekonk River, where he spent the winter with three companions in filthy, smoke-filled huts belonging to Indian friends. The next spring the Puritan leaders notified them that they were residing illegally in the Plymouth Colony and should remove themselves.

New Hampshire and Stephen Bachiler

While most radicals expelled from Massachusetts moved to Rhode Island, a number of Antinomians, Anabaptists, Quakers, and other freethinkers relocated north of the Merrimack River, which runs to the sea through Essex County, Massachusetts, and was at the time generally thought to be the northern boundary of the Massachusetts Bay Colony.[25] Early New Hampshire settlement concentrated in the four towns of Hampton, Exeter, Dover, and Portsmouth. The towns fell within a radius of ten miles, so early New Hampshire settlement was confined to a small area close to the sea.[26] By 1650, approximately one thousand English had settled there. In the early 1640s, Boston disputed the assumption that the Merrimack was the northern border, and it was 1679 before New Hampshire finally attained full autonomy.

The earliest New Hampshire settlers came not for the sake of religion but for economic gain. They came to till the soil, fell the trees, and hunt in the rich lands bordering the sea and to fish the waters. Explorations of that land had taken place as early as 1602, and by 1623 settlers founded a plantation near the Piscataqua River. William and Edward Hilton, who had been fishmongers in London, are usually regarded as the fathers of New Hampshire.[27] William arrived in Plymouth on the ship *Fortune* on 11 November 1621; his wife and two children came two years later on the ship *Anne.* His brother Edward probably settled in New Hampshire in 1623, a bit earlier than William.[28]

A third settler, Thomas Roberts, was born in Woolaston, England, in 1600; he sailed to America on the *Providence* in the spring of 1623 and migrated soon thereafter to New Hampshire.[29] He resided in Dover, where he married Rebecca Hilton, likely a relative of the Hilton brothers.[30] Even though they came for economic gain, the Hilton brothers and Roberts appear to have held to certain esoteric beliefs, though these were temperate in comparison to later New Hampshire residents.

For instance, Hanserd Knollys, a Dover minister in the late 1630s, had claimed to have had a number of profound spiritual experiences leading to his involvement with Antinomianism and Anabaptism.[31] In 1638, John Underhill came with Knollys to establish a new church. Underhill was born in Warwickshire, England, and had served as a soldier in England, holding the rank of captain. After coming to America, he held political offices and performed honorable and faithful military service both in the Massachusetts Bay and Connecticut Colonies. However, he was a casualty of the Antinomian crisis and was required to give up the sword. He returned for a time to England but later came back and settled in Dover with Knollys. The residents of Dover knew him well, and rather than shun him for his religious position, they welcomed him, commending him for his military role, cordially inviting him to become a part of their community.

Accounts of Knollys and Underhill should not suggest that all Dover residents were religious heretics, though a number of residents who were ancestors of LDS converts openly declared allegiance to radical beliefs. When Quaker missionaries came to Dover, Thomas Roberts, one of the earliest settlers of New Hampshire, spoke out in favor of giving them a fair hearing.[32] Edward Starbuck, known for his radical beliefs, was tried in 1648 by the general court for the "profession of Anabaptism" and for disturbing the peace of the church,[33] because he refused "to join with the church in the ordinance of baptisme."[34] This was the same court to which he earlier had been elected, in 1643 and again in 1646, as the first representative of Dover.[35] Prominence did not deter him from continuing his "heretical" mission, and in 1651 he parted company with the church and moved to Nantucket, where he converted to Quakerism.[36]

Also implicated in a number of radical activities was the Tristram Coffin family. In 1609, Coffin, who was the father of Judith Coffin, a fifth-generation LDS ancestor of Mary Thurston Rand, was born in Brixton, near Plymouth, England, and he came to New England in 1642, bringing his extended family. He eventually bought much of Nantucket and encouraged the spread of Quakerism on the island. The religious attitudes of Coffin and other LDS ancestors gave New Hampshire a reputation for being open to extreme ideas. This status contributed to the exodus to that area of certain ministers who took their entire congregations with them when they left Massachusetts.

The total number of identified fifth-generation LDS ancestors from what is today New Hampshire was 188, 120 of whom have unique names; this represents about 9 percent of the midcentury population. Because about one-fifth of the entire population of New England were fifth-generation LDS ancestors, New Hampshire was underrepresented in terms of Mormon ancestors. They were clustered in three towns: 75 from Hampton, 24 from Exeter, and 38 from Portsmouth.

In 1632, one of the earliest groups of dissidents more radical than Puritans and Pilgrims to arrive in Massachusetts was led by Stephen Bachiler (1561–1660 or 1661),[37] a seventy-one-year-old minister. He declared the group to be Puritans, but they inclined so toward Familism that Boston's leaders considered them too radical to remain in the town. Bachiler and his small band of faithful sought peace by migrating first to Lynn, then Yarmouth, and then Newbury. They finally left Massachusetts and in 1638 settled the town of Hampton, north of the Merrimack River, beyond the northern boundary of the Massachusetts Bay Colony in the fertile lands of coastal New Hampshire.[38] Bachiler is said to have given the town its name.[39]

The Familists (Family of Love) were followers of the Dutch mystic Hendrik Niclaes (1502–80), who had established his church in the 1540s. The movement had come to England by the 1570s, when a number of Niclaes's works were revised and translated into English. Niclaes wrote that the church of Christ had fallen from the truth, and a veil had descended between God and his people: "The spirit was replaced by the flesh," according to Alastair Hamilton, "the Scriptures read as a dead letter, the ceremonies and sacraments of the Church observed out of superstition."[40] His was intended to be a universal religion, and all people, whether Christian, Jew, Mohammedan, or heathen, were invited to give up their contention over theological dogma and join together in the body of Christ.

Niclaes claimed he had been anointed by God to become his medium in restoring a relationship between the divine and humankind. He claimed to have received a number of vivid and dramatic spiritual visions that provided the insight necessary to fulfill scriptural prophesies relating to the restoration of the true gospel. His Family of Love was thought to be a community capable of breaking the veil between the heavens and earth.[41] Familists identified themselves as a fraternity or fellowship, signifying powerful feelings of cohesion and mutual support in Christ.[42] The group grew quickly in the fertile soil of England, but it experienced a brief life and died by the 1660s. Certain Familists appeared in other American colonies, and they presaged the universalists of the eighteenth century.

The treatment Familists received by established religious institutions in England typify the difficulties encountered by radical religious communities. Church ministers delivered many sermons against the Family of Love and its doctrines of inclusion;[43] opponents wrote pamphlets, describing them in derogatory terms. They were given the label of a "sect," signifying a group that was subversive to the social order. In 1580, Queen Elizabeth issued a proclamation ordering these "dangerous Heretikes and Sectaries to be severely punished."[44] Public officials regularly interrogated them and threw many into prison. Eventually, the members were either incorporated into a new movement arising in England, the Quakers, or they left England to seek peace abroad.[45]

Bachiler attended St. John's College at Oxford from 1581 until February 1586, where Puritanism had by that time taken firm root. After completing his studies, Bachiler moved to the vicarage of Wherwell in Hants, a small village near Andover in Hampshire, southwest of London, where he remained off and on for the next twenty years. During this time, persecution of the Puritans increased, particularly after the death of Queen Elizabeth and the ascension to the throne of James I, who in 1604 called together the famous Hampton Court Conference. This conference led directly to the removal of many Puritan ministers, including Bachiler, who was "ejected" as vicar and excommunicated from the church.[46] The formal charges against him, according to Philip Marston, were that he "disregarded authority" and sought to take away "the chastity of his neighbor's wife."[47]

Even after he was excommunicated, several of his children were born in Wherwell in Hants, so we know he likely remained there at least until 1609, when the last child was born. We also find that two of his daughters were born in Norfolk: Joanna in 1600, and Ann in 1601; this suggests he probably resided northeast of London for a time prior to being excommunicated. Eventually, he fled to Holland, and many of his parishioners followed him.

In Holland, Bachiler became involved in a venture to form a colony in Maine, known both as the Plough Patent and the Company of Husbandmen. John Winthrop described the group as Familists, who "professed the principle that religion lay in love irrespective of faith, a tenet no doubt harmless when intelligently held, but liable in rude minds to run into licentious extremes."[48] Leaders of the Plough Patent expected Bachiler to serve as the minister in Maine; however, the venture failed.

Bachiler was already elderly, age seventy-one, when in March 1632 he arrived in America with his family aboard the *William and Frances*.[49] He decided to settle in Newtown but was soon urged to move to Saugus, where he began duties as the pastor. It took less than four months for him to be notified by the general court of the colony of Massachusetts to cease his responsibilities as a preacher, because his "contempt of authority" and independent ideas had created a scandal in the colony.[50]

And so he moved north through Essex County, where he was a "private member" of the community, but he soon became restless and traveled to Cape Cod in search of a location to establish a new settlement. He gave that idea up in favor of a new community in New Hampshire. In the spring of 1638, Bachiler became the minister in Hampton and Timothy Dalton the teacher of the church.

Dalton had joined Bachiler because his wife was related to the minister. However, Dalton was also related to John Winthrop and was ideologically inclined toward the governor's point of view, or the mainstream religious orientation of the Puritans. Therefore, Bachiler and Dalton quickly broke into open dispute. The main incident cited by those opposed to Bachiler comes from Winthrop's journal, stating that Bachiler, at the time eighty years of age, had proposed to a woman in the congregation that they commit adultery.[51] A large literature surrounds this and subsequent events, but finally, in 1654, Bachiler returned to England, where he died six years later.

Bachiler had four wives in his lifetime. He married his third wife while the second was yet living, and because he had failed to record this marriage, he was advised to remove himself from Hampton, New Hampshire. After he returned to England, he married his fourth wife. The other wives remained in America, and their families are prominent in New Hampshire history.

Of the thirty-six heads of household and total of fifty-six settlers in the first group to arrive in Hampton, at least twenty-two have thus far been identified as ancestors of no less than seventy-two early LDS converts.[52] Unfortunately, because only the names of heads of household were recorded, we have no record of most of the women and children among Bachiler's followers. Mary Perkins, the sister of Abraham and Isaac Perkins, is an exception; she was the ancestor of LDS convert Abigail Glidden. Mary Thurston Rand, another early LDS convert, could claim to have direct-line connections with seven of the first thirty-six heads of household in Hampton. In addition, Rand is related to two of the nine heads of household who came the following year. Within two years, about sixty families had moved to Hampton, and many of them were ancestors of early LDS converts.[53] Not only were these settlers dedicated to each other through the gospel of Jesus Christ but they were tightly bound together as a social and economic community.

Most of the people who settled Hampton had been living in Massachusetts, some for up to a decade, though other members of the group had arrived in New England only a few months before they removed to New Hampshire. Their incentive was clearly to escape the press of the center of Puritanism and to help establish a community where they could bind themselves "by the grace and help of Christ, and in his name" to "live quietly and peaceably together in all godliness and honesty."[54]

One remarkable aspect of Hampton was its dedication to equality. Of course, just as most other New England towns, the townspeople decided who could and could not live in Hampton. They also determined who was a "freeman," and they disposed of land tracts according to the status of the freemen. That is, the more important freemen received larger and more attractive tracts of land than did the less important. However, their dedication to communal decisions was strong. Most heads of household were given the title of freeman, and most important decisions, at least in the first years, were made in frequently held town meetings, where attendance of all freemen was required.[55]

Each LDS ancestor among the early settlers had an important story to tell. For example, Robert Tucke, a sixth-generation ancestor of LDS converts Mary Thurston Rand, Lydia Smith, and Daniel Sanborn Miles, was one of the original settlers in Hampton whose family name remains today among residents of the town.[56] Tucke was born about 1590 in Gorleston in Norwich County, England, and he likely arrived in Boston in 1636. It is not clear when he married the daughter of Stephen Bachiler, Joanna, but the marriage surely took place in England, because four of their children were born there before they emigrated. Joanna is also recorded as having been born in Gorleston, so Robert and Joanna likely knew each other as children.

In addition, as a boy and young man, Tucke would certainly have come to know Stephen Bachiler. After arriving in America, he lived first in Watertown, very near to New Town, where Bachiler resided. Watertown is significant because in 1634 it initiated the "town meeting," a concept the residents of Hampton carried even further. When Bachiler moved on to Essex County, Tucke moved to Salem and then joined his father-in-law when Hampton was settled. Tucke's daughter Mary would marry the son of John Sanborn, who, with his brother William, was another of the first settlers in Hampton. John himself had married another daughter of Stephen Bachiler in England, so the ties were not only congregational but familial.[57]

Some of Bachiler's followers took an even more radical course than he. William Marsten, for example, had followed Bachiler from Salem to Newbury and on to Hampton, but he eventually opted to become a Quaker. His family history describes him as a kind-hearted, benevolent, and godly man.[58]

Richard Swaine, another ancestor of LDS converts, was a known Antinomian. Swaine had come to Massachusetts from England in 1635 on the *Truelove,* though his wife Elizabeth Basselle had already preceded him. He had not been associated with Bachiler prior to arriving in the colonies, having been born in Rowley, England, and grown up in Darbyshire, some distance north of Bachiler's parish. The Swaines settled first in Rowley, Massachusetts; however, three years after Swaine's arrival, he was dismissed from the church during the Antinomian crisis.[59] Swaine had embraced Hutchinson's and Wheelwright's doctrine that no man, through his own efforts and on his own behalf, could gain salvation. Relying rigidly on Calvinist doctrine, he believed a person to be utterly dependent on God's free grace rather than capable of gaining adequate merit in God's eyes through works.[60] He believed that a person's knowledge of having received grace would come directly via a witness of the Spirit, without any intermediary such as the Scriptures. The Holy Spirit, he believed, was none other than the Holy Ghost, who dwells in the justified person. In Hampton, Richard Swaine's property did not face the prestigious meetinghouse green but was located just off it, on the road leading toward Salisbury. He was among the first three town commissioners and eventually died at sea in the Caribbean, while traveling on a commercial venture.[61]

7. The Antinomian Crisis

The Meaning of Antinomianism

In the first years of colonial New England, individual dissidents occasionally disrupted life in their immediate circle of relationships; Antinomianism was the first major crisis that involved large numbers of people. The term "Antinomian" means "against law."[1] Its doctrine was based on mystical tenets of Martin Luther as interpreted by his disciple, Johann Agricola (1494–1566), who held that grace freed believers from legalistic obedience to civil laws. According to this view, the good life does not come from simple obedience but from the inner workings of the Holy Spirit, which progressively reforms the individual until the attributes of God become the individual's attributes. The Holy Spirit harmonizes and makes humans one with the divine.[2]

Antinomianism is now associated mainly with the religious crisis in Boston surrounding Anne Marbury Hutchinson. While it is difficult to document the pervasiveness of Antinomian sentiment in and around Boston, it is possible to identify specific persons who participated in the Hutchinson movement. Emery Battis names 38 males who formed a core group and 187 marginal participants. Almost all of the persons identified by Battis were men, and it is less certain how many women were involved, but it is safe to note that married males and their spouses usually professed similar views on matters of religion.[3] Our discussion of Antinomianism in New England will center on Hutchinson and her brother-in-law, John Wheelwright. Both had a large number of followers, many of whom were ancestors of early LDS converts.

Anne Marbury Hutchinson and Her Disciples

Anne Marbury Hutchinson (1591–1643), a central figure of the early radical religious movement, has inspired the imagination of interpreters of the time. For example, Thomas Bicknell summarizes her spiritual orientation in the following way: "In matters of religion and theology Anne Hutchinson was a seer, a prophetess, 'a Daniel, come to jedgment.' Three great spiritual concepts possessed her. She believed that the human soul could and did hold close communication with the Divine Over-Soul. She believed in direct and special revelations from the divine to the human,—from God to her own soul. She also believed in a spiritual justification of the soul of man, with God, through faith."[4]

Anne was born in Alford, Lincolnshire, England, the daughter of Francis Marbury and his second wife, Bridget Dryden. Both Francis and Bridget came from known Puritan families. Francis, a rigid and tough Anglican minister, was a schoolmaster at Alford Grammar School and a preacher at the local church. Just prior to Anne's birth, he had denounced the Church of England for its failure to institute ecclesiastical reform. This was not the first time he had attacked the church, and the bishops in London responded to this "impudent Puritan" by temporarily releasing him from his duties at school and the local parish. It was Anne's good fortune to be born into a family with a highly educated father who had nothing to do but give his attention and time to his baby daughter. At the time, Queen Elizabeth reigned, and she had set an example for the education of a bright girl by mastering classical and modern languages, poetry, the harpsichord, and rhetoric. Francis was intent on his daughter's emulating the example of the queen; he proved to be the ideal teacher and she the ideal pupil.[5]

When Anne was fourteen, her father received a new appointment in London as the minister of Saint Martin Church at the Vintry, near St. Paul's Cathedral. In the rectory where the Marbury family lived, religious controversies were regularly discussed and debated. According to Selma Williams's account, Anne remained silent but absorbed the conversations of visitors reflecting mainstream as well as dissenting opinions. With her father now actively engaged in his pastoral duties, Anne increasingly turned to her mother for further education. She learned to "compound herbal ointments, salves, and medicines" for nursing family, friends, and even pets back to health.[6]

The seeds of radical rebellion were planted in Anne when she came in contact with Familism, responding especially to its beliefs in "direct communication between each individual—female as well as male—and God," and its disregard for original sin, a doctrine that places blame on Eve and all women for the evils of the world.[7] She was touched by Familism's call to join together into a Family of Love.[8]

Her father died when Anne had reached marriageable age, and one month after turning twenty-one she married William Hutchinson, a wealthy sheep farmer and textile merchant from her hometown of Alford. Her husband, mild-mannered and devoted, was well thought of in the Lincolnshire countryside as a "businessman of ample substance and ability."[9] Within a year she gave birth to her first child and eventually bore fifteen children, the last in 1636 during the Antinomian crisis that sent her into exile. Throughout her married life she was an ardent student of midwifery. She had become not only her own nurse, giving birth to a child every fifteen to twenty-three months, but a midwife to others. In Alford she served as an informed community medical practitioner and healer.

The most important person in her mature spiritual development was John Cotton. As a young minister, Cotton took a church position at Boston, in England, twenty-four miles north of Alford. Although initially Anne did not hear Cotton's sermons, the whole area was constantly churning with details of his activities, which soon tore Boston apart with dissent and factions. He was an outstanding orator, and his eloquence and rhetorical style moved the entire region. Soon Anne and William were regularly making the one-and-one-half-day trips to Boston to hear the minister. However, Cotton's activities became so inflammatory that in 1633 he migrated to New England.

A year later, Anne Hutchinson and her husband followed her spiritual and theological hero to the shores of Massachusetts. In Boston, the Hutchinsons moved into a house diagonally opposite the large and prosperous home of Governor John Winthrop. They were immediately admitted without opposition to membership in the congregation and to the inner circle of Saints. The nursing skills Anne had acquired in England soon came to good use. She had brought medicinal herbs and roots, including tansy, catnip, pennyroyal, sage, and spearmint, which served her well in administering to the sick and afflicted.[10]

As she went among the sick, she found they were often suffering as much from spiritual as from physical ill health. She found them to be in great pain and under the spiritual bondage of guilt, and she was soon offering them comfort and advice about how the Holy Spirit could relieve their feelings of pain and guilt.[11]

When Hutchinson arrived in Massachusetts, she found that John Cotton had touched off a sort of religious revival in the community. With great force and simplicity, Cotton proclaimed Calvin's doctrines. Two covenants were at issue. First, God had given Adam a commandment (covenant) to be anxiously engaged in activities (works) that would satisfy divine law. Second, with the fall of Adam, God had provided a new covenant (grace) that would allow humankind to obtain salvation.[12] The payment for this grace would be the crucifixion of his only begotten son, Jesus Christ. Puritan ministers engaged in great efforts to meld the two covenants, but Hutchinson believed that Cotton had tilted toward the covenant of grace. She took his argument to its logical conclusion and pressed the importance of grace to the point that works became irrelevant in the scheme of salvation.

Hutchinson's keen memory and intellect came to good use as she began to help others understand more clearly what Cotton's sermons were all about. Of course, she also propagated her own points of view in the weekly meetings she held to instruct others. She claimed that good works were never enough to merit inclusion as a predetermined member of the select, chosen few. Her disciples soon began to visit different towns to question ministers and to challenge them when their teachings were at variance with those of Cotton. Her beliefs were soon labeled Antinomianism (against law), and she became the central figure of what has been called the Antinomian crisis of 1636–38.[13]

The first major published account of Antinomian activities appeared in 1644 under the authorship of the Reverend Thomas Welde, a man who traveled across the ocean to Massachusetts in 1634 and toiled as a pastor in Roxbury until 1641, when he returned to England.[14] The account was entitled *A Short Story of the Rise, Reign, and Ruin of the Antinomians, Familists, and Libertines, that infected the Churches of New England.*[15] Welde exclaimed that the first great storm sent among the people in the new land came from persons propagating a species of Gnosticism. This had infected "multitudes of men and women, Church-members and others," who were "streight infected before they were aware, and some being tainted conveyed the infection to others."[16] He cataloged what he claimed were the erroneous opinions brought into the fold, refuted each "error" by way of the Scriptures, and reserved most of his story for accounts of general court actions against specific individuals, including the Reverend John Wheelwright, William Aspinwall, John Coggeshall, William Baulstoon, Edward Hutchinson, Thomas Marshal, William Dinely, William Dyer, and the worst of them all, a woman named Anne Hutchinson.[17]

One sees in Anne Hutchinson's attitudes and activities a foreshadowing of many Mormon beliefs and practices, though there are obvious differences. For example, Mormons are true Universalists because they believe Christ's atonement has universal application, that his sacrifice gave both the sinner and the saint assurance that they would be resurrected. But Mormons do not accept Hutchinson's claim that works are irrelevant. While they believe that God's grace has universal application, they also believe that every person gains merited spiritual reward to the extent he or she performs good works.[18]

Two issues related to Hutchinson have particular relevance to Mormon radicalism. First, Hutchinson practiced the gift of healing, which accounts for some of the negative attitudes the Puritan hierarchy held toward her, because the healing arts were considered to be closely connected with witchcraft. Puritan attitudes toward healing and witchcraft are revealed in the account published by Thomas Welde.[19] At the end of his *Short Story,* Welde gives a number of specific accounts of "satanic activity," including a description of Mary Dyer giving birth to a premature, monster child while attended by Anne Hutchinson and a midwife friend by the name of Mrs. Hawkins. According to Welde's account, the baby was stillborn, and on the advice of John Cotton, it was buried without any formal announcement of the event. However, because their names were associated with Familism and witchcraft, Anne and Mrs. Hawkins were rumored to have been somehow responsible for the whole hideous event.[20] When Anne Hutchinson was banished, Mrs. Hawkins was one of those who traveled with her to Rhode Island.[21]

Those around Hutchinson and Mrs. Hawkins believed they, indeed, possessed special healing powers. Part of their healing technique was to inquire of a woman who was ill whether she "did believe," and if she said she believed, they claimed they could help her. In other words, the healing arts were dependent on exercising faith. Orthodox Puritans were appalled to find these women using "magical techniques," signifying what they interpreted to be not only spiritual corruption but satanic practices.[22]

Second, Anne Hutchinson took radical positions concerning the way a person comes to know God, how God interacts with his children on earth, and how God blesses some with the gifts of the Holy Spirit. In each respect she challenged Puritan doctrines. Hutchinson claimed her spiritual knowledge had come directly from God through the Scriptures and the Holy Spirit.

Deeply personal crises in England had led Hutchinson to make this claim. The Reverend John Cotton had been her inspiration, but in 1630 Cotton fell ill and made no public appearances for some time. During this period, she lost two of her daughters, fourteen-year-old Susanna and eight-year-old Elizabeth. She found herself cast spiritually adrift, and on one occasion she withdrew to her chamber and in the gloomy stillness of her room pleaded with God to help her. Immediately, she felt the spirit of God descend over her.[23] This event led to "long hours at silent meditation in her chamber or poring restlessly over familiar pages of Scripture." During these times, "God came often to her," giving direction and meaning to her life.[24] She developed an intimacy with the Holy Spirit that was profound but unsettling to those around her.

Consequently, Hutchinson advocated that though the Scriptures were powerful and helpful, a person could develop a direct means of reaching God through the "indwelling of the divine." When the voice of God speaks, one knows the truth by direct and "private revelation."[25] The concept of the indwelling Spirit parallels the Mormon belief of having the "Gift of the Holy Ghost." In both cases, the Holy Ghost is said to reside within the person, giving light, comfort, and guidance.

It is instructive to review part of the formal court proceedings leading to Hutchinson's conviction and expulsion from Massachusetts. The formal theological issue on which the court focused was the position she took regarding grace versus works. Because beliefs were respected as matters of conscience, she could never have been expelled over the issue of grace and works alone. Rather, her expulsion was ensured when, asked why she was so certain of her position, she explained: "I shall give you the ground of what I know to be true. . . . The Lord . . . by his prophetical office must open it to me." Her examiner, John Winthrop, pushed her on her meaning, asking how she was so certain of her knowledge, and she replied again, "So to me by an immediate revelation." Thus, her admission that she had received her knowledge directly from God sealed her fate; she claimed to know by "the voice of his own spirit to my soul."[26]

Because she was ill, the court allowed her to remain in Roxbury for the winter, but the following spring Hutchinson moved with her family to Aquidneck, in what would later be known as Rhode Island. When her husband died in 1642, she moved to Long Island Sound, known then as New Netherlands, near the current Pelham Bay. There in 1643, Indians massacred her and all the children except the baby daughter, Susanne, whom they carried away and later sold to the Puritans. That only surviving daughter of Anne Marbury Hutchinson formed the link to early LDS converts John Portineus Greene, Evan Molbourne Greene, Anson Pratt, Parley Parker Pratt, Orson Pratt, William Dickinson Pratt, and Meritable Sawyer; however, many other ancestors of LDS converts were her disciples.

Within a few months after the verdict against Hutchinson, at least thirty-four heads of household suffered the most severe punishment rendered for conviction of Antinomianism: eviction from Massachusetts. Most of them journeyed to Aquidneck,[27] but some others went elsewhere, such as John Wheelwright, who took his congregation to New Hampshire. Thus, even though only a few LDS ancestors were located in the center of Puritanism, a significant portion of them reflected radical religious tendencies, sympathizing and identifying with movements such as Antinomianism.

Among those traveling to Rhode Island was William Coddington, one of the wealthiest men in Massachusetts Bay Colony; he had served as treasurer to the colony as well as assistant in the general court. John Coggeshall, an ancestor of several LDS converts, was a dealer in expensive fabrics and also served on the general court. Samuel Cole was a well-known innkeeper in Boston.

It is also possible to identify some direct-line ancestors who were family members of those implicated in Antinomianism. The Robert Harding family is a good case in point. Robert came with Winthrop's fleet in 1630 and was one of the earliest members of the First Church in Boston, having penned the eleventh signature on the church covenant. He moved into a house on the corner of School and Washington Streets, close to the home of Governor Winthrop and across from what was to become Anne Hutchinson's home. Robert served several times on the Board of Selectmen, beginning in 1634, the first year it was convened. He had married Philippa Hammond in Boston in 1631, and it is likely that she was the first in the family attracted to meetings being held by Anne Hutchinson; her husband was soon active in Antinomianism.[28] After Hutchinson was convicted, both Robert and Philippa were disciplined for their participation, and they moved to Newport, Rhode Island.[29]

Robert and Philippa Harding did not have direct-line descendants among early LDS converts because they soon moved back to London, where he continued his work as a merchant. However, Robert's younger brother, Abraham, who was only a teenager at the time of the crisis but was then living with Robert, was undoubtedly a family participant. However, he was too young to be charged with Antinomianism. Abraham was the ancestor and namesake of Dwight Harding, baptized a Mormon in 1831.[30]

Not only did people convicted of Antinomianism suffer personal trials but their names were later reviled by scholars who sympathized with Puritanism. For example, Justin Winsor, librarian of Harvard University toward the end of the nineteenth century, wrote a four-volume history of Boston, and he noted, "it is easy to see what possible mischief of dangerous self-delusion and utter recklessness about the demands of strict virtue and even common morality was wrapt up in this beguiling heresy." He observed that Antinomianism often led to a "private mystical experience, real or imagined, that one was in a state of grace." Pointing to John Underhill, Winsor noted: "Thus, that sad reprobate Captain Underhill, . . . when detected in gross immorality, had the assurance to tell the pure-hearted Governor Winthrop, 'that the spirit had sent in to him the witness of Free Grace.'"[31]

John Wheelwright and His Congregation

Because of the Antinomian crisis, the Reverend John Wheelwright (1592–1679) and members of his congregation were banished from Massachusetts for heresy and sedition, and they migrated north and settled Exeter, New Hampshire. Wheelwright, the brother-in-law of William Hutchinson, had begun church service in Bilsby, Lincolnshire, England, where he married Marie Storre, the vicar's daughter. Vicar Storre soon died, and Wheelwright took over direction of the church. Marie died while giving birth to their third daughter, and John then married Mary Hutchinson, the sister of William Hutchinson, husband of Anne Marbury. The Hutchinson family lived in Alford, within walking distance northeast of Bilsby, so the two towns shared much in common.

John Wheelwright was a man of deep spiritual conviction; he believed God spoke directly to his children on earth. He preached the covenant of grace as forcefully as had John Cotton, with the added conviction that he had come to such knowledge by the influence of the Holy Spirit.[32] Wheelwright believed that anyone who knew God and his gospel received that knowledge through the gift of the Holy Ghost, or an "indwelling of the divine." After serving as vicar in Bilsby for eight years, he was released because of his nonconformist and "heterodox" views.

In 1636, having lost his permanent appointment in the clerical profession, Wheelwright sailed to the Massachusetts Bay Colony to join his two brothers-in-law, William and Edward Hutchinson. In Boston, the Puritan hierarchy received him warmly, even though they knew he was sympathetic with Anne Marbury Hutchinson's views on grace. In his inaugural address at Boston, he discussed the nature of faith and the relationship between the believer and the divine. Wheelwright explained that faith represents a union between the believer and the Holy Ghost, who bestows an inner light on the faithful. This proclamation brought adulation from those assembled, though Governor John Winthrop, who was in attendance, stirred uneasily because he felt such claims had no scriptural footing.[33]

Minister Wheelwright arrived in Boston when the Antinomian crisis was at its peak. The crisis had so infected the churches of Massachusetts that the general court proclaimed a fast and injudiciously invited Wheelwright to deliver the sermon at the end of the fast. His remarks were sympathetic with the views of Anne Hutchinson and further inflamed the crisis. He was subsequently tried for holding "Antinomian and Familistic" beliefs and was found guilty of "sedition and contempt." Sedition was particularly apt, because it suggested that Wheelwright's language and conduct were intended to incite the people to rebel against the constituted authority. The court attempted to reconcile him with the community; but "he persisted to justify his sermon and his whole practice and opinions, and refusing to leave either the place or his public exercisings, he was disfranchised and banished."[34]

In July 1638, Wheelwright and eight of his banished friends arrived in New Hampshire, purchased land on the banks of the Swamscot River, and settled Exeter.[35] Established from the beginning as a religious community, Exeter was founded on the basis of a religious covenant. The town soon expanded to thirty-four heads of household, all of whom signed the "Combination," a covenant or contract to be independent, subject only to the authority of God and the king of England. The townspeople "combined" themselves solemnly together "by the grace & helpe of christ & in his name & feare to submit our selves to such godly and christian laws as are established in the Realme of England . . . yt we may liue quietly and peaceably together in all godliness and harmony."[36] When Massachusetts asserted its claim over New Hampshire in 1643, Wheelwright and members of his inner circle left Exeter and removed further north to Wells, Maine. Within a short time, Wheelwright and others returned to New Hampshire, where he served as minister in Hampton,[37] where were located the largest number of LDS ancestors from New Hampshire.[38]

Many of those signing the town Combination, including Wheelwright, were sixth-generation ancestors of at least forty-three early LDS converts.[39] Of the thirty-four signatories of the 1639 Combination, John Cram, Godfrey Dearborn, George Rabone, Thomas Wight, and William Wentworth came from Wheelwright's old Bilsby parish in England. Significantly, twenty-two of the forty-three LDS converts with ancestors in the group were direct-line descendants of those coming from Bilsby. In addition, William Wentworth, Christopher Lawson, and Christian Helme were cousins of Wheelwright, and Augustine Storre was his brother-in-law.[40] Certain other ancestors were not members of Wheelwright's original congregation but soon became closely identified with his cause. For example, Edmund Littlefield, ancestor of six LDS converts, came from the parish of Titchfield, Hants, England, near the parish where Stephen Bachiler, discussed in the previous chapter, was minister. When Wheelwright moved north to Wells, Maine, Littlefield decided to go with him.

Whereas most exiles became permanent residents of specific towns, Exeter was an unusual case, because many who came there moved on to other towns because of continuing difficulties with Massachusetts authorities over their religious convictions. Large numbers of ancestors of LDS converts were among the first Exeter settlers, including William and Thomas Wardell. The Wardells had come from Leicestershire, England, and were acquainted with Anne Hutchinson in Alford, where the two families were neighbors. It was natural that as soon as Wheelwright arrived in Boston, William Wardell would affiliate himself with Wheelwright's congregation and become a part of his inner circle. William was a "servant" of Edmund Quincy, but on 20 February 1636, after William had arrived in the New World, he was granted two acres of land in Boston at Mount Wollaston, and he was granted additional land in 1637 at the same place.[41] He became a member of Hutchinson's "core group" in the Antinomian crisis and was charged and convicted of being an Antinomian.[42] He was one of the signers of the Exeter Combination, but as was true of many of those who first settled Exeter, he was a resident of the town for only a short time. He soon converted to Gortonism and moved to Rhode Island; he was subsequently brought to trial and convicted of heresy, as were other Gortonists.[43]

Exeter was also a town where some Scottish prisoners of war lived as indentured servants, having been sold into servitude to the highest bidder for a number of years to pay off their debts. Scotland had been in conflict with England, and in the Battle of Worcester, 272 Scottish prisoners were taken and sent to America, where they arrived on 24 February 1652. They were, by and large, devoted Presbyterians, who were indentured to pay the cost of their passage. While most of the Scots remained in Boston to work in the iron mills, six were sold to Nicholas Lissen, owner of two sawmills near Exeter. Among them were fifth- and sixth-generation ancestors John Bean, Alexander Gordon, and John Sinclair.[44] These Scots were a deeply religious "covenant" people, prone to revivalism and "superstitious beliefs." Their traditions were filled with a tendency for self-mythologizing and prophesying related to Arthurian and other legends.[45] To escape arrest, many religious radicals in Scotland had been forced to hold church services in caves, swamps, and out-of-the-way places.[46]

8. Anabaptists, Quakers, and Gortonists

Following the Reformation, the radical spiritualist awakening contributed to the establishment of many Christian church communities claiming an esoteric, mystical foundation. When New England was colonized, representatives of most of these groups migrated to the New World. According to George Washington Greene, Cotton Mather expressed frustration with developments in Rhode Island, which he declared was "a colluvies of Antinomians, Familists, Anabaptists, Anti-Sabbatarians, Arminians, Socinians, Quakers, Ranters, everything in the world but Roman Catholics and true Christians."[1] Anabaptism, Quakerism, and Gortonism were the three religious movements thought to pose the greatest threat to Puritanism. Ancestors of LDS converts played active roles in all three groups.

Anabaptists

The first European Anabaptists, or rebaptizers, followers of Huldrych Zwingli (1484–1531), believed the ancient church and the Holy Spirit already had been restored through contemporary divinely inspired apostles. Anabaptists belonged mainly to the disinherited classes, peasants, poor handicraftsmen, and the economically oppressed, who attempted to translate the idea of a primitive church into institutional reality.[2] One of their important tenets was adult baptism, withheld until the believer was old enough to be able to distinguish between good and evil.

A number of Anabaptist branches sprang up in Europe, taking on a number of different names, each with its own peculiar orientation. While "Anabaptist" was a pejorative term, believers identified themselves by names such as the "Brethren." In England they called themselves "Christian Brethren," but generally they were known by the name of the culture they represented, including the Bohemian Brethren, Swiss Brethren, and Hutterian Brethren.[3]

One significant group was the Münster Anabaptists, initiated in 1534 by a group of Dutch religious radicals who claimed their church had been founded by twelve apostles representing the twelve tribes of Israel. They claimed Christ had charged them to go two by two, proclaiming an apocalyptic dispensation had begun that would usher in the "new world," the "millennial kingdom," the "restitution of all things," the "reign of the saints," and the "Kingdom of God on earth."[4]

Münster in Westphalia, Germany, was designated the new Jerusalem, which would prepare the way for the second coming of Christ. The city of Münster was a hothouse for radical Protestants, and its residents quickly responded to the efforts of Anabaptist missionaries. A wave of apocalyptic excitement overwhelmed the city, and its leaders instituted what they proclaimed to be the fullness of the restored gospel as revealed in the Old and New Testaments. This restoration included a theocracy, a communal economy, and a patriarchal order based on household-centered polygamous marriages.[5]

The Münster experiment died almost as quickly as it was born, mainly because it alienated all who refused to embrace this glimpse into the radical spirit of Christianity—one that would spill over into England and then New England and would anticipate, even prophesy, Mormonism in America three hundred years later.

Within three decades after the first settlers arrived in New England, Anabaptists, or rebaptizers, were present in a number of towns. They believed God had taken the church of Jesus Christ from the earth but that God was now restoring that church, and Anabaptists were to be part of its restoration. In the mid-seventeenth century, most Anabaptist activity in New England took place in the Rhode Island and Plymouth Colonies, though there was also a presence in Massachusetts, Connecticut, New Hampshire, and Maine.

Rhode Island Anabaptists

In 1639 in Providence, Rhode Island, Roger Williams and his companions established the first Anabaptist congregation in America, and it is therefore appropriate to frame the beginnings of Anabaptism around him.[6] The group consisted of about twelve households, including those of Stukely Westcott, William Arnold, Thomas James, Robert Cole, John Greene Sr., John Throckmorton, William Harris, William Carpenter, Thomas Olney, Francis Weston,

Richard Waterman, and Ezekiel Holliman. At least twenty-six early LDS converts could claim one or more of these men as direct-line ancestors.[7]

Williams's religious beliefs are important to a discussion both of Mormon cosmology and Mormon practices. He was clearly a Separatist and adopted many Separatist principles. For example, as early as 1590 the Separatists rejected the practice of written prayers, and Williams concurred that prayers on paper extinguish the spirit of God.[8] He agreed with other Puritans that conversion was founded on an inward alteration of a person's spirit, so that the power of Satan would cease and the power of God would take over. Such a change would be as if "an old man became a new Babe . . . yea, as amounts to God's new creation in the soule."[9] But Williams went beyond conventional Separatism. For a time he was attracted to Anabaptism, and he and twenty others set up the first Anabaptist congregation in America; however, after a few months he withdrew from the congregation because of his personal struggle over whether or not he had the authority to act in God's name.

Williams developed a millenarian theory of the nature and function of the ministry. He believed the Antichrist had destroyed the original church of Jesus Christ along with its true ordinances and had reigned for 1,260 years as the Catholic Church. He claimed the Church of England was no more legitimate than the Church of Rome. In important respects, he insisted, mainstream Puritans were among the false prophets, because they had not yet withdrawn themselves from the influence of the Antichrist. He believed they had strayed by allowing their ministers to accept ordination at the hands of English bishops. Separatists, he believed, had received sufficient spiritual light to reject ordination from the prelates, but their purported separation was inconsistent and incomplete because they continued to accept infant baptism as practiced within the Church of England. Baptism, to be valid, Williams argued, must include the recipient's personal affirmation of faith, which requires maturity and accountability.[10]

Attempting to be consistent with his reasoning, Williams made arrangements for Ezekiel Holliman to rebaptize him; he then, in turn, rebaptized others, including Stukely Westcott and John Greene Sr.[11] But Williams became increasingly uncomfortable with this procedure and eventually declared rebaptism invalid, claiming, as Mormons would claim two hundred years later, that true ordinances, such as baptism, could be restored only by special commission of God. Eventually, he declared that without a divine commission, no man had authority to perform sacred ordinances.[12] No church had the power and authority to act in the name of God. As Mormons would later claim, he held that God's plan was to restore the church of Jesus Christ in its original form, and Christ's true church would be restored only through the millennial appearance of new apostles.[13]

If God was to restore the authority and the church, what roles were Williams and other so-called Seekers to play? He declared that in the long historical interim between the apostasy and the revival of the true church, the "secret motion" of the Holy Spirit stirred up individual witnesses to wage verbal battle against the Antichrist and the errors brought into the Roman church. This permitted individuals, such as himself, to preach and organize groups in anticipation of the restoration of the church of Jesus Christ.[14] But it did not permit them to baptize anyone.

Williams refused to collect wages for his work. Christ, he believed, drew a clear distinction between a shepherd and a hireling. The shepherd cares only about God's sheep, while the hireling cares only about wages, haggling and bargaining for his or her keep. From "Popery to Protestantism," he said, the hireling has worried only about comfort and salary.[15] Two hundred years later, the Mormon Church held that the ministry must come from the laity and not be looked upon as a profession or occupation and that professional studies do not qualify one to assume a role as a religious leader; this role must come as a calling from God.

Williams anticipated the difficulties that reliance on the Holy Spirit would bring. If people relied entirely and solely on the Holy Spirit, there was no way, according to Williams, they could differentiate between God's revelation and the devil's whisperings. External criteria must combine with spiritual experience to determine its veracity.[16] He believed the true Holy Spirit manifested itself in rational thought harmonizing with scriptural truth.

Williams left his Anabaptist congregation after only a few months, claiming that church authority must be traced by unbroken succession to the original apostles of Christ and that this was impossible to do. Doubting the validity of anyone's authority to baptize, he withdrew from all churches and became a "Seeker," anticipating the day when the authority to perform ordinances would be restored to the earth.[17]

In 1644, John Clarke, a physician and one of the most highly educated of the early colonists, established a second "rebaptizing church" in Newport, Rhode Island.[18] After arriving in America in 1637, Clarke was attracted to Anne Marbury Hutchinson and her Antinomian cause. When she was banished, he accompanied her to Rhode Island, to a location soon to be known as Newport. There was a considerable difference between the populations of Newport and Providence. Whereas the people of Newport were generally sophisticated and well-read, the residents of Providence were mainly less-educated and of peasant stock. While the Newport families followed the New

England fashion of founding the town on the basis of a covenant or compact, Providence chose not to do so. However, the Newport covenant differed from those of Massachusetts and Connecticut in that it specifically prohibited the town from debarring those whose conscience "may scruple the giving or taking an oath."[19] Thus, the covenant confirmed and maintained the rights of individuals to live as conscience dictated.

John Clarke was the first to publish a report in Europe on the persecutions of Anabaptists taking place in New England, which was printed in London in 1652.[20] In the introduction, Clarke exclaims that the world is engaged in a struggle between darkness and light. The darkness is so pernicious that its "seducing spirits . . . shall deceive if it were possible the very elect of God." However, he continued, the spirit of Christ shall destroy the tempter with the brightness of his coming and enlighten seekers after Christ by convincing, converting, transforming, and creating them anew. Clarke provides graphic details of the persecutions the leaders of "Mathatusets Bay" had administered against seekers after Christ. As early as 1644, Massachusetts had targeted radicals such as Clarke by passing laws making Anabaptistry illegal.[21]

In the 1640s, an infusion of missionaries from England further strengthened Anabaptism. Mark Lucar, the most prominent of the missionaries, arrived in Newport in 1648. Lucar advocated a new mode of adult baptism through immersion or "dipping," a practice that he claimed had scriptural foundation. Lucar also introduced the doctrine that Christ's atonement was for all people. That is, whoever declared faith in Christ was eligible for salvation through repentance and baptism. Anabaptists had previously taken the Calvinist notion for granted that Christ's atonement was for the "elect." The universalist doctrine advocated by Lucar led to a split in the Anabaptists between one faction, thereafter known as General Anabaptists, who believed the atonement of Christ was for everyone and salvation was available to all of God's children, and the other, Particular Anabaptists, who believed salvation was reserved for the elect.[22]

The major practice separating the two groups of Anabaptists was an additional rite among General Anabaptists of the ordinance, after rebaptism, of the "laying on of hands," which meant that the Holy Spirit would thenceforth dwell with the person as a companion and guide.[23] This practice was akin to the Mormon principle of the laying on of hands for the Gift of the Holy Ghost.[24]

In both the Newport and Providence congregations, difference of opinion reigned over Particular and General salvation issues. The Newport branch, which had been Particular in orientation, was so severely affected by the issue of universal salvation and the laying on of hands that in 1656 the congregation broke apart, and two separate Anabaptist branches were organized. There had been fewer than fifty members before the split, but twenty-one broke away to form the core group of a new General Anabaptist branch.[25]

In 1671, the original Newport congregation (Particular Anabaptists) experienced yet another division when dissident members formed the first congregation of Seventh Day Baptists.[26] Members of the new congregation differed from their Anabaptist neighbors in that they believed the Lord had designated his Sabbath to be on Saturday, the last day of the week and the day the Lord had "rested" after the Creation. The first Seventh Day Baptist had arrived in America from England in 1664.[27] Among those converted to the Seventh Day Baptists was John Crandall, who in 1651 had been one of three people tried and convicted of Anabaptism in Boston.

More Anabaptist ancestors of LDS converts have been identified who were associated with the Providence than with the Newport congregation. Among the eleven associates of Williams who settled in Providence and founded the first Anabaptist congregation, eight were direct-line ancestors of many LDS converts, including Catharine Slauson, Lydia and Celinda Ackermann, the Pratt brothers, Reynolds Cahoon and his son, William Farrington Cahoon, the Morley family, and the Peck family. A direct-line Wightman, Erastus, was baptized in 1835. These ancestors also included Stukely Westcott, John Greene Sr., and John Greene Jr., all important political and religious figures in early Rhode Island. Westcott settled first in Salem, where the congregation "passed censure" on him and his wife for claiming the Massachusetts churches were not "true churches."[28] As a consequence of the Antinomian affair, the Westcotts removed to Rhode Island, where they became attracted to Roger Williams and committed themselves to Anabaptism.

By midcentury, a number of other LDS ancestors had joined the Providence group. We see from the 1650 map of Providence (figure 5), that fifty-three households were located in the town. They were lined up along the Great Salt River, and members of at least twenty-two of these families were ancestors of LDS converts.

Even though more ancestors so far have been identified in Providence, there were also important connections with Newport Baptists. John Clarke, the founder of the Newport branch, had no issue and so had no direct-line descendants; however, Clarke's brothers, Joseph, Thomas, and William, were all ancestors of some important LDS converts, including Martin Harris and the Pratt brothers.[29]

Plymouth Colony Anabaptists

Plymouth Colony had its own Anabaptists, who were concentrated mainly in Rehoboth and Swansea. In general, fifth-generation LDS ancestors were

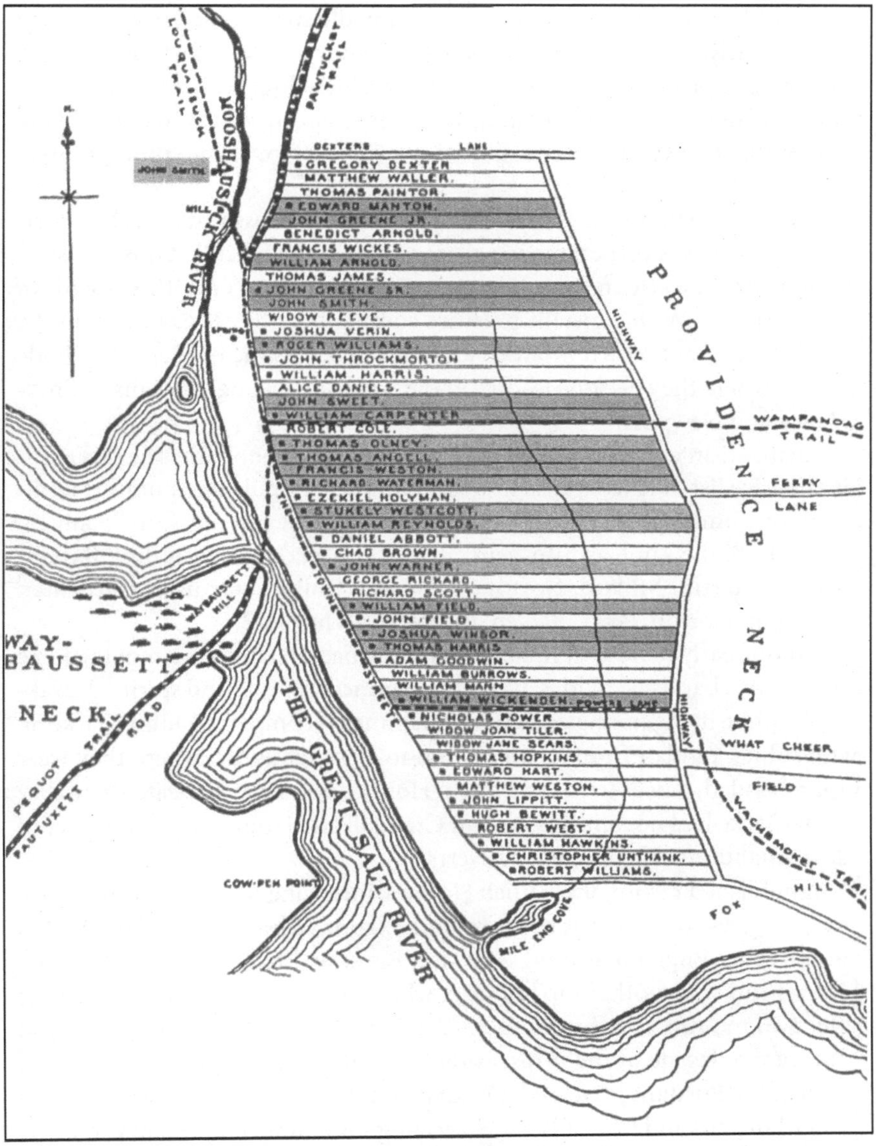

Figure 5. Providence about 1650, with Lots of LDS Ancestors Shaded (*Source:* Welcome Arnold Greene, *The Providence Plantations for 250 Years* [Providence: N.p., 1886], 37)

concentrated in these towns, and a large portion of them were Anabaptists. Swansea, in particular, was known as an Anabaptist town.

No less than seventy-nine fifth-generation ancestors of LDS converts have been identified from Swansea, an astounding number considering the small size of the settlement.[30] Although no register of Anabaptist names was available until the eighteenth century, undoubtedly many LDS ancestors were party to early radical activities in Swansea. Some early Swansea residents were ancestors of prominent LDS Church figures, including William Cahoon and Amasa Lyman. No formal congregation was established in Swansea until the end of the 1660s, so it is impossible to provide a complete account of direct links.[31]

Plymouth had no law against rebaptism, as did Massachusetts, but Puritan leaders in Boston became so agitated over the prospect that this "disease" would spread to them that they pressed Plymouth to curb the growth of Anabaptists.[32] With constant pressure coming from Boston, almost all the original Anabaptists left Swansea and moved across the border into Rhode Island, where they became leaders in the Anabaptist congregations of Providence and Newport.[33]

Anabaptism was also strong in the larger town of Rehoboth. The first comprehensive list of Anabaptists in Rehoboth was not published until 1734, almost one hundred years after it was settled, but the last names of many on this list are the same as fifth-generation LDS ancestors, including Barney, Round, Martin, Millard, Norton, Bosworth, Bullock, Ormsby, Carpenter, Wheaton, Horton, Perry, Bowen, Pierce, and Thurber.[34]

Among early Rehoboth Anabaptists was Obadiah Holmes, a moving force in early Anabaptist activities; he had experienced a profound spiritual awakening while living in England. In 1651, Holmes accompanied John Clarke Sr. and John Crandall from Rhode Island to Massachusetts, where they were apprehended, jailed, tried, and fined. Holmes was severely beaten as well.[35] John Clarke had no family issue, but Crandall and Holmes had a number of descendants among the early converts.[36]

A published record of Obadiah Holmes, including his "last will and testimony," gives some clue as to his radical religious ideas.[37] He had been born in northern England around 1607, and his early life appears to have been uneventful. His mother died in 1630, which signaled a turning point in his life. Two months after his mother's death he married Katherine Hyde, and during the decade of the 1630s, as Bishop William Laud's public campaign against the Puritans increased, Obadiah and Katherine joined thousands of other Puritans and left for Boston, arriving sometime in 1638. They first settled in Salem, where they joined the Congregational Church led by Hugh Peter. Later, Peter would be executed for treason in England, in 1660.[38]

Holmes was a good member of the Salem congregation, but by 1643 he became restive and decided to move to the newly settled town of Rehoboth, forty miles south of Boston and ten miles east of Providence. There Holmes found his own peace by accepting Anabaptism's saving claims. He later recounted his life had been shadowed by "death and darkness" until his rebirth with Anabaptists, which was "brought to light in my soul." His life had been "like a wave tossed up and down" until God had helped him see how he gave "His own love to poor lost man."[39]

Holmes's involvement with Anabaptists brought him into difficulty with the Puritan minister in Rehoboth. The Rehoboth Anabaptists had become pawns in the struggle between Boston and Plymouth. Boston Puritans had long complained that Plymouth Colony was far too lax in its response to the threat of Anabaptism, and they urged the leaders of Plymouth to stamp it out. In June 1650, the Plymouth general court brought charges against Holmes and eight others for infecting the area with Anabaptist heresies. In October of that same year, the Anabaptists were again brought back into court for continuing to meet on the Lord's day. These were the actions that convinced Holmes to remove from Rehoboth to Rhode Island, where he hoped to find a more accepting environment.

Massachusetts Anabaptists

It has been estimated that in 1650 there were only eleven Anabaptists in Massachusetts.[40] This meager number reinforces the argument outlined in chapter 2 that Massachusetts was not where most of those engaged in radical religious practices settled. Although the names of many of the early Massachusetts Anabaptists have not been found, some important individuals are known. For example, Henry Duster was president of Harvard College from 1640 to 1654; he was released from his position when he embraced the Anabaptist faith. No connections have been made between him and early LDS converts. But other known Massachusetts Anabaptists were LDS ancestors, including John Russell Jr., a shoemaker in Woburn who was active in Anabaptism from his youth. He was the fifth-generation ancestor to LDS converts Ellis and Julietty Eames.[41] John George, another known Massachusetts Anabaptist, was the ancestor of early converts John F. and Olive Boynton, as well as of Silas Knapp.[42]

Connecticut Anabaptists

Anabaptists appeared in Connecticut a little later than in Rhode Island and Massachusetts. Valentine Wightman is especially important in the story of Connecticut Anabaptists, though his account begins in the early 1700s, much later than is our focus in this study. As a young man, Valentine came to Groton, Connecticut, to begin the first Anabaptist church. That church remains today the first Baptist church in Connecticut; it will be discussed in chapter 11.

The first Connecticut Anabaptist ministry began in New London County in 1674, and by 1678 the congregation could count about ten members.[43] In 1680, the Connecticut governor submitted a report to England that "there are 4 or 5 Seven-day men, in our colony, and about so many more Quakers."[44] It is likely, however, that the numbers were larger.

Among the first converts to Anabaptism in Connecticut were family members of James Rogers Sr., a man who arrived in America in 1635 at the age of twenty on the *Increase.* He lived first in Stratford, where he married Elizabeth Rowland, and then in the mid-1650s he began commercial interests in New London. He soon established a plantation there, becoming wealthy and influential in local affairs. He owned an important bakery, engaged in shipping interests, was elected six times to the general court, and was active in ecclesiastical affairs.[45]

Rogers had a family of five boys and two girls, and most of the family would leave its mark on New London radical religious history. In 1674, two of his sons, John and James Jr., embraced Sabbatarian principles professed by the Newport Seventh Day Anabaptist congregation, and in 1675 a third son, Jonathan, was also baptized; he was followed in 1676 by James Sr., James's wife Elizabeth, and one of their daughters, Bathsheba. They formed the core of a New London branch.

Connections with the Newport Seventh Day Anabaptists in Rhode Island were cemented when Jonathan Rogers married Naomi Burdick, the daughter of Robert Burdick, a strong and faithful member of the Newport branch. Robert Burdick's wife, Ruth Hubbard, was the sister of an elder in the Newport branch. Naomi Burdick's sister, Deborah, would marry Joseph Crandall, the son of John Crandall, one of three Newport Anabaptists tried and convicted of heresy in Boston in 1651.

The crucial insight to be gained from these contact points between the New London and Newport congregations is that there were multiple connections between various families. Early Mormons such as Lydia and Celinda Ackermann, David Crandall, Eliza Ann Beebe, Ira and Lydia Ames, and others were related to several sixth-generation LDS ancestors among the Seventh Day Anabaptists sin Newport and New London. Of course, not all members of these family circles were a part of the movement. The wife of John Rogers, Elizabeth Griswold, for example, had come from Saybrook, and when John declared himself an Anabaptist, her family became enraged, and a long battle ensued to take Elizabeth away from what they considered an infestation of Satanism.[46]

In 1677, a crucial incident occurred that defined the religious course taken by John Rogers. At the time Joseph Rogers's wife was to be baptized, Elders Hubbard and Hiscox, from the Newport Seventh Day Anabaptist branch, came to officiate in the ordinance. The New London civil authorities requested that the elders do the baptism outside of New London, so that townspeople would not cause difficulties. The Newport Anabaptist leaders agreed with this "reasonable" request, except for John, who refused to compromise; he demanded that the baptism proceed according to its original plan. From that day, John expressed unhappiness with the Seventh Day Anabaptists and eventually broke away to form his own religious movement. He maintained that true believers ought to disrupt normal religious activities of the Puritan congregations and invite persecution on the part of Puritans. The movement inspired by John Rogers eventuated in the formation of a separate religious organization, known generally as the Rogerenes, a radical religious group that emphasized spiritual gifts, particularly divine healing.[47]

Many Rogerenes were ancestors of early LDS converts. One of the more important connections comes through the Mack family. Lucy Mack was Joseph Smith Sr.'s wife, and her grandfather, Ebenezer Mack, had belonged to the Open-Communion Baptist Church in Lyme, Connecticut. Ebenezer's father, John Mack Jr., had married the niece of Rogerenes Samuel and Bathsheba Fox. Lucy's uncle, Elisha Mack, had also married into a family connected to the Rogerenes.[48]

New Hampshire Anabaptists

There is some record of Anabaptist influence in New Hampshire prior to the middle of the seventeenth century, mainly through the influence of Hanserd Knollys, a notable English radical who spent approximately four years in the colonies. While Knollys himself was not an LDS ancestor, many LDS ancestors invited him to head their congregation and were sympathetic to his religious views.

Hanserd Knollys had been an ordained minister in England, but he came to feel he had not received a clear call and commission from Christ to do this work, so in the early 1630s he renounced his ordination. While in England, Knollys sought counsel from John Wheelwright, the brother-in-law of Anne Marbury Hutchinson.[49] Following several discussions with Wheelwright and a period of time in seclusion, Knollys came forth declaring he had received a profound spiritual experience that filled his "soul with joy and peace in believing." Consequently, he again commenced his work, convinced of Antinomian doctrines of salvation and of Anabaptist principles.[50]

Because Knollys met with so much resistance from the Anglican Church, he journeyed to Boston, where he met further resistance from the Puritans. He then went north to Dover, New Hampshire, on the fringe of the colonies, where he served for a time as minister. In Dover, he ran into further trouble with a rival minister, so in 1641 he returned to London.

Knollys was a religious radical who was well known by members of the Dover congregation. His views resonated with many early residents in New Hampshire, and many in the Dover community sided with them. Thomas Roberts, for example, an LDS ancestor who eventually became a Quaker, was sympathetic with Knollys.[51] In 1623, Roberts and William and Edward Hilton were the first settlers of New Hampshire. Edward Starbuck, another member of the Dover congregation, whose family name would eventually be associated with Quakerism, was convicted in 1647 "with the profession of Anabaptism."[52] These examples could be multiplied, but evidence is abundant that strong family connections are to be found between early New Hampshire Anabaptists and significant numbers of early LDS converts.

Maine Anabaptists

Maine Anabaptist inclinations first appeared in Kittery in 1681, and within a short time there were several people professing the Anabaptist faith. These Anabaptists were first led by William Screven, born in 1629 and an early emigrant from England; he was married to Bridget Cutts. The first members of the branch had been part of the Boston congregation, but their minister, Isaac Hull, recognized Screven's talents and suggested they unite under him into a separate church. Screven was commissioned by the Boston Baptist Church to serve as the minister. As quickly as this was done, the local magistrate, Mr. Huck, began to awaken, in the words of Joshua Millet, "prejudice and hatred against these conscientious disciples in Kittery. Slanderous abuses and legalized tyranny were now to be endured by them," as the magistrate fined each person visiting the Anabaptist church five shillings for every such offense.[53]

These actions failed to prevent further baptisms, and so the General Assembly of the province tried and convicted Screven of contempt for continuing his public preaching and for declaring his resolution to persist in his work. He was fined ten pounds and threatened with further penalties for every future offense against the established order. In September of 1682, the church published the names of the following men as members: William Screven, minister; Humphrey Churchwood, deacon; Robert Williams, John Morgandy, Richard Cutts, Timothy Davis, Leonard Brown, William Adams, Humphrey Azell, and George Litter. There were also several women.[54] As persecution continued, the group was formally dissolved and its members scattered. To avoid further problems, William Screven gathered the remaining members with his family, and they removed to South Carolina, where they became the first congregation of Baptists in the South. No LDS ancestors have so far been found among the Baptists who came out of Maine and settled in South Carolina.

Quakers

While Anabaptist impulses were already evident as early as the late 1630s, the Quaker movement did not gain visibility in New England until more than a decade later. In 1653, the *Woodhouse* arrived in America carrying thirteen Quakers. Two went to New York and eleven to Newport, where they were cordially greeted. Newport residents found Quaker doctrines and conduct so acceptable that many of the most influential, educated, and wealthy of the island converted to the faith. Governor Coddington, his son William, John Cranston, William Brenton, Nicholas Easton, Henry Bull, Walter Clarke, John Easton, Caleb Carr, William Wanton, and John Wanton—all of whom were at one time or another governors of Rhode Island—became disciples of George Fox, the father of Quakerism.[55]

It has been estimated that by the beginning of the 1700s half of all residents of Rhode Island had declared themselves Quakers. Certain LDS ancestors stand out among them, including Mary Dyer, later executed in Boston for her beliefs, and her husband William, who served as the secretary of Rhode Island for more than ten years. Another was William Coddington, a man of great wealth and social status, who served on the board of the Massachusetts Bay Company and was also its treasurer. After Coddington sided with Anne Hutchinson in the Antinomian crisis, he was forced into exile to Rhode Island. He was an ancestor of John Portineus Greene.

Quakerism was an important option for those in the colonies wishing to organize alternative religious communities. By 1658, in Salem alone, more than thirty people were engaged in Quaker meetings. Though the less educated and poor were more heavily represented, those attracted to Quakerism were drawn from a surprisingly broad range of social levels and professions.[56] By 1670, fifty-seven Quakers were recorded as residing in Salem. At least twenty of them have been identified as ancestors of early LDS converts, almost all of whom had multiple direct-line connections.[57]

Local Puritan authorities, wishing to quell Quakerism, dealt harshly with the local converts but especially with the "visiting Quakers," missionaries from foreign parts who were circulating throughout New England. There has been speculation that Puritan resolve against Quakerism was strong because Puritan leaders worried that colonists were tiring of the Puritans' brittleness and might feel that Quakers were satisfying their resolve to seek after a more spiritual, more inward faith.[58] At first, Puritan authorities simply harassed those involved in Quaker meetings, but they soon resorted to more severe tactics, such as fines, imprisonment, and whippings.

In 1655, Massachusetts passed a law that anyone who "entertained" a Quaker would be fined, which led to widespread legal action against those sympathetic with the movement. For example, Chu has found that all fifty-nine identified Quakers in Salem in the early period paid fines for their heretical behavior.[59] LDS ancestors Richard Swaine and John Heard were two of those so punished.[60] Authorities also attempted to starve Quakers by denying them food while they served prison sentences.[61] Other LDS ancestors sympathetic with Quakerism, such as William Marsten of Hampton, New Hampshire, were often apprehended and their dwellings searched to determine if they were harboring Quakers.[62] On one occasion, two Quaker tracts were found; Marsten paid a twenty-pound fine.[63]

In 1658, persecution of visiting Quakers intensified. At that time, at least nine Rhode Island Quakers came to Boston, including Thomas Harris, the ancestor of early LDS leader Martin Harris.[64] Thomas was arrested for attempting to speak in a Congregational church after the minister had concluded his sermon. His companion, William Brend, was so severely beaten that the attending physician gave up any hope of saving his life. Remarkably, Brend recovered.[65] Soon after this occurrence, three other Rhode Island ancestors of a number of early LDS converts, Christopher Holder, John Copeland, and John Rouse, traveled north to Massachusetts.[66] They came to a Boston meetinghouse and attempted to speak to the congregation at the conclusion of the church service but were apprehended and jailed.[67] Tensions reached such an extreme that Quakers were banished from the colony and informed that if they returned they would suffer the pain of death. Such threats only reinforced Quaker commitment, and the movement continued to grow.

The most crucial episode in this tragic story was the execution of LDS ancestor Mary Dyer, who had converted to Quakerism after accompanying Anne Marbury Hutchinson to Rhode Island.[68] Dyer returned to England for a period of time but eventually came back to the colonies as a Quaker missionary.[69] In 1657, Dyer was traveling from New Hampshire to Rhode Island with a fellow Quaker, Ann Burden, who wished to stop in Boston to settle her deceased husband's estate. After arriving in Boston, both women were apprehended and thrown into prison, and Dyer was placed in solitary confinement so she could not influence other prisoners. She was soon released but expelled from Massachusetts. She resided for a time in New Haven, but in 1658 she returned to Boston with a group of Quakers from Plymouth and Rhode Island. The two leaders of this group were Quaker missionaries from England, William Robinson and Marmaduke Stephenson, who were arrested when they attempted to address a Boston Puritan congregation after the minister had finished his Sunday sermon.

Even though the Puritans focused their hostile energies on visiting Quakers, local residents sympathetic with Quakerism were not exempt. At the time Robinson, Stephenson, and Dyer were arrested in Boston, three Salem residents, all ancestors of several LDS converts, were also apprehended. Two of these Salem residents, Lawrence and Cassandra Southwick, were jailed because they had entertained the two Quaker missionaries in their Salem home.[70] The other Quaker sympathizer from Salem, Samuel Shattuck, was jailed for interfering with the arresting magistrate at the church by stuffing a glove and handkerchief into the magistrate's mouth.[71] The three Salem prisoners protested by refusing to work in the prison, so Governor Endecott ordered them whipped, with the understanding that each day they persisted, the number of whippings would increase. To their credit, the townspeople protested against such severe treatment of their neighbors, and all three prisoners were soon released.[72]

The three missionary Quakers, Robinson, Stephenson, and Dyer, were also soon released but were told they must leave Massachusetts and return only "upon pain of death."[73] Dyer went to Rhode Island but returned to Boston to visit another Quaker prisoner, Christopher Holder, also an ancestor of several LDS converts. Dyer was apprehended there, as were Robinson and Stephenson, who had decided not to leave Boston. All three were brought to trial, and the men caused great disturbance when they demanded to read a statement about their convictions and mission. All three were convicted of being in Boston, and the day of execution was set. The two men were hanged, but because she was a woman, Mary was returned to her prison cell and given a reprieve, which she refused. When she was brought before Governor Endecott, she exclaimed that if he did not repeal the death penalty for Quakers "the Lord would send others of his servants to witness against them." He rebuked her, asking if she considered herself a prophetess. And she exclaimed that she only spoke the words the Lord had spoken to her.[74] That declaration of personal spiritual communication with the Lord, with all it implied, sealed her fate, and she was hanged the next day.

What drove the Quakers to such behavior? The Quaker movement had originated about 1644 in Leicestershire, England, when a certain group of piously disposed people joined into an association centered on George Fox.

By the early 1650s, a full missionary effort was under way.[75] The message of George Fox was that Christian churches had departed from the primitive purity and simplicity of the true church, but the "day of the Lord was at hand." God was pouring his spirit out upon the earth, Fox asserted, and those touched by his spirit must dedicate themselves to preaching his everlasting gospel to every one of God's creatures. God "did not dwell in temples made with hands" but in persons, through "that inward light, spirit, and grace by which all might know their salvation and their way to God." This inner light was available to every one of God's children, for "Christ had died for all men to profit rather than for the elect." In this respect, Fox argued a universalism that was akin to the General Anabaptists of his time and to the Mormons two hundred years later.[76] Every believer was called to the work; there were ministers called by God, but they did not constitute a trained, professional ministry. As would the Mormons, the Quakers relied on a lay clergy.

Fox demanded that his followers throw off the old religions of the world and take upon themselves the true church of Christ. Believers gathered together without liturgy or prearranged preachers, believing either that the inner light of God would come in silence or his inner light would inspire those who might speak. While Quaker services have little in common with typical Mormon worship services, three practical elements of the two religious traditions are similar. First, there is no professional ministry among Latter-day Saints or Quakers. Second, once a month the Mormons hold a so-called testimony meeting, where anyone in the congregation may stand and bear testimony if moved by the spirit to do so, much like what is done in the typical Quaker service. Third, Mormons are intent that each person in the "ward" or congregation is visited each month by the "home teachers." Similarly, Quakers are diligent in making family visits and reporting on these visits at each monthly meeting.[77]

The number of Quakers in northern New England grew faster than the population.[78] Quaker activity occurred in New Hampshire, Maine, and Essex County, Massachusetts.[79] Puritans reacted by harshly persecuting anyone engaged in Quaker affairs. A number of Salem ancestors of LDS converts were targets of persecution. The Wardell family is a good case in point. In 1664, Eliakin Wardell, a son of Thomas Wardell of Hampton, New Hampshire, and nephew of William Wardell, was fined for entertaining a Quaker missionary and for engaging in disruptive behavior.[80] His wife, for example, had completely disrupted a Newbury congregation by going naked into the meetinghouse in an attempt to shame the Puritans for stripping women to the waist and whipping them through the center of towns.

In New Hampshire, LDS ancestors sympathetic with Quakerism were also badly treated by resident Puritans. At Dover, where Quakers visited in the winter of 1662, Thomas Roberts, the former governor of the town and an ancestor of several LDS converts, recommended giving them a fair hearing.[81] However, the Dover church enforced the rules coming out of Massachusetts and stripped to the waist Anna Coleman, Mary Tomkins, and Alice Ambrose, three Quaker women, tying them to the back of a horse-drawn cart and whipping them with ten lashes as they passed through each township on the way to Boston.[82]

In spite of actions taken against Quakers by the Dover church, some residents remained sympathetic with former governor Roberts's protestations against Puritan mistreatment. The Coffin family, ancestors of LDS convert Mary Thurston Rand, were influenced positively by the Quaker visitors to New Hampshire and later adopted Quakerism after moving to Nantucket. Peter Coffin, the son of Tristram Coffin Sr. and the brother of Tristram Coffin Jr., was the secretary at Dover in 1662; he attempted to document these injustices by recording the charges for and against the Quaker missionaries visiting that town.[83]

During the summer of 1659 a number of people from Hampton, New Hampshire, visited Nantucket as a possible place to settle and decided to organize a group to buy all rights and interest in the island. Later, Nantucket became a focal point of Quaker activity. Members of the group founding Nantucket included LDS ancestors Tristram Coffin Sr., Peter Coffin, Richard Swaine, John Swaine, Christopher Hussey, and Stephen Greenleaf.[84] Several LDS converts, including Samuel Jones Rolfe, Mary Thurston Rand, Lydia Chamberlain, and Dwight Harding, could trace their direct-line ancestry to one or more of these individuals.

Gortonists

Gortonists were followers of Samuell Gorton (1592–1677), who was called at various times an "arch-heretic," a "beast," a "miscreant," a "proud and pestilent seducer," and a "prodigious minter of exorbitant novelties."[85] Though he never identified himself with the Family of Love, he was often regarded as a Familist, because both he and they "believed in mystical communion with the Holy Spirit."[86]

Gorton arrived in Boston in 1636, in the middle of the Antinomian crisis, a few months after Roger Williams had been banished from the colony. While in England, he had led a relatively conventional life. His father was from a good family, connected with the local gentry of Gorton, a town located near Manchester that carried the family name. Though the father, a prosperous merchant, chose not to send Samuell to the university, he did give him, likely through a home tutor, a grasp of the Scriptures. As a young man, Samuell worked as a clothier and also became involved in local religious debates, declaring himself opposed to the established church. He had not yet formed a systematic religious view but was so opposed to the religious pretensions of English orthodoxy that by 1636 he had decided to remove himself and his family from England.[87]

Upon arriving in Boston, Gorton found that everywhere he went he became the center of religious disruption and protest. He quickly determined that Boston Puritans were mainly intent on "the outward carriage of one man toward another" but failed to observe the barest "principles of divinity wherein we had been instructed." So he moved on to Plymouth but came again into difficulty with the authorities over religious matters. He began holding meetings in Plymouth where he gave religious instruction, and the wife of the local minister, John Smith, regularly attended these meetings; her involvement caused unusual stress within the church hierarchy. The house servant of the Gortons was another woman to cause grief; she disrupted public meetings by speaking out and voicing her opinions. The minister indicted her for disrupting church services, but Gorton complained, noting that the only specific charge against his house servant was "that she had smiled in your congregation."[88]

Gorton was soon charged with alienating the community and causing dissension in the regular ministry. In 1638, he was banished from Plymouth Colony and traveled to Rhode Island, where he threw in his lot with Anne Marbury Hutchinson, who was then living in Portsmouth. In 1641, he relocated to Providence, where he questioned every exercise of civil authority, causing even Roger Williams to wonder at his behavior.

He then moved to Warwick, south of Providence, but had to fight off Indian and Massachusetts claims to the land. At one time, a force of forty men from the Massachusetts Bay Colony sought him out and carried him and others to Boston for trial. There he was beaten, jailed, and persecuted because he emphasized the indwelling of the Holy Spirit. In 1646, he returned to England for a time, where he published a tract entitled *Simplicities Defence against Seven-Headed Policy, or Innocence Vindicated, being unjustly Accused, and sorely Censured, by the Seven-Headed Church-Government United in New-England.* In the tract he attacked those in the Massachusetts Bay Colony who had persecuted him and his fellow sufferers. After four years in England, he returned to the colonies, where he left a profound legacy of radical religious thinking.

While his prose style has been described as "relatively inaccessible" to those of us not living in his time and place, it does provide glimpses of how his theology came into direct conflict with the most fundamental tenets of mainstream Puritanism.[89] For example, he challenged the prevailing notion of trinitarianism, which since the Nicene Creed was adopted in A.D. 325, had dictated that God, Christ, and the Holy Ghost were "of one essence." He characterized this as "a most dangerous and pernicious doctrine," a creed that rejected the simple fact that Jesus was human in form and had been resurrected in human form.[90] His beliefs about the Godhead helped open the way to challenges against the trinitarianism that had dominated Christianity for thirteen centuries.

One aspect of Gortonism that coincides with Mormonism was his claim that there is an essential divine spark in human nature. Every human soul is said to possess that spark; it is neither created nor will it pass away. It is eternal and everlasting. There is an indwelling divinity found in all people.

Gorton also anticipated Mormon dualist theology in his belief that good and evil are in eternal conflict: good tending toward eternal life, evil toward eternal damnation. Gorton claimed, as do Mormons, there is no single arbitrary event upon which people will be judged. The good and the evil weigh intrinsically and naturally on every action. Righteousness is movement in the direction of life eternal, while sin is movement toward damnation. All humankind participates in a continuous, eternal flow of moments, and the "now" is one moment of eternal existence. Gorton did not look for some future condition so much as strive to attain the heavenly in every action and decision. He believed heaven is not so much a place as a condition of the soul.

Gortonists, holding themselves outside the confines of civil and ecclesiastical law, were accused of advocating a communal way of life, including plural marriage, that closely paralleled the English Diggers and the Ranters.[91] Gortonists believed both men and women could partake of the Holy Spirit. They were against all formality in worship, the sacraments, taxes to support religion, and a college-educated clergy. They believed God should appoint ministers, not the qualifications bestowed by a school.[92]

Gorton's direct-line descendants among early LDS converts included Celinda and Lydia Ackermann and Lebbeus T. Coons Sr. While Gorton's first disciple, John Wickes, who followed him from Plymouth, does not appear to have had descendants among early LDS converts, other disciples do. Gortonist John Greene Sr., the first of a long line of important Greene leaders of Rhode Island, was an ancestor of a number of early converts.[93] Greene was a highly educated surgeon who probably arrived in Massachusetts in 1636 and removed to Providence, where he lived with his three wives and five children from his first wife, Joanne Tattershall.

Samuell Gorton proclaimed other views as well. His spiritual mysticism was strikingly similar to what Brooke calls the "paradisal universalism of Familists and of other Continental mystics" who practiced a spiritually egalitarian form of Christianity.[94] Gorton's near pantheist universalism was radically expressed in his injunction to "goe and preach the Gospell in every creature."[95] He proclaimed the beginning of a new dispensation based on the doctrine, as is the case in Mormon doctrine, that everyone was free from original sin.

Probably the closest disciple of Gorton was Randall Holden, who accompanied Gorton on his return trip to London, but Holden came back two years later to help establish a permanent Gortonist settlement around Warwick Cove, Rhode Island.[96] Holden had many connections to early LDS converts, including the Knight and Peck families.[97] Other Gorton disciples who were LDS ancestors include Richard Waterman, John Warner, and William Wardell.[98]

9. LDS Ancestors Engaged in Alchemy and Astrology

Divergent Views

There are divergent opinions on the extent to which the Mormon Church has a mystical and magical worldview. Michael Quinn, a Mormon historian, startled contemporary Mormons with the publication of his *Early Mormonism and the Magic World View,* in which he claims that nineteenth-century Mormonism was infused with practices that today would be identified with the occult, including treasure seeking and folk magic. It is Quinn's position that early Mormons reflected widespread attitudes about magic typical of the time that were generally considered to be rational, self-evident, and Christian. He notes that "occult beliefs and magic practices were part of early America's heritage," and that Mormons shared in these beliefs and practices. He also notes that the worldview of Mormons and Americans in general has changed since that time.[1]

Even though Quinn suggests any beliefs of early LDS leaders concerning magic predated Mormonism, he does not elaborate on the issue, and it was left to John Brooke to suggest a possible historical account of the ways in which Mormonism was rooted in America's pre-Mormon magical and mystical cosmology.[2] Significantly, while Brooke has received great praise from non-Mormon scholars, those within the LDS Church have been less enthusiastic about his work, probably in part because he attempts to give a human rather than a divine face to Mormonism's origins; but also because his work is cast in a language with terms such as "hermeticism," "gnosticism," "the occult," "cosmology," "mythology," "cabalism," and "primitivism," words that feel alien to Mormons and do not resonate with their concepts and emphases.[3]

Quite a different approach to the magic worldview of Mormons is reflected in a 1994 publication by Jan Shipps and John W. Welch, *The Journals of William E. McLellin,* which they feel are some of the most important documents related to the earliest years of the LDS Church. McLellin joined the LDS Church in 1831, and within a year he was excommunicated; then, in 1833, he was rebaptized. In 1835, he was ordained an apostle, but within months he was again excommunicated, and within a month reinstated, and then excommunicated again in 1838.[4] Throughout all this on-again, off-again relationship with the church, he meticulously recorded the missionary work of the LDS Church in its first decade, including sermons and biblical references in church meetings.

If the works of Brooke and Quinn reflect the core and essential character of early Mormonism, one would expect McLellin's journals to indicate, at least at some level, "occultism and hermetic hocus-pocus" in the church.[5] Instead, these journals make no reference to the occult or magic. Mystical experience is another matter. Early Mormonism involved "revelations, prophesying, seeing visions, and dreaming dreams," but Shipps and Welch believe almost all such expressions can more easily be associated with miracles, as recounted in the Bible, than with the occult.[6] And, indeed, even in today's world, Mormons are at ease with accounts of these types of mystical experiences.

It is indisputable that early Mormons' views of magic and the occult were at least consistent with what Americans in general believed. And Mormons held to mystical beliefs that went beyond the norm. Early Mormons were comfortable, as are Mormons today, with the unseen world, the world of the spirit, and the gifts imparted by the Holy Spirit. According to Welch, McLellin gives rich accounts of miracles: "He reports twenty-three cases of healing the sick, an instance of discerning of spirits, two acts of casting out devils, seven occurrences of speaking in tongues, and four times when divine help was received along the way."[7] For Mormons, the window between the visible and invisible world was open, and wonders, including seer-stones, amulets, anointings, divining rods, and buried treasures, were a part of their life experience. Part of the radicalism of Mormons was surely inherited from the beliefs and practices of their forebears. We ought to explore briefly the world of magic that belonged to their early American ancestors.

Magic and the New World

Most early Christians in the New World, whatever their confession, believed in the reality of magic and spiritual gifts. They took for granted the validity of sciences based on what is today associated with the occult, particularly alchemy and astrology. Most Christians accepted the presence of supernatural forces that empowered human beings to perform miracles, to be conduits of divine intervention, to use magic and thereby predict the future, heal the sick, destroy enemies, and defend against evil.[8] They commonly "offered techniques to invoke other-worldly powers to control nature and affect mankind."[9]

But Puritans and many other Protestants were also ambivalent about the astral sciences. Ministers saw their authority undercut by those who embraced occult techniques. Puritan leaders recognized the influence of alchemy and astrology but were suspicious because these sciences took people beyond the boundaries of a perfect faith; ministers were supposed to be in charge of supernatural powers, and so they railed against the corruption represented by the occult.

Puritan leaders were apprehensive of people who claimed to possess spiritual gifts. Mainstream Protestantism associated folk magic and spiritual gifts with corrupt Catholicism. The older Christian tradition took magic for granted, and in the seventeenth century theirs remained a "syncretic Christianity," where the lines between the supernatural spirit world and the natural world were blurred.[10] The Catholic Church taught that there were people who wielded supernatural power through magic and rituals. The holy saints possessed the power to perform amazing feats, such as predict the future, heal the sick, and perform other acts requiring divine assistance.[11]

Puritan reformers challenged this tradition. They denounced acts of magic and claims of spiritual gifts as fraudulent and deceptive and inevitably decided such acts were evidence of wizardry, witchcraft, and sorcery. These were described as debased "folk magic," in contrast to the true Christian magic of the original church. Mainstream Protestants attempted to cleanse the church of mystical, magical, and ethereal elements. They abolished confession, cast away the practice of exorcism, turned the Lord's sacrament from a miraculous transubstantiation of bread and wine to a symbolic representation, took away the pomp and ceremony of the mass, and rid the church of statuary, stained glass windows, and other ornamentation. In other words, the Reformation tended to create a colder, more sterile set of religious practices.

The Reformation went even further, in that most spiritual experiences were challenged. Earliest Christianity had been based on the notion of revelation and the role of the Holy Spirit in the lives of believers, including the possibility of spiritual gifts, such as prophecy, visions, healing, and speaking in tongues. But, as early as the second century, church leaders recognized that claims to prophecy and revelation threatened their political power. Consequently they persecuted any factions within Christianity, such as the Montanists, who advanced the idea that these gifts were real and readily available. Church leaders maintained that even though the divine Christ, the cornerstone of the church, and his apostles possessed powerful spiritual gifts, after their departure God had withdrawn these gifts. God's revelation was then transferred to the Scriptures, which, according to the church, contained the fullness of God's word on earth.

Nevertheless, aspects of supernatural expression continued in the Roman as well as the Orthodox Eastern Church, and even as the Reformation spread throughout Northern Europe, pockets of spiritualism remained. Scotland, for example, was redolent with spiritualism, particularly with prophetic themes. The Arthurian legend, in many ways a replay of the Christian myth, predicted that a new Arthur would emerge, reunite the whole of Britain, and drive the accursed Anglo-Saxon back into the North Sea.[12]

When Protestant leaders deinstitutionalized mystical, magical, and sensory aspects of religion, the common, ordinary believer simply turned to sources of mystical experience outside the church. Everywhere people were found who claimed they possessed some form of "white" magic. They could heal the sick by prescribing healing ceremonies and herbal remedies, dictate special dietary practices for good health, provide love potions, find stolen goods, drive rats away from households, and discover hidden treasure.

It is unclear who was eligible to participate in such rites. Both males and females engaged in magical practices. Some thought the seventh son of a seventh son had special abilities. Typically, however, those exercising gifts of the Holy Spirit gained their status through the performance of acts of white magic, relying on word of mouth to publicize their powers.

Radical religionists in colonial New England were among those who professed to exercise the gifts of the Holy Spirit. Quakers extolled the miracles of their founder, George Fox, who was known to have healed the wife of a governor in the New World.[13] And John Rogers, founder of the Connecticut Rogerenes, claimed to be a healer through the Holy Spirit.[14]

The Reformation presents a paradox. On the one hand, its leaders attempted to stamp out mystical practices. On the other hand, the Reformation contributed to a religious awakening, which had the effect of revitalizing various aspects of mysticism. On the continent, the first major German mystic of the time was likely Ægidius Gutmann (1490–1584) of Swabia, who wrote a long, complex text entitled *Revelations of Divine Majesty*, wherein he intertwined contemporary religious fancy with natural science (alchemy), prophecy, and what Waite calls an "inner awakening."[15]

Gutmann was followed by Valentine Weigel (1533–88), who composed tracts anticipating Rosicrucianism. Jakob Böhme (1575–1624), the most prominent German mystic, a Lutheran in Silesia, professed a number of spiritual experiences, the most important coming in 1600, when he looked into a pewter dish and saw "the Being of Beings, the Byss and the Abyss, the eternal generation of the Trinity, the origin and descent of this world, and of all creatures through the Divine Wisdom."[16] He was deeply Christian but raised to a new level the importance of firsthand inward experience and the possibility that the human spirit or soul might engage in divine union.[17] Böhme had a great impact on the mystical movement of continental Europe, but he was almost unknown in England until English translations of his works were published in 1624.

Prior to Böhme, mystical initiation rites of study, discipline, and even research were demanded before anyone could gain esoteric knowledge. But for Böhme, a simple, unschooled shoemaker, the most important factor in gaining esoteric knowledge was purity of life. This attitude was adopted by scholars committed to the budding natural sciences, who believed the pure life would contribute to insight in science and experimentation.

Rosicrucians, who emerged in Kassel, Germany, around 1614, just prior to the Thirty Years War (1618–48), were committed to "knowledge by revelation" more than to knowledge by study, logic, and experimentation. At that time, a spate of tracts and manifestos circulated throughout Europe announcing the reemergence of a secret brotherhood of philosophers who were connected with the mystic figure, Christian Rosenkreutz, who was said to have lived in the late fourteenth and early fifteenth centuries.[18]

Rosicrucians announced they had discovered tablets in Rosenkreutz's tomb in 1604 bearing secret inscriptions and that their translation had restored the secret knowledge of the brotherhood that showed how to unfold the inner power residing in each person. German Lutheran theologian Johann Valentin Andreä translated these manuscripts into two anonymously published English-language tracts. Radical religious circles of Europe circulated hopeful rumors that a new dispensation would take place based on the knowledge of ancient mysteries. Every member of humankind would be able to tap into the vast, deep reservoir of the totality of humankind's experience and bring it forth to yield a wealth of personal meaning and illumination.

One reason Puritans reviled and abused Anabaptists and Quakers was because these groups believed the Holy Spirit dwelled within them and gave them special powers to heal the sick, prophesy, and gain special insight. Puritans believed such powers were real but that they more likely came from the devil than from God. Seventeenth-century New England Puritans dedicated themselves to purging from Christian life what they considered to be magic and superstition.[19] In spite of their efforts, folk magic associated with the occult continued to find expression and was so pervasive that civil authorities eventually responded by ruling occult practices to be illegal.[20]

The practice of occult ritual in the early colonial period was primarily noninstitutional; thus, it is impossible to determine how extensive it was. But scholars such as John Brooke feel that in New England the hermetic tradition was relatively insignificant. He suggests that the Mormon roots linked to that tradition are best explained by connecting Joseph Smith to the mystical traditions in the Middle Atlantic states, particularly Pennsylvania and New Jersey.[21] Certainly, there was a strong expression of the occult in the middle states of America, and it is possible that Joseph Smith learned of this tradition while in seclusion in the Pennsylvania countryside. However, such explanations do not explain why the hundreds of converts who first joined the LDS Church were so attracted to its cosmology, even though their experience was entirely of New England and they were rooted in its historical traditions. The parallels between Mormonism and hermeticism, "concepts of the coequality of matter and spirit, of the covenant of celestial marriage, and of an ultimate goal of human godhood," are so obvious that the responsiveness of the LDS converts to this cosmology indicates it must have existed in New England.[22]

The two most familiar institutions often identified today with occult ritual are Freemasonry and Rosicrucianism. Freemasons claim roots going back as far as King Solomon and his temple in Jerusalem; however, as an organized unit in its present-day form, Freemasonry first became evident in 1717 with the establishment of the English Grand Lodge.[23] Rosicrucians claim to have discovered documents that suggest a presence as early as 1614; however, organized groups identifying themselves as Rosicrucians do not appear until the eighteenth and even nineteenth centuries.[24] Brooke finds Masonic and Rosicrucian expressions of hermeticism particularly attractive in his treatment of Mormon roots, but these groups came to America from abroad long after the ancestors of LDS converts had arrived and were well established in their New England communities. The two practices that today are considered part of the occult, but which in the sixteenth century had wide acceptance as sciences, are alchemy and astrology.

Alchemy

Alchemy has been regarded as a transitional natural science, a precursor to chemistry. It might also be seen as learned occultism, in that it occupied the attention of some of the most brilliant minds of the seventeenth and eighteenth centuries. It is likely that alchemy was as commonly believed in at the time as chemistry is today, but it began to be overshadowed by chemistry when revolutionary chemical discoveries of the eighteenth century undermined alchemy's claims.

Alchemy was not just a study of chemicals and their transformation; it was ultimately about the metamorphosis of the soul. Almost synonymous with hermeticism, alchemy claimed to be an exact science, studying the regeneration of the soul. In the mortal world, alchemists believed, the soul is immersed in a physical, sensate state, but alchemy promised to show the way for the soul's transformation into a state of perfection and nobility, its state prior to the fall to mortality.[25]

As alchemy began to decline in influence, it continued to retain some credibility with the general public and even with the educated, though this was increasingly unusual. In the seventeenth century, the strongest advocates of alchemy in the English-speaking world lived in England, and they included such people as John Dee and Robert Child; however, the New World could also claim a number of prominent alchemists. Probably the most famous in the early New England colonies was John Winthrop Jr. He was the son of the governor of Massachusetts, but he moved to Connecticut, where he himself became governor. He was celebrated in poetry by Benjamin Thompson for his fame as an alchemist; Cotton Mather, the renowned Puritan cleric, characterized him as the "Hermes Christianus."[26] Winthrop, a trained physician, assembled a large library of alchemical and mystical literature.[27] He belonged to a circle of intellectuals who followed the hermetic, Paracelsian tradition.[28] Paracelsus, a Swiss chemist, physician, and philosopher of the sixteenth century, had drawn on a combination of the Scriptures, German mysticism, alchemy, and magic to construct his "science-based" worldview.[29]

Robert Starkey (or Stirk) was another respected New World alchemist. He was born in 1627 in what is now Bermuda, the son of the Reverend George Stirk, and when he reached the age of sixteen his father enrolled him in Harvard College.[30] He engaged in conventional humanistic and religious studies but ultimately chose to concentrate on medicine and chemistry, which led him into the study of alchemy, particularly pyrotechnics. He read Paracelsus, Galen, and Helmont, and he met Robert Child in Boston during Child's visit in 1645–47. European alchemists such as Samuel Hartlib followed Starkey's work, especially with furnaces, medical treatments, and processes for transmuting tin into silver and silver into gold.[31] It is clear that while a young man in America, Starkey was able to gain a firm grounding in alchemy.

The importance of alchemy in America is well illustrated by the works of an anonymous alchemist, an interesting figure known as Eirenaeus Philalethes, or the Cosmopolitan. After he had published a large number of tracts and reports, his first book appeared in London in 1654; but because Starkey edited the first edition, some claim he was its pseudonymous author. Others have also been "identified" as the author of Philalethes's many works.[32] For example, Jon Butler speculates Philalethes was John Winthrop Jr.[33]

Among Philalethes's contemporaries was Christian Lodowick of Newport, Rhode Island, a "Quaker, mystic, physician, musician, and mathematician," who is best known for his linguistic work in producing a German-English dictionary. However, Lodowick was also known for his work in alchemy.[34] It is not surprising that the science would have been practiced in Rhode Island, the site of so much other radical religious activity.

Samuel Lee, a noted preacher and theologian, migrated in 1686 from England to Bristol, Rhode Island, to become the minister of a church. He had a large collection of alchemical and astrological writings, which eventually found its way to the Winthrop library after Lee died in 1691.[35]

Some alchemists of that time were ancestors of LDS converts. Robert Starkey had no American progeny because he moved back to England in 1650. But one known sixth-generation ancestor was Jonathan Brewster, son of the *Mayflower* Pilgrim and Separatist William Brewster. Jonathan was an alchemist living in the small village of Moheken, Connecticut, just north of New London, in a major region of religious radicalism in southern New England.[36]

During William Brewster's stay in Leyden, the Netherlands, his faith was caught up in the Arminian controversy swirling around the University of Leyden.[37] Some commentators connect Arminianism with magic and the occult.[38] The followers of Jacob Arminius, centered at Leyden, became known as anti-Calvinists because they taught a modified view of grace, rejecting Calvin's notion of predestination as well as the notion of an "elect." Arminians affirmed the controversial doctrine that Christ died for everyone, suggesting that those who fall from grace do so by their own choice. Their belief that God was aware of who would fall was a notion somewhat akin to the Mormon emphasis on God's foreknowledge about who will accept His gospel and who will not.

Jonathan Brewster had been born in Scrooby in 1593, and he was a young man when the *Mayflower* first sailed to the New World carrying his father. A year after the *Mayflower*'s voyage Jonathan arrived in Plymouth on the *Fortune*. In 1630, he moved to Duxbury, Massachusetts, and by 1636 had moved further from Boston to the belt of religious radicalism located along the southern coast of New England. He took command of a trading house and experimented with alchemy.[39] Brewster borrowed a number of books from

Winthrop's alchemical library and wrote to Winthrop that he believed he had attained the "red elixir" or the philosopher's stone, in his experiments.[40]

Alchemy was by no means restricted to areas known for religious radicalism. Though Boston was not a healthy place for advocates of magic, Harvard College was known for its work in "learned occults of alchemy and astrology." Samuel Danforth, ancestor of LDS converts Ebenezer and John Edward Page, was one of those engaged in alchemical experiments and the pursuit of the philosopher's stone. Born in 1696 in Dorchester, Massachusetts, Danforth was a Harvard student when he was exposed to Charles Morton's *Compendium Physicae,* which for a half-century after 1686 was the primary scientific text at Harvard College. Morton had devoted considerable space in the text to topics such as "The Artifice of Gold by Alchymy" and "the finding of the Phylosophers Stone." The philosopher's stone was thought to be a catalyst that would not only transmute base metals into gold but also transmute mere mortals into a state of immortality.[41]

According to David Lovejoy, a student of "enthusiasm" during the colonial period, the most enthusiastic, zealous, and radical pioneers in New England were alchemists. They "believed they were on the way to extracting from the New World experience the holy presence of Christ, the philosopher's stone," which had been denied them in England and was not available to most of the Saints. The New World was where they as "spiritual Chymists" would be able to distill and enjoy the essence of Christ. Lovejoy was speaking here of the Antinomians, followers of Anne Hutchinson, many of whom were ancestors of early LDS converts.[42]

It is difficult to identify which ancestors of LDS converts engaged in alchemy in early America. Because alchemy was not part of a formal institution with membership records, only court prosecutions and other legal records provide testimony of its pervasiveness. Brooke claims that alchemy was pervasive among the ancestors of early LDS leaders, although his evidence for "pervasiveness" is mainly circumstantial.[43]

Astrology

Along with alchemy, astrology was also an important transition science, and people in the colonies interpreted astrology in different ways. Many people in the colonies committed to a rational, scientific worldview held astrology to be a credible and serious means of interpreting the cosmos. Astrology represented a mechanistic understanding of the universe, somewhat as we view contemporary astronomy, and many New Englanders believed that God's will was expressed in the movement of heavenly bodies and that careful attention to both their position and movement would provide insights into the weather, farming conditions, and physical health. Some people who were not especially committed to a scientific worldview linked astrology with the occult, even believing that the positions of the planets and zodiacal signs at the time of birth informed people of the course their lives were to take.

Astrology was based on the view that the earth was the center of the universe, a view destroyed by the Copernican revolution. Consequently, astrology as a science declined precipitously in the seventeenth century. However, astrology continued as a strong force among the common people and even among the nonscientific educated classes.

The Puritan fathers saw occult astrology as dangerous and blasphemous because it touched on an invisible world, a secret world that God had "forbidden and concealed from discovery by lawful means."[44] They connected this astrology to the devil and held that its practitioners relied on the services of the devil to perform their wizardry. And yet, the Puritan clergy itself was captivated by the lure of astrology's potential and power. For example, from 1660 to 1686, in Hampton, New Hampshire, where a relatively large number of LDS converts' ancestors lived, the pastor was Seaborn Cotton, the eldest son of the Reverend John Cotton of Boston. Seaborn Cotton kept a diary of theological notes, church records (births, marriages, deaths), and genealogical information. In that diary, he devoted eighteen pages to a discussion of astrology, including the influence each planet exercises over an individual born under its particular phase.[45] One might assume that he conveyed this interest to members of his parish.

The eighteen pages of Cotton's book were written in the hand of his first wife, Dorothy Bradstreet, daughter of Simon and Anne Bradstreet of Ipswich, Massachusetts.[46] Anne was the first poetess of note in New England, and her widely read poems were filled with astrological symbolism. The poems were surely known and appreciated by the many Ipswich ancestors of LDS converts.

It is difficult to connect specific individuals directly with astrology during that time. There were no associations or professional groups that would allow one to identify membership or subscription lists. However, based on the contents of almanacs of the day, it is clear that astrology was of general interest.[47] Prior to 1740, no newspapers or regular magazines were available. Almanacs, the most important information outlet of the day, had become extremely popular since the Gutenberg printing press was invented in Germany in the mid-1400s. Almanacs were plentiful in England.

A printing press was brought to the colonies in 1638, and a year later a New

England almanac edition was first published. In 1645, alchemist Samuel Danforth began to publish an almanac series, whose size, format, and contents became the model for a host of subsequent almanacs in the colonies.[48] Cotton Mather remarked in 1683 that almanacs had come "into almost as many hands as the Bible itself."[49] Four-fifths of all secular literature published at the time were almanacs, and they even outsold the Bible.

Most early almanacs were published by tutors of Harvard College; they devoted much attention to astronomical information, the telling of time, important meetings or dates, the weather, sailing information, and farming advice. The greatest space was given to monthly calendars, which contained the time of the new and full moon and so on. The famous "man of the signs," a drawing of a human figure surrounded by the twelve signs of the zodiac, was always a part of the publication.

By 1687, Harvard had lost its monopoly, but most New England almanacs continued to be published in Boston.[50] In 1728, Benjamin Franklin's brother, James, printed the first *Rhode Island Almanac.* It became one of the most popular yearly editions. An excellent almanac was published in the second half of the eighteenth century (from 1762 onward) by Nathaniel Low of Ipswich, where many LDS converts' ancestors were located. All almanacs contained astronomical information and astrological predictions, as well as more general material. They inevitably carried astrological signs and charts for charting the destiny of a person. Astrology held a special place within the occult, in that it was considered to be as much a science as a form of magical expression. Most of the almanacs were published by clerics, who otherwise denounced magic.[51]

The fifth-generation ancestors of LDS converts were surely as captivated by astrology as other people of the time, and it may be possible to make some inferences about their involvement in it by examining, for instance, marriage dates. Almanacs were important sources of astrological information when making such important personal decisions. A number of special days were considered to be particularly advantageous ones on which to marry, such as the first week or any multiple of seven days after the new moon.

Birth, marriage, and death dates are available for many early residents of New England, but it is awkward to establish the exact dates on present-day calendars because the events were recorded according to the Julian calendar, which had been in use since Julius Caesar authorized its use in 46 B.C.[52] Western Europe slowly adopted the more accurate Gregorian calendar, named after Pope Gregory XIII, but the British were so hostile to the pope that they failed to adopt it until 1752. This posed difficulties for early English and colonial almanac makers. The authors of the so-called Tully Almanac, first published in 1687, moved the New Year from March to January, but until 1752, almanac makers retained the dating system of the Julian calendar.

In spite of the problem of conflicting calendars, I was interested in exploring just how much might be learned about the involvement of LDS ancestors in astrology by analyzing their marriage dates. It was only possible to consider a small number of them because the specific day, month, and year of marriage are rarely provided in genealogical data. I took a sample of sixty-six marriage dates that did have the necessary information and engaged in a number of calculations to see if any astrological arrangements might be deduced. When I looked at the conjunction of the planets Venus, Mars, and Jupiter with the moon and the sun, I found no more marriages among the ancestors than might be expected through random choice. I considered the multiples of seven, beginning with the new moon, and again found no more dates than might be randomly expected. But when I calculated the marriages taking place in the first week following the new moon, I found that twenty-six of the sixty-six marriages took place then, which means that almost 40 percent of all marriages took place in that time period. If the marriage dates had been randomly selected, we would expect to find that approximately 25 percent of all marriages had taken place then. This higher-than-expected percentage of marriages taking place in the first week after the new moon tantalizingly suggests that many early LDS ancestors deliberately chose that period of time for their marriage date, but the evidence is suspect.

I have no evidence that the LDS ancestors relied on astrology more than other New Englanders in selecting marriage dates. But it is likely that those who lived in the context of a radical religious tradition were incorporating astrology into their decision making for a much longer time than the general population, even as late as the nineteenth century. Among early Mormons, Joseph Smith's family members were greatly interested in astrology. They owned a magic dagger inscribed with Mars and magic parchments inscribed with astrological symbols, and Joseph Smith married all of his wives on days that coincided with favorable astrological signs.[53] However, it would be a mistake to connect these activities with occult practices that extended beyond the boundaries of the beliefs and practices common to those living in the American colonies during the period of the Second Great Awakening.

10. Witchcraft among LDS Ancestors

Witchcraft has always been a special type of magic. Witches often claimed supernatural gifts, including the ability to perform miracles such as healing, to prophesy in the name of Christ, discern diverse spirits, speak in tongues, and interpret the words of those who speak in tongues. Witches also claimed the gift of wizardry, divining and fortune-telling. In other words, witchcraft has always manifested both a spiritual and a shadow side. Those individuals claiming to be inspired by the Holy Spirit have contended with the fraudulent and the charmers, with the counterfeiters and the sorcerers; those engaging in the miraculous have competed with cunning conjurers; white witches have contended with black and maleficent witches.[1]

In general, Catholics have always acknowledged positive spiritual experiences, while Protestant leaders have considered both white and black witches to be of the devil. The Protestant point of view developed simultaneously with the first whisperings of the Reformation. As early as the fourteenth century, witch hunting had become a major enterprise of civil and ecclesiastical authorities, who did not distinguish between white and black witches. Individuals were often put to death because they practiced special medical skills. Some were burned at the stake because they claimed to have "asked in spirit" and to have then been granted special gifts of the Holy Spirit.

The extent of witchcraft convictions and live burnings is startling. Certain German cities averaged six hundred executions a year;[2] city officials in Würzburg executed as many as nine hundred in one year. Town leaders in Como, Italy, executed one thousand in one year, while in Toulouse, France, they executed four hundred in a single day. Millions may have been put to death, and it is estimated that 85 percent were women and children. England does not appear to have engaged in as many executions as the Continent; nevertheless, as many as one thousand were carried out.[3]

When the American colonies were established, witchcraft practices soon followed. In early New England, ministers often railed against occult practices, and they were particularly preoccupied with witchcraft. Cotton Mather was so concerned about its popularity that he delivered entire sermons on the subject. Two years before the 1692 witchcraft trials, he gave a sermon against using magical techniques to cure illnesses and to settle interpersonal conflicts. In that sermon he explained how the congregation could defend against witchcraft, enchantments, and charms. The only "amulets" they needed were "fervent prayer," "a lively faith," and "a holy life."[4]

In the early colonial period, folk magic was widespread among the common people.[5] Katherine Harrison of Hartford and Wethersfield claimed she was able to tell fortunes. She predicted, for example, that the daughter of her employer, who was being courted by one William Chapman, would never marry anyone named William but, rather, would marry someone called Simon. This proved to be an accurate prediction. She was accused of fortune-telling in 1668 but was later acquitted.[6] One Alice Metherill, mother of a "black bastard child," once commented that Peter Wittem had read her fortune and told her that her seed would be mixed with that of another nation. In 1672, a fortune-teller reportedly told Goody Whitteridge of Wenham that she would meet with a strange death; after she related this to her son, she left her house in agitation, only to be found dead the next morning.[7] In Salem, in 1691–92, several girls were said to have formed a fortune-telling group and fashioned "a primitive crystal ball by suspending the white of an egg in a glass." One girl, who wanted to know of her future husband, claimed she saw in the crystal ball the likeness of a coffin. Soon after, several members of the group apparently fell ill and began to suffer fits.[8]

Episodes of witchcraft began in New England at least a half-century prior to the famous Salem witchcraft craze of 1692. It is not clear when the first witch was convicted, though as early as 1647 John Winthrop, governor of Massachusetts, recorded a witchcraft conviction. Unfortunately, no corroborating records are available.[9] Such convictions were based on laws passed in Massachusetts (1641), Connecticut (1642), and New Haven (1655), all of which were founded on British precedent. In Massachusetts the law stated: "If any man or woman be a witch, (that is hath or consulteth with a familiar spirit) they shall be put to death."[10]

Between 1640 and 1690 in New England, prior to the Salem witchcraft delusion of 1692, at least ninety-two people were indicted, sixty-one brought to trial, and sixteen convicted of witchcraft.[11] In table 11, I have clustered the accusations, trials, and convictions in the counties of New England into three distinct groups according to whether they were dominated by a single religious practice (Puritans, Separatists, or radical spiritualists) or whether there was active struggle for dominance among the religious practices. The results are striking. Where mainstream Puritanism monopolized the population, such as in Suffolk County, Massachusetts, or where there was little mainstream Puritan presence and Separatism or religious radicalism dominated, such as in Plymouth Colony, Rhode Island, and New London, Connecticut, charges of witchcraft and witchcraft trials rarely or never occurred. But in areas dominated by Puritans where there was also a strong presence of radical spiritualism, such as in New Hampshire, in Essex County, Massachusetts, and in most of the counties of Connecticut, witchcraft trials occurred more often. It should be no surprise that witchcraft trials took place only where tension between religious radicals and mainstream Puritans were part of everyday life.

A notable example of an episode that likely would have been recorded as witchcraft, had it taken place in an area of tension between Puritans and religious radicals, was the case of Elizabeth Knapp, born in 1655 in Watertown, Massachusetts, the daughter of James Knapp.[12] As a young girl, Elizabeth began working as a maidservant in the town of Lancaster, near Groton, and then she moved to Groton and began attending a school run by Samuel Willard, the local Puritan minister. In the summer of 1671 at the age of sixteen, she moved into the Willard family home as their maidservant.

Table 11. Indictments, Trials, and Convictions for Witchcraft in New England Counties between 1640 and 1690

County	Indictments	Trials	Convictions
Suffolk County, Mass.	0	0	0
Plymouth Colony Counties	1	1	0
Rhode Island Counties	0	0	0
New London County, Conn.	0	0	0
Rockingham County, N.H.	6	5	1
Essex County, Mass.	14	7	0
Middlesex County, Mass.	30	18	5
Hampden County, Mass.	3	3	1
Hartford County, Conn.	20	16	7
Fairfield County, Conn.	9	4	2
New Haven County, Conn.	6	5	0
Middlesex County, Conn.	3	2	0

Source: John Putnam Demos, *Entertaining Satan: Witchcraft and the Culture of Early New England* (Oxford: Oxford University Press, 1982), appendix.

Note: The figures in Demos's *Entertaining Satan* are not exhaustive. See, for example, Samuel G. Drake, *History of Boston* (Boston: Luther Stevens, 1856), 495–97, for a discussion of one witch executed in Boston.

On 15 October 1671, her affliction began. Minister Willard took care of her and made a daily record of her troubles. On 30 October, she suddenly cried out, "Oh, my legs!" "Oh, my breast!" and "Oh, I am strangled!" and engaged in fitful and frenzied movements of her body. At times it took six people to hold her down and to control her violent body movements. The nature of her fits shifted over time. Once, she began to bark like a dog and bleat like a calf. Her fits came and went, so that at times she was rather calm and could even discuss somewhat rationally what had happened to her during her periods of chaos and agitation. At these times she would describe the role the devil played in her condition and how he attempted to recruit her as a member of his corps of followers. The devil appeared as a "black rogue," she said, and she taunted him, telling him: "Thou art a liar and a deceiver, and God will vindicate His own truth one day."[13]

There were many witnesses to these episodes eager to jump into the fray. But Minister Willard assisted her and attempted to help her maintain control and to rely on the forces of God, rather than allow the devil to reign over her. Willard's diary ends suddenly on 15 January 1672, and it is not clear when and how the case was finally resolved. However, since Elizabeth eventually married and raised a family, her adult life was apparently both normal and conventional.

The Willard diary was sent to Increase Mather in Boston and may be found among his archived papers. Mather wrote a brief account of the case in his *Illustrious Providences.* Consequently, the case of Elizabeth Knapp has been widely cited in the historical literature on witchcraft, in spite of the fact that Minister Willard's treatment of Elizabeth was quite different than that of others who were thought to suffer from fits and mystical experiences. Because witchcraft was not a pressing social issue in Boston, it was treated as an illness rather than as a satanic episode.

A significant number of the ancestors of early LDS converts were accused of involvement with witchcraft even prior to the Salem delusion. The ancestors were not only among the accused but also among the accusers claiming to have witnessed witches exercising special satanic powers from the invisible world. In other words, some LDS ancestors were indicted and convicted of witchcraft while others were involved in charging or convicting. It is not clear whether the accused or the accusers in the witchcraft trials were more prone to radical and mystical beliefs, but the two sides of the controversy suggest there was widespread belief in the practice. Clearly, accusing someone of witchcraft implies the accuser believes in witches.

The most damaging evidence accusers presented was that the accused possessed one or more supernatural attributes. For example, six people testified that George Burroughs, of Wells, Maine, could perform the superhuman feat of lifting a heavy gun at arm's length with a single finger stuck into the end of the gun barrel. Such evidence was enough to convict and execute the man.[14]

Our discussion will concentrate on those witchcraft cases that were either related directly to ancestors of early LDS converts or to communities where large numbers of these ancestors were located. These cases are found mainly in New Hampshire, Connecticut, and Essex County, Massachusetts.

New Hampshire

New Hampshire was one of the places where radical spiritualists contended actively with Puritans. As early as 1656, two Portsmouth, New Hampshire, residents were accused of witchcraft,[15] but the most famous New Hampshire cases occurred in Hampton, where large numbers of ancestors of LDS converts were located. The first case involved Eunice Cole, a forebear of Aaron, Amasa F., Olive, and Selah Cheney. Eunice, an unfortunate widow living in a hut, had been accused of witchcraft in 1656 and again in 1673. Finally, in 1680, she was committed to prison "on suspicion of being a witch" and secured "with a lock to be kept on her legg." Witnesses claimed her charms were responsible for drowning Peter Johnson and James Philbrick, both ancestors of several LDS converts, though the testimonies against her were not sufficient to obtain a conviction.[16] When Cole died, people reportedly dragged her body to a hole, threw it in, covered it up with all speed, and then drove a stake into the grave. The stake had a horseshoe attached to it to prevent Cole from doing further harm.[17]

In 1680, again at Hampton, Isabel Towle, forebear of early LDS convert William Walker Rust, was accused of witchcraft.[18] She was implicated with Rachel Fuller, likely the sister of another LDS ancestor, Rebecca Brabrooke.[19] Unfortunately, the court records do not indicate the substantive charges. They simply state: "Rachel Fuller and Isabella Towle, being apprehended and committed upon suspicion of witchcraft . . . still continue in prison till bond be given for their good behavior of £100 apiece, during the Court's pleasure." Rachel, age twenty-five at the time, had the distinction of being one of the youngest women to be charged with witchcraft. Isabel and Rachel were both discharged the following year.[20]

Connecticut

Prior to the Salem delusion in 1692, at least thirty-eight formal indictments were made in Connecticut, twenty-seven of which led to trials and nine to convictions. Most of the towns of Connecticut were settled with the intention of establishing small spiritual utopias. In spite of attempts to suppress religious liberty, from the beginning the colony experienced crises between Puritans and radical spiritualists.[21] These crises were accompanied by accusations and convictions of witchcraft.

The first trial of witchcraft in Connecticut occurred in Windsor in 1647, when Alice Young was convicted. The Winsor congregation, home of many LDS ancestors, was especially subjected to admonitions from Minister John Warham that the devil was behind witchcraft, with the consequence that witches were thought to be everywhere. At least three witch trials took place in that town.[22] For example, in 1662 Elizabeth Seager, forebear of Maria Sagers, was charged with having "intimatt familliarity" with bad spirits but was acquitted.[23] One of Elizabeth Seager's accusers was Daniel Pratt, the son of John Pratt, William Pratt Jr.'s twin brother. William was the ancestor of the four LDS Pratt brothers. Four witnesses, including Daniel Pratt, testified that they had seen Seager in the woods with three other women, dancing around two black creatures who were standing near a kettle hung over a fire.

Early trials (1653 and 1655) also took place in New Haven, where many LDS progenitors resided, although the three accused were not convicted. Elizabeth Goodman, for example, was charged with engaging in "spiritual love" and other strange behaviors. When she was tried, witnesses claimed she was in possession of information that she could never have gained through natural channels.[24]

Most incidents of witchcraft occurred in the area of Hartford; in a single two-year period, 1662 to 1663, no less than eight people were accused, and three of these were ultimately executed.[25] At the time, magistrates in Hartford included Thomas Wells, an LDS ancestor, who ruled over the witchcraft trials.[26] The magistrates were aided by juries, and in a case involving one John Carrington and his wife, the jury consisted of Wells and other "foremost citizens" giving civic service, including John Pratt.[27]

In Wethersfield, just south of Hartford, where large numbers of LDS ancestors resided, one man claimed he saw Katherine Harrison as a red calf's head on top of a cart of hay, and a young girl said Harrison appeared at night as an ugly-shaped thing like a dog but with her own head.[28] The court referred her case to the general assembly, which dismissed Harrison from imprisonment after she paid all fees and agreed to leave Wethersfield. She resettled in New York that same year.[29]

In 1692, the same year as the Salem witchcraft trials, a number of people in Fairfield, Connecticut were convicted of witchcraft, a notable case being that of LDS ancestor Mercy Disborough, who apparently had bewitched not only people but a pig; she reportedly had cast mesmeric influences of light and darkness on people and had tormented others through divination.[30]

Massachusetts

While there were almost no episodes of witchcraft in and around Boston, where the core of mainstream Puritanism was found, in 1688 Goody Glover was executed for having bewitched the children of John Goodwin.[31] All other cases of witchcraft in Massachusetts took place outside of Suffolk County. In 1661 in Springfield, LDS ancestors Hugh Parsons and his wife were charged with a number of strange acts, including casting afflictions on their neighbor Mrs. Bedortha, setting off strange lights in meadows, casting fits on Martha Moxon and her sister, and causing the death of a neighbor's child and a cow; and Mrs. Parsons was charged with murdering her own child.[32] The Parsons were convicted of witchcraft a year later.[33]

And in Ipswich, Henry Bachiler's wife was accused of witchcraft because she had told Thomas Medcalfe and Francis Bates several times that their cattle would die. They believed she had bewitched the cattle.[34] Henry Bachiler was the son of Stephen Bachiler, settler of Hampton, New Hampshire, and forebear of many LDS converts. Henry settled across the border, south of New Hampshire, in Essex County, Massachusetts.

Salem, Essex County

Although the witchcraft trials of 1692 are identified with Salem, they involved at least twenty-three other villages in Massachusetts, New Hampshire, and Maine. These areas were formally Puritan but also contained strong elements of Separatism and radical spiritualism. Based on our analysis of witchcraft episodes prior to 1690, these were likely areas of New England where a witchcraft delusion might occur, where conflicts between religious radicals and mainstream Puritans were a part of everyday life. Of course, other factors played a role in Salem, including property interests, social-class conflicts, and political power struggles.

The 1692 Salem witchcraft delusion remains the most excessive episode of magic gone wrong in the American colonies; it involved 156 accusations, 44 confessions, 30 convictions, and 19 executions. In addition, 4 more people died while imprisoned, and a fifth, Giles Corey, was crushed by a heavy weight laid on him in an attempt to force a confession during interrogation.[35]

Even prior to 1692, witchcraft episodes had occurred in Salem. As early as 1650, the wife of Erasmus James had been accused of being a witch, and in 1680 Bridget Oliver was accused of the same crime.[36] But in early 1692, accounts of witchcraft were rampant after the children of Minister Samuel Paris accused their neighbors of bewitching them. Panic quickly spread through the town. A number of residents were either accusers or the accused; the jails of Salem were soon full, and the overflow was imprisoned as far away as Boston.

The first people accused were three women: Sarah Good, Sarah Osborne, and an Indian named Tituba. It is no coincidence that an Indian would be implicated. The Puritans believed that Satan dwelled in the souls of the Native American, and they equated Indian supernaturalism with witchcraft.[37] The first person to be executed was Bridget Bishop, who was hanged on 10 June 1692, but within a month five others were hanged, and in the following months the number of executions continued to grow. The episode ended in January of 1693, but it left a permanent mark on the history of Essex County.

LDS Ancestors' Involvement in Salem

Because so many people in the Salem area were involved in the witchcraft mania, it was inevitable that the many ancestors of LDS converts who lived in Essex County would also be implicated. Family relationships extended the network of witchcraft involvements. Seventeenth-century family ties reached far beyond nuclear families and included direct and indirect relationships with a multitude of relatives. At that time, obligations to remote family members were often as far-reaching as those to immediate ones, and these familial ties were important in defining the attitudes and beliefs of LDS ancestors.

Even though many LDS ancestors were accused of witchcraft, there were also many accusers among them. Jonathan Walcott and Nathaniel Ingersoll, ancestors of some LDS converts, were among the accusers, submitting a number of formal complaints.[38] Walcott was involved in at least nineteen accusations, and Ingersoll in at least thirteen.[39] Members of the Putnam family, also LDS ancestors, were also active in bringing formal complaints for witchcraft.[40] Thomas and Edward Putnam were responsible for no less than forty-eight complaints against their neighbors.[41] Clearly, they believed in the spirit world and in witches who had easy access to that world.

The fourth person accused in the Salem witchcraft delusion was Rebecca Nurse, a citizen of Essex County and a direct-line ancestor of several LDS converts.[42] Even though the formal complaint was signed by Thomas Putnam, Deacon Edward Putnam, Joseph Hutchinson, and Thomas Preston, there were others who also gave testimony. In the early stages of the examination, magistrates showed great sympathy for Rebecca Nurse, a respected elder citizen, but the young girls who had started the ordeal quickly brought about pandemonium in the hearing. One of the girls fell into convulsions, followed by the others, who screamed and shrieked until everyone within hearing fell back in fear. The children writhed in their fits in such a fearful display that Rebecca Nurse had no chance.[43] Her neighbors vainly signed a petition that she "had brought up a great family of children and educated them well, so that there is in some of them [the] apparent savor of godliness."[44] In spite of this effort, Rebecca Nurse was executed.

Another case involved John Proctor, his wife Elizabeth, and their young son William, all LDS forebears.[45] One witness against John Proctor was Joseph Bayley, the brother-in-law of Thomas and Edward Putnam. Bayley explained that he was riding on horseback with his wife in sight of the Proctor house near Ipswich when he felt two hard blows to the midsection of his body, "which caused great pain in my stomach and amazement in my head."[46] In spite of thirty-one neighbors' signing of a petition questioning the legitimacy of such evidence, the Proctors were held responsible for these blows.[47] This and similar evidence led to the execution of John Proctor and his wife. Their son William was never executed, although authorities attempted to extract a confession from him and two others by tying "Neck and Heals till the Blood was ready to come out of their Noses."[48]

Ancestors of William Walker Rust

While there are many examples of direct-line connections between LDS ancestors and the witchcraft delusion, the connections multiply on both sides of the issue—accusers and accused—when one weaves in the extended family. For illustrative purposes, I present the example of my own great-great-grandfather, William Walker Rust, through his direct-line ancestors and their extended families. William was a descendant of Henry Rust, who likely arrived in Boston in 1633.[49] Henry settled initially in Hingham but moved to Boston and then to Ipswich, just northwest of Salem, where he raised a family of three sons, Samuel, Nathaniel, and Israel. William Walker Rust's direct-line ancestry runs through Nathaniel and his wife, Mary Wardell.

The first known witchcraft episode concerning the Rust family occurred in Ipswich five years prior to the 1692 trials.[50] Mary Wardell Rust was among several people filing formal charges against one Rachel Haffield Clinton, who had been involved for over a decade in altercations with various neighbors. William Baker, an employee of Nathaniel Rust, submitted one of the depositions, recalling a time when some newly brewed beer mysteriously disappeared. At the time, Rachel Clinton was involved in an altercation with Nathaniel's wife, Mary, and Mary reported that "Rachel went backward and forward six or seven times up and down the lane that leads to our house." When Goodwife Rust went down to the basement to check on the beer, she found the barrel empty, "and neither was there any appearance of wet upon the floor." Subsequent testing showed the barrel to be leak-proof, and the obvious conclusion everyone drew was that Rachel Clinton had something to do with the beer's mysterious disappearance.[51] Other neighbors also gave depositions against Rachel, and she suffered arrest, trial, conviction, and imprisonment. She remained in prison for several months before she regained her freedom as part of the general reprieve of January 1693. In this case, Mary Rust was an accuser, but there were also many in the extended family who were accused.

Mary Wardell Rust was the daughter of William Wardell.[52] William and his brother Thomas had been involved in the Antinomian crisis and had been among those driven from Boston to Exeter, New Hampshire, with Minister John Wheelwright. In 1692, Samuel, the son of Thomas Wardell and cousin of Mary Rust, was convicted of witchcraft and hanged in Salem.

The case of Samuel lends a human face to the trials. He has been described as "an inoffensive man" of about fifty-five years of age at the time, who owned a farm in Andover, northwest of Salem. Even though the laws of England prescribed punishments for those able to read the future, for many years Samuel "had been a fortune teller, strolling about, reading palms and solving life's mysteries from the broken tea leaves in the bottom of the cup. . . . The chief complaint against Wardell was that his predictions too often came true. This proved he was a wizard."[53]

Samuel was "charged with bewitching Mary Sprague, a sixteen year old girl," and he was arrested and placed in the Salem jail. After a few days he confessed that he was, in fact, a wizard. The full confession has been preserved.[54]

Samuel explained in his confession that he had encountered a black man, the devil, who demanded that Wardell serve him. The man baptized Samuel in Shaws River, where he "was dypt all over."[55] At the hearing, when Samuel was asked what ought to be done to him, he replied, "I think I ought to dye for it." However, after a few days he denied his confession. The denial of his confession prompted an immediate trial. Testimony was given by several people: Mary Sprague said he "afflicted me many times by pinching and sticking me with pinns and striking me down"; Mary Warren and Mary Walcott,[56] LDS ancestors, believed Wardell had "afflicted" them; Ephraim Foster explained that Wardell had told the fortune of Dorothy Eames, Foster's sister-in-law;[57] Thomas Chandler claimed that from time to time he overheard Samuel telling young people their fortunes; and Abigail Martin said she had heard Samuel tell John Farnam and Jean L. Briggs their fortunes. In the Farnam and Briggs deposition, they explained that Wardell had told them of their love for teenage girls, and in both instances, it had proved to be true, though neither had spoken of it. Finally, the evidence included statements by Wardell's wife, Sarah, and daughter, Mercy, who testified that Samuel had engaged in "strange antics."[58]

On 22 September 1692, along with seven others, Wardell was hanged. As he was standing on the gallows, he again proclaimed his innocence, but while doing so, he began to choke on the smoke emanating from the pipe of his executioner. The young girls who had brought the original charges were sitting in the front row, and they began to chant: "The Devil hinders Wardwell with smoke! The Devil hinders Wardwell with smoke!"[59]

More stringent rules for conviction of witchcraft began to be applied toward the end of 1692, and of the last thirty accused, only three, all women, were found guilty. Significantly, among those three women was Sarah Wardell, the wife of Samuel. Sometime after he was executed, she also confessed to being a witch and was hanged. Mercy Wardell, their daughter, also confessed but was not convicted.[60]

My namesake, William Walker Rust, was also a direct-line descendant of William Beamsley, who arrived in Boston in 1632. William and his wife, Anne, had nine children, including three daughters: Mercy, Hannah, and Anne. Members of the extended families of all three of these daughters were accused of witchcraft. Mercy, through whom the William Walker Rust family line runs, was the grandmother of John Sadie Jr., who on 9 September 1692, at the age of thirteen, was imprisoned for witchcraft, though he was never convicted.[61] John was the son of Mercy's daughter, Elizabeth Peters Sadie, the sister of Andrew Peters Jr., through whom the Rust line runs.

Hannah, the second Beamsley daughter, married Abraham Perkins. The Perkins family had settled Hampton, New Hampshire, with Stephen Bachiler, where many LDS ancestors resided.[62] On 28 May 1692, Abraham's sister, Mary Perkins Bradbury, was imprisoned for witchcraft.[63] Mary was seventy-seven years old when she was convicted and sentenced to hang, but fortunately her family had enough money to smuggle her out of prison and hide her until the whole witchcraft episode had subsided.[64]

Hannah Beamsley and her husband, Abraham Perkins, had a daughter, also named Hannah, who married Daniel Ringe Jr. After Hannah Perkins Ringe died, her husband, Daniel, married Mary Rust, the daughter of Nathaniel and Mary Wardell Rust,[65] thus bringing the Rust family connection back full circle with the Beamsley family.[66]

The witchcraft connections with Hannah Beamsley continue. Hannah's husband, Abraham Perkins, had an uncle, Thomas, who along with his wife, Phoebe, as well as Phoebe's sister, Priscilla, and her husband, John Wildes, were all implicated in witchcraft. Their relationship with William Walker Rust is tenuous, but they were direct-line ancestors of his wife, Mary Thurston Rand, as well as a number of other early LDS converts.[67]

John and Priscilla Wildes had two daughters, Sarah and Phoebe. Sarah married Edward Bishop Jr.; both were convicted of witchcraft because they were thought to be able to read minds; however, they escaped from jail and were not executed.[68] The connections continue to multiply. When Priscilla died, her husband, John, married Sarah Averill, who, on 19 July 1692, was hanged for witchcraft in Salem for bewitching Goody Reddington and her two step-sons. These sons had died approximately sixteen years earlier, the one in 1676 and the other in 1677.[69] Depositions were given by John Gould, the brother-in-law of Priscilla through her first husband, and by many other people.[70]

Anne Beamsley Solart, the third Beamsley daughter, had a daughter, Sarah, who was one of the first three people accused of witchcraft in 1692. Sarah had first married a Mr. Poole, and after his death she then married William Good, a well-to-do innkeeper who owned a large estate. The second marriage did not work out, and the Good family fell into debt, which deepened after Mr. Good died.

Sarah Good was soon forced to beg, and her main offense was the way she begged. She did so in what was interpreted as an unpleasant manner, because she had once been among the wealthy herself and approached her neighbors with an air of equality. This gave offense to those whom she visited. When people refused to give an offering, Sarah reacted with hostility, and some neighbors thought she cast a spell on their household. For this crime, she was hanged on 19 July 1692.[71]

When Sarah Beamsley Good was committed to prison, she was the mother of two small children. The baby was less than a year old, and Sarah had no choice but to take Infant Good with her to prison, where it soon died. At the time, the older daughter, Dorcas, was approximately four years of age. The teenage girls who were making so many of the witchcraft complaints formally claimed Dorcas had tortured them and had asked them to write in the devil's book. Dorcas was imprisoned the next day, and the warden chained the little girl's hands and feet. Four months later Sarah Good was hanged, but Dorcas remained in prison for another six months. She was five when she was released. Her father wrote in 1710 that the girl had been so terrified by the ordeal that she was thereafter unable to "govern herself."[72]

Clearly, there was a whole web of relationships between the families of people indicted for witchcraft. The Wardells, the Rusts, the Perkins, and the Beamsleys were all actively involved both as accusers and accused. On the one hand, many LDS ancestors, including Mary Rust, the wife of Nathaniel Rust,

Mary's cousin's wife, and many others, provided evidence against those accused. On the other hand, at least eleven members of the extended Rust family were among those accused; eight were convicted, four hanged, and three were scheduled to hang but escaped from prison. Another victim was Infant Good, who died in prison where her mother had taken her.

It would take us far beyond the scope of this book to trace the web of relationships of all ancestors of LDS converts who trace their family lines back to the Salem area. Such complex and extensive networks are surely to be found among other ancestors who lived in areas rife with tensions among Puritans, Separatists, and radical spiritualists. The importance of familial connections in spiritual radicalism must always be kept in mind. We conclude that significant numbers of LDS convert ancestors defied the demands of Puritan leaders that they refrain from spiritualist activities; instead, they insisted that they and others had received special gifts or possessed special powers from the invisible world.

11. Generational Connections

There is ample evidence demonstrating a close affinity between early LDS converts and their fifth-generation ancestors. But what about the fourth, third, second, and first generations? Even though many of the fifth-generation ancestors may have had spiritual dispositions similar to the first Mormon converts, a number of changes in values and perspectives occurred through the middle generations, particularly among those coming from the South and slavery, as well as those participating in the First and Second Great Awakenings. Some of these changes in the culture of America were so significant that scholars such as Jon Butler feel the contribution of early colonial New England to the formation of American society was overshadowed by them.[1] We shall find, however, that these changes did not always represent a shift away from the fundamental spiritual dispositions of the original settlers of New England.

Clearly, many of the ancestors of early LDS converts were among the religious radicals of the early colonial period. And surely pockets of religious radicalism remained in New England even after Puritanism disappeared, because religious radicals were less inclined than mainstream Puritans to moderate their spiritual orientations in response to social and political pressures. One reason it was possible for them to retain their extreme attitudes over several generations was because they had strong community support. A limited number of small towns harbored the collective strength of early LDS convert ancestors. Far more than half of the 10,415 fifth-generation LDS ancestors so far identified were located in twenty-six of the approximately three hundred New England towns and hamlets listed as birthplaces of ancestors. They were clustered in a relatively small number of communities and were usually bound together in their neighborhoods and kinship groups.[2]

Location of LDS Ancestors across Generations

Families in New England expressing radical religious attitudes shared their lives with each other over a number of generations until many began to migrate west when the American frontier opened up in the early 1800s. For example, of the twenty-four known fifth-generation forebears of LDS convert Jonathan Harriman Hale, eighteen were born in Rowley, Essex County, Massachusetts, four others came from nearby Newbury, and one each from Boxford and Roxbury. Every one of his known fourth-, third-, second-, and first-generation ancestors were also born in Essex County, as was Jonathan himself.

Of the thirty-two fifth-generation ancestors of LDS convert Laura Clark, fourteen were born in the tiny town of Milford in New Haven Colony. And the majority of her ancestors in subsequent generations began their lives in what became New Haven County. She herself was born in nearby New Fairfield, Connecticut.

Of the twenty-three known fifth-generation ancestors of Lebbeus Thaddeus Coons Sr., six were born in Westerly and another six in Newport, Rhode Island. Another seven also came from nearby hamlets of Rhode Island. Almost without exception, Coons's ancestors in later generations were also born in Rhode Island, where he himself was born.

Of Mary Thurston Rand's twenty-seven known fifth-generation ancestors, eight were born in Hampton and five in nearby Exeter, New Hampshire, while another four came from Newbury, within walking distance just across the border in Essex County, Massachusetts. All the others except three lived within a ten-mile radius of Hampton. Mary's ancestors for the next two hundred years were born in Rockingham County, New Hampshire. Mary herself was born in Gilford, New Hampshire, less than fifty miles from Hampton, and she resided there almost to adulthood, when, in the early 1800s, she and her family finally left New Hampshire, migrated west, and settled in Vermont.[3]

In sum, these ancestors lived in a small cluster of communities for several generations. As they married and formed new families, they found spouses in the same town or in a neighboring community who usually shared a similar heritage, values, and habits, as well as the spiritual perspectives they had grown up with and had incorporated as their own. In contrast, large metropolitan areas such as Boston soon lost their religious direction through trade and expansion and became increasingly secular.

Many of the smaller towns failed to gain the notice of the larger world for their spiritual radicalism simply because they and their neighbors shared a common outlook. There was little tension or struggle among them. The town of Hampton, Rockingham County, New Hampshire, for example, where many ancestors of LDS converts lived, was begun as a congregation of disenfranchised Saints under the leadership of Stephen Bachiler. When he returned to England, the Hampton congregation invited John Wheelwright, who had been convicted of sedition and contempt, to become its spiritual leader. But once congregation members had firmly established themselves in Hampton, isolated from the broader world, they settled into a peaceful state, and their tranquil lives attracted no further attention.

Even when the values of a New England town did not uniformly reflect a radical spiritual perspective, there was usually within the town a cluster of neighbors who provided the kind of friendship and kinship network that supported and reinforced their sense of shared heritage. It is not only possible but probable that elements of radical spiritualism that had characterized early New England persisted in individual families and towns through successive generations.

Some migrants to the frontier discovered that they were, indeed, different from the rest of the world only after they had left their safe New England havens during the period of westward expansion in the nineteenth century. So they sought refuge by joining religious communities that were also charged with radical spiritualism. Other migrants chose to leave the New England towns where their families had lived for generations and journey into the frontier because their religious zeal had contributed to their being ostracized and marginalized. They also sought haven in new spiritual communities. In the nineteenth century, many of them began to see the Mormon Church as an ideal place of refuge. In addition, it offered a comforting and somehow familiar message, that the gospel of Jesus Christ had been restored through divine intervention, that everybody possessed a spark of the divine and was able to gain a personal knowledge of God, and that each individual might receive as well as exercise gifts of the Holy Spirit.

While the main focus of this study has been on the fifth- and sixth-generation ancestors of early Mormon converts, the question of continuity from the fifth-generation ancestors to the generation of converts is an apt one. In support of my argument, I will trace a small number of strands through the generations. An obvious starting point is the generational strands of the founder and first prophet of the LDS Church, Joseph Smith Jr.

Joseph Smith Jr.

Many of Joseph Smith's biographers have cast his ancestors in a negative light. His supporters want his family to be seen as simple, uneducated folk because such a background would make his contribution to humankind all the more remarkable. His detractors wish to cast his family as shiftless, no-account fortune seekers who sold the world a faulty bill of goods. In fact, Joseph Smith Jr. comes from a long tradition of notable ancestors, leaders in their local communities, who held the most radical of religious inclinations. Among his earliest American ancestors, through his mother, Lucy Mack, one finds seven passengers of the *Mayflower*, including the Fullers, the Tillies, and John Howland.[4] These *Mayflower* ancestors developed close ties to John Lathrop's Separatist congregation in Barnstable. For instance, Samuel Fuller, also of the *Mayflower*, married Jane, daughter of John Lathrop. John Howland's daughter, Hannah, married a member of Lathrop's Barnstable congregation, Jonathan Crocker.

The Mack family arrived in America somewhat later than most of the LDS ancestors. Whereas most fifth-generation ancestors of LDS converts were born in America, John Mack, Lucy's third-generation ancestor, was born in Scotland and did not arrive in America until 1669 as a sixteen-year-old teenager. John Mack came from a long line of Scottish clergymen. He settled in Lyme, New London, Connecticut, a town where, in the 1740s, at the time of the Great Awakening, the so-called New Lights of evangelism would become especially active. He and other members of his family married into families affiliated with the Rogerenes, and later generations of his family belonged to the Open-Communion Baptist Church in Lyme.[5]

Lyme was a center of both the First and Second Great Awakenings. Lyme's mainstream Congregational minister during the 1740s was Jonathan Parsons, one of the active initiators of revivals in the town and elsewhere. His revivals were so wrenching that there was said to be "plentiful Weeping, Sighs and Sobs."[6] The Macks, along with other Baptists, were undoubtedly involved.

On his father's side, Joseph Smith Jr. could claim descent from some of the earliest settlers of several towns in Essex County, Massachusetts.[7] His first American paternal ancestor, Robert Smith (fifth-generation ancestor), was an early resident of Topsfield, Essex County, Massachusetts. Robert was born in 1626, in Kirton, Lincolnshire, England, and came to Massachusetts with a brother in 1638 at the age of twelve. After working as a tailor in Boston for some time, he married the daughter of Thomas French, one of the early settlers, and first constable, of Ipswich.[8] The Smiths lived first in Boxford and then Topsfield, where Robert was active in civic and religious affairs. He chose not to join the Puritan Congregational Church in Topsfield, and some critical historians of religion in America see this as an act of what Hall refers to as a "horseshed Christian," someone who hangs back from a total commitment to religion.[9]

But this interpretation misrepresents many deeply committed individuals who differed with Calvinism and its brittle religious point of view. Robert Smith and his family may have remained separate from Congregational membership because of their commitment to radical religious ideas. While I do not have direct evidence for the beliefs of Robert and his wife, we shall see that later generations clearly chose not to join the Congregational church because they were decidedly more radical in their religious views. At his death, Robert Smith left an estate of three hundred acres valued at £189, which was about four times the average for an estate of that day.[10]

Robert's son Samuel (Joseph's fourth-generation ancestor) was born in 1666 in Boxford, Massachusetts, although he grew up in Topsfield. Like most children in Topsfield, Samuel was taught to read the Scriptures and to write.[11] Even though he, too, did not join the Congregational church, he held a number of public offices and was listed in town records as a "gentleman." It was inevitable that, because Topsfield was only about ten miles from Salem, Samuel would become entangled in many religious issues in the surrounding towns. For example, in the 1692 Salem witchcraft hysteria, he was a major witness in the trial of Mary Towne Easty, the sister of Rebecca Towne Nurse and Sarah Towne Cloyce. All three sisters were accused of witchcraft. Here is the testimony of Samuel Smith against Mary:

> The deposition of Samuell Smith of Boxford about 25 yers who testifieth and saith that about five years sence I was one night att the house of Isaac Estick sen'r. of Topsfeild and I was as farr as I know to Rude in discorse and the above said Esticks wife Mary Towne uld not have you be so rude in discorse for I might Rue it hereafter and as I was agoeing whom that night about a quarter of a mille from the said Esticks house by a stone wall I Received a little blow on my shoulder with I know not what and the stone wall rattleed very much which affrighted me my horse also was affrighted very much but I cannot give the reson of.[12]

Clearly, Samuel Smith did not say that Mary was a witch, but his explanation provided support for her conviction and ultimate hanging.

Zacheus Gould, the first settler in Topsfield, was another direct-line fifth-generation ancestor of Joseph Smith Jr. The Smith family line runs through Zacheus's son, John (Joseph's fourth-generation ancestor), whose sister Priscilla was connected, albeit obliquely, to witchcraft. Priscilla married John Wildes in 1663 in Topsfield, but she soon died; her widower husband then married Sarah Averill. Tension arose between the Gould, Wildes, and Smith families over the question of land ownership. In 1676, John Gould charged that Sarah Averill Wildes, his former brother-in-law's new wife, was a witch.[13] In 1692, when Sarah was charged a second time with witchcraft, John Gould gave testimony about mishaps occurring in 1674. He blamed Sarah for certain apparitions that he and his brother experienced while they were haying.[14] Sarah was imprisoned, and on the basis of their testimony, hanged for her "misdeeds." Although a dedicated civil servant, John Gould created a stir when he refused to attend the Lord's Table, in protest against the disregard of Sir Edmund Andros, the British governor in Boston, for civil rights in the colonies.[15]

The Gould family is most notable for its involvement in an ironworks project in Boxford. The ironworks was built on John Gould's property with the financial backing of Simon Bradstreet, husband of Anne Bradstreet, whose poetry contains many magical allusions. Subsequent Smiths were involved in the ironworks activities, and some commentators have speculated that this metallurgical tradition provided the alchemical, magical, and well-digging know-how employed by the Joseph Smith Sr. and his son at the time the LDS Church was being formed.

The Smith family was undoubtedly exposed to widespread occult activities taking place in Essex County, Massachusetts. The Reverend John Wise, of neighboring Ipswich, advocated the use of the philosopher's stone to bring about transformation through alchemical processes, leading, for instance, to economic development.[16] According to John Brooke, Salem had been a hermetic center; and not only was it the focal point of witchcraft activity but its residents had often been accused of dabbling in white magic and of harboring Quakers and Anabaptists.[17]

Samuel Smith Jr. (Joseph's third-generation ancestor), born in 1714, was a young man when the First Great Awakening took place. Inspired particularly by the Anglican itinerant George Whitefield, the movement attracted crowds of unprecedented size and enthusiasm, taking on a broad and stirring form as the "new birth" of the American religious community.[18] It began in New England, and the people responding to it lived where large numbers of fifth-generation ancestors of LDS converts had settled and where their descendants now lived. It was seen as a revival of the spiritual vitality found in the earliest days of the New England colonies. The new birth proclaimed by Whitefield, according to Stephen Marini, "was a self-validating sacred event in which the Holy Spirit implanted itself directly in the soul." Whitefield declared it a spiritual and physical transformation bestowed on the Saints by the Holy Spirit.[19]

When Whitefield traveled through New England, he began in Boston, going on to Roxbury, Marblehead, Ipswich, and Newbury, Massachusetts; Hampton and Portsmouth, New Hampshire; and York, Maine. Then he retraced his steps. He included Salem on his return route but failed to reach any inland towns, such as Topsfield. Other well-known evangelists, operating mainly in Connecticut, also never ventured as far north as Topsfield.[20] However, lesser known evangelists would have a direct impact on the town. David and Nathaniel Rogers of the Second Parish Church in Ipswich, only nine miles from Topsfield, were zealous and tactless advocates of revivalism.[21]

Without question, Samuel Smith Jr. and his wife were touched by the First Great Awakening. In 1734, Samuel had married Priscilla Gould, the granddaughter of John Gould. The Goulds were ardent New Lights of evangelism and opposed the Old Lights of those wishing to maintain the status quo.[22] Samuel and Priscilla had two sons and three daughters; after Priscilla died, he married her cousin, who also carried the name of Priscilla; it was she who raised the children to adulthood. Joseph Smith's line runs through the third child, Asael Smith. Samuel was an important figure in and beyond Topsfield; he served six terms in the state legislature and twelve terms as a selectman, and in 1774 he was a delegate to the First Provincial Congress in Massachusetts.[23] When he died, the *Salem Gazette* noted that he had been "a sincere friend of the liberties of his country and a strenuous advocate for the doctrines of Christianity."[24]

Asael (Joseph's second-generation ancestor) was born in 1744 in Topsfield; at the age of twenty-three he married Mary Duty. It is not known when her family first arrived in America, though in 1658 her great-grandfather was born in Rowley, and the family continued to live in Rowley for the next one hundred years. In 1772, Asael moved his family to Windham, Rockingham County, New Hampshire, and two years later to Dunbarton, New Hampshire. When the Revolutionary War began, Asael enlisted in Colonel Joshua Wingate's regiment. Three years later, he returned to become the town clerk at Derryfield, where he worked until 1786. His father, Samuel, had passed away in 1785, and Asael decided to move back to his father's home in Topsfield. By this time Asael's family numbered eleven children; Joseph, the father of the prophet, was the ninth child. Because his father had incurred a number of debts, Asael found it necessary to sell the Topsfield farm and for a brief time rented a dairy near Ipswich. But with eleven children, he recognized he was not going to make ends meet, so he and his son Joseph moved west and purchased a farm of eighty-three acres in the state of Vermont. Within a short time Asael had become active in civic affairs "serving as selectman, grand juror, surveyor of highways and over the years came to hold nearly every office in Tunbridge."[25]

During all this time, Asael had chosen not to be a member of the local Puritan congregations where he lived. Rather, true to the tradition of his fathers, he chose a more radical course of action. During the Second Great Awakening, radical evangelism "blossomed into the first indigenous religious sects of independent America: Shakers, Freewill Baptists, and Universalists."[26] Asael chose to be a Universalist, someone who believed that God determined all individuals would be saved and who challenged the Calvinist notion of an elect.

Essex County, Massachusetts, where Asael was born, was a center of Universalist activity. John Murray, who was particularly responsible for initiating Universalism in the region,[27] had settled in Gloucester, a small fishing village about fifteen miles from Topsfield. As a result of his influence, a number of residents whose families had been in Gloucester for several generations were suspended from the traditional First Parish Church; they then declared themselves Universalists.[28] John Murray's influence spread far beyond Gloucester, affecting the thinking of many ancestors of early LDS converts. Asael Smith readily accepted Murray's claim that Christ took on the sins of everyone, thereby redeeming them from eternal damnation,[29] a doctrine comfortable to Mormons, for whom there is no such thing, except in rare cases, as eternal damnation.

In 1797, Asael chaired a meeting to organize one of the first Universalist societies in Vermont. He and sixteen others, including his sons Jesse and Joseph (the prophet's father), joined together to formally declare that they did not wish to be taxed under state law for the Congregational church.[30] Thus, it is clear that Asael had passed on to the prophet's father his own religious values. These values included the notion that the "perfect kingdom" of God would soon be restored, fulfilling Daniel's prophecy. In fact, Asael believed the American Revolution was the beginning of the new millennium under the rule of God.[31]

In 1796, Joseph Smith Sr. and his wife, Lucy Mack, parents of the prophet, were married in Tunbridge, Massachusetts, under relatively favorable circumstances. Joseph's father gave him a share of the ownership of a good farm. And Lucy received one thousand dollars as a wedding gift from her brother. Until 1802, life appears to have moved relatively smoothly for the young couple. Then they chose to move to Randolph, seven miles west of Tunbridge, where they opened a store.

Joseph decided to buy ginseng, which grew wild where he lived, and to ship it to China, where ginseng was highly prized because it was thought to increase vitality and extend life. The venture failed because of a dishonest partner, and Joseph lost everything, including his store and farm. For the next thirty years the Smith family lived in abject poverty. Moving from town to town, trying to make a new start, they finally made the decision to migrate west to New York in 1816.[32] In spite of his economic problems, Joseph Sr. was actively engaged in the spiritual life. According to family tradition, he had refused to join the local Congregational church. He was, however, deeply religious. At the time of a religious revival in 1811, he had important dreams and visions. His wife Lucy recorded verbatim the first of these dreams.

> I seemed to be traveling in an open, barren field, and as I was traveling, I turned my eyes towards the east, the west, the north, and the south, but could see nothing save dead, fallen timber. Not a vestige of life, either animal or vegetable, could be seen; besides, to render the scene still more dreary, the most deathlike silence prevailed; no sound of anything animate could be heard in all the field. I was alone in this gloomy desert, with the exception of an attendant spirit, who kept constantly by my side. Of him I inquired the meaning of what I saw, and why I was thus traveling in such a dismal place. He answered thus: This field is the world, which now lieth inanimate and dumb, in regard to the true religion, or plan of salvation; but travel on, and by the wayside you will find on a certain log a box, the contents of which, if you eat thereof, will make you wise, and give unto you wisdom and understanding.[33]

Joseph Smith Sr. surely was made of the same fiber as his ancestors and his prophet son.

Catharine Slauson

Whereas Joseph Smith's family came from the northern part of New England, mainly in Essex County, Massachusetts, Catharine Slauson's ancestors lived in the southern New England colonies, mainly in the radical areas of Rhode Island and New London County, Connecticut. Catharine was born on 28 May 1806 in Remsen, Oneida County, New York. The Slauson family members were devout Methodists, and they came from distinguished lines of religious radicals of early colonial New England, including such fifth- and sixth-generation direct-line ancestors as Roger Williams, Obadiah Holmes, John Lathrop, George Denison, and his well-known wife, Ann Borodell, as well as many others.[34]

Some descendants of these early ancestors eventually moved from Connecticut, Rhode Island, and Long Island up the Hudson River Valley and westward into what is now upper New York State. Catharine's grandfather, who had been born in Fairfield County, Connecticut, died in Pittstown, Rensselaer County, New York. Her father was born in 1773 in Salem, Westchester County, New York. During the Revolutionary War, the Slausons were living in Oneida County, New York, and were among the earliest settlers in Remsen, where Catharine was born. Following her birth, the family moved to Waterford, Erie County, Pennsylvania, where she met her husband, Ezekiel Brown.[35] Together, Ezekiel and Catharine began their family of five girls and two boys. As was typical of the times, Ezekiel was multifaceted; he was a carpenter, farmer, and livestock man, and he built a textile mill on the banks of the local creek that ran through Beaver Dam Township.[36]

In examining Catharine's Wightman ancestors, it is instructive to begin with Edward Wightman (1566–1612), her seventh-generation ancestor, who died in England during the reign of King James I. Edward had been known as a Montanist and an Anabaptist, and he had the distinction of being the last man burned at the stake in England.[37] He was apprehended in his hometown of Litchfield, England. According to the written order issued by the king, he was to be executed because he had "stubbornly and perniciously, knowingly and maliciously" engaged in behavior that was "blasphemous," and so he was eventually charged with eleven heresies, including the "abominable" belief that infants should not be baptized.[38] The king ordered Edward to be plucked as a "diseased sheep out of the flock of the Lord, lest our subjects he do infect by his contagion."[39]

Edward's son John (Catharine's sixth-generation ancestor) left England with four of his five sons and fled to America. John was the direct-line ancestor of three early Mormon converts found in this study and the namesake ancestor of Joseph and Erastus B. Wightman, who were baptized after 1835.[40] The date of the first record of John in Rhode Island is 1654, though by that time Valentine, John's eldest son, had been employed for six years as an interpreter to the Indians at a trading post at Wickford in the Narragansett country owned by Richard Smith.

The Wightman brothers were deeply religious. Two were preachers, two were deacons, and one was a professor of religion, all in the Anabaptist faith.[41] The brothers settled in Rhode Island, where Anabaptism was a dominant religious creed, and they became leading forces in the movement.

John Wightman's son George (1632–1722), Catharine's fifth-generation ancestor through whom her family line runs, settled on a farm in North Kingstown, where he and his wife Elizabeth Updyke reared five sons and three daughters. He owned more than one thousand acres of land, and though it was divided among family members it was held in the family for more than six generations. George's son Daniel, became a Baptist minister in Newport, Rhode Island, and is known to have been one of twenty-one members of the First Baptist Church who broke away from the group to form a Second Baptist Church, known thereafter for its General Baptist beliefs.

Another of George Wightman's sons, the youngest, named Valentine, was

Catharine's fourth-generation ancestor. He distinguished himself by extending Anabaptist influence to Connecticut. At the turn of the eighteenth century, Valentine was still a young man of twenty-four, but he traveled to Connecticut as a missionary for the General or Six Principle Baptists. Settling in Groton, seven miles north of New London, he declared himself pastor of the First Baptist Church of Connecticut. He held Anabaptist meetings in various homes until, a decade after his arrival, a chapel was built. Valentine's efforts initially drew much opposition, but Connecticut had already developed a tradition of free expression of conscience, and while serving as pastor for forty years, he eventually enjoyed the liberty to conduct his religious affairs as he saw fit.

Valentine maintained close contact with the mother General Anabaptist Church in Rhode Island. His son Daniel (Catharine's third-generation ancestor) would return to that colony to find a wife, Catherine Westcott, granddaughter of Stukely Westcott, a close companion of Roger Williams. The family of Valentine Wightman illustrates well the fact that many radical families would remain bound together for many generations. Valentine's wife was Susannah Holmes, the granddaughter of Obadiah Holmes, the second pastor of the First Baptist Church of Newport, and the great-granddaughter of John Sayles and Roger Williams, all prominent early Anabaptists, all of whom were ancestors of several early LDS converts.[42]

Valentine Wightman was still the pastor in Groton when the First Great Awakening took place. Evangelists in Connecticut, such as George Whitefield, James Davenport, and Benjamin Pomeroy canvassed Connecticut, calling on the people to restore their resolve to live the pure Christian life. Their revivals converted large numbers to the cause. Although the movement took place mainly within the ranks of the mainstream Congregationalist churches, it also had a profound effect on other denominations. In Groton, where Valentine resided, the pastor of the local Congregational church, John Owen, actively agitated for revival and reform. In 1741, Owen became a partner with Valentine Wightman, and they afterward celebrated a "glorious year" of revival;[43] they continued working together until Valentine's death in 1747.

The First Great Awakening also inspired a rash of occult and mystical activities, many of which occurred in and around Groton.[44] In New London, for example, witches' pulpits were a part of the meetinghouse ensemble of the Rogerenes. In 1743, the itinerant James Davenport repeated the actions that might have been expected of the earlier Rogerenes. He led a group of New London men and women out of the local church house onto the town wharf, where they built a huge bonfire and burned not only the symbols of worldliness but the great works of Puritan authors.[45] It was surely no accident that his great-grandfather was John Davenport, one of the founders of New Haven Colony, where so many LDS ancestors lived.

Except for the brief pastorate of Daniel Fisk, the Wightmans served as pastors to the Groton Baptist Church until 1841. Valentine's son Timothy served for decades and was replaced by his son, John Gano Wightman. Timothy would serve as pastor during the remainder of the First Great Awakening, and he sponsored at least four different "awakenings" in an attempt to reintroduce the people to the religious zeal of the previous century.[46] John Wightman served during the Second Great Awakening and organized at least ten awakenings before his death in 1841.[47]

Catharine Slauson's direct line runs through Daniel Wightman, Timothy's brother. Daniel lived for most of his adult life in Norwich, Connecticut, north of New London along the Thames River, where he was a prosperous farmer and served as a deacon in one of the local Baptist churches. In 1752, prior to his death, Daniel was still in Norwich. At about the same time, Elizabeth Backus, who had been attending a Baptist church for seven years, refused to pay taxes to the Congregational church. In the aftermath, her son Isaac chose to break away from the Congregationalists and became what many call the "father of American Baptists." In so doing, he placed what had previously been, in Stanley Grenz's words, an "outcast group within the Protestant myth of reformation theoretically and then helped to win for them a place of equality among the leading denominations of America." Isaac drew many Congregational churches into the ranks of Baptist congregations. These churches initially transformed independently, but they quickly discovered each other and united to form a spiritual and institutional bond.[48]

During the Second Great Awakening, four congregational separations took place in Norwich, all the congregations having been touched by the New Light and their members having become dissidents. Most of these "separates" finally went over to the Baptists. Daniel, Catharine Slauson's great-great-grandfather, and Valentine Dea Wightman, her great-grandfather, had been lifelong Baptist members even before the transformation took place.[49]

Many of the Wightmans, including Valentine Dea Wightman's youngest son Joseph, began moving to New York State before the Revolutionary War. It was in New York that Joseph Wightman and his son, Erastus B. Wightman, became acquainted with the Mormon Church. Even though Joseph himself never joined, he spent his last years in Kirtland, where the LDS Church was located. Three of his children, Erastus, Jane Elizabeth, and Charles Billings did join.[50] Jane Elizabeth and Charles Billings made the long and difficult trek cross the plains with other Mormon pioneers and devoted many years of their lives to the LDS Church before they died in Payson, Utah.

Conclusion

Many examples may be found of family lines remaining consistently radical across many generations. The original ancestors of many LDS converts engaged in radical religious activities from the earliest days of colonial New England. Some of their descendants were active participants in what is today identified as white and black spiritualist activities, including witchcraft. Others were engaged in the establishment of radical churches such as the Rogerenes and the Seventh-day Baptists. Many were active in the First and Second Great Awakenings, and they participated in the establishment of what are generally considered to be the first indigenous religions of America, including Shakers, Freewill Baptists, and Universalists.

In spite of variations of religious expression through the periods under question, there were clear commonalities. Those people we have identified with early religious radicalism lived clustered in a small number of villages and towns of New England. Their families tended to remain in these communities for many generations. They lived in areas where the First and Second Great Awakenings had significant impact. In the early 1800s, the population of the New England colonies began to flow westward. But many individuals migrating out of New England belonged to families that had proclaimed spiritual powers and gifts for many generations.[51] Many of the New England migrants joined the Mormon Church after they had moved west, or they moved west soon after they had joined the church. The newly formed LDS Church encouraged them to continue to express, practice, and incorporate the shared radical spiritual attitudes and traditions that had been so much a part of their New England family heritage.

12. Ancestors of the American Religions

Roots of America's Religions

Mormons believe the gospel of Jesus Christ has been restored to the world by divine intervention in these, the latter days. They also believe forerunners played a crucial role in preparing the way for this divinely inspired restoration. This book has been about special forerunners, the ancestors of the earliest converts to the Mormon church, who were among the earliest settlers of the New England colonies. Seventeenth-century settlers included a polyglot of Europeans: Scots, Germans, Dutch, Swiss, and French. But most were English, and they participated in the creation of the first elements of what would become "American" society, a society that would be distinctive in terms of its economic, political, and social orientation, as well as it secular and religious life.

These earliest settlers, Jon Butler has pointed out, probably would not have recognized America of the nineteenth century; especially they would not have recognized the major indigenous expressions of religious faith that took root and flourished in the young, nineteenth-century republic.[1] New churches included not only the Mormons but Christian Scientists, Seventh-day Adventists, and the Jehovah's Witnesses, as well. Scholars sometimes add Pentecostals and the breakaway Southern Baptists to this list. But, I would argue, although the early settlers might not have recognized the forms these indigenous churches took, they might well have been comfortable with many of the beliefs and impulses the new religions expressed.

Historians John Brooke and Jon Butler discount the importance of early New England contributions not only to the foundations of American society as a whole but especially to its indigenous religions. Brooke argues, instead, that the Middle Atlantic and southern regions of the United States were critically influential in forming new religious expression in America.[2] And, clearly, radical impulses coming into these regions did help shape America's religious traditions.

As early as the seventeenth century, but especially in the eighteenth, religionists from across the Atlantic brought radical traditions of individual conscience and separatism into the Middle Atlantic region of this country. Reacting against cultural accommodation and moral laxity in mainstream and secular thought, Quakers, Mennonites, Pietists, Anabaptists, and Moravians, living lives of intense religious fervor, stressed spiritual renewal; they believed each person to be, literally, a child of God, able to communicate directly with God and the spiritual world. These so-called perfectionists moved to the hospitable lands south of New England, particularly into Pennsylvania and New Jersey.

Many perfectionists came from Britain, but substantial numbers came from the Continent. As early as 1663, Dutch Mennonites established a communal colony along the Delaware River separating Pennsylvania from New Jersey. A few years later, German and Swiss Mennonites immigrated to Pennsylvania. Over time, Dutch and German Pietists swelled the ranks of radical reformers in New Jersey. By 1681, William Penn, the most prominent Quaker in American history, received a charter for his colony of Pennsylvania, which became a refuge for Quakers from both the Old and New World. And in 1710, the first Amish migrated from Germany and Switzerland to America, settling particularly in Pennsylvania. There were Baptists residing in New England since 1639, but the following century, they, as well, began to settle the Middle Atlantic region. In Philadelphia in 1705, five Baptist churches united to form the Philadelphia Baptist Association, the first Baptist association in America.

Although the South was never as attractive as the Middle Atlantic region to religious migrations, the first group of Moravians to settle in North America arrived in 1735, in Savannah, Georgia; but six years later, they resettled at Bethlehem, Pennsylvania. Early in the eighteenth century, Baptist missionaries were at work in the South, where congregations were to be found in Virginia and North Carolina; in 1751, the Charleston Baptists Association was formed.

Scholars focus their historical interpretations not only on geography but on time. Butler suggests that "the eighteenth century may have left a far more indelible impression on the American religious tradition than did the seventeenth century." He urges us to abandon the notion that Puritanism was the crucial force in the formation of America's religious tradition.[3] Butler argues that the evangelical revivals of the eighteenth century were so compelling that they, rather than Puritanism, shaped America's most distinctive religious patterns. He finds, for example, that African spiritual life contributed greatly to America's relationship to religion. He feels belief in the occult and magic world of the early colonial period, which had declined precipitously toward the end of the seventeenth century, was revived in novel and radical ways during the eighteenth. He suggests movements such as Freemasonry and Rosicrucianism gained increasing prominence in America in that century. In this interpretation, the early period of American religious life would have contributed little to the forces moving converts to join the LDS Church.

Certainly, Puritanism stopped being a social force by the second half of the colonial period.[4] By the eighteenth century, Puritan New England had become Yankee New England, having discarded many of the old values imported from abroad.[5] But there were religious forces in the early New England colonies far more radical than Puritanism. Whereas Puritans generally did not believe, for example, that God did business with them directly, they believed that he certainly had the power to intervene through visions, revelations, miracles, and such but chose to restrict himself to his record of interaction with the Saints to the Bible. But, contrary to mainline Puritanism, numbers of the early New England faithful believed God spoke to them in a personal and direct way and bestowed on them gifts of the Holy Spirit.

Colonial New England was characterized by a wide diversity of religious expression. It was racked with dissent and challenges against the norms of the dominant Puritan fathers. I have argued that these pockets of dissent and radical expression persisted into the First Great Awakening and beyond. Seen from this point of view, the religious revivals of the eighteenth century take on a somewhat different meaning. The First Great Awakening, inspired particularly by the Anglican itinerant George Whitefield, attracted crowds of unprecedented size and enthusiasm.[6] The movement took on a broad and stirring form in terms of a "new birth" of the American religious community. But notably, the First Great Awakening began in New England, and the people responding to it lived where large numbers of fifth-generation LDS progenitors and their descendants continued to live. The awakening was a revival of the kind of spiritual vitality that had existed previously. Of course, Jon Butler is correct in emphasizing new and vital forces taking place in eighteenth-century America, but the importance of radical religious elements coming out of early New England should not be discounted. Early Mormons could trace the forerunners of their religious convictions back to virtually all the radical religious forms of early America, including Anabaptists, Quakers, Familists, Montanists, Ranters, Gortonists, Seekers, and so on.

Indigenous American Religions

I have argued for recognition of the importance of forerunners in early colonial New England who prepared the way for the formation of the LDS Church. But in order to establish the possible links of radical colonial New England more fully with the American religious tradition, the genealogical roots of other groups such as Christian Science, Seventh-day Adventists, and Jehovah's Witnesses should be considered. Even though it is clear that the genealogical roots of the founding Mormons and their converts can be traced to early colonial New England, the question arises whether other indigenous religions have a different religious heritage. Mormon genealogy might be an anomaly in the religious landscape of America, a fluke of American religious history. The organizers and developers of other indigenous churches in this country might have had quite different backgrounds and origins.

It is not possible to engage here in a full genealogical study of the founders and early converts to other indigenous religions, but it might be instructive to provide some sense of the connections these founders had with early colonial America. I do not intend to go into the theological beliefs of these religions but to identify significant individuals who have genealogical records. There is some evidence that all of these religions, at least with regard to their founders, reflect a background similar to that of Mormons, although at this point the evidence is suggestive rather than conclusive. However, to the extent that it does suggest the importance of early colonial New England in their religious foundations, it also suggests the general notion that radical spiritual values are transmitted across several generations.

Christian Science

Christian Science, formally founded in 1879 by Mary Baker Eddy, can be placed in a broader context known generally as New Thought, of which Mary Baker Eddy's work was one strand. Eddy, born in 1821 in Bow, New Hampshire, was reared in a strict Congregationalist home. Though she rejected the Calvinist determinism of her parents, she continued to be Bible-centered. Her early life was filled with personal illness, and her search for ways to overcome these misfortunes eventually led her to experiment with various alternative therapies, including homeopathy. In 1862, she was apparently cured by Phineas Parkhurst Quimby, a charismatic healer living in Maine. Quimby would sit opposite his subject, holding both hands in his, and look the subject "intently in the eye for a short time, when the subject would go into that state known as the mesmeric sleep." Quimby felt that he was then able to look into the patient, read the "opinion of the mind," and prescribe remedies.[7] Quimby's cure spurred Eddy to study the possibilities of New Thought therapy, based on the notion that illness is largely mental in nature.

Quimby, born in 1802 in Lebanon, was also from New Hampshire. He came from a family that had lived many generations in that state. He died in 1866, but his disciples, the most prominent being Annetta and Julius Dresser, carried on his work. The Dresser family had lived for many generations in Maine. Annetta and Julius first met in Quimby's office; they married in 1863. For the rest of their lives, they remained disciples of Quimby's therapy, and they claimed his approach was far superior to Mary Baker Eddy's subsequently developed "mind cures."

In 1866, some weeks after Quimby died, Eddy was living in Lynn, Massachusetts, studying the healings of Jesus, when she suffered a mysterious, severe accident. Subsequently, on her own, she experienced a sudden healing; this led her to even more intense study and the eventual development of Christian Science doctrine. In 1870, she began teaching others her art and eventually organized a formal church.[8]

In 1875, Eddy authored *Science and Health,* in which she claimed that Christianity as taught by Jesus "was not a creed, nor a system of ceremonies, nor a special gift from a ritualistic Jehovah; it was the demonstration of divine love that cast out error and healed the sick, not merely in the *name* of Christ, or Truth, but in demonstration of Truth, as must be the case in cycles of divine light."[9] For Eddy, there was no objective material world, rather reality was thought to be completely spiritual, either for good or evil. Thus, physical health was a matter of spiritual enlightenment and divine understanding, while illness was little more than falling prey to evil influences. Each person, she maintained, was a child of God; the spiritually enlightened can draw directly from God's spiritual forces.

In 1892, Eddy formalized the largest and most important congregation in her ministry, the mother Christian Science Church in Boston, and she appointed a board of directors to oversee the church. Key persons on this board included Augusta Emma Simmons Stetson, Ira O. Knapp, Edward A. Kimball, and Brigham Bicknell Young, all of whom exerted a lasting influence on Christian Science theology and practice.

Through Brigham Bicknell Young, a nephew of the second Mormon prophet, Brigham Young, some founders of early Mormonism have close family ties to early Christian Scientists. Bicknell was a gifted musician and had been sent to study music in London. After returning to America, and while in Chicago, he became gravely ill. He was referred to a Christian Science practitioner, who healed him; thereafter, he devoted himself to Christian Science.[10]

Eddy, the Dressers, Stetson, Knapp, and Young all have available pedigrees sufficient to trace some lines of their ancestry back at least six generations.[11] These pedigrees indicate that the ancestors of the first Christian Scientists would fit comfortably within the profiles of the ancestors of early Mormon converts.[12] Almost all the known ancestors of these Christian Science founders originated in Britain, and the sixth-generation ancestors began to migrate to America, all of them to New England. Nearly all of the known fifth-generation ancestors were born in New England. Young's ancestors came from Connecticut and Massachusetts. Eddy's ancestors had settled mainly in Essex County, Massachusetts, where many Mormon ancestors were located. Julius Dresser's ancestors settled in Maine, New Hampshire, and Massachusetts, while Annetta Seabury Dresser's known ancestors were from Duxbury, Massachusetts. Augusta Emma Simmons Stetson's forebears were mainly from Plymouth and Rhode Island, while the few Knapp ancestors so far identified settled in Connecticut. *Mayflower* Pilgrim John Alden, an ancestor of several early Mormons, was also ancestor to Augusta Emma Simmons Stetson. Moses William Simmons, born in Leyden, the Netherlands, where the Pilgrims had resided while in exile, was ancestor to early Mormons Noah Packard and Lucy Simmons, and he was also namesake to Augusta. A simple count shows that of the seventy-nine sixth-generation Christian Science founders' ancestors I have so far identified, no less than thirty-nine (49 percent) are identical with one or more fifth-generation Mormon ancestors.[13]

Seventh-day Adventists

The Seventh-day Adventists derived from the so-called Millerite movement in nineteenth-century America. The Adventists formally organized as a church in 1860, but the characteristic aspects of the religion had already been expressed in the activities of William Miller (1782–1849), who led a movement predicated on the belief that the second coming of Christ would occur in 1843 or 1844. Miller, a self-educated man, was born in Pittsfield, Massachusetts. Although in his early life he was a Deist, he eventually came to believe that the Lord is involved in the everyday life of humankind and that the Bible is the literal word of God.[14]

Miller was assisted in the organization of conferences by ministers such as Charles Fitch and Henry Dana Ward, as well as a former sea captain, Joseph Bates. In these conferences, Miller proclaimed that he had calculated from the Scriptures the imminent return of Christ. He argued that any formal organization of the faithful would "automatically transform the body into a—'Babylon'—a world conforming apostate body."[15] Even though the second coming did not occur at the appointed time, the Millerite movement "bequeathed a system of prophetic interpretation and biblical literalism that helped shape the character of Adventism that arose from its ruins."[16]

Among those disciples who remained committed to Adventism after 1844 were Joseph Bates, James White, and his wife, Ellen Harmon White, a woman given to visions, dreams, and "charismatic experiences."[17] In 1850, the Whites and the Bates founded an Adventist magazine, and at an 1855 conference of the faithful in Battle Creek, Michigan, Ellen White had a prophetic vision that told her it was necessary to organize.[18] This significant vision marked the beginning of the church, which was later formally constituted. Among those initially associated with the newly organized church was Dr. John Harvey Kellogg, a physician, the inventor of corn flakes, and a strong advocate of hygiene. Even though a number of other Adventist bodies have emerged from the Millerite movement, the Seventh-day Adventists remain the most prominent.

I have been able to locate some genealogical records of individuals noted above who were associated with the Millerite movement and early Seventh-day Adventism: William Miller, Joseph Bates, Henry Dana Ward, Ellen Gould Harmon White, and John Harvey Kellogg. All their genealogies would fit comfortably within the profiles of ancestors of early Mormons. The known birthplaces of the sixth-generation ancestors were by and large Britain or New England, and all of the birth and death places of the fifth generation that have been identified were in New England. Miller's ancestors settled almost exclusively in the Springfield area, where the condemned spiritualist, William Pynchon, had led many early settlers. The few known ancestors of Henry Dana Ward and John Harvey Kellogg settled in Massachusetts. Ellen White's ancestors settled in Essex County, Massachusetts, and New Hampshire.[19] A number of fifth- and sixth-generation ancestors in common were found for Seventh-day Adventists and Mormons, particularly those of William Miller, Joseph Bates, Ellen Gould Harmon, and John Harvey Kellogg.[20]

In his book *The English Connection,* B. W. Ball draws parallels between New England Puritan thought and the true Christian life represented by Adventism.[21] Ball makes no distinction between mainstream Puritans, Separatists, and radical spiritualists, but he attempts to find a thread of Adventism in the debates of the times. He notes that some doctrines of the early radicals, such as the authenticity of Scripture, the witness of Christ, the justification and sanctification of the sinner, and the regeneration of humankind, were broadly accepted, while other doctrines, such as baptism, the Sabbath day, the imminent second advent of Christ, and the millennium, were broadly discussed and disputed.

Jehovah's Witnesses

The Jehovah's Witnesses were a direct outgrowth of the nineteenth-century American Adventist movement. When William Miller's movement fell apart after his prediction of the second coming of Christ failed to materialize in 1844, a number of Adventist sects came into being, including the Advent Christian Church, the Life and Advent Union, and the Seventh-day Adventists. Those people instrumental in organizing the Jehovah's Witnesses, such as Charles Taze Russell, were all connected in some way with one or another of the Adventist groups. In 1870, Russell heard a sermon by an Adventist preacher, Jonas Wendall, explaining the second coming of Christ. This introduction to Adventism moved Russell to study the Bible, and he soon gathered a small band of students together. He did not want to be called anything but a Christian, and so the church had a number of informal labels, including Bible Students and Watch Tower, before it took on its permanent name.

Russell was born in 1852 in Pittsburgh, Pennsylvania, into a devout Presbyterian family. While in his early life he appears to have been a practicing member of his family faith, he lost that faith when he was a young man and then moved from religion to religion, including the Adventists, before he finally began organizing his own Bible study groups.

Russell indicated that George Washington Stetson and George Storrs were particularly important in helping him in his spiritual formation.[22] Storrs was the more important of the two. A disciple of William Miller, Storrs had proclaimed far and wide that Christ would return in the early 1840s, but when Christ did not return, Storrs left the movement. By 1863 he had helped establish an Adventist branch known as the Life and Advent Union. However, in 1871, Storrs broke with that group and began publishing a newspaper known as the *Bible Examiner,* which came to influence Russell's doctrines.

In 1876, Russell came in contact with Nelson H. Barbour, a magazine editor in Philadelphia, who had proclaimed that Christ had returned to earth two years earlier, in 1874. Russell made his own study of history and was responsible for the publication of *The Divine Plan of the Ages,* which outlined the history of the world, culminating in the spiritual return of Christ, although, Russell argued, he would not begin his visible reign until 1914. Russell maintained that he was Christ's voice on earth and was given a prophetic office to communicate the word of the Lord both directly and through scriptural interpretation. In 1884, he organized the Watch Tower Bible and Tract Society, a loosely knit association of groups devoted to the study of the Scriptures.

Russell died in 1916 and was succeeded by Joseph Franklin Rutherford, considered to be the organizer of Jehovah's Witnesses as a formal institution.[23] Rutherford was born in 1869 in Morgan County, Missouri, to a devout Baptist family, but he associated himself with Russell's Bible Students in 1894 and was instrumental in bringing about a more formal organizational structure of the faithful.

Genealogical records on Russell and Rutherford are scanty. The birthplaces of Russell's parents are not even known, though they were of Scotch-Irish descent, which suggests that they likely arrived in America in the eighteenth century and could easily have come directly to the Middle Atlantic colonies or the South.[24] Rutherford's father was born in 1825 and his mother in 1827, both in Ireland. This means that the two main figures in the early life of the Jehovah's Witnesses probably had little connection with early colonial New England, although the two people most influential in Russell's spiritual life, George Washington Stetson and George Storrs, do have strong New England roots. Nine of Stetson's fifth-generation ancestors came from Plymouth Colony, including a daughter of John Lathrop, founder of Barnstable. Three more ancestors were from New London County, Connecticut, the most religiously radical of the Connecticut counties.

Of Storrs's twelve known fifth-generation ancestors, all were from Massachusetts and include several ancestors in common with the second Mormon prophet, Brigham Young. A member of the Jehovah's Witnesses' early board of directors, Clayton J. Woodworth, had family lines that run back to early Connecticut. It is evident that influences on the Jehovah's Witnesses came not only from New England but from the Middle Atlantic region and the South.

Southern Baptists

Prior to 1845, there was little formal difference between Baptists in the North and in the South. However, in 1840, the secretary of the Foreign Mission Society of the Baptists declared that the society would no longer appoint slaveholders as missionaries.[25] It was inevitable that the Southern Baptists would break away from the Northern Baptists, and in 1845 the Southern Baptist Convention was established.

The Southern Baptist Convention exemplifies the ecstasy and "mystical enthusiasm," to use Ronald Knox's language, that characterizes, to some extent, all indigenous American religions.[26] Southern Baptists sought to join with Christ, to be one with Christ. They hoped to have an absolutely intimate relationship with the Savior. They claimed each believer could have direct access to God; there was no mediator, such as the mother Mary or even the Scriptures, but there was the immediacy of the Holy Spirit, an inward awakening of the individual Baptist to Christ. The Baptist experience in knowing Christ was solitary and individual; it was prior to the community, to public worship, and to acts of sacrifice and charity; it was an utterly singular relationship with the Savior.

The roots of Southern Baptists come directly out of early colonial New England. The first Baptist congregation in the South had been established in 1696, when William Screven, the leader of a band of Baptists from Kittery, Maine, took his small congregation to South Carolina in an attempt to escape the hostility he and his group had experienced in conservative Maine. Screven's group consisted exclusively of early New England settlers.[27] Half a century later, Baptists came from other parts of America. For example, in 1751 Oliver Hart, from Pennsylvania, was active in the Philadelphia Baptist Association and used that group as a model in organizing the Charleston Baptist Association.

Without question, the most important Southern Baptist leader prior to the Civil War was Richard Furman. In 1755, at the age of sixteen, Furman was converted by the revivalist Separate Baptists and later became the pastor of the First Baptist Church in Charleston. He was the first president of the South Carolina Baptist Convention and served in that capacity for more than twenty-five years. He was born in Long Island, New York, but also had family roots in Wethersfield, Connecticut, where many ancestors of LDS converts had lived.

Today, the Southern Baptists understandably make little reference to their northern roots. The name of Roger Williams, the first Anabaptist in America, rarely appears in their historical literature; however, Southern Baptists would likely resonate with his Baptist beliefs more than with those of other Baptist conventions, simply because Southern Baptists have retained their traditional roots far more zealously than the Northern Baptists.

Roger Finke and Rodney Stark explain why Southern Baptists were transformed less over time than other Baptists. First, Southern "congregations are extremely autonomous and democratic. They locally hire and fire their preachers as they please and need not submit to any directives, theological or otherwise, from above." This has been crucial in that the South has remained resistant to social change, and the local congregations inevitably reflect the values of the community. Second, the very autonomy of the congregations prevents them from rooting out factions within the congregation. Consequently, as long as dissidents remain within the framework of the church, they are free to stay and fight for their values and points of view. Third, the autonomous congregations have not allowed their seminaries to become professionally separate, thus holding them in check from becoming "modern" and "secularized."[28] The conservative tradition among the clergy is further reinforced by the fact that the Southern Baptist minister is as much a lay, as he is a professional, minister. His salary is usually so small that he must maintain some other means of support, which situates him much more within, than above the congregation.

Obviously, although there have been influences on the Southern Baptists that have come from the Middle Atlantic and Southern regions of America, we must conclude from this brief discussion of Southern Baptists that it is clear that New England radicalism, at least in the early phases of this Baptist church, was a strong, though not exclusive, source of inspiration. Whereas we have attempted to make genealogical connections between LDS ancestors and the other indigenous religions, this has not been possible regarding Southern Baptists, simply because there are almost no LDS ancestors in the South. It has therefore been necessary to draw some parallels in values and points of view rather than ancestral relationships.

The American Religious Tradition

The American religious tradition has been described as reflecting an "inner faith" akin to our identity as a nation.[29] The American faith is expressed not only in spiritual doctrines and practices but in specific kinds of social reconstruction. Indigenous religions emphasize a tangible spirit world and spiritual gifts accessible to everyone in the mortal world. These believers pay homage to prophets within their ranks, who prophesy in a language inspired by God. They regard God as a loving, caring, personal father, actively involved in the everyday life of his children. Their God speaks directly to them, giving guidance and consolation. Indigenous American churches retain an allegiance to the sacraments and ordinances of Protestantism but attempt to recover primitive biblical patterns through practices such as baptism by immersion and expressing gifts of the Holy Spirit.

The American religious tradition manifests itself especially in traits characteristic of the Second Great Awakening, which took place in the latter half of the eighteenth and early nineteenth centuries; these traits include not only evangelism, universalism, millennialism, adventism, communalism, and spiritualism but also equality, democracy, temperance, and a belief in the unlimited worth and potential of all human beings.

However, each of the indigenous churches discussed here emphasizes some aspects of the American religion more than others. Christian Science is noted for its theory and practice of spiritual gifts, particularly religious healing. Although Mary Baker Eddy's *Science and Health and Key to the Scriptures* is not considered to be equivalent to Scripture, it does hold a special place as an inspired "text." However, there is, for instance, little discussion among Christian Scientists about modern-day prophets or the imminent return of Christ. Seventh-day Adventists focus their attention on the imminent return of Jesus Christ. They believe God has raised up in this day prophets and messengers who convey the word of God just as did the prophets of old. Their religious practices include baptism by immersion and partaking of the Lord's Supper. They also emphasize social reconstruction in health practices and diet. Jehovah's Witnesses recognize the prophetic offices of its leaders, who are thought to receive direct revelation from God and an authoritative understanding of God's word as found in the Scriptures. They, like the Adventists, believe in the imminent return of Christ. Charles Taze Russell maintained that Christ had returned in 1874, but that claim has since been modified by the church. Jehovah's Witnesses practice baptism by total immersion, which consecrates the 144,000 believers destined to attain heavenly salvation. Southern Baptists are committed evangelists; they subscribe to the Bible as the ultimate authority defining ecclesiastical and social programs. Southern Baptists intend to bring about a conversion of the human soul such that it melds with the spirit of Christ. Believers are baptized through immersion by ministers who have themselves been immersed in a recognized church.

Whereas each of these religions has its own distinct focus, many scholars hold that Mormons exemplify most elements of the American religious tradition, and their doctrines and practices reflect many facets of the spiritual, cultural, and social ferment of early nineteenth-century America. Harold Bloom even asserts that the spirit of Joseph Smith Jr. best manifests what he calls "the American Religion."[30]

The main intent of this book has been to provide a historical account of the Mormon religion's spiritual roots by tracing family histories of early LDS converts. In doing so, we have gained a new perspective on America's religious tradition. Of course, the beliefs of early LDS converts were not identical to those of their progenitors. There were characteristic manifestations of religious radicalism in each era, from the beginning days of the Protestant Reformation, to the early American colonial period, through the First Great

Awakening, the Second Great Awakening, and the Mormon's 1830 restoration of the gospel of Jesus Christ.

Millennialism and adventism were on the minds of the faithful from the beginning of New England's colonial history. Witchcraft came to an end prior to the beginning of the eighteenth century, even though other manifestations of spiritualism, including white and black magic, were to be found in every era. Evangelism was found as early as Thomas Hooker's congregation in Hartford but became prominent in the First Great Awakening and remained thereafter a force in the American religion. Various forms of universalism first began to be fully expressed at the time of the Second Great Awakening. Communalism manifested itself in the early part of the nineteenth century.

Of course, aspects of religion commonly identified with the American Revolution appeared at different times. The aspects of American particularism associated with divine destiny came with the Pilgrims and Puritans at the early stages of the colonial period. However, nationalism, individualism, and democratic impulses came much later. Finally, social justice and reconstruction, at least on a national scale, were part of organized churches and directed toward the new federal American government, whose constitution was not ratified until 1789.

Postscript

This book began as my quest to gain some perspective on the radical religious roots of my own family. But perhaps because I am a historian, it soon blossomed into a study of the roots of an indigenous American church, the Mormons, and it ultimately became a study of the role of early colonial religious radicals in the development of American religious culture. I hope the book serves as an inspiration for others to learn more about their own family roots, to find out about the antecedents and forerunners of their own religions, and to inquire more about the role that religion has had in the formation the world in which they live. When I began this study, almost a decade ago, the difficulties of gaining access to the necessary resources were formidable. Since then, advances in technology have made the quest far easier for both the curious seeker after genealogical data and for the serious academic scholar asking broader questions about religion and history.

Appendix

Listed below are the names of the 583 early Mormon converts, noted in bold, who form the base of this study and their known fifth-generation ancestors. Although the spelling of some names has changed over time, I have retained the spelling that appears in the genealogical records. Where a woman's maiden name is not known, I have listed her by her husband's surname and used "Mrs." before her given name or, if that is unknown, before her husband's given name, unless that is also unknown; and I have used "Mr." where a man's given name could not be found. Duplicate names indicate either more than one person with the same name or the same person as an ancestor through more than one family line.

Abbott, Lewis: Abbott, George; Abbott, Mrs. Elizabeth; Farnham, Ralph; Farnham, Mrs. Alice; Rice, Edward; Bent, Anne; Russell, William; Russell, Mrs. Martha; Merrick, William; Tracy, Rebecca; Trowbridge, James; Atherton, Margaret; Harrington, Robert; George, Susannah; Bigelow, John; Warren, Sarah;

Ackermann, Celinda and Lydia: Ackerman, Lodawyck; Bleyck, Jannetie; Sie, Jacobus; Sie, Mrs. Catherine; Lewis, Jonathon; Steere, John; Wickenden, Hannah; Arnold, Stephen; Smith, Sarah; Carpenter, Ephraim; Harris, Susannah; Crandall, Samuel; Burdick, Deborah; Longworthy, Samuel; Longworthy, Mrs. Rachel; Crandall, John; Gorton, Elizabeth; Tefft, Samuel; Jenckes, Elizabeth;

Adams, Alta: Adams, James; Vassell, Frances; Davis, Robert; Davis, Mrs. Robert; Adams, Samuel; Adams, Mrs. Mary; Monroe, William; Ball, Mary; Howe, Samuel; Nutting, Mary; Herrick, Ephraim; Cross, Mary; Hill, Ebenezer; Hill, Mrs. Sarah; Yerrington, Peter; Woodward, Abial; Day, Anthony; Matchett, Susannah; Rowe, Hugh; Langton, Rachel;

Aldrich, William: Aldrich, John; Thayer, Huldah; Hayward, Samuel; Thompson, Mehitable; Bartlett, John; Aldrich, Sarah; Aldrich, John; Thayer, Huldah; Capron, Banfield; Callender, Elizabeth; Aldrich, John; Thayer, Huldah; Hayward, Samuel; Thompson, Mehitable;

Alger, Samuel: Alger, Andrew; Alger, Mrs. Agnes; Baker, Alexander; Farrar, Elizabeth; King, John; Blucks, Mary; Whitman, John; Whitman, Mrs. Ruth; Thayer, Ferdinando; Hayward, Huldah; Bass, Thomas; Wood, Sarah;

Allen, Andrew Lee: Allen, Charles; Huggins, Susanne; Locke, John; Bowles, Elizabeth; Clark, Matthew; Dow, Mrs. Mary; Smith, Nicholas; Gordon, Mary; Hall, Samuel; Walker, Hannah; Avery, John; Chesebrough, Abigail; Griswold, John; Bemis, Mary; Wentworth, Ezekiel; Wentworth, Mrs. Elizabeth; Waldron, John; Ham, John; Heard, Mary; Stockbridge, John; Stockbridge, Mrs. John; Godfrey, John; Cox, Mary; Smith, Jonathon; Holdridge, Mehitabel;

Allen, Charles: Allen, Daniel; Wilder, Mary; Wheelock, Gershom; Stoddard, Hannah; Rice, Henry; Moore, Elizabeth;

Allen, Daniel and Joseph Stewart: Allen, Nehemiah; Woodford, Sarah; Wright, Judah; Burt, Mercy; Grant, John; Hull, Mary; Cook, Nathaniel; Cook, Mrs. Nathaniel; Dibble, Zachariah; Waterbury, Sarah; Clements, William; Clements, Mrs. Elizabeth; Abbott, George; Weed, Mary; Hayes, George; Hayes, Mrs. Sarah; Stewart, Robert; Forsythe, Janet; Clark, John; Adams, Agnes; Stewart, Robert; Forsythe, Janet; Clark, John; Adams, Agnes

Allred, Hannah Caroline, Isaac, Martin Carrell, Reuben Warren, and William Hackley: Aldridge, William; Fallin, Alice; Hamilton, James; Hamilton, Mrs. Grace;

Allred, James: Aldridge, Clement; Tills, Elizabeth; Fallin, Charles; Fallin, Mrs. Jane;

Alvord, Charlotte: Alvord, Alexander; Vore, Mary; Baker, Joseph; Holton, Ruth; Wright, Judah; Burt, Mercy; Hunt, Jonathon; Hosmer, Clemence; Chapin, Japhet; Cooley, Abilene; Sheldon, Isaac; Woodford, Mary; Dickenson, Nathaniel; Beardsley, Hannah; Gibbs, Samuel; Dibble, Hepsibah; Wellington, Joseph; Straight, Elizabeth; Whitmore, Samuel; Gardener, Rebecca; Stone, Samuel, Jr.; Jones, Dorcas; Adams, Joseph; Eames, Margaret; Richardson, Ezekiel; Swan, Elizabeth; Holden, Sarah; Chinery, John; Stratton, Elizabeth; Fuller, Joshua; Griggs, Hannah; Swan, Gershom;

Alvord, Thaddeaus: Alvord, Thomas; Hawkins, Joan; Vore, Richard; Vore, Mrs. Ann; Baker, Edward; Baker, Mrs. Jane; Holton, William; Winche, Mary; Wright, Samuel; Wright, Mrs. Margaret; Burt, Henry, Jr.; March, Eulalia; Hunt, John; Webster, Mary; Hosmer, Thomas; Bushnell, Frances; Chapin, Samuel; Penny, Cecily; Coley, Samuel; Prudden, Ann; Sheldon, Ralph; Stone, Barbara; Woodford, Thomas; Blott, Mary; Dickinson, Nathaniel; Gull, Anne; Beardsley, William; Harvey, Mary; Gibbs, Giles; Gibbs, Mrs. Katharine; Dibble, Thomas; Grant, Mary;

Ames, Ira and Lydia: Ames, John; Willis, Sarah; Hayward, John; Mitchell, Sarah; Jennings, Thomas; Jennings, Mrs. Anne; Bassett, Joseph; Lapham, Mary; Clark, Jeremiah; Latham, Frances; Audley, John; Audley, Mrs. Margaret; Wilcox, Daniel; Cooke, Elizabeth; Cooke, John; Borden, Mary; Rogers, Jonathon; Champion, Alice; Beckwith, Matthew; Rayner, Elisheba;

Anderson, John: Anderson, John; Starrot, Isabelle; Thayer, Shadrach; Priest, Deliverance; Brown, John; Buckland, Lydia; Mason, John; Peck, Anne; Rugge, John; Prescott, Hannah; Monroe, William; Ball, Mary; Hall, John; Farmer, Bethia; Mathews,

James; Mathews, Mrs. James; Wood, Thomas; Hunt, Ann; Hunt, Nehemiah; Toll, Mary; Hanks, Joseph; Hanks, Mrs. Joseph; Heiford, John; Atkins, Abigail; White, James; Baker, Sarah;

Anderson, Mary Ann: Pierce, Benjamin; Adams, Martha; Cowing [Cowan?], Israel; Litchfield, Hannah; Howard, Jonathan; Dean, Sarah; Field, John; Ames, Elizabeth;

Andrews, Benjamin: Andrews, John; Jordan, Jane; Rindge, Daniel; Kinsman, Mary; Cross, Robert; Jordan, Anna; Burnham, Thomas; Burnham, Mrs. Anna; Coggswell, William; Hawkes, Susannah; Goodhue, William; Dane, Hannah;

Angell, James William: Angell, Thomas; Ashton, Alice; Field, William; Fairbank, Ruth; Olney, Thomas; Marsh [March?], Elizabeth; Burnes, Thomas; Albie, Prudence; Smith, Christopher; Smith, Mrs. Alice; Angell, Thomas; Ashton, Alice; Mowry, Roger; Johnson, Miss; Inman, Edward; Inman, Mrs. Edward; Tripp, John; Paine, Mary; Anthony, John; Potter, Susanna; Manton, Shadrach; Smith, Elizabeth; Thornton, John; Thornton, Mrs. Sarah; Ames, William; Ames, Mrs. Hannah; Willis, John; Hodgkins, Elizabeth; Howard, John; Hayward, Martha; Latham, Robert; Winslow, Susanna;

Angell, Solomon and Truman Osborn: Angell, John; Field, Ruth; Olney, Thomas; Burns, Lydia; Smith, Edward; Angell, Anphillis; Mowry, Nathaniel; Inman, Joanna; Tripp, John; Anthony, Susannah; Manton, Edward; Thornton, Elizabeth; Ames, John; Willis, Sarah; Howard, John; Latham, Sarah; Morton, Abraham; Kellogg, Sarah; Waite, Jeremiah; Graves, Mary; Dexter, Benjamin; Arnold, Sarah; Clark, John; Tobey, Mary; Langford, Thomas; Holderbee, Comfort; Northup, Joseph; Smith, Hopestill; Sanford, Samuel; Nathaniel, Esther; Clark, Joseph; Parker, Mary;

Arey, Mary: Arey, Richard; Marchant, Sarah; Norton, Joseph; Lewis, Ebenezer; Lothrop, Anna; Crow, Thomas; Crow, Mrs. Deborah; Crosby, Simon; Nickerson, Mary; Sears, Paul; Freeman, Mercy; Sparrow, Jonathan; Young, Sarah; Doane, Joseph; Godfrey, Mary; Marchant, Abishai; Taylor, Mary; Gage, Benjamin; Lombard, Elizabeth; Ripley, Abraham; Farnsworth, Mary; Jenkins, Peter; Jones, Sarah; Raynes, Nathaniel; Harmon, John; Johnson, Deborah; Moulton, Jeremiah; Young, Mary;

Avery, Arvin: Avery, James; Greenslade, Joanna; Chesebrough, Samuel; Ingraham, Abigail;

Avery, Daniel: Avery, James; Greenslade, Joanna; Stallion, Edward; Stallion, Mrs. Margaret; Rose, Thomas; Rose, Mrs. Joanna; Allyn, Robert; Allyn, Mrs. Sarah; Williams, William; Thompson, Arabella; Wheeler, John; Larkin, Sarah; Bayley, Thomas; Redfield, Lydia; Smith, Edward; Bliss, Elizabeth; Parke, Thomas; Parke, Mrs. Martha; Rose, Robert; Rose, Mrs. Rebecca; Brewster, Benjamin; Addis, Ann; Gager, John; Gore, Elizabeth; Treat, James; Lattimer, Rebecca; Noyes, James; Stanton, Dorthy;

Babbitt, Almon Whiting: Babbit, Elkanah; Briggs, Elizabeth;

Babbitt, Ira: Babbitt, Edward; Tarne, Sarah; Briggs, William; Macomber, Sarah;

Badger, John: Badger, Nathaniel; Lunt, Mary; Roath, Robert; Saxton, Sarah; Wait, William; Wait, Mrs. Abiah; Rockwood, Josiah; Twitchell, Mary; Lowell, Thomas; Lovell, Ann; Herrick, George; Herrick, Mrs. Martha; Sawyer, Thomas; Lewis, Hannah; Houghton, John, Jr.; Farrar, Mary; White, Josiah; Rice, Mary; Whitcomb, Josiah; Waters, Rebecca; Farrar, Jacob; Hayward, Hannah; Rediat, John; Goodenow, Susanna;

Bailey, Mary: Bailey, John; Mighill, Mary; Wood, John; Hazen, Esabel; Rolfe, Ezra; Bond, Abigail; Jackson, John; Palmer, Sarah; Boutelle, John, Sr.; Davis, Hannah; Burnap, Thomas; Pearson, Mary; Foster, Samuel; Steward, Sarah; Roberts, Abraham; Burnap, Sarah; Eames, Robert; Eames, Mrs. Elizabeth; Peabody, Francis; Foster, Mary; Roberts, David; Brooks, Joanna;

Baldwin, Caleb: Bruen, Mary; Camp, Edward; Canfield, Mary; Tomlinson, Henry; Tomlinson, Mrs. Alice; Parmelee, Nathaniel; French, Sarah; Kelsey, John; Disborough, Hannah; Bushnell, Samuel; Rudd, Patience;

Baldwin, Charles Nelson and Nathan Bennett, Sr.: Greene, Thomas; Hills, Rebecca; Upham, Phineas; Wood, Ruth; Potter, John; Cooper, Hannah; Hill, John; Grannis, Hannah; Munson, John; Cooper, Sarah; Clark, Samuel; Tuttle, Hannah;

Ballou, Lillis: Ballou, Maturin; Pike, Hannah; Wightman, Valentine; Wightman, Mrs. Mary; Hall, Zuriel; Tripp, Elizabeth; Phillips, Michael; Phillips, Mrs. Barbara; Mowry, John; Mowry, Mrs. Mary; Bishop, Edward; Wild, Sarah; Hooper, William, I; Marshall, Elizabeth; Mighill, John; Batt, Sarah; Claflin, Robert Mack; Warner, Joanna;

Barden, Jerusha: Barden, William; Barker, Deborah; Booth, John; Sampson, Samuel; Nash, Esther; Eddy, John; Owen, Deliverence;

Barlow, Israel and Jonathan Watson: Barlow, Edmund; Pemberton, Mary; Huxley, Thomas; Spencer, Sarah; Harmon, John; Cummins, Elizabeth; Skinner, John; Filley, Mary; Purchase, Thomas; Williams, Elizabeth; Cook, John; Buxton, Mary; Worthington, Nicholas; Bunce, Sarah; Scott, John; Bliss, Sarah; Gillett, Jonathan; Barber, Mary; Bancroft, Thomas; Gardner, Hannah; Barlow, James; Huxley, Sarah; Harmon, Nathaniel; Skinner, Mary; Phelps, Timothy; Crow, Martha; Stiles, Robert; Bridges, Ruth;

Barnes, Amanda Melissa: Barnes, Thomas; Howe, Mary; Gilbert, Henry; Belding, Elizabeth; Ould, Robert; Hanford, Susannah; Walker, Edward; Dean, Elizabeth; Hayward, John; White, Anna; Chadwick, John; Manning, Sarah; Wheeler, Obadiah; White, Elizabeth; Woolcott, John; Emerson, Joanna;

Barnes, Anna: Barnes, William; Barnes, Mrs. Elizabeth; Linsley, John; Griffin, Hannah; Brockett, John, Jr.; Doolittle, Elizabeth; Grannis, Edward; Wakefield, Hannah;

Barney, Aramel, Edson, Philania, and Royal, Jr.: Barney, Joseph; Davis, Constance; Clark, Aaron; Eddy, Hannah; Martin, Ephraim; Bullock, Thankful; Peck, Jathniall; Smith, Sarah; Shepardson, John; Fuller, Elizabeth; Barney, Joseph; Davis, Constance; Clark, Aaron; Eddy, Hannah; Martin, Ephraim; Bullock, Thankful; Peck, Jathniall; Smith, Sarah; Marsh, Samuel; Ellison, Mary; Gillett, Joseph; Gull, Esther; Mattoon, Philip; Hawkes, Sarah; Boltwood, Samuel; Lewis, Sarah;

Barney, Rachel Marsh and Royal, Sr.: Barney, Jacob; Witt, Ann; Davis, James; Eaton, Elizabeth; Clark, Aaron; Lange, Sarah; Eddy, Obadiah; Ellis, Benet; Martin, John; Esten, Joanna; Bullock, Samuel; Rouse, Thankful; Peck, John; Peck, Mrs. Hannah;

Smith, Daniel; Chickering, Esther; Marsh, John; Webster, Anne; Ellison, Richard; Ellison, Mrs. Thomasina; Gillett, Joseph; Hawks, Elizabeth; Gull, William; Smith, Elizabeth; Mattoon, Hubartus; Hawkes, John; Hawkes, Mrs. Elizabeth; Boltwood, Robert; Gernor, Mary; Lewis, William; Hopkins, Mary;

Bearce, Rebecca: Bearse, Austin; Hyanno, Mary; Taylor, Richard; Wheldon, Ruth; Tuspaquin, Benjamin; Tuspaquin, Mrs. Weecum; Bruen, Mary; Warrups, Chicken; Warrups, Mrs. Catoonah; Canfield, Thomas; Crane, Phebe; Hine, Thomas; Lane, Elizabeth; Baldwin, Richard; Warrups, Anne; Waramaug, Mr.; Waramaug, Mrs.; Mallory, Peter; Preston, Mary; Macky, Hugh; Thorp, Nathaniel; Ford, Mary;

Beebe, Eliza Ann: Beebe, Jonathon; Brockway, Bridget; Coley, Peter, Jr.; Couch, Hannah; Beebe, William; Rogers, Ruth; Rogers, James; Stevens, Sarah; Traine, John; Stubbs, Mary; Jennison, Samuel; Macomber, Judith; Corse, James; Catlin, Elizabeth; Munn, Benjamin; Nims, Thankful; Cummings, John; Towne, Susanna; Larabee, Isaac; Towne, Mary; Allard, Andrew; Haven, Zerviah;

Beman, Alvah: Parke, Thomas; Thompson, Dorothy; Geer, George; Allyn, Sarah; Tracy, Thomas; Mason, Mary Conway; Griswold, Francis; Tracy, Mary; Parrish, Thomas; Danforth, Mary; Wattles, John; Goole, Mary;

Beman, Mary Adeline: Beman, Simon; Young, Alice; Parke, Nathaniel; Geer, Sarah; Tracy, Jonathan; Griswold, Mary; Parish, John; Wattell, Mary; Lee, Thomas, Jr.; de Wolf, Mary; Marvin, Reinold; Clark, Sarah; Grimes, Henry Graham; Grimes, Mrs. Mary;

Benner, Henry: Thomas, Phillip; Iddings, Esther;

Bennett, David: Bennett, Samuel, Jr.;

Bent, Samuel: Bent, John; Blanchard, Martha; Brown, William; Beseech, Mary; Foster, Hopestill; Bates, Mary; Stone, Simon; Whipple, Mary; Jones, John; Jones, Mrs. Dorcas; Reed, George; Jennison, Elizabeth; Pierce, Thomas; Cole, Elizabeth;

Bicknell, Jane A.: Bicknell, John; Porter, Mary; Smith, James; Brandon, Mary; Cadwell, Edward; Butler, Elizabeth; Bunce, John; Barnard, Mary; Field, Zechariah; Webb, Sarah; Bennett, James; Broughton, Mary; Spofford, Samuel; Burkby, Sarah; Haseltine, Abraham; Longhorne, Elizabeth;

Billings, Titus: Billings, Richard; Billings, Mrs. Margery; Fellows, William; Church, Richard; Marsh, Anne; Hopkins, Stephen; Hopkins, Mrs. Elizabeth; Parsons, Joseph; Bliss, Mary; Strong, John; Scott, Ann; Stebbins, Thomas; Wright, Hannah; Munn, Benjamin; Burt, Abigail; Bishop, Stephen; Bartlett, Hannah; Stevens, Nathaniel; Stevens, Mrs. Sarah; Meigs, John; Wilcoxson, Sarah; Willard, Josiah; Hosmer, Hannah;

Billington, Rebecca Delight: Billington, Joseph; Billington, Mrs. Grace; Huntley, Aaron; Champion, Mary; Mack, John; Bagley, Sarah; Huntley, Aaron; de Wolf, Deborah; Beckwith, Matthew; Marvin, Reinold; Clark, Sarah;

Bingham, Erastus: Bingham, Thomas; Rudd, Mary; Odell, John; Walker, Mary; Abbe, Samuel; Knowlton, Mary; Allen, Joshua; Warner, Isaac; Boltwood, Sarah; Leffingwell, Thomas; Bushnell, Mary; Babcock, Samuel; Fenno, John; Tucker, Rebecca;

Perry, Ezra, Sr.; Burgess, Elizabeth; Swift, William; Swift, Mrs. Ruth; Joy, Joseph, Jr.; Andrews, Elizabeth; Ford, Joseph; Stetson, Lois; Bliss, Ephraim; Bliss, Mrs. Ephraim; Whitaker, Richard; Cooper, Rebecca; Peck, Israel; Bosworth, Bethia;

Bird, Benjamin Freeman: Freeman, William; Orrell, Mary; Bowne, William; Bownes, Mrs. Anne; Holmes, Obadiah; Hyde, Katherine; Marsh, John; Baldwin, Grace; Hinds, James; Knight, Mary; Cutter, Richard; Williams, Elizabeth; Rolfe, John; Pike, John; Turvell, Mary; Stout, Richard; van Princin, Kent;

Bird, Charles: Bird, Joseph; Bird, Mrs. Elizabeth; Freeman, John; Bowne, James; Holmes, Lydia; Marsh, Samuel; Mann, Comfort; Hindes, Joseph; Hindes, Mrs. Anne; Cutter, William; Rolfe, Rebecca; Pike, John; Stout, Sarah; Reeves, Hezekiah; Hallock, Jerusha; Corwin, John; Corwin, Mrs. Sarah; Fairchild, Zachariah; Beach, Hannah; Fairchild, Alexander; Jackson, Deborah; Taylor, Samuel; Horseman, Susannah; Foulke, Thomas; Curtis, Elizabeth; Quicksall, Mary;

Blackman, Sarah: Blackman, John; Pond, Mary; March [Church?], John; Tucker, Mary; Long, Thomas; Wilcox, Sarah; Evarts, James; Guttridge, Lydia; Crampton, Dennis; Munger, Sarah;

Blanchard, Aseph: Ackley, Nicholas; Ackley, Mrs. Hannah; Spencer, John; Howard, Rebecca; Mott, Nathaniel; Shooter, Hanna; Brockway, Wolston; Briggs, Hannah;

Boynton, Abram, Clarissa, John Farnum, and Olive: Boynton, Joshua; Burnap, Hannah; Dole, William; Brocklebank, Mary; Stickney, Amos; Morse, Sarah; Palmer, Samuel; Pearson, Mary; Hardy, Thomas; Hardy, Mrs. Lydia; Eaton, Thomas; Singletery, Eunice; Kimball, Benjamin; Hazeltine, Mercy; Day, John; Pengry, Sarah; Nichols, Thomas; Moulton, Mary; Sargent, William, Jr.; Stainwood, Naomi; George, James; Jordan, Sarah; Hadlock, James; Hutchinson, Rebecca;

Boynton, Eliphalet: Boynton, William; Jackson, Elizabeth; Burnap, Robert; Burnap, Mrs. Ann; Dole, Richard; Rolfe, Hannah; Brocklebank, Samuel; Brocklebank, Mrs. Hannah; Stickney, William; Dawson, Elizabeth; Morse, Anthony; Waldro, Ann; Palmer, Thomas; Palmer, Mrs. Ann; Pearson, John; Pearson, Mrs. Dorcas; Hardy, Thomas; Eaton, Peter; Crossman, Ann; Singletery, Richard; Cooke, Susanna; Kimball, Richard; Scott, Ursula; Haseltine, Robert; Haseltine, Ann; Day, Robert; Pingry, Hannah; Pengry, Moses; Clements, Lydia;

Brim, Alexander: Merrick, Thomas; Tilley, Elizabeth; Dumbleton, John; Dumbleton, Mrs. Mercy; Moore, Joseph; Hayward, Lydia; Allis, Samuel; Allis, Mrs. Alice; Lawrence, Enoch; Whitney, Ruth; Jewell, Nathaniel; Smedley, Mary; Parkhurst, Joseph; Spaulding, Eunice; Cady, Nicholas; Redland, Patience;

Brown, Albert: Brown, Peter, Jr.; Gillett, Mary; Loomis, Nathaniel; Moore, Elizabeth; Ellsworth, Josiah; Holcomb, Elisabeth;

Brown, Charles: Elwell, Eleazer; Mariner, John; Sawyer, Sarah; Knight, John; Knight, Mrs. Elizabeth; Tucker, William; Tucker, Mrs. Grace; Riggs, Thomas; Millett, Mary; Witham, Henry; Somes, Sarah; Babson, James; Hill, Elinor; Baker, Cornelius; Woodbury, Hannah; Allen, Joseph; Griggs, Rachel;

Brown, Samuel: Brown, James, Sr.; Howse, Hannah; Kelly, John; Knight, Sarah; Pike, Hugh; Brown, Sarah; Kelly, John; Knight, Sarah; George, Francis; Hadlock, Sarah;

George, Francis; Hadlock, Sarah; Webster, Stephen; Ayer, Hannah; Goodwin, Christopher, Jr.; Crouch, Mercy; Haynes, Jonathan; Moulton, Sarah; Harriman, Matthew; Swan, Elizabeth; Hall, Richard; Hall, Mrs. Sarah; Kimball, Henry; Marsh, Hannah; Kimball, Benjamin; Hazeltine, Mercy;

Brunson, Amanda and Seymour: Brownson, Richard; Wilbour, Abigail; Gibbs, Jacob; Andrus, Elizabeth; Peet, John; Osborn, Sarah; Morehouse, Thomas; Keeler, Elizabeth; Bentley, William, III; Leithfield, Sarah; Clark, John; White, Elizabeth; Whitmore, Francis; Harris, Hannah; Smith, Jonathan; Bushnell, Martha; Averill, William; Jackson, Hannah; Walker, Philip; Bowen, Mary; Cogswell, William, Jr.; Emerson, Martha; Browne, Nathaniel; Perkins, Judith;

Brunson, Jabez, Jr.: Weybourne, John; Gibbs, Giles; Gibbs, Mrs. Katharine; Andrus, Joseph; Andrus, Mrs. Elizabeth; Peate, John, Sr.; Allcock, Sarah Margaret; Osborn, Richard; Townsend, Mary; Morehouse, Thomas; Keeler, Isabel; Keeler, Ralph; Whelpley, Sarah; Bentley, William, Jr.; Bentley, Mrs. William; Eldred, William; Lumkin, Anne;

Bundy, Sophia: Bundy, John; Chandler, Martha; Prentice, Thomas, Jr.; Stanton, Sarah; Hammond, Nathaniel; Griffin, Mary;

Bunnell, David Edwin: Bonnel, Nathaniel; Whitehead, Susanna; Frazee, Joseph; Osborne, Mary; Wade, Benjamin; Looker, Ann; Ogden, Joseph; Whitehead, Sarah; Baker, John; Pierce, Alice;

Burbank, Hannah Marie: Burbank, Caleb; Smith, Martha; Gage, Daniel; Kimball, Sarah; Savory, William; Savory, Mrs. Hannah; Adams, Nathaniel; Kimball, Abigail; Palmer, Joseph; Jackman, Sarah; Green, Thomas; Weeks, Mary; Savory, William; Savory, Mrs. Hannah; Adams, Nathaniel; Kimball, Abigail; Dow, Joseph; Dow, Mrs. Mary;

Burdick, Alden, Elias, Rebecca, and Thomas: Burdick, Robert; Hubbard, Ruth; Foster, Thomas; Parker, Susannah; Maxon, John; Mosher, Mary; Clarke, Joseph, Jr.; Hubbard, Bethiah;

Burgess, Harrison Joseph and Horace: Newland, Anthony; Austin, Easter; Caswell, Stephen; Thresher, Hannah; Woodward, John; Crossman, Sarah; Stockwell, William; Lambert, Sarah; Singletary, John; Greeley, Mary; Kinne, Daniel; Richards, Mary; Stockwell, William; Shaw, Elizabeth; Gale, Ebennezer; Green, Elizabeth; Kinne [Kenney], Jonathon; Nurse, Rebecka;

Burgess, William, Sr.: Newland, Jeremiah; Newland, Mrs. Catherine; Austin, Jonah; Read, Esther; Caswell, Thomas; Caswell, Mrs. Ann; Thrasher, Christopher; Woodward, Nathaniel; Jackson, Mary; Crossman, Robert; Kingsbury, Sarah;

Burr, Maria: Stevens, James; Wakeley, Mary; Barnes, John; Betts, Mercy; Kelsey, John; Disborough, Hannah; Crane, Henry; Meigs, Concurrence; Johnson, Isaac; Miller, Margaret; Brainard, Caleb; Bidwell, Elizabeth; Pelton, John; Johnson, Jemima; Burr, Jonathan; Hubbard, Abigail;

Burtts, Sally: Lee, Thomas; Browne, Phoebe; de Wolf, Balthazar; de Wolf, Mrs. Alice; Marvin, Reinhold; Marvin, Mrs. Marie; Clark, James; Harvey, Sarah;

Butler, John Lowe: Butler, William; Butler, Mrs. William; Lowe, Thomas;

Butterfield, Josiah: Butterfield, Benjamin; Butterfield, Mrs. Ann; Ballard, William; Berwick, Grace; Heald, John; Royle, Dorothy; Dane [Dean?], Thomas; Dane [Dean?], Mrs. Elizabeth; Farnsworth, Richard; Marshe, Elizabeth; Farr, George; Stowers, Elizabeth; Shattuck, William; Hayden, Susanna; Whitney, John; Reynolds, Ruth;

Butterfield, Thomas Jefferson: Butterfield, Joseph; Ballard, Lydia; Heald, John; Dane [Dean?], Sarah Frances; Farnsworth, Matthias; Farr, Mary; Shattuck, John; Whitney, Ruth; Knowlton, Mr.; Knowlton, Mrs.; Batchelder, Joseph; Moulton, Miriam; Fellows, Isaac; Bordman, Joanna; Potter, John; Kimball, Sarah;

Cahoon, Mary and Reynolds: Cahoon, Mr.; Peck, Deliverance; Reynolds, James; Potter, Deborah; Greene, James; Anthony, Elizabeth; Vaughn, David [Davy?]; Vaughn, Mrs. Mary; Bull, Isaac; Parker, Sarah;

Cahoon, William Farrington: Cahoon, Joseph; Cahoon, Mrs. Elizabeth; Reynolds, Francis; Greene, Elizabeth; Vaughan, John; Bull, Elizabeth; Bassett, Samuel; Weaver, Alice;

Calkins, Chauncy Ira: Calkins, John; Royce, Sarah; Gifford, Stephen; Gore, Hannah; Strong, John, Jr.; Warriner, Elizabeth; Gillett, Josiah; Tainter, Joanna; Burgess, Joseph; Worden, Mary; Storrs, Samuel; Huckins, Mary; Cole, John; Rogers, Mary;

Call, Anson: Call, John; Kettell, Hannah; Lowden, Richard; Cole, Mary; Sprague, Samuel; Crawford, Rebecca; Greene, John; Wheeler, Sarah; Sanderson, Jonathan; Bartlett, Abiah; Stratton, John; Smith, Mary; Green, William; Hills, Elizabeth; Sprague, Samuel; Green, Sarah; Ellis, Matthias; Nye, Mercy; Blackwell, Joshua; Fish, Mercy; Hammond, Seth; Randall, Mary; Jenney, Mark; Barlow, Elizabeth;

Call, Cyril: Call, Thomas; Harrison, Bennett; Kettell, Richard; Ward, Esther; Cole, Ryse [Rice?]; Phipps, Arrold; Sprague, John; Warren, Joanna; Crawford, John; Crawford, Mrs. Winifred; Greene, Thomas; Lynde, Elizabeth; Wheeler, Isaac; Cook, Frances; Sanderson, Edward; Eggleston, Mary; Bartlett, Thomas; Bartlett, Mrs. Hannah; Stratton, Samuel; Stratton, Mrs. Alice; Smith, Thomas; Knapp, Mary; Greene, William; Wheeler, Elizabeth; Hills, Joseph, Jr.; Smith, Hannah; Sprague, Samuel; Crawford, Rebecca; Greene, John; Wheeler, Sarah;

Carlisle, Sally: Pierce, Stephen; Parker, Tabitha; Fletcher, Mr.; Dryer, William; Locke, Anna; Wilmarth, Jonathon; Peck, Esther;

Carter, Charity: Carter, Edward; Carter, Mrs. Margaret; Lucas, William; Cornwall, Hester Clark; Nettleton, John; Hull, Maratha; Woodmansee, Gabriel; Ricks, Sarah; de Wolf, Balthazar; de Wolf, Mrs. Alice; Lee, John; Lay, Sarah; Waterman, Robert; Bourne, Elizabeth; Tracy, Thomas; Mason, Mary; Doude, Henry; Dowd, Mrs. Elizabeth; Bartlett, George; Cruttenden, Mary; Grinnell, Daniel; Wordell, Mary; Pabodie, William; Alden, Elizabeth; Parmalee, Nathaniel; French, Sarah; Kelsey, John; Disborough, Hannah;

Carter, Dominicus and William Fulsbury: Carter, Richard; Carter, Mrs. Elizabeth; Peavey, Edward; Peavey, Mrs. Rachel; Pine, Charles; Balster, Grace; McKenney, Robert; Sparks, Rebecca; Jameson, William; Holmes, John; Abbott, Mary; Pevy, William; Pevy, Mrs. Sarah; Libby, David; Libby, Mrs. Eleanor; Hanscom, Thomas;

Rogers, Alice; Larrabee, Thomas; Roe, Elizabeth; Ingersoll, John; Phoenix, Deborah; Andrews, William; Woodward, Margaret; Smith, Samuel; Smith, Martha A.; Seavey, William; Jackson, Hannah; Knight, Nathan; Westbrook, Mary;

Carter, Gideon: Carter, Edward; Blackburne, Elizbeth; Nettleton, Samuel; Nettleton, Mrs. Maria Mary; Hull, Josiah; Loomis, Elizabeth; Woodmansee, Thomas; Ricks, John; Waterhouse, Jacob; Waterhouse, Mrs. Jacob; Clark, John; Porter, Rebecca; Stark, Aaron; Stark, Mrs. Sarah; Shaw, Thomas; Shaw, Mrs. Mary;

Carter, Gideon Hayden, Jerusha, John Sims, Luman, Prudence, Simeon Dagget, Susannah Abigail, and Jared: Carter, Edward; Carter, Mrs. Margaret; Nettleton, John; Hull, Martha; Woodmansee, Gabriel; Ricks, Sarah; Waterhouse, Abraham; Clark, Rebecca; Stark, Aaron; Shaw, Mehitable;

Carter, Jabez: Manning, William; Manning, Mrs. Dorothy; Stearns, Isaac; Barker, Mary; Spalding, Edward; Elliot, Margaret; Underwood, William; Pellett, Sarah; Carter, Thomas; Carter, Mrs. Mary; Burnham, Robert; Andrews, Mary; Tuttle, John; Tuttle, Mrs. John;

Case, Nancy: Case, William; White, Mary; Smith, John; Smith, Mrs. Margaret; Phenix, Alexander; Sewall, Abigail; Wightman, George; Updyke, Elizabeth;

Chadwick, Polly: Chadwick, John; Chadwick, Mrs. Joan; Brewer, John; Rice, Elizabeth; Jones, Josiah; Treadway, Lydia; Merriam, Joseph; Stone, Sarah; Cutler, Thomas; Dewey, Abigail; Allen, Joseph; Sabin, Hannah; Wight, Ephraim; Morse, Lydia;

Chamberlain, Electa: Chamberlain, Richard; Gilbert, John; Wright, Samuel; Burt, Elizabeth; Taylor, John; Woodward, Thankful;

Chamberlain, Lydia: Chamberlain, Thomas; Poulter [Parker?], Mary; Proctor, John; Proctor, Mrs. Martha; Hill, Ralph; Hill, Mrs. Margaret; Holmes, Robert; Holmes, Mrs. Jane; Cram, John; White, Hester [Esther?]; Weare, Nathaniel; Swaine, Elizabeth; Short, Elizabeth; Ballard, William; Berwick, Grace; Powers, Walter; Shepard, Trial; Poulter, John; Elliot, Rachel; Russell, John; Fiske, Elizabeth; Craggens, John; Dawes, Sarah; Skelton, Joseph; Howe, Deborah; Barker, William; Dix, Mary; Hayward, Joseph; Hosmer, Hannah;

Chamberlain, Soloman: Chamberlain, Daniel; Addington, Rebecca; de Lannoy, Phillippe; Dewsbury, Hester; Warren, Nathaniel; Walker, Sarah; Hatch, Jonathan; Rowley, Sarah; Allen, James; Partridge, Elizabeth; Deane [Dean?], Walter; Strong, Eleanor; Wood, Ellis; Wood, Mrs. Catherine; Peck, Joseph; Peck, Mrs. Mary; Bosworth, Jonathan; Bosworth, Mrs. Elizabeth; Beebe, James; Boltwood, Mary; Colver, Edward, Jr.; Backus, Sarah; Hebard, Robert; Walden, Mary;

Chapman, Huldah: Chapman, Edward; Symonds, Mary; Brewer, John, Sr.; Whitmore, Mary; Wentworth, William; Kenney, Elizabeth; Stewart, Duncan; Winehurst, Ann; Chase, William, Jr.; Holder, Elizabeth; Baker, Francis; Twining, Isabel; Gowell, Mr.; Remick, Christian; Remick, Mrs. Hannah; Berry, Richard; Berry, Mrs. Alice; Bell, John; Bell, Mrs. John; Gray, John; Lumpkin, Hannah; Dillingham, John; Feake, Elizabeth;

Chase, Darwin and Eli: Chase, John; Baker, Elizabeth; Berry, John; Berry, Mrs. Susannah; Maker, James; Maker, Mrs. Rachel; Hopkins, Stephens; Merrick, Mary;

Chase, Stephen: Chase, William, Jr.; Holder, Elizabeth; Baker, Francis; Twining, Isabel; Berry, Richard; Berry, Mrs. Alice; Hopkins, Giles; Wheldon, Catherine; Merrick, William; Tracy, Rebecca;

Cheney, Aaron: Cheney, Daniel; Bailey, Sarah; Dustin, Thomas; Emerson, Hannah; Littlefield, Anthony; Page, Mary; Mott, Nathaniel; Shooter, Hanna; Stewart, Duncan; Winehurst, Ann; Allen, Walter; Holmes, Mary; Barsham, John; Barsham, Mrs. Mehitable; Hubert, Jean; Le Gallais, Elizabeth; Goodwin, Daniel; Spencer, Margaret; Heard, James; Conley, Shuah; Cole, Nicholas; Cole, Mrs. Nicholas; Neal, John; Searle, Joan; Furbish, William; Furbish, Mrs. William; Johnson, Peter; Moulton, Ruth; Green, Abraham; Sweet, Esther;

Cheney, Amasa F., Elijah, Nathan Calhoon, Olive Mehitable, and Selah: Cheney, Daniel, II; Dustin, Hannah; Littlefield, Edmund; Mott, Elizabeth; Stewart, Samuel; Barton, Dorcas; Allen, James; Barsham, Dorothy; Hubbard, Philip; Goodwin, Elizabeth; Heard, John; Cole, Jane; Neal, Andrew, Jr.; Furbish, Catherine; Johnson, Edmund; Green, Abigail; Wells, Joshua; Tuthill, Hannah; Brewster, Timothy; Hawkins, Mary; Reeves, James; Terry, Mrs. James Mary; Salmon, John; Barnes, Sarah; Tuthill, John; Wells, Mehitable; Reeves, James; Satterly, Deborah; Wells, Joshua; Tuthill, Hannah; Brewster, Timothy; Hawkins, Mary;

Chidester, John M.: Peck, John; Morris, Esther; Mygatt, Joseph; Stevens, Elizabeth; Starr, Benjamin; Taylor, Eunice; Gifford, Samuel; Calkins, Mary; Hough, William; Lathrop, Anne;

Chubuck, Polly: Chubbuck, John; Beal, Martha; Bate, James; Hilliard, Esther; Whitman, John; Hollis, Abigail; Pratt, Matthew; Hunt, Sarah; Terrill, William; Pratt, Abigail; Nash, Joseph; Marsh, Phebe; Gurney, Zachariah; Bensen, Mary; Perkins, Thomas; Woodman, Remember; Wilkins, John; Gengill, Mary; Southwick, Daniel; Boyce, Esther; Curtis, John; Looke, Mary; Gould, John; French, Phebe; Ingalls, Robert; Harker, Sarah;

Clapp, Benjamin L.: Clapp [Clap?], Nikolas; Potter, Elizabeth; Clapp, Nikolas; Potter, Elizabeth;

Clark, Laura: Clark, George; Clark, Mrs. Mary; Baldwin, Timothy; Mepham, Mary; Beard, John; Hawley, Anna; Rogers, Eleazer; Knowls, Elizabeth; Clark, Samuel; Clark, Mrs. Mary; Clark, Samuel; Tuttle, Hannah; Fowler, William; Beard, Anna; Keeler, John; Rockwell, Mehitable; Saint John, James; Comstock, Mary; Betts, Samuel; Reynolds, Judith; Brinsmade, Daniel; Kellogg, Sarah; Bearse, Joseph; Taylor, Martha; Newcomb. Andrew; Bayes, Anna; Barrett, Moses; Barrett, Mrs. Sarah; Spaulding, Andrew; Warren, Abigail;

Clark, Timothy Baldwin: Clark, George; Bodye, Grace; Clark, George; Bodye, Grace; Baldwin, Richard; Harding, Isabell; Beard, James; Beard, Mrs. Martha; Rogers, John; Rogers, Mrs. Ruth; Knowles, Alexander; Clark, George; Clark, Mrs. Mary; Clark, James; Harvey, Sarah; Tuttle, John; Lane, Catherine; Fowler, William; Tapp, Mary; Beard, John; Hawley, Anna;

Clements, Albert: Clements, Nolgen; Seeley, Joseph; Seeley, Mrs. Martha;

Cleveland, Henry Alanson: Cleveland, Samuel; Hildreth, Persis; Hyde, Jonathan; Kidder, Dorothy; Lawrence, Enoch; Whitney, Ruth;

Clisbee, Lydia: Clisbee, Ezekiel; Clisbee, Mrs. Sarah; Frothingham, Nathaniel; Hett, Mary; Lewis, Joseph; Jones, Mary; Hugh, Jones; Foster, Mary; Howe, Abraham; Ward, Hannah; Martin, Thomas; Martin, Mrs. Joanna; Rice, Edward; Bent, Anne; Graves, Benjamin; Hoar, Mary; Goddard, William; Miles, Elizabeth; Davis, William; Davis, Mrs. Jane; Clayes, Peter; Littlefield, Hannah;

Cluff, David: Clough, John; Page, Mercy; Merrill, Nathaniel; Kinney, Joanna; Clough, John; Clough, Mrs. Jane [Jone?]; Connor, Cornelius; Brown, Sarah; Meader, John; Tuttle, Abigail; Pittman, William; Roberts, Ann; Runnels, Job; Huckins, Robert; Thomas, Welthen;

Coe, Joseph: Coe, Robert; Mitchell, Hannah; Hawley, Joseph; Birdsey, Catherine; Robinson, Thomas; Welles, Mary; Kirby, John; Hinds, Elizabeth; Curtis, John; Welles, Elizabeth; Judson, Joshua; Porter, Sarah; Johnson, Peter; Johnson, Mrs. Elizabeth; Holbrook, John; Streame, Elizabeth;

Colburn, Thomas: Hoagland, Christofeel; Cregier, Catherine; Middagh, Jan Aertse; Potter, Adrianna;

Colby, Alanson: Colby, John; Eldredge, Sarah; Bartlett, Christopher; Weed, Deborah; Worthen, Ezekiel; Martin, Hannah; Carter, John; Browne, Martha; Flanders, John; Sargent, Elizabeth; Prince, Thomas, Jr.; Harradaine, Elizabeth; Galpin, Philip; Smith, Elizabeth; Brown, Francis; Lawrence, Martha; Hawley, Samuel, Sr.; Thompson, Mary; Curtiss, Benjamin; Judson, Esther; Bunnell, Benjamin; Mallory, Rebecca; Wheeler, Joseph; Holbrook, Patience;

Cole, Edith: Coles, Robert; Hawkshurst, Mary; Cole, Samuel; Cole, Mrs. Anne; Brown, Abraham; Brown, Mrs. Lydia Ann; Shattuck, William; Hayden, Susanna; Davis, Dolor [Dolar?]; Willard, Margery; Meaddows, Philip; Iggleden, Elizabeth;

Coltrin, Graham, and Zebedee: Maxam, Samuel, Sr.; Maxam, Mrs. Samuel; Perry, Ezra, Jr.; Freeman, Rebecca; Freeman, Ellis; Ellis, Mercy; Clark, Thomas; Miller, Susanna;

Coltrin, John, Jr.: Maxham, Mr.; Perry, Ezra, Sr.; Burgess, Elizabeth; Freeman, Edmund [Edward?]; Prence, Rebecca; Ellis, John, Jr.; Freeman, Elizabeth; Clark, James; Lathrop, Abigail; Miller, Mr.;

Conrad, Sarah: Kaufmann, Hans; Arnold, Katrina; Kneisley, Mr.; Kneisley, Mrs. Magdelena;

Coons, Lebbeus Thaddeus, Sr.: Maccoon, John; Maccoon, Mrs. Annie; Ross, William; Ross, Mrs. Hannah; Lewis, John; Crandall, Samuel; Burdick, Deborah; Longworthy, Samuel; Longworthy, Mrs. Rachel; Crandall, John; Gorton, Elizabeth; Tefft, Samuel; Jenckes, Elizabeth; Crandall, Samuel; Burdick, Deborah; Longworthy, Samuel; Longworthy, Mrs. Rachel; Crandall, John; Gorton, Elizabeth; Tefft, Samuel; Jenckes, Elizabeth; Lewis, James; Babcock, Sarah;

Covert, Betsy: Covery, Lucas Teunis; Sprong, Barbara;

Covey, Benjamin: Covey, James; Covey, Mrs. Mary; Covey, James; Covey, Mrs. Mary;

Cowdery, Phebe L., Oliver, and Warren: Cowdery, Nathaniel; Cowdery, Elizabeth; Parker, Hannaniah; Brown, Elizabeth; Damon, Thomas; Emerson, Joseph; Bulkley, Elizabeth; Fuller, Samuel; Lathrop, Jane; Rowley, Moses; Fuller, Elizabeth; Cornwell, William; Bull, Mary; Ward, John; Harris, Mary; Spencer, Gerard; Hills, Hannah; Bate, James; Withington, Ann; Bogue, John; Walkley, Richard; Walkley, Mrs. Rebecca;

Cowles, Austin: Cowles, Samuel; Stanley, Abigail; Woodruff, John; Winchell, Mary; Johnson, Isaac; Harris, Mary; Miller, Thomas; Nettleton, Sarah; Woodworth, Joseph; Stockbridge, Sarah; Torrey, James; Rawlins, Elizabeth; Buck, Isaac; Turner, Eunice;

Crandall, David: Crandall, Samuel; Burdick, Deborah; Crandall, John; Gaylord, Hannah; Cottrell, John; Cottrell, Mrs. Elizabeth; Closson, Josiah; Williamson, Mary; Wells, Peter; Sweet, John; Jeffreys, Mrs.; Hamilton, William; Berry, Mercy; Reynolds, Joseph; Reynolds, Mrs. Mary; Badcock, John; Lawton, Mary; Spencer, John; Griffin, Susanna; Whaley, Theophilus; Mills, Elizabeth;

Crosby, Jonathan: Crosby, Nathaniel; Bennett, Elizabeth; Wicom, Daniel; Hazen, Sarah; Houghton, Jonas; Burbeen, Mary; Moore, Jonathan; Sawyer, Hannah; Osgood, Stephen; Hooker, Mary; Woodman, Joshua; Stevens, Elizabeth; White, Josiah; Rice, Mary; Wilder, Nathaniel; Sawyer, Mary; Barnes, Thomas; Goodenow, Abigail; Howe, Samuel; Bent, Martha; Eager, William; Hill, Ruth; Woods, John; Stevens, Cyprian; Willard, Mary; Rice, John; Stone, Tabitha; Stevens, Cyprian; Willard, Mary; Wilder, Nathaniel; Sawyer, Mary;

Cummings, Rhoda E.: Whiton, James; Beal, Mary; Rickard [Richard?], Giles; Dunham, Hannah; Wilson, John; James, Hannah; Willson, Jonathan; Sibley, John; Leach, Rachel; Follett, William; Nicholas, Rich, Jr.; Greene, Abigail; Marsh, Samuel; Thompkins, Prescilla; Newton, Richard; Loker, Anna; Morse, Joseph; Shattuck, Susannah; Belknap, Samuel; Jones, Sarah; Ayers, Nathaniel; Turloar, Tameson;

Curtis, Enos: Curtiss, Thomas; Merriman, Mary; Parker, John; Bassett, Hannah; Calkins, John; Royce, Sarah; Gifford, Stephen; Gore, Hannah; Grannis, Edward; Wakefield, Hannah; Russell, John; Russell, Mrs. Hannah; Avery, William; Allright, Margaret;

Curtis, Lyman: Curtis, Zacheus; Blake, Mary; Jafford, David Francis; Jafford, Mrs. Francis; Buzzell, Samuel; Keyes, Sarah; Stiles, Robert; Frye, Elizabeth; Meacham, Jeremiah; Trask, Mary Margaret; Cash, William; Lambert, Elizabeth; Hawkins, Thomas; Hawkins, Mrs. Agnes; Humphries, John; Humphries, Mrs. Elizabeth; Waite, Joseph; Oaks, Hannah; Sargent, John; Chipman, Lydia; Bancroft, John; Eaton, Elizabeth; Clark, Thomas; Brighton, Mary; Stratton, John; Prentice, Abigail; Coolidge, Thomas; Eddy, Sarah; Miller, Elizabeth; Estabrook, Joseph, II; Leavitt, Hannah;

Cutler, Alpheus: Cutler, James; King, Mary; Bigelow, John; Warren, Mary; Flagg, Thomas; Flagg, Mrs. Mary;

Cutler, Lois Huntington: Cutler, Thomas; Dewey, Abigail; Bigelow, Samuel; Flagg, Mary; Day, Robert; Dresser, Elizabeth; Louthrup, Iferell Israel; Bliss, Rebecca; Waterman, Thomas; Allyn, Elizabeth; Hough, John; Post, Sarah; Wetherall, Mary Brewster; Denison, George; Huntington, Christopher; Adgate, Sarah; Gifford, Samuel; Calkins, Mary B.; Hyde, John; Abell, Experience;

Daley, Abigail Jane and Moses: Ennis, William; Viervant, Cornelia; Quick, Thomas; Dekker, Margriete; Hornbeck, Evert; Cuddeback, Eleanor; Cuddeback, Abraham; Gumaer, Esther; DeWitt, Andrews, Sr.; Egbertsen, Jannetje; Nottingham, William; Rutsen, Margaret Bergjen; De Puy, Moses; Wynkoop, Maria; Schoonmaker, Joachim H.; Hussey, Anna;

Daniels, Sheffield: Daniels, Joseph; Fairbanks, Mary; Partridge, John; Bullard, Magdalene; Adams, Peter; Newcome, Rachel; Cook, Samuel; White, Lydia; Hill, John; Johnson, Hannah; Twitchell, Benjamin; Riggs, Mary; Sheffield, William; Webb, Mary; Bullard, Benjamin; Pidge, Martha;

Dayton, Hyram: Baldwin, Richard; Alsopp, Elizabeth; Canfield, Thomas; Crane, Phebe; Beecher, Eleazer; Prindle, Phoebe; Peck, Paul; Baysey, Elizabeth;

Decker, Isaac: Frere, Hugo; Wibou, Jannetje; van Wagenen, Jacob A.; Pels, Sarah; Vanaken, Pieter; Damen, Russia; de Grauw, Gerrit; Hyer, Dorothea;

de Mille, Freeborn: de Mille, Anthony; van der Liphorst, Elizabeth; van Syssen, Joost Carelzen; Jans, Christina Styntje; Provost, David; Ten Waert, Margaretta; Janszen, Albert; Emich, Hans; Emich, Mrs. Hans;

Dibble, Lydia: Holcombe, Thomas; Ferguson, Elizabeth; Bliss, Nathaniel; Chapin, Catherine; Pettibone, John; Pettibone, Mrs. John; Eggleston, Bygod; Wall, Mary; Granger, Launcelot; Granger, Mrs. Launcelot; Adams, Robert; Wilmot, Eleanor; Younglove, Samuel; Legatt, Margaret;

Dibble, Philo, Sr.: Dibble, Abraham; Tefft, Lydia; Benjamin, Caleb; Hale, Mary; Hayes, Robert; Malster, Margaret; Dibble, Samuel; Grant, Mary; de Cosse, Capet; Porter, Richard; Hocombe, Ruth; Hillier, John; Wakefield, Mary; Hayes, George; Dibble, Abigail; Pomeroy, Medad; Woodward, Experience; Seymour, Richard; Woodruff, Hannah; Remington, Thomas; Walker, Mehitable; Hovey, Nathaniel; Fuller, Sarah; Austin, John; Atwater, Mercy; Royce, Samuel; Churchill, Hannah; Benham, Joseph; Merriman, Hannah; Cook, Samuel; Parker, Hope;

Draper, Fannie, Lydia, Phoebe, William, Jr., and Zemira: Draper, James; Stansfield, Marie; Jackson, Sebastian; Baker, Sarah; Hyde, Job; Fuller, Elizabeth; Prentice, Thomas, Jr.; Jackson, Rebecca; Rogers, Noah; Tainter, Elizabeth; Goodsell, Thomas; Hemingway, Sarah; Byington [Boynton?], John; Westover, Jane; Lathrop, Samuel; Scudder, Elizabeth; Bliss, Thomas; Birchard, Elizabeth; Otis, John, Jr.; Jacob, Mary; Thomas, Nathaniel; Jacob, Deborah; Pike, James; Cutler, Hannah; Welch, James; Welch, Penelope, Jr.; Clother, Jeremiah; Clother, Mrs. Ruth; Brown, Peter, Jr.; Gillett, Mary;

Draper, Lavina: Draper, Mr.; Braman, James; Babcock, Jane; Carr, Caleb; Slocum, Johanna; Richmond, Edward; Thurston, Rebecca;

Draper, William, Sr.: Draper, William; Mitchell, Grace; Stansfield, Gideon; Eastwood, Grace; Jackson, Edward; Jackson, Mrs. Frances; Baker, Thomas; Baker, Mrs. Elizabeth; Hyde, Samuel, Sr.; Hyde, Mrs. Temperance; Fuller, John; Cole, Elizabeth;

Prentice, Robert; Prentice, Mrs. Grace; Jackson, Edward; Jackson, Mrs. Frances; Rogers, William; Hall, Ann; Tainter, Michael; Rose, Elizabeth; Goodsell, Thomas, Sr.; Hemingway, Samuel; Cooper, Sarah; Boynton, Caleb; Moores, Mary; Westover, Jonah; Griswold, Ann;

Drollinger, Samuel: Drollinger, Wendel; Drollinger, Mrs. Margaretha; Funck, Anastasius; Funck, Maria; Clemmer, George; Clemmer, Mrs. Elizabeth; Altergott, Michael; Kneier, Barbara; Lotholz, Johannes; Lotholz, Mrs. Magdalena; Welsz, Andreas; Fuess, Hans; Fuess, Mrs. Maria; Deeg, Erhard; Deeg, Mrs. Anna Elisabeth;

Drury, Joel: Drury, John; Weare, Mary;

Duncan, John: Duncan, George;

Dunning, Eunice: Dunning, Benjamin; Dunning, Mrs. Mary; Miner, John, Jr.; Rose, Sarah; Shepard, John; Peck, Hannah; Allen, Gideon; Prudden, Sarah; Colvin, Mr.; Colvin, Mrs.; Allen, Matthew; Kirby, Sarah; Briggs, Thomas; Briggs, Mrs. Martha;

Durfee, Edmond and James: Durfee, Thomas; Durfee, Mrs. Thomas; Earle, William; Earle, Mrs. Prudence; Chase, William, Jr.; Hale, Abigail; Borden, John; Earle, Mary; Borden, John; Earle, Mary; Wadell, Gersham; Tripp, Mary; Mumford, Stephen; Mumford, Mrs. Ann; Peery, Ezra, Sr.; Freeman, Mary; Salisbury, William; Salisbury, Mrs. Susannah; Ormsby, Thomas; Fitch, Mary;

Durfee, Tamma and Martha: Durfee, Benjamin; Earle, Prudence; Chase, Benjamin; Borden, Amey; Borden, Richard; Wadell, Innocent; Mumford, John; Perry, Peace; Salisbury, William; Ormsbey, Mary;

Duzett, Philemon: Wing, Daniel; Swift, Hannah; Spooner, William; Pratt, Hannah;

Duzette, Edward Peas and Mariah Elizabeth: King, William; Elwill, Agnes; Fuller, John; Farrington, Elizabeth; Hall, Samuel; White, Elizabeth; Pease, John; Goodell, Mary; Adams, James; Vassell, Frances; Spencer, Thomas; Bearding, Sarah; Pratt, John, Sr.; Boosey, Hannah; Morgan, Miles; Gilbert, Prudence; Pease, John; Goodell, Mary; Randall, William; Randall, Mrs. Elizabeth;

Eames, Ellis and Julietty: Bacon, John; Hall, Rebecca; Loker, John; Rice, Sarah; Cooledge, John; Cooledge, Mrs. Mary; Morse, Joseph; Badcock, Hannah; Russell, John; Palmer, Elizabeth; Winn, Increase; Sawtell, Hannah;

Eddy, Wealthy: Eddy, John; Owen, Deliverance; Fuller, Benjamin; Darling, Mary; Wheaton, Jeremiah; Amidon, Hannah [Joanna?]; Phelps, Timothy; Crow, Martha; Dewey, Nathaniel; Burroughs, Margaret; Eddy, John; Owen, Deliverence;

Edwards, Elisha: Edwards, Thomas; Birch, Marie; Moore, William; Wellman, Mary; Searle, John; North, Mary; Moore, William; Wellman, Mary;

Egglestone, Amanda: Eggleston, James; Williams, Esther; Mills, Peter; Eggleston, James; Williams, Esther; Hoskins, Anthony; Browne, Isabel; Curtis, Joseph; Deming, Mercy; Goodridge, John; Allen, Rebecca; Woodford, Joseph; Newell, Rebecca; Fowler, Ambrose; Alvord, Joan; Baker, Joseph; Baker, Mrs. Joseph; Tuttle, Thomas; Powell, Hannah; Hotichiss, Samuel; Talmage, Sarah; Bradley, Isaac; Danish, Elizabeth; Chidsey, Ebenezer; Thompson, Priscilla;

Elliott, David, III: Elliott, Daniel; Cloyce, Clayes Hannah; Provender, John; Aldridge, John; Thayer, Hulda; Hayward, Samuel; Thompson, Mehitable;

Emmett, James: Emmot, James; Lawrence, Mary; Rittinghousen, Nicolas; Dewees,

Wilhelmina; Trowbridge, William; Lamberton, Elizabeth; Sherwood, Matthew; Fitch, Mary; Stephens, Mr.; Borden, Sarah;

Estabrook, Sarah B.: Estabrook, Joseph; Mason, Mary; Hobart, Nehemiah; Jackson, Sarah; Paddock, Zachariah; Sears, Deborah; Hall, John; Bearse, Priscilla; Palmer, Samuel; Kinsley, Elizabeth; Abbe, Samuel; Knowlton, Mary;

Evans, David J.: Alexander, James; Alexander, Mrs. James; McKnitt, Mr.;

Farr, Winslow, Sr.: Farr, Thomas; Farr, Mrs. Thomas; Taylor, William; Merriam, Mary; Powers, Walter; Shepard, Trial; Winslow, Kenelm; Worden, Mercy; King, Thomas; Clap, Elizabeth; Ewar, Thomas; Lovell, Elizabeth; Conant, Nathanial; Mansfield, Hannah; Snow, John; Greene, Mary; Cutler, James; Page, Phoebe; Brigham, Thomas; Rice, Mary; Warren, Joseph; Wheelock, Experience; Trowbridge, James; Jackson, Margaret; Ward, John; Spring, Mary; Park, Richard; King, Sarah; Fuller, John; Griggs, Hannah;

Farwell, Olive: Hovey, James; Dane, Priscilla; Barlow, Edmund; Pemberton, Mary; Farwell, Joseph; Learned, Hannah; Hyde, Jonathon; Kidder, Dorothy; Johnson, William; Wiswell, Esther; Gardner, Richard; Rolfe, Hanna; Davis, Joseph; Davis, Mrs. Joseph; Patten, Thomas; Paine, Rebecca; Freeman, Edmund; Perry, Margaret; Presbury, John; Bessey, Dorcas; Skiffe, Stephen; Snow, Lydia; Freeman, Edmund, Jr.; Presbury, Kezia; Johnson, William; Davis, Hannah; Hovey, Edmund; Farwell, Mary; Farwell, John; Baldwin, Dorothy;

Fausett, Eliza McKee, John McKee, and William McKee: Fawcett, Christopher; Fawcett, Mrs. Dorothy; Stonhewer, Richard; Mckee, Robert; Mckee, Mrs. Agnes;

Felshaw, William: Davis, John; Davis, Mrs. Mary; Chamberlain, Jacob; Child, Mary; Towne, John; Smith, Mary; Hicks [Hix?], Daniel; Hammer, Rebecca; Kingsley, John; Sabin, Sarah; Moulton, William, II; Webster, Abigail; Chase, Thomas; Follansbee, Rebecca;

Finch, Hannah B.: Finch, Nathaniel; Hoadley, Mary; Bartholomew, William; Johnson, Mary; Frisbie, John; Bowers, Ruth; Blakeslee, John; Ventrus, Grace; Benton, Samuel; Chatterton, Sarah;

Fisk, Alfred, Hulda, Ira, Rhonda, Russell W., and Sterry: Fisk, John; Baldwin, Hannah; Bowen, Obadiah; Bullock, Abigail; Sterry, Roger; Palmer, Hannah; Rose, Daniel; Goodrich, Elizabeth; Wilbour, Joseph; Brownell, Ann; Irish, Jonathan; Taylor, Mary; Knight, Jonathan; Bennett, Hannah; Stone, Hugh; Potter, Mary; Walker, Thomas; Parris, Elizabeth; Coggeshall, Joshua; Timberlake, Elizabeth; Newby, George; Newby, Mrs. Elizabeth; Round, John; Bowen, Abigail; Seamans, Thomas; Salisbury, Susannah; Eddy, John; Owen, Deliverance;

Fisk, Hezekiah: Fisk, John; Gott, Remember; Baldwin, John, Jr.; Bruen, Mary; Bowen, Obadiah; Clifton, Mary; Bullock, Richard; Ingraham, Elizabeth; Palmer, William; Short, Rebecca; Rose, Thomas; Rose, Mrs. Joanna; Allyn, Robert; Allyn, Mrs. Sarah; Wilbor, William; Holmes, Martha; Brownell, William; Smitton, Sarah; Irish, John; Irish, Mrs. Elizabeth; Taylor, John; Taylor, Mrs. John; Knight, Richard; Rogers, Sarah; Bennett, Robert; Bennett, Mrs. Rebecca; Stone, Hugh; Bussaker, Abigail; Potter, Abel; Warner, Rachael;

Follett, King: Follett, Robert; Black, Persis; Kellum, Mackum;

Foote, Timothy Bradley: Foote, Robert; Potter, Sarah; Palmer, Micah; Bulkeley, Elizabeth; Sutcliffe, Nathaniel; Plympton, Hannah; Brockett, Benjamin; Barnes, Elizabeth; Hand, Stephen; Stratton, Sarah; Pierson, Abraham; Clarke, Abigail; Walstone, John; Wright, Anna; Barnes, John; Betts, Mercy; Bradley, Stephen; Smith, Hannah; Leaming, Christopher; Burnet, Esther; Hand, Stephen; Stratton, Sarah; Pierson, Abraham; Clarke, Abigail;

Ford, Asanath and William: Ford, Joseph; Hovey, Elizabeth; Holt, George; Farnham, Elizabeth; Davison, Thomas; Tracy, Hannah; Herrick, Stephen; Trask, Elizabeth;

Ford, William Martin: Ford, Joseph; Waldo, Deborah; Hovey, Nathaniel; Fuller, Sarah; Holt, Henry; Ballard, Sarah; Farnham, Ralph, II; Holt, Elizabeth; Davison, Daniel; Davison, Mrs. Daniel; Tracy, Jonathan; Griswold, Mary; Herrick, Ephraim; Cross, Mary; Trask, Mr.; Trask, Mrs.;

Foster, Julia: Glidden, Richard; Gilman, Sarah; Jones, Benjamin; Sinclair, Sarah; True, William; Stevens, Eleanor; Allen, Stillson; Stillson, Margaret; Prescott, Joshua; Clifford, Sarah; Ambrose, Nathaniel; Eastman, Hannah;

Foster, Solon: Foster, Christopher; Stevens, Frances; Hildreth, Thomas; Hildreth, Mrs. Hannah; Jessup, John; Lupton, Christopher; Raynor, Abigail;

Fowler, Nancy: Lake, Thomas; Peat, Sarah; Case, James; Case, Mrs. Hannah; Crapeau, Mr.; White, Samuel; Lapham, Rebecca; Manter, John; Lambert, Martha; Whitten, Jerimiah; Doggett, Elizabeth; Coleman, John; Folger, Joanna;

Freeman, Isaac Farwell and Olive Hovey: Freeman, Edmund, Jr.; Perry, Margaret; Presbury, John; Bessey, Dorcas; Skiffe, Stephen; Snow, Lydia; Johnson, William; Wiswell, Esther; Gardner, Richard; Rolfe, Hannah; Davis, Joseph; Davis, Mrs. Joseph; Patten, Thomas; Paine, Rebecca; Hovey, James; Dane, Priscilla; Barlow, Edmund; Pemberton, Mary; Farwell, Joseph; Learned, Hannah; Hyde, Jonathan; Kidder, Dorothy; Farwell, Joseph; Learned, Hannah; Hyde, Jonathan; Kidder, Dorothy; Baldwin, John; Heywood, Sarah; Kidder, Ephraim; Crosby, Rachel;

Gates, Jacob, Lucinda, and Thomas, Jr.: Gates, Stephen; Woodward, Sarah; Benjamim, Joseph; Clark, Sarah; Hubbard, Jonathan; Rice, Hannah; Clark, Samuel; Nichols, Rachel; Wheeler, Deliverance; Davis, Mary; Gates, Simon; Benjamin, Hannah; Darby, Thomas; Browne, Mary; Butterick, John; Blood, Mary; Plumly, Joseph; Plumly, Mrs. Jane; Drew, John; Churchill, Hannah;

Gates, Thomas, Sr.: Gates, Stephen; Veare, Anne; Woodward, George; Woodward, Mrs. Mary; Benjamin, John; Eddy, Abigail; Clark, Arthur; Clark, Mrs. Sarah; Hubbard, John; Merriman, Mary; Rice, Samuel; King, Elizabeth; Clark, Arthur; Clark, Mrs. Sarah; Nichols, William; Nichols, Mrs. Mary [Rachel?]; Wheeler, Thomas; Wood, Ruth; Davis, Simon; Blood, Mary; Gates, Stephen, Jr.; Woodward, Sarah; Benjamin, Joseph; Clark, Sarah; Darby, John; Makepeace, Hester; Browne, John; Makepeace, Hester; Butterick, William; Bateman, Sarah; Blood, Robert; Willard, Elizabeth;

Gee, George Washington: Gee, Richard; Gee, Mrs. Mary; Huntley, Aaron; De Wolf, Deborah; Mack, John; Bennett, Love; Hill, Charles; Fox, Abigail; Beckwith, Joseph; Lee, Mary; Smith, Francis; Huntley, Mary; Harris, Joseph; Stevens, Mary; Champlin, John; Champlin, Mrs. Elizabeth; Crane, Abraham; Griswold, Hannah; Curtis, William; Butler, Ruth; Watson, Cyprian; Steele, Elizabeth; Moody, John; Everts, Sarah;

Gee, Salmon: Gee, Ezechiell; Crossman, Elizabeth; Huntley, Aaron; Champion, Mary; De Wolf, Stephen; Jones, Hannah; Mack, John; Bagley, Sarah; Bennett, Henry; Champion, Sarah; Harris, Gabriel; Abbot, Elizabeth; Stevens, William; Meigs, Mary; Champlin, Christopher; Champlin, Mrs. Christopher; Raymond, Joshua; Sands, Mercy; Beckwith, Joseph; Lee, Mary; Smith, Francis; Huntley, Mary; Harris, Joseph; Stevens, Mary; Champlin, John; Champlin, Mrs. Elizabeth;

Gifford, Alpheus: Giffard, Philip; Turner, Mary; Mills, John; Gregory, Sarah; Shepherd, Ralph; Lord, Thankful; Sherman, Peleg; Lawton, Elizabeth; Wilbor, William; Holmes, Martha; Burman, Thomas; Annabel, Hannah; Harper, Robert; Perry, Deborah; Burgess, Joseph; Freeman, Patience;

Gilbert, Algernon Sidney: Gilbert, M; Baker, Jane; Parker, Sarah; Todd, Christopher; Middlebrook, Grace; Brown, Eleazer; Bulkley, Sarah; Alcott, Phillip; Mitchell, Elizabeth; Heaton, James; Street, Sarah; Hemmenway, Ralph; Hewes, Elizabeth; Cooper, John; Woolen, Mary; Morris, Thomas; Morris, Mrs. Elizabeth; Bishop, James; Lewen, Mary; Tuttle, Joseph; Munson, Hannah; Sanford, Thomas; Payne, Elizabeth; Thompson, John; Powell, Priscilla; Mansfield, Moses; Glover, Mercy;

Gilbert, Mary Harriett: Gilbert, Thomas; Combe, Joan; Crane, Henry; Kingsley, Tabitha; Walker, James; Phillips, Elizabeth; Brooks, Gilbert; Simmons, Elizabeth; Bobet [Babbitt?], Edward; Babbitt, Sarah; Tisdale, John; Walker, Sarah;

Glidden, Abigail: Glidden, Charles; Shore, Eunice; Gilman, John; Treworgye, Elizabeth; Jones, George; Jones, Mrs. Mary; Sinkler, John; Sinkler, Mrs. Mary; True, Henry; Bradbury, Jane; Stevens, Benjamin; Barnard, Hannah; Allen, William; Harris, Mary; Prescott, James; Boulter, Mary; Clifford, Israel; Smith, Ann; Ambrose, Henry; Worcester, Susannah; Eastman, Nathaniel; Hudson, Elizabeth;

Goddard, Mary Adaline: Gozzard, Nicholas; Gillett, Elizabeth; Hayes, George, Sr.; Dibble, Abigail; Pettibone, John; Eggleston, Sarah; Bissell, Samuel; Holcomb, Abigail; Cornish, James; Browne, Phoebe; Hillyard, Andrew; Burr, Hannah; Barber, Thomas; Buell, Abigail; Case, Samuel; Westover, Mary; Phelps, Nathaniel; Phelps, Mrs. Eunice; Loomis, William; Morley, Martha;

Goodall, Persis: Emerson, Joseph; Bulkley, Elizabeth; Boutwell, James; Kendall, Mary;

Gould, Harriet: Gould, Robert; Bosworth, Elizabeth; Jacob, John; Russell, Mary; Chappel, Caleb; Royce, Ruth; Sill, Joseph; Clark, Sarah; Lord, Richard; Hyde, Elizabeth; Noyes, Moses; Picket, Ruth; Ely, Richard; Marvin, Mary;

Gould, John: Gold, Nathan; Talcott, Hannah; Bradley, Abraham; Thompson, Hannah; Wakeman, Joseph; Hawley, Elizabeth; Sherwood, Benjamin; Sherwood, Mrs. Sarah; Bradley, Francis, II; Jackson, Sarah;

Granger, Oliver: Granger, Launcelot; Granger, Mrs. Launcelot; Adams, Robert; Wilmot, Eleanor; Younglove, Samuel; Legatt, Margaret;

Grannis, Ruth: Grannis, Edward; Wakefield, Hannah; Russell, John; Russell, Mrs. Hannah; Thompson, John; Powell, Priscilla; Potter, John; Hitchcock, Mary;

Grant, Carolina A., George Davidson, and Jedediah Morgan: Grant, Noah; Billings, Mercy; Parke, William; Frink, Hannah; Woodward, Daniel; Dana, Elizabeth; Parke, Robert; Rose, Mary; Howard, Thomas; Jones, Ruth; Spencer, Thomas Lawrence; Bates, Elizabeth; Miner, Clement; Mould, Martha; Turner, Ezekiel; Keeney, Susannah; Davies, Thomas; Davies, Mrs. Thomas;

Grant, Joshua: Grant, Samuel; Porter, Mary; Billings, William; Atherton, Mary; Parke, Thomas; Thompson, Dorothy; Frink, John; Stevens, Grace; Woodward, George; Woodward, Mrs. Mary; Dana, Richard; Bullard, Ann; Parke, Thomas; Parke, Mrs. Martha; Rose, Robert; Rose, Rebecca;

Greene, Evan Molbourne: Jefferay, William; Gould, Mary; Coddington, William; Brinley, Anne; Hutchinson, William; Marbury, Anne; Brown, James; Carr, Elizabeth; Clark, James; Clark, Mrs. Hope; Sanger, Richard; Smith, John, I; Hinckley, Susannah; Reynolds, Mary; Cutter, Richard; Williams, Elizabeth; Peake, Jonathan; French, Sarah; Leavens, John; Wood, Hannah;

Greene, John Portineus: Greene, John L.; Jefferey, Mary; Coddington, William; Brinley, Anne; Hutchinson, Edward; Hamby, Katharine; Browne, John; Carr, Elizabeth; Clark, James; Clark, Hope; Smith, John; Smith, Mrs. Elizabeth; Sanger, Richard; Reynolds, Mary; Cutter, Richard; Williams, Elizabeth; Peake, Jonathan; French, Sarah; Leavens, John; Wood, Hannah;

Greenleaf, Rebecca W.: Townsend, James; Price, Elizabeth;

Griswold, Hannah: Griswold, Edward; Blencow, Margaret; North, Thomas; Price, Mary; Stevens, William; Meigs, Mary; Hubbell, Richard; Gaylord, Elizabeth; Bushnell, John; Scranton, Sarah;

Grover, Thomas: Grover, Mathew; Davis, Mary; Buck, Ephraim; Brooks, Sarah; Bacon, Michael; Richardson, Sarah; Wyman, Francis; Reed, Abigail; Sherman, Joseph; Winship, Elizabeth; Bullen, Ephriam; Bullen, Mrs. Grace; Perham, John; Shipley, Liddiah; Fletcher, Samuel; Hailston, Margaret; Spalding, Andrew; Jefes, Hannah; Warren, Jacob; Hildreth, Mary; Underwood, Joseph; Bond, Elizabeth; Parker, Nathaniel; Polley, Bethia; Browne, John; Browne, Abigail; Wheeler, Josiah; Worster, Elizabeth;

Groves, Elisha Hurd: Groves, Nicholas; Sallows, Hannah; Wallis, James; Wallis, Mrs. James;

Gunn, Lucy: Gunn, Nathaniel; Day, Sarah; Wyatt, John; Brownson, Mary; Belden, Samuel; Belden, Mrs. Mary; Wells, Thomas; Beardsley, Mary; Marsh, John; Webster, Anne; Ellison, Richard; Ellison, Mrs. Thomasina; Gillett, Joseph; Hawks, Elizabeth; Gull, William; Smith, Elizabeth; Gunn, Jasper; Gunn, Mrs. Mary [Christian?]; Day, Robert; Stebbing, Editha; Wyett, Stephen; Mullins, Leah; Brunson, John; Hills, Frances; Root, Joseph; Haynes, Hannah; Russell, John, Sr.; Russell, Mrs. Phoebe; Church, Edward; Hopkins, Mary;

Hadlock, Samuel: Hadlock, Mr.; Hadlock, Mrs.; North, Richard; North, Mrs. Ursula; Thurlow, Richard; Thurlow, Mrs. Jane; Morse, Anthony; Waldro, Ann; Merrill, Nathaniel; Peabody, Susannah; Webster, John; Batt, Anne; Petty, William; Petty, Mrs. Mary; Whitmarsh, John; Harding, Sarah; Stowell, Samuel, Sr.; Farrow, Mary;

Cox, William; Cox, Mrs. Mary; Pope, John; Pope, Mrs. Margaret; Blackman, John; Scotlow, Sarah; Weekes, William; Atherton, Elizabeth;

Hale, Emma: Heald, John; Royle, Dorothy; Vinton, John; Vinton, Mrs. Ann; Hodge, John; Denslow, Susanna; Bunnell, Benjamin; Mallory, Rebecca; Ward, Andrew; Meigs, Tryal; Beach, John, Jr.; Royce, Mary; Towner, Richard; Towner, Mrs. Mary; Barnes, Thomas; Frost, Abigail; Lewis, Edward; Cobb, Hannah; Huckins, John; Chipman, Hope; Maltby, William; Maltby, Mrs. Mary; Lord, William; Buckland, Lydia; Tuttle, Thomas; Powell, Hannah; Hotchkiss, Samuel; Talmage, Sarah; Bradley, Isaac; Danish, Elizabeth; Chidsey, Ebenezer; Thompson, Priscilla;

Hale, Jonathan Harriman: Hale, Thomas; Hutchinson, Mary; Palmer, Samuel; Pearson, Mary; Haseltine, Abraham; Longhorne, Elizabeth; Spofford, Samuel; Burkby, Sarah; Johnson, John; Crosby, Hannah; Wicom, Daniel; Smith, Mary; Boynton, John; Keyes, Hannah; Haseltine, Robert; Jewett, Elizabeth; Harriman, Leonard; Palmer, Margaret; Elithrope, Nathaniel; Batt, Mary; Plumer, Joseph; Cheney, Sarah; Wood, Thomas; Hunt, Ann;

Hall, Benjamin Kimball and Levi: Hall, Richard; Collicot, Elizabeth; Kimball, Henry; Wyatt, Mary; Marsh, Onisiphorus; Cutler, Hannah; Kimball, Benjamin; Hazeltine, Mercy; Hazen, Edward; Grant, Hannah; Peabody, John; Andrews, Hannah; Harriman, Matthew; Swan, Elizabeth; Page, Joseph; Dow, Martha; Eaton, Thomas; Singletery, Eunice; Webster, Stephen; Ayer, Hannah;

Hancock, Clarrisa, Levi Ward, Sr., Solomon, and Thomas, Jr.: Hancock, Thomas; Leonard, Rachel; Webb, John; Webb, Mrs. Hanna [Anna?]; Wright, Benjamin; Chapin, Mary; Miller, Lazarus; Burbank, Mary; Wright, Abel; Kitcherel, Martha; Chapin, Henry; Cooley, Bethia; Miller, Obadiah; Cogan, Joan; Burbank, John; Merrill, Susannah; Ward, William; Ward, Mrs. Judith; Jones, Benjamin; Wildes, Elizabeth; Ward, Obadiah; Ward, Mrs. Mary; Jones, Thomas; North, Mary; Wildes, John; Gould, Priscilla;

Hanson, Melinda: Gunn, Samuel; Wyatt, Elizabeth Bronson; Belding, Stephen; Wells, Mary; Marsh, Samuel; Ellison, Mary; Gillett, Joseph; Gull, Esther; Gunn, Nathaniel; Day, Sarah; Wyatt, John; Brownson, Mary; Root, Joseph; Root, Mrs. Hannah; Russell, Phillip; Church, Mary;

Harding, Dwight: Harding, Abraham; Adams, Elizabeth; Mason, Thomas; Partridge, Margery [Margaret?]; Hill, John; Johnson, Hannah; Twitchell, Benjamin; Riggs, Mary; Corbin, Clement; Buckminster, Dorcas; Morse, Anthony; Barnard, Mary; Cutler, James; Moore, Lydia; Snow, John; Greene, Mary; Goodale, Isaac; Cook, Patience; Titus, John; Redway, Lydia; Bugbee, John; Bugbee, Mrs. Joanna;

Harmon, Alpheus A., Oliver, and Jesse Pierse: Harmon, John; Cummins, Elizabeth; Skinner, John; Filley, Mary; Austin, Richard; Austin, Mrs. Elizabeth; Huggins, John; Green, Bridget; Norton, George; Machias, Mary; Barber, Thomas; Coggins, Jane [Joan?];

Harriman, Henry: Brocklebank, Samuel; Platts, Elizabeth; Spofford, Samuel; Burkby, Sarah; Fowler, Philip; Herrick, Elizabeth; Jacob, Thomas; Howe, Abraham; Peabody, Sarah; Andrews, Joseph; Perley, Sarah;

Harris, Emer, Preserved, and Martin: Harris, Thomas; Harris, Mrs. Thomas; Tew, Richard; Clarke, Mary; King, Clement; Reyner, Mary; Baker, John; Baker, Mrs. Elizabeth; Mowry, Nathaniel; Inman, Joanna; Bull, Isaac; Parker, Sarah; Paine, Stephen; Chickering, Anna; Rainsford, Urania; Lapham, John; Mann, William; Hopkins, Frances; Arnold, Richard; Angell, Mary;

Haskins, Hopestill: Haskins, William; Hinds, Ann; Caswell, Thomas; Caswell, Mrs. Ann; Godfrey, Richard; Turner, Mary; Richmond, John; Hayward, Susanna; Briggs, Clement; Allen, Joan; Harvey, William; Hucker, Joanne; Andrews, John; Jackson, Hannah; Shaw, John; Phillips, Alice;

Hastings, Sarah Sawyer: Hastings, Thomas; Cheney, Margaret; Sanderson, William; Sanderson, Mrs. Sarah; Hartwell, William; Hartwell, Mrs. Jasan; Wright, Edward; Mellows, Elizabeth; Wheeler, Thomas; Harwood, Hannah; Davis, Simon; Blood, Mary; Burt, David; Holton, Mary; Cowles, John; Bartlett, Deborah; Severence, John; Severance, Mrs. Mary; Sawyer, Caleb; Houghton, Sarah; Wheelock, Joseph; Wheelock, Mrs. Elizabeth;

Hathaway, Elizabeth: Hathaway, Abraham; Wilbor, Rebecca; Shaw, Benjamin; Bicknell, Hanna; Gilbert, Thomas; Blake, Anne; Bradford, Samuel; Rogers, Hannah; Williams, Nathaniel; Rogers, Elizabeth; King, Philip; Whitman, Judith; Atherton, Joshua; Gulliver, Mary; Leonard, James; Gulliver, Lydia;

Haven, Elizabeth: Haven, Moses; Ball, Mary; Walker, Thomas; Howe, Martha; Bullard, Benjamin; Fairbank, Martha; Morse, Samuel; Thurston, Sarah; Marsh, Alexander; Belcher, Mary; Wilson, John; Newton, Sarah; Howe, Samuel; Bent, Martha; Mixer, Isaac, Jr.; Garfield, Rebecca; Howe, Samuel; Bent, Martha; Death, John; Peabody, Mary; Goddard, William; Miles, Elizabeth; Stone, Simon; Whipple, Mary; Brigham, Samuel; Howe, Elizabeth; Moore, Richard; Collins, Mary;

Hendrickson, Polly: Rauh, Nicholas; Steenhop, Gertrude; Winter, Henrich;

Higbee, Elias, Isaac, and John Somers: Higbee, Edward; Adams, Abigail; Andrews, Mordecai; Andrews, Mrs. Mary; Risley, Richard; Adams, Rebecca; Conover, Peter; van Couwenhoven, Mary; Smith, John; David, Ruth; Somers, John; Somers, Mrs. Elizabeth; Hand, Thomas;

Higgins, Nelson: Daggett, John; Pease, Sarah; Atwater, David; Sayre, Damaris; Allen, John; Bradley, Ellen; Benham, John; Smith, Mercy; Beecher, John; Roberts, Elizabeth;

Hillman, Mayhew: Cottle, Edward; Cottle, Mrs. Judith; Sampson, Henry; Plummer, Ann; Whitman, John; Whitman, Mrs. Ruth; Look, Thomas; Bunker, Elizabeth; Lewis, George; Lewis, Mrs. Elizabeth; Lewis, George; Lombard, Mary; Folland, William; Folland, Mrs. Elizabeth; Butler, John; Lynde, Mary; Doggett, Thomas; Mayhew, Hannah; Hatch, Jonathan; Rowley, Sarah;

Hills, Julia: Hills, Joseph, Jr.; Smith, Hannah; Metcalf, Michael; Fairbanks, Mary; Fisher, Samuel; Snow, Meletiah; Fisher, Cornelius; Heaton, Leah; Whitney, Jonathan; Jones, Lydia; Mann, William; Jarred, Mary; Hunting, Margaret; Ellis, John, Jr.; Lombard, Susan; Herring, Thomas; Herring, Mrs. Mary; Partridge, John;

Bullard, Magdalene; Smith, Samuel; Turner, Elizabeth; Metcalf, Michael; Fairbanks, Mary; Fisher, Samuel; Snow, Meletiah; Colburn, Nathaniel; Clark, Priscilla; Partridge, George; Tracy, Sarah;

Hitchcock, Seth: Hitchcock, Matthias; Rogers, Elizabeth; Merriman, Nathaniel; Lines, Joan; Andrews, Samuel; Peck, Elizabeth; Parker, John; Bassett, Hannah; Parker, John; Bassett, Hannah; Beach, John, Jr.; Royce, Mary; Curtiss, Thomas; Merriman, Mary; Howe, Zachariah; Gilbert, Sarah; Barnes, Thomas; Andrews, Mary; Tappen, James; Tappen, Mrs. Anna; Heaton, James; Street, Sarah; Todd, Samuel, Sr.; Bradley, Mary; Mansfield, Joseph; Potter, Mary; Thomas, John; Parker, Lydia; Cooper, John; Thompson, Mary; Smith, Thomas; Patterson, Elizabeth;

Holbrook, Chandler, Phebe, and Joseph: Holbrook, Peter; Godfrey, Alice; Chapin, Josiah; Brown, Lydia; Fisher, John; Metcalf, Mary; Rockwood, Benjamin; Ellis, Judith; Bobet [Babbitt?], Edward; Tisdale, Abigail; Cooper, Timothy; Whitman, Elizabeth; Marcy, John; Hadlock, Sarah; Morris, Samuel; Mayo, Mehitable; Morton, Abraham; Kellogg, Sarah; Waite, Jeremiah; Graves, Mary; Dexter, Benjamin; Arnold, Sarah; Clark, John; Tobey, Mary; Langford, Thomas; Holderbee, Comfort; Northup, Joseph; Smith, Hopestill; Sanford, Samuel; Nathaniel, Esther; Clark, Joseph; Parker, Mary;

Holman, James Sawyer and Joshua Sawyer: Holman, Jeremy; Pratt, Mercy; Tarbell, Thomas; Knight, Jonathan; Wright, Ruth; Butterick, Samuel; Blood, Elizabeth; Farr, Stephen; Taylor, Mary; Stone, Simon; Farnsworth, Sarrah; Sawyer, Thomas; Lewis, Hannah; Houghton, John; Farrar, Mary; Sawyer, James; Marble, Mary; George, Joshua; George, Mrs. Elizabeth;

Houghton, Ornon: Houghton, John; Walker, Beatrix; Farrar, Jacob; Farrar, Mrs. Ann; White, John; West, Joane; Rice, Thomas; King, Mary; Houghton, John; Walker, Beatrix; Burbeen, John Duke; Gould, Sarah; Jones, Samuel; Potter, Elizabeth; Hall, Richard; Hall, Mrs. Sarah; Chapman, William; Smith, Elizabeth;

Hubbard, Marshall Moore: Hobart, Caleb; Faxon, Elizabeth; Newcomb, Peter; Cutting, Susanna; Copeland, John; Newcomb, Ruth; Moore, Benjamin; Wright, Dorothy; Rice, John; Stone, Tabitha; Gibbs, John; Cutler, Sarah; Parmenter, Joseph; Gibbs, Mary; Powers, William; Bank, Mary; Perham, John; Fletcher, Lydia; Pierce, Stephen; Parker, Tabitha; Fletcher, Mr.;

Hulet, Sylvester and Charles: Howlet, John; Powell, Michael; Bedle, Abigail; Newton, Richard; Loker, Anne; Larkin, Edward; Hale, Joanna; Evans, Richard; Evans, Mrs. Rebecca; Hathorne, John; Breed, Sarah; Gott, Daniel; Morice [Morrice?], Mary;

Hunter, Edward: Maris, John; Lewis, Susannah; Massey, Thomas; Taylor, Phebe; Owen, Robert; Owen, Rebecca; Maris, George; Maddock, Jane; Hunter, John; Hunter, Mrs. Ann; Albin, James; Albin, Mrs. Margaret; Woodward, Richard; Nye, Jane; Edge, John; Edge, Mrs. Jane;

Hutchins, Elias: Hutchins, Mathew; Hutchins, Mrs. Mathew; Southwick, Lawrence; Buffum, Cassandra; Follett, Robert William; Black, Persis; Stowell, Samuel, Sr.; Farrow, Mary; Fuller, Samuel; Fuller, Anne; Cheney, Daniel, I; Bailey, Sarah; Wiswall, Noah; Jackson, Theodocia; Page, John; Dunster, Faith; Lawrence, Nathaniel; Morse, Sarah; Boynton, Joseph; Swan, Sara; Jewett, Joseph; Law, Rebecca;

Hyatt, Olive: Hoit [Hoyt?], Thomas; Russell, Elizabeth; St. John, Mark; Seeley, Elizabeth; Smith, Henry; Gorges, Hannah; Marvin, Matthew; Bouton, Alice Kellogg; Whitney, Henry; Whitney, Mrs. Henry; Smith, Richard; Northrup, Joseph; Norton, Mary; Haughton, Robert; Phippen, Sarah;

Hyde, Heman Tilton: Hide, John; Rumsey, Rachel; Perry, Arthur; Judson, Anna; Clark, Ephraim; Belding, Hester; Loring, Nehemiah; Cunningham, Elizabeth; Pennock, Samuel; Wilson, Mary; Bordman, Samuel; Cadwell, Mehitabel; Seeley, John; Benjamin, Martha; Bartlett, Josiah; Tilton, Daniel; Sanborn, Mehitabel; Page, Francis; Smith, Meribah; Flanders, Stephen; Carter, Abigail; Smith, Richard; Smith, Mrs. Elizabeth;

Hyde, Orson: Hide, John; Harvey, Elizabeth; Rumsey, Robert; Frost, Rachel; Perry, Arthur; Crow, Elizabeth; Judson, Joshua; Tuttle, Anne; Bouton, Joseph; Gregory, Mary; Raymond, Samuel; Palmer, Judith; Fitch, Thomas; Lane, Elizabeth;

Ingersol, Hannah and Peter: Ingersol, John; Bascom, Abigail; Ashley, David; Glover, Hannah;

Ivie, James Russell: Aldridge, William; Fallin, Alice; Hamilton, James;

Jackman, Levi: Jackman, James, Sr.; James, Joanna; Plumer, Samuel; Bidfield, Mary; French, Joseph; Stacy, Susanna; Jackman, James, Sr.; James, Joanna; Merrill, Daniel; Clough, Sarah; Allen, John; Getchell, Samuel; Jones, Elizabeth; Carr, George; Oliver, Elizabeth; Greeley, Philip; Ilsley, Sarah; Walker, Shubael; Jewett, Patience; Stevens, Benjamin; Barnard, Hannah; Greeley, Philip; Ilsley, Sarah;

Johnson, Alice, John, Jr., Luke Samuel, Lyman E., and Nancy Marinda: Johnson, John; Ward, Deborah; Lamb, Joshua; Alcock, Mary; Richardson, Nathaniel; Peacock, Mary; Green, Samuel; Upham, Elizabeth; Higgins, Jonathan; Rogers, Elizabeth; Collins, Joseph; Knowles, Ruth; Doane, John; Bangs, Hannah; Horton, John; Horton, Mrs. Hannah; Jacob, John; Russell, Mary; Allen, Samuel; Walley, Hannah; Wilson, John; James, Hannah; Willson, Jonathan; Beal, William; Trafton, Jane; Wood, Samuel; Davis, Mary; Crowell, John; Crowell, Mrs. Margaret; Allen, Samuel; Williams, Abigail;

Johnson, Almera Woodard, David, Delcena D., Joel Hills, Julia Ann, Nancy Maria, Seth Garnzey, and Susan Ellen: Johnson, Jonathan; Newton, Mary; Rider, William; Lovett, Hannah; Thayer, Isaac; Ward, Mercy; Thayer, Josiah; Bass, Sarah; Garnsey, John; Titus, Elizabeth; Millard, Nathaniel; Gladding, Susanna; Lee, Richard; Edwards, Sarah; Millard, Ephraim; White, Experience; Hills, Samuel; Hills, Mrs. Sarah; Metcalf, Eleazur; Fisher, Meletiah; Fisher, Cornelius; Whitney, Anna; Mann, Samuel; Ware, Esther; Ellis, John, II; Herring, Mary; Partridge, Eleazer; Smith, Elizabeth; Colburn, Samuel; Partridge, Mary;

Johnson, Ezekiel: Johnson, William; Story, Elizabeth; Newton, Richard; Loker, Anne; Rider, Thomas; Lane, Elizabeth; Lovett, Daniel; Blott, Joanna; Thayer, Ferdinando; Hayward, Huldah; Ward, John; Jackson, Hannah; Thayer, Ferdinando; Hayward, Huldah; Bass, Thomas; Wood, Sarah; Garnsey, Henry; Munnings, Hannah; Titus, John; Miller, Sarah; Millard, Robert; Sabin, Elizabeth; Gladding, John; Rodgers, Elizabeth; Lee, Thomas; Lee, Mrs. Alice; Edwards, Rice; Edwards, Mrs. Elnor; Millard, Robert; Sabin, Elizabeth; White, Joseph; Rogers, Lydia;

Johnson, John, Sr.: Johnson, Solomon; Crafts, Eleanor; Ward, William; Ward, Mrs. Elizabeth; Lamb, Thomas; Harbottle, Dorothy; Alcock, John; Palsgrave, Sarah; Richardson, Thomas; Baldwin, Mary; Greene, Thomas; Hills, Rebecca; Upham, Phineas; Wood, Ruth; Higgins, Richard; Chandler, Lydia; Rogers, Joseph; Rogers, Mrs. Hannah; Collins, Joseph; Collins. Mrs. Ann; Knowles, Richard; Bowers, Ruth; Doane, John; Doane, Mrs. Ann; Bangs, Edward; Hobart, Rebecca;

Keeler, Mary: Keeler, Ralph; Whelpley, Sarah; Rockwell, John; Weed, Elizabeth; St. John, Mathias; St. John, Mrs. Elizabeth; Comstock, Christopher; Platt, Hannah; Betts, Thomas; Betts, Mrs. Mary; Reynolds, John; Huested, Rebecca; Brinsmead, John; Carter, Mary; Kellogg, Daniel; Bouton, Bridget; Bearse, Austin A.; Hyanno, Mary; Taylor, Richard; Wheldon, Ruth; Newcomb, Andrew; Rix, Grace; Bayes, Thomas; Baker, Anna; Barrett, Moses; Smith, Anna; Spalding, Andrew; Jefes, Hannah; Warren, Jacob; Hildreth, Mary;

Kellogg, Lydia: Kellogg, Joseph; Foote, Joanna; Merrill, John; Watson, Sarah; Moore, John; Goffe, Hannah; Griswold, George; Holcomb, Mary; Spencer, Obadiah; Disbrow, Mary; Kelsey, Mark; Hoskins, Rebecca; Kellogg, Samuel; Day, Sarah; Dickenson, Nathaniel; Beardsley, Hannah; Miller, Thomas; Nettleton, Sarah; Turner, Edward; Sanford, Mary; Strong, Jedediah; Woodward, Freedom; Ingersoll, John; Bascom, Abigail; Adams, John; Pinney, Abigail;

Kellogg, Sarah: Kellog, Joseph; Terry, Abigail Martha; Boltwood, Samuel; Lewis, Sarah; Williams, Thomas; Williams, Mrs. Ann; Hitchcock, Matthias [Matthew?]; Rogers, Elizabeth; Meyrick, John; Bishop, Dorothy; Jones, Griffith; Jones, Mrs. Sarah; Graves, John; Smith, Mary; Foote, Nathaniel; Smith, Elizabeth; Bliss, Nathaniel; Chapin, Catherine; Clothier, Ambrose; Clothier, Mrs. Hanna;

Kennedy, Mary Ann: Churchhill, John; Pontus, Hannah; Hicks, Samuel; Doane, Lydia; Harlowe, William, Sr.; Bartlett, Rebecca; Cushman, Thomas; Allerton, Mary; Sylvester, Joseph, Jr.; Bartlett, Hannah;

Kent, Celia: Kent, Samuel; Woodall, Frances; Hunter, William; Corish, Priscilla; Hosford, John; Thrall, Phillipi; Austin, Richard; Austin, Elizabeth; Huggins, John; Green, Bridget; King, William; Elwill, Agnes; Fuller, John; Farrington, Elizabeth; Hanchett, John; Pritchard, Esther; Hayward, Joseph; Treadway, Elizabeth; Sheldon, Thomas; Hinsdale, Mary; Smith, John; Roote, Mary; Sheldon, Issac; Gunn, Mehitable; Southwell, William; Stebbins, Sarah; Hathaway, Abraham; Wilbor, Rebecca; Kent, John; Dudley, Abigail;

Kent, Daniel: Kent, Richard; Kent, Mrs. Emma; Griswold, Francis; Griswold, Mrs. Mary; Gannett, Matthew; Andrews, Hannah; Combs, Henry; Combs, Mrs. Elizabeth; Wheaton, Robert; Bowen, Alice; Prince, John; Honor, Alice; Beal, Jeremiah;

Ripley, Sarah; Lane, Andrew; Lane, Mrs. Triphena; Barnes, Thomas; Goodenow, Abigail; Howe, Abraham; Ward, Hannah; Gilbert, Thomas; Chapin, Catherine; Belden, Samuel; Belden, Mrs. Mary;

Killian, John: Kilian, Phillip; Lotter, Susanna;

Kimball, Heber C.: Kimball, Benjamin; Hazeltine, Mercy; Gage, Samuel; Stickney, Faith; Head, Arthur; Reynolds, Sarah; Atwood, Phillip; Tenney, Sarah; Roberts, Thomas; Downing, Susan; Hendrick, Daniel; Pike, Dorothy; Belknap, Samuel; Jones, Sarah; Ayer, Nathaniel; Turloar, Tameson; Spalding, John; Heald, Hannah; Brackett, John; French, Hannah; Cleveland, Moses; Winn, Ann; Pierce, Samuel; Pierce, Mrs. Mary; Gates, Stephen, Jr.; Woodward, Sarah; Geer, George; Allyn, Sarah; Coit, Joseph; Harris, Martha; Wheeler, Isaac; Parke, Martha;

King, Elizabeth Jane: King, William; Elwill, Agnes; Fuller, John; Emerson, Elizabeth; Hall, Samuel; White, Elizabeth; Bourne, Jonathan; Bourne, Mrs. Jonathan; Pease, John; Goodale, Mary; Adams, William; Stacy, Elizabeth; Spencer, Thomas; Bearding, Sarah; Pratt, John; Boosey, Hannah; Morgan, Miles; Gilbert, Prudence; Pease, John; Goodale, Mary; Randall, William; Randall, Mrs. Elizabeth;

King, Sarah: Kinge, James; Fuller, Elizabeth; Huxley, Thomas; Spencer, Sarah; Seymour, Richard; Woodruff, Hannah; Hollister, Stephen; Treat, Abigail; Austin, Anthony; Huggins, Esther; Hall, Samuel; Bourne, Jonathan; Winchell, Benjamin; Moore, Sarah; Coy, Mathew; Brewster, Ann; Reed, Josiah; Holloway, Grace; Amsden, Isaac; Rutter, Jane; Hall, Samuel; Bourne, Elizabeth; White, Elizabeth; Moore, Andrew; Phelps, Sarah;

Kingsbury, Joseph C.: Kingsbury, Joseph; Ayer, Love; Denison, John, Jr.; Ayer, Ruth; Loomis, Thomas; Porter, Hannah; Terry, Samuel; Boreman, Martha; Collins, Nathaniel; Adams, Alice; Kellogg, John; Moody, Sarah; Ashley, Samuel; Kellogg, Sarah; Pease, John; Cummings, Ann; Osborn, John; Eggleston, Abigail; Pease, John; Adams, Margaret; Spencer, Gerard; Pratt, Hannah;

Kingsbury, Nancy: Kingsbury, Joseph; Ayer, Love; Denison, John, Jr.; Ayer, Ruth; Smith, Edward; Bliss, Elizabeth; Abell, Joshua; Smith, Mehill; Rust, Israel; Clark, Rebecca; Atcheson, John; Atcheson, Mrs. Deliverance; Hatch, Jonathan; Rowley, Sarah; Eddy, John; Doggett, Hepzibah; Carleton, Edward; Kimball, Elizabeth; Kimball, John; Bradstreet, Mary; Ladd, Samuel; Corliss, Martha;

Knapp, Silas: Knapp, John; Young, Sarah; Park, Thomas; Dix, Abigail; Whitney, John; Reynolds, Ruth; Beach, Richard; Beach, Mrs. Martha; Bartlett, Robert; Warren, Mary; Waite, Richard; Waite, Mrs. Elizabeth; Hyde, Jonathan; French, Mary; Kidder, James; Moore, Anna; Chadwick, John; Chadwick, Mrs. Joan; Bemis, Joseph; Bemis, Mrs. Sarah; Harrington, Robert; George, Susannah; Barnard, John; Barnard, Mrs. Elizabeth; Stone, John; Bass, Sarah;

Knight, Anna, Esther, Hyruna, Joseph, Jr., Newell, and Polly: Knight, John; Bridge, Mary; Chase, Isaac; Tilton, Mary; Eames, Thomas; Blanford, Mary; Patten, Nathaniel; Adams, Rebecca; Peck, Nicholas; Bosworth, Rebecca; Cooper, Thomas, Jr.; Slye, Mary; Carder, John, Sr.; Holden, Mary; Paine, William; Reed, Daniel;

Peck, Hannah; Ide, Timothy; Cooper, Elizabeth; Robbins, William; Gowing, Priscilla; Clark, Joseph; Wight, Marie;

Knight, Joseph, Sr.: Knight, John; Knight, Mrs. Mary; Bridge, William; Pierce, Persis; Chase, Thomas; Philbrick, Elizabeth; Tilton, Thomas; Philbrick, Elizabeth;

Knight, Mary: Knight, Toward; Dimery, Alice; Buffington, Thomas; Buffington, Mrs. Ann;

Knight, Vinson: Knight, David; Backus, Sarah; Crane, Jonanthan; Griswold, Debra; Hutchins, John; Whitney, Abigail; Bushnell, Joseph; Leffingwell, Mary; Elderkin, John; Fowler, Abigail; Lee, John; Smith, Elizabeth; Waterman, Thomas; Allyn, Elizabeth; Griswold, Samuel; Huntington, Susannah; Lee, Joseph; Woodia, Mary; Heywood, John; Blodgett, Sarah; Morse, Samuel; Morse, Mrs. Grace; Newton, Daniel; Morse, Sussana; Miles, John; Goodenow, Susanna; Foster, Samuel; Keyes, Sarah; Lee, Joseph; Woodia, Mary; Heywood, John; Blodgett, Sarah;

Lake, James, Jr.: Lake, John; Spicer, Anne; Smit, Claes Claeszen; Willekens, Geertruyd; Hendrickson, Jan; Bastianese, Annetje; Mynderts, Korten; Pia, Marye Maria; Hegeman, Adrian; Margits, Catherine; Dollen, John; Gridley, Miss; de Mont, Wallerand; Hendricks, Marguarite; van Huysen, Jan P.; Jans, Grietje; Prat, Pierre; Philippe, Marie;

Lamoreaux, Andrew Losee: Masse, Daniel; Masse, Mrs. Daniel; Mersereau, Jean; Dubois, Elizabeth; Pearsall, Daniel; Bassett, Emma;

Lampson, Nancy: Lampson, Joseph; Rice, Elizabeth; Adams, James; Ramesden, Prescilla; Bliss, Samuel; Cadwell, Thomas; Lampson, Joseph; Stebbins, Elizabeth; Loomis, Nathaniel; Moore, Elizabeth; Rice, Elizabeth; Rockwell, Samuel; Norton, Mary; Gleason, Joseph; Russell, Martha; Adams, James; Livermore, John; Sherman, Grace; Noyes, Joseph; Darvill, Mary; Ramesden, Priscilla

Lathrop, Lois: Lathrop, Samuel; Scudder, Elizabeth; Bliss, Thomas; Birchard, Elizabeth; Waterman, Thomas; Tracy, Miriam; Allyn, John; Gager, Elizabeth; Huntington, Christopher; Rockwell, Ruth; Adgate, Thomas; Marvin, Marie; Gifford, Stephen; Gore, Hannah; Caulkins [Calkins?], John; Royce, Sarah; Hyde, Samuel, Sr.; Lee, Jane; Abell, Caleb; Post, Margaret;

Lathrop, Lydia: Lathrop, John; Howse, Hannah; Scudder, Thomas; Lowers, Elizabeth; Bliss, Thomas; Hulins, Margaret; Birchard, Thomas; Robinson, Mary; Otis, John, I; Otis, Mrs. Margaret; Jacob, Nicholas; Gilman, Mary; Thomas, Nathaniel; Thomas, Mrs. Mary; Pike, James; Pike, Mrs. Naomi; Cutler, Samuel; Cutler, Mrs. Elizabeth; Clothier, Ambrose; Clothier, Mrs. Hanna; Brown, Peter; Foorde, Martha; Gylette, Jonathan; Dolbere, Mary;

Le Baron, David: Pecton, Louis; Wilder, Edward; Eames, Elizabeth; Benson, John, Jr.; Marsh, Elizabeth; Briggs, Samuel; Ellis, Elizabeth; Chatfield, George; Nettleton, Isabel; Kelsey, John; Disborough, Hannah; Crane, Henry; Meigs, Concurrence; Kinge, James; Fuller, Elizabeth; Hall, Samuel; Bowine, Elizabeth; Ould, Robert; Granger, Dorothy;

Littlefield, Waldo: Littlefield, Edmund; Littlefield, Mrs. Edmund; Waldo, Daniel;

Adams, Susanna; Williams, Benjamin; Macey, Rebecca; Howard, Ephraim; Keith, Mary; Cole, Hugh; Foxwell, Mary; Gray, Edward; Lettice, Dorothy; Stephens, Edward; Churchill, Eleazer; Gardner, Thomas; Porter, Mary; Orne, Bejamine; Orne, Mrs. Sarah; Ingersoll, Samuel; Ingersoll, Mrs. Sarah;

Lowell, Olive: Lowell, John; Goodale, Elizabeth; Woodman, Edward; Salway, Joanna; Davis, John; Davis, Mrs. Elinor; Carter, Thomas E.; Dalton, Mary E.; Bradbury, William; Wheelwright, Rebecca; Cotton, John, Jr.; Rossiter, Joanna; Greeley, Andrew; Moyse, Mary; Wilford, Gilbert; Dow, Mary;

Lyman, Amasa Mason: Lyman, Richard; Cowles, Elizabeth; Woodward, John; Dewey, Ann; Strong, Joseph; Allen, Sarah; Parker, Thomas; Griswald, Samuel; Huntington, Susannah; Sanders, John; Thompson, Susannah; Hewett, Soloman; Waterman, Sarah; Gifford, Samuel; Calkins, Mary; Mason, Sampson; Butterworth, Mary; Brooks, Timothy; Russell, Mary; Ormsby, Thomas; Fitch, Mary; Salisbury, Samuel; Brooks, Mary; Barney, Joseph; Davis, Constance; Martin, John; Hayward, Marcy; Martin, Ephraim; Bullock, Thankful; Washburn, Jonathan; Vaughn, Mary;

Lyman, Asa: Lyman, Richard; Ford, Hepzibah; Cole, John; Hart, Hannah; Woodward, Henry; Woodward, Mrs. Elizabeth; Dewey, Mr.; Dewey, Mrs.; Strong, Thomas; Holton, Rachel; Allen, Nehemiah; Woodford, Sarah; Loomis, Nathaniel; Moore, Elizabeth; Rockwell, Samuel; Norton, Mary; Warner, Andrew; Warner, Mrs. Mary; Boltwood, Robert; Gernor, Mary; Huntington, Christopher; Rockwell, Ruth; Backus, William, Jr.; Pratt, Elizabeth; Bassett, Nathaniel; Joyce, Dorcas; Borden, John; Hough, Hannah;

Mack, Almira: Bagley, Orlando; Colby, Sarah; Huntley, Aaron; Champion, Mary; de Wolf, Stephen; Jones, Hannah; Gates, George; Olmstead, Sarah; Dutton, Joseph; Merriam, Rebecca; Fuller, John; Rowley, Mehitable; Crocker, Jonathoa; Howland, Hannah;

Mack, Lucy: Colby, Anthony; Colby, Mrs. Susanna; Huntley, John; Huntley, Mrs. Jane; Champion, Henry; Champion, Mrs. Sarah; de Wolf, Balthazar; de Wolf, Mrs. Alice; Jones, Lewis; Palmer, Deborah; Olmstead, N.; Loomis, Sarah; Dutton, Thomas; Dutton, Mrs. Susanna; Merriam, William, Sr.; Breed, Elizabeth; Fuller, Samuel; Lathrop, Jane; Rowley, Moses, Sr.; Fuller, Elizabeth; Crocker, John; Bodfish, Mary; Howland, John, Jr.; Lee, Mary;

Marsh, Ann and Thomas B.: Marsh, John; Marsh, Mrs. Sarah; Hartshorn, Thomas; Buck, Susanna; Marsh, John; Marsh, Mrs. Sarah; Partridge, William; Colburn, Sarah; Wight, Ephraim; Morse, Lydia;

Marsh, Editha: Marsh, John; Baldwin, Grace; Webster, John; Smith, Agnes; Ellison, Lawrence; Ellison, Mrs. Lawrence; Gylette, Jonathan; Dolbere, Mary; Hawkes, John; Hawkes, Mrs. Elizabeth; Gull, Thomas; Gull, Mrs. Margaret; Smith, Samuel; Chileab, Elizabeth; Trumbull, James; Straker, Janet; Chandler, John;

McBride, James, Martha, Reuben, Samuel, Abigail, and Margaret: Mead, John; Hardy, Ruth; Butler, Walter; Reynolds, Rebecca; Friske, William; Kilham, Sarah; Brown, Josiah; Fellows, Mary; Mead, John; Potter, Hannah; Leone, Mr.; Leone, Mrs.;

Mead, Abigail: Mead, John; Potter, Hannah; Hardy, Richard; Husted, Anne; Butler, Evan; Penoyer, Johane; Reynolds, John; Huested, Rebecca; Fiske, William; Muskett, Bridgett; Kilham, Austin; Gorball, Alice; Brown, Nicholas; Leids, Elizabeth; Fellows, William; Ayer, Mary;

Mead, Betsy: Mead, John; Hardy, Ruth; Butler, Walter; Reynolds, Rebecca; Mead, John; Hardy, Ruth; Butler, Walter; Reynolds, Rebecca; Newcomb, Simon; Newcomb, Mrs. Deborah; Woodworth, Benjamin; Damon, Hannah; Dennard, John; Spencer, Rebecca;

Merriam, Edwin Parker: Royce, Samuel; Churchill, Hannah; Benedict, Thomas; Messenger, Mary; Scoville, John; Barnes, Sarah; Richards, Obadiah; Andrus, Hannah; Baldwin, Jonathan; Ward, Hannah;

Miles, Daniel Sanborn: Mills, Samuel; Pimbrook, Frances; Heath, Bartholomew; Moyce, Hannah; Davis, John; Linnell, Hannah; Sanborn, Richard; Moulton, Ruth; Philbrick, James; Perkins, Hannah; Rawlins, Thomas; Coxe, Rachel; Lawrence, David; Taylor, Mary; Swett, Banjamin; Weare, Esther; Dow, Henry; Page, Hannah; Shaw, Benjamin; Richardson, Esther;

Miller, Eleazer: Bradway, Edward; Bradway, Mrs. Mary; White, Christopher; Angell, John; Field, Ruth; Winsor, Samuel; Williams, Mercy;

Miller, Mary Thompson: Primblecomb, Philip;

Millett, Artemas: Millett, Thomas; Greenoway, Mary; Lester, Andrew; Lester, Mrs. Barbara; Batchelder, John; Batchelder, Mrs. Mary; Goodale, Richard; Killiam, Catherine; Morgan, Robert; Norman, Margaret; Dixey, John; Allen, Elizabeth;

Miner, Albert: Miner, Clement; Burcham, Frances; Beckwith, Joseph; Tallman, Susanna; Willey, John; Harvey, Elizabeth; Munson, Samuel; Farnes, Martha; Merriman, Caleb; Preston, Mary; Cruttenden, Abraham; Kirby, Susannah; Sutliff, Nathaniel; Savage, Sarah;

Morley, Lucy Diantha: Morley, Thomas; Wright, Martha; Wickham, William; Churchill, Sarah; Wood, Solomon; Haseltine, Mary; Webster, Jonathan; Judd, Ester [Esther?]; Marsh, Samuel; Ellison, Mary; Gillett, Joseph; Gull, Esther; Trumble, Judah; Trumble, Mrs. Mary; Gunn, Samuel; Wyatt, Elizabeth Bronson; Belding, Stephen; Wells, Mary; Gunn, Nathaniel; Day, Sarah; Wyatt, John; Brownson, Mary; Root, Joseph; Root, Mrs. Hannah; Russell, Phillip; Church, Mary;

Morley, Diantha, Horace, and Isaac: Morley, Marmaduke; Brewer, Mary; Wright, Abel; Kitcherel, Martha; Wickham, Thomas; Wickham, Mrs. Sarah; Churchill, Josiah; Foote, Elizabeth; Marsh, John; Webster, Anne; Ellison, Richard; Ellison, Mrs. Thomasina; Gillett, Joseph; Hawks, Elizabeth; Gull, William; Smith, Elizabeth; Wood, Thomas; Hunt, Ann; Haseltine, Abraham; Longhorne, Elizabeth; Webster, Jonathan; Hopkins, Dorcas; Judd, Benjamin; Lewis, Mary; Marsh, John; Webster, Anne; Ellison, Richard; Ellison, Mrs. Thomasina; Trumble, John; Chandler, Elinor;

Morley, Thomas: Morley, Thomas; Dolman, Mary; Brewer, Thomas; Wright, John; Richall, Jane; Ketcherel, Samuel; Chapman, Martha; Wickham, Thomas; Wickham, Mrs. Thomas; Churchill, Josiah; Churchill, Mrs. Josiah; Foote, Nathaniel; Deming, Elizabeth; Wood, Edward; Mousall, Ruth; Hunt, Enos; Hunt, Mrs. Enos; Hazeltine, Robert; Hazeltine, Mrs. Anna; Longhorne, Nicholas; Crosby, Mary; Webster, Robert; Treat, Susannah; Hopkins, Stephen; Brownson, Dorcas; Judd, Thomas; Lewis, William; Hopkins, Mary;

Morrill, Laban: Morrill, Jacob; Whittier, Susanna; Wadleigh, John; Marston, Abigail; Morrill, Isaac; Gill, Phoebe; Sargent, William; Colby, Mary; Carpenter, Joseph; Sutton, Margaret; Weekes, William; Atherton, Elizabeth; Loomis, Nathaniel; Moore, Elizabeth; Graves, Mitchel George; Mitchell, Mrs. Elizabeth;

Morse, Justus: Montague, John; Smith, Hannah; Benton, Samuel; Chatterton, Sarah; Adkins, Josiah; Whitmore, Mrs. E.; Whitmore, Thomas, Sr.; Hubbard, Elizabeth; Clark, Samuel; Tuttle, Hannah; Bassett, John; Todd, Mercy;

Morton, Phebe Ann: Morton, Richard; Morton, Mrs. Ruth; Kellogg, Samuel; Root, Sarah; Waite, Benjamin; Leonard, Martha; Graves, John; White, Sarah; Dexter, William; Vincent, Sarah; Arnold, Samuel; Holmes, Sarah; Clark, John; Smith, Sarah; Tobey, John; Tobey, Mrs. Jane; Langford, Thomas; Cook, Mary; Holderbee, Joseph; Holderbee, Mrs. Elizabeth; Northup, Stephen; Harrington, Elizabeth; Smith, John; Gereardy, Phillis; Sanford, Thomas; Payne, Elizabeth; Clark, Samuel; Tuttle, Hannah; Parker, John; Bassett, Hannah;

Moses, Julian: Moses, John, II; Brown, Mary; Thrall, Timothy; Gunn, Deborah; Brown, Joshua; Sawyer, Sarah; Tilton, Abraham; Shaw, Deliverance; Dike, Anthony; Dike, Mrs. Margery; Baker, Cornelius; Woodbury, Hannah;

Mott, Mary: Mott, Adam; Hulet, Jane; Walcott, John; Walcott, Mrs. Mary; Wentworth, Sylvanus; Key, Mary; Armstrong, Benjamin; Raymond, Sarah; Armstrong, Benjamin; Armstrong, Mrs. Rachel; Dewey, Thomas; Dewey, Mrs. Abigail; Mosely, Consider; Bancroft, Elizabeth;

Murray, Roswell and Vilate: Bradley, Nathan; Griswold, Hester; Way, George; Nest, Susannah; Sprague, John; Goffe, Lydia; Gould, John; Baker, Sarah; Stone, Daniel; Goodwin, Patience;

Myers, Angeline: Meyer, Adolph; Verveelen, Maria; Waldron, Johannes; van Dalsen, Anna; Rogers, Jonathan; Wicks, Rebecca; Scudder, Thomas; Ludlam, Mary; Wiltsee, Martin Hendricksen; Vanwyck, Maritje; Smith, Jermiah; Cornell, Anne;

Nash, Anna: Noyes, John; Poor, Mary; Poor, Henry; Hale, Abigail;

Nelson, David: Nelson, Thomas; Lambert, Ann; French, Samuel; Brown, Abigail; Batcheler, John; Goodale, Sarah; Stone, Samuel; Stearns, Sarah; Brown, Jonathan; Shattuck, Mary; Garfield, Benjamin; Bridge, Elizabeth; Goddard, William; Miles, Elizabeth; Stone, Simon; Whipple, Mary;

Nickerson, Caroline Eliza, Elezer Freeman, Levi Stillman, Moses Chapman, and Uriel Chittendon Hatch: Nickerson, Nicholas; Derby, Mary; Baker, John; Pierce, Alice; Bearse, Joseph; Taylor, Martha; Cobb, Samuel; Taylor, Elizabeth; Chase, John; Baker, Elizabeth; Gowell, Richard; Remick, Hannah; Berry, Samuel; Bell, Elizabeth; Gray, William; Dillingham, Rebecca; Chapman, Simon; Brewer, Mary; Wentworth, Paul; Steward, Catherine; Chase, John; Baker, Elizabeth; Gowell, Richard; Remick, Hannah; Berry, Samuel; Bell, Elizabeth; Gray, William; Dillingham, Rebecca;

Nickerson, Freeman: Nickerson, William; Busby, Anne; Derby, John; Derby, Mrs.

Alice; Baker, Francis; Twining, Isabel; Pierce, Abraham; Pierce, Mrs. Rebecca; Bearse, Austin A.; Hyanno, Mary; Taylor, Richard; Wheldon, Ruth; Cobb, Henry; Hinkley, Sarah; Taylor, Richard; Wheldon, Ruth; Chase, William, Jr.; Holder, Elizabeth; Baker, Francis,; Twining, Isabel; Gowell, Mr.; Remick, Christian; Remick, Mrs. Hannah; Berry, Richard; Berry, Mrs. Alice; Bell, John; Bell, Mrs. John; Gray, John; Lumpkin, Hannah; Dillingham, John; Feacke, Elizabeth;

Noble, Joseph Bates: Noble, Thomas; Warriner, Hannah; Dewey, Thomas, II; Hawes, Constance; Callendar, John; Callendar, Mrs. Elizabeth; Eaton, Jonas; Mason, Hannah; Eggleston, Samuel; Payne, Patience; Deming, Ebenezer; Grant, Sarah; Steele, James; Welles, Anna; Kellogg, Martin; Hinsdale, Anna; Chester, Stephen, Jr.; Treat, Jemima;

Norton, Clarissa: Welton, John; Upson, Mary; Upson, Stephen; Lee, Mary; Sutcliffe, Nathaniel; Plympton, Hannah; Brockett, Benjamin; Barnes, Elizabeth;

Osgood, Levi: Osgood, John; Booth, Sarah; Hooker, Richard; Woodman, Edward; Salway, Joanna; Stevens, John S.; Parker, Elizabeth; White, John; West, Joane; Rice, Thomas; King, Mary; Wilder, Thomas; Eames, Hannah [Anna?]; Sawyer, Thomas; Prescott, Mary;

Packard, Noah: Packard, Samuel; Stream, Elizabeth; Howard, John; Hayward, Martha; Alden, Joseph; Simmons, Mary; Allen, Samuel, Sr.; Partridge, Sarah; Richards, Joseph; Richards, Mrs. Susan; Ford, Andrew, Jr.; Pierce, Abiah; Whitmarsh, Ebenezer; Baley, Christian; Hamblin, James; Dunham, Mary; Sears, Paul; Willard, Deborah; Mayo, Nathaniel; Prence, Hannah; Hopkins, Giles; Wheldon, Catherine [Catone?]; Shaw, John; Phillips, Alice;

Page, Ebenezer and John Edward: Linsley, John; Ware, Sarah; Johnson, Nathaniel; Smith, Mary; Hoadley, William; Hoadley, Mrs. Mary; Pollard, William; Farmer, Mary; Farmer, Edward; Farmer, Mrs. Mary; Danforth, Jonathan; Parker, Rebecca; Shed, John; Chamberlain, Sarah;

Parker, Mary: Parker, John; Bassett, Hannah; Curtiss, Thomas; Merriman, Mary; Barnes, Thomas; Barnes, Mrs. Mary; Leek, Thomas; Hitcheson, Sarah; Hitchcock, John; Merriman, Abigail; Andrews, William; Parker, Hannah; Parker, John; Bassett, Hannah; Beach, John, Jr.; Royce, Mary; Hull, John; Kelsey, Abigail; Hull, Thomas; Sheather, Hannah; Crane, Henry; Meigs, Concurrence; Doggett, Thomas; Mayhew, Hannah; Parmelee, Nathaniel; French, Sarah; Kelsey, John; Disborough, Hannah; Hull, Josiah; Loomis, Elizabeth; Sheather, John; Sheather, Mrs. Susanna;

Parker, Mary Lovisa: Parker, Edward; Wood, Elizabeth; Bassett, William; Dickerman, Hannah; Kibbe, Edward; Partridge, Mary; Cook, Henry; Birdsall, Judith; Beach, John; Staples, Mary; Wilcoxson, Timothy; Birdseye, Joanna; Cook, Henry; Birdsall, Judith; Hall, John; Woolen, Jeanne; Parker, Edward; Wood, Elizabeth; Bassett, William; Dickerman, Hannah; Beach, John; Staples, Mary; Royce, Johnathan; Spinning, Mary; Blakesley, Samuel; Potter, Hannah; Lupton, Thomas; Morris, Hannah; Doolittle, Abraham; Moss, Abigail; Cornwell, John; Peck, Martha;

Partridge, Edward, Sr.: Partridge, William; Smith, Mary; Crow, John; Goodwin, Elizabeth; Williams, Isaac; Parke, Martha; Cotton, Seaborn; Bradstreet, Dorothy; Williams, Isaac; Parke, Martha; Cotton, Seaborn; Bradstreet, Dorothy; Stoddard, Anthony; Downing, Mary; Warham, John; Dabinott, Jane; Bidwell, John; Wilcox, Sarah; Scott, Edmund; Scott, Mrs. Mary; Webster, John; Devotion, Edward; Curtis, Mary; Pond, Daniel; Shepard, Abigail; Taylor, John; Holt, Rhoda; Wyllys, Samuel; Haynes, Ruth;

Patten, Archibald, David Wyman, Elizabeth, Ira J., John M., and Polly: Patten, Nathaniel; Adams, Rebecca; Luxford, Rueben; Luxford, Mrs. Margaret; Pomeroy, Joshua; Lyman, Elizabeth; Weeks, Joseph; Atherton, Mary; Makepeace, William; Johnson, Ann; Tisdale, John; Walker, Sara; Aldrich, John; Thayer, Huldah; Cook, Samuel, Sr.; White, Lydia; Cole, John; Cole, Mrs. Ann; Weeden, Edward; Cole, Elizabeth; Brown, Jonathan; Shattuck, Mary; Davis, Samuel, Sr.; Meaddows, Mary;

Pearce, Keziah: Wilbor, William; Holmes, Martha; Potter, Nathaniel; Stokes, Elizabeth;

Peck, Ann Eliza, Martin Horton, Nancy F., and Sally Ann: Peck, John; Peck, Mrs. Hannah; Smith, Daniel; Chickering, Esther; Whitaker, Richard; Cooper, Rebecca; Williams, Seth; Dean, Mary; Barney, John; Throop, Mary; Horton, Thomas; Harmon, Sarah; Garnsey, John; Titus, Elizabeth; Millard, Robert; Sabin, Elizabeth; Gladding, John; Rodgers, Elizabeth; Brayton, Francis; Fish, Mary; Butts, Zacheus; Conklin, Sarah; Wheaton, John; Carpenter, Elizabeth; Slade, William; Holmes, Sarah;

Peck, Berthena, Esther, Ezekiel, Hezekiah, Nicholas, and Polly: Peck, Joseph; Burwell, Alice; Camp, Nicholas; Beard, Sarah; Ford, Timothy; Knowls, Elizabeth; Fitch, Thomas; Clarke, Ruth; Smith, Ephraim; Briscoe, Abigail; Clark, George; Gold, Deborah; Cooley, Samuel; Curtis, Mary; Peck, Joseph; Burwell, Alice; Baldwin, Joseph; Whitlock, Hannah; Stream, John; Beard, Martha;

Perry, Asahel: Perry, Anthony; Perry, Mrs. Elizabeth; Miller, John; Wilmarth, Thomas; Bliss, Elizabeth; Peck, John; Hunting, Elizabeth; Fisher, Daniel; Hill, Hannah; Eddy, John; Owen, Deliverence; Lane, Andrew; Lane, Mrs. Triphena; Briggs, William; Macomber, Sarah; Wolcott, William; Ingersoll, Alice; Sibley, John; Leach, Rachel; Bailey, John; Emery, Eleanor; Putnam, John; Prence, Rebecca; Abbott, George; Weed, Mary; Ruscoe, John; Beebe, Rebecca;

Perry, Hiram, Isaac, and William Chadwick: Perry, Samuel; Miller, Mary; Wilmarth, Jonathan; Peck, Esther; Fisher, Eliezer; Eddy, Hannah; Lane, John; Briggs, Sarah; Walcott, Jonathan; Sibley, Mary; Bailey, Joseph; Putnam, Priscilla; Jackson, Jedidah; Abbott, John; Ruscoe, Ruth; Chadwick, John; Manning, Sarah; Brewer, John; Jones, Mary; Merriam, Robert; Cutler, Abigail; Allen, Joseph; Wight, Miriam;

Pettigrew, David: Hardy, Thomas; Hardy, Mrs. Lydia; Jackman, James, Sr.; James, Joanna; Hardy, John; Jackman, Mary; Burbank, Caleb; Smith, Martha;

Phelps, Charles Morris: Phelps, Nathaniel; Martin, Grace; Burnham, William; Loomis, Elizabeth; Parsons, Joseph; Strong, Elizabeth; Sheldon, Isaac; Warner, Sarah; Miller, Ebenezer; Keep, Hannah; Bush, Ebenezer; Bush, Mrs. Miriam; Noble, Mark; Marshall, Mercy;

Phelps, William Wines: Phelps, Timothy; Griswold, Mary; Crow, Christopher; Burr, Mary; Dyer, Samuel; Hutchinson, Anne;

Pickle, Magdalena: Wagner, Hans; Wagner, Mrs. Hans; Geissig, Wilhelm; Geissig, Mrs. Anna Margretha;

Pierce, Isaac Washington, Sr.: Pierce, Ephraim; Low, Mary; Round, John; Round, Mrs. Elizabeth; Martin, John; Esten, Joanna; Brooks, Timothy; Russell, Mary; Hicks, Daniel; Hammer, Rebecca; Edmunds, Andrew; Hearnden, Mary; Luther, Samuel; Abel, Mabel; Shepardsen, Joannah; Taylor, William; Merriam, Mary;

Pitkin, George White: Pitkin, William, III; Goodwin, Hannah; Stanley, Caleb; Cowles, Hannah; Welles, Samuel; Hollister, Elizabeth; Judson, Joshua; Porter, Sarah; White, Domingo; Crow, Sarah; Bissell, Thomas; Moore, Abigail; Hunt, Jonathan; Hosmer, Clemence; Williams, Samuel; Parke, Theoda; Lathrop, Samuel; Scudder, Elizabeth; Bliss, Thomas; Birchard, Elizabeth; Baker, Samuel; Robinson, Fear; Annabel, Samuel; Allyn, Mehitable; King, Philip; Whitman, Judith; Deane, Isaac; Leonard, Hannah;

Plumbley, Patty: Plumly, Alexander; Plumly, Mrs. Esther [Hester?]; Drewe, William; Churchill, John; Pontus, Hannah;

Porter, Sanford: Porter, John; White, Anna; Hart, Stephen; Stanley, John; Lancocke, Susan; Morrice, Timothy; Sanford, Thomas; Meadows, Sarah; Paine, Thomas; Ware, Rebecca; Beach, Richard; Cook, Catherine; West, Matthew; Tanner, Francis; Tanner, Mrs. Francis; Badcock, John; Crandall, Jane; Bailey, William; Parsons, Grace;

Pratt, Anson, Orson, Parley Parker, and William Dickinson: Pratt, John, Jr.; Parker, Margaret; Hough, William; Lathrop, Anne; Pratt, Samuel; Peck, Elizabeth; Chalker, Abraham; Barber, Deborah; Tolls [Tolles?], Henry; Tolls [Tolles?], Mrs. Sarah; Thomas, Daniel; Thompson, Rebecca; Sperry, Nathaniel; Dickerman, Sarah; Wilmot, John; Clark, Sarah; Dickinson, Charles; Greene, Phillippa; Cole, William; Pinder, Ann; Griffith, Stephen, Sr.; Ryder, Rebecca; Norcross, Richard; Sanders, Hannah;

Pulsipher, Daniel, Elias, Iona Almira, and Mariah: Pulsipher, Benedictus; Waters, Susanna A.; Stowell, David; Stedman, Mary; Harrington, John; Winter, Hannah; Dutton, Thomas; Brabrooke, Rebecca; Burge, John; Thayer, Tryall; Hill, Jonathan; Hartwell, Mary; Page, Nathaniel; Page, Mrs. Joanna;

Pulsipher, Zerah: Pulsipher, Benjamin; Waters, Richard; Plaise, Joyce; Stowell, Samuel; Farrow, Mary; Stedman, Nathaniel; Wills, Temperance; Harrington, Robert; George, Susannah; Winters, John, Jr.; Winters, Mrs. Hannah; Dutton, Thomas; Dutton, Mrs. Susannah; Brabrook, John; Brabrook, Mrs. Elizabeth; Burge, John; Upham, Rebecca; Thayer, Shadrach; Barnett, Mary; Hartwell, William; Hartwell, Mrs. Jasan; Page, Richard; Whitecliffe, Elmira; Hill, Ralph; Hill, Mrs. Margaret;

Putnam, Betsy Taylor: Putnam, Thomas; Holyoke, Ann; Carr, George; Oliver, Elizabeth; Whipple, John; Reynor, Martha; Nurse, Francis; Town, Rebecca; Smith, John; Thompson, Margaret; Mitchell, Thomas; Moulton, Mary; Atwood, Phillip; Bachelor [Batcheldor?], Rache; Taylor, Richard; Burgess, Ruth; Rice, Henry; Moore, Elizabeth; Powers, Walter; Shepard, Trial; Barrett, Joseph; Gould, Martha; Houghton, Ralph; Stowe, Jane; Sawyer, Thomas; Prescott, Mary;

Rand, Mary Thurston: Rand, John; Ault, Remembrance; Marden, John; Berry, Rachel Berry; Philbrick, James; Perkins, Hannah; Moulton, Joseph; Swain, Bethia; Sanborn, John; Coffin, Judith; Dennett, Alexander; Tetherley, Mehitable; Smith, Nicholas; Gordon, Mary; Gilman, Moses; Heard, Anne; Bean, John; Gilman, Sarah; Fifield, Jonathon; Huse, Abel; Milton, Mary; Webster, Israel; Lunt, Elizabeth; Graves, Abraham; Hayward, Anna; Perkins, James; Cox, Leah;

Rappleye, Jeremiah: Williamson, William; Wykoff, Myke Pieters; van Voorhees, Steven; Janse, Agatha; Tillier, William; Tillier, Mrs. Mary;

Rappleye, Tunis: Brinkerhoff, Abraham; Field, John; Field, Mrs. Margaret; Williamson, William; Wykoff, Myke Pieters; van Voorhees, Steven; Janse, Agatha; Tillier, William; Tillier, Mrs. Mary;

Redfield, Hanna: Redfield, James; Howe, Elizabeth; Grinnell, Daniel; Pabodie, Lideah [Lydia?]; Ward, Peter; Joye, Mary; Parmelee, Nathaniel; Kelsey, Esther;

Redfield, Zina: Redfield, William; Redfield, Mrs. Rebecca; Howe, Jeremiah; Howe, Mrs. Elizabeth; Grinnell, Daniel; Wordell, Mary; Pabodie, William; Alden, Elizabeth; Ward, Andrew, Jr.; Meigs, Tryal; Joy, Jacob; Spencer, Elizabeth; Parmelee, Nathaniel; French, Sarah; Kelsey, John; Disborough, Hannah;

Reed, Clarissa: Reed, John; Holden, Elizabeth; Pierce, Benjamin; Reed, Mary; Proctor, James; Wilson, Hannah; Byam, Abraham; Ong, Sarah; Cowdery, Nathaniel, Jr.; Parker, Elizabeth; Blanchard, Thomas; Adams, Ruth; Parker, Nathaniel; Nutting, Lydia; Bearse, Joseph; Taylor, Martha; Sissell, Isaac; Tuspaquin, Mary; Baldwin, Richard; Warrups, Anne; Waramaug, Mr.; Waramaug, Mrs.; Canfield, Jermiah; Hine, Alice; Baldwin, John; Caroline, Mercy; Roberts, Eli; Mallory, Mary; Macky, John; Thorpe, Mary;

Reed, John: Reed [Read?], Ralph; Pierce, Mary; Holden, Richard; Fosdick, Martha; Pierce, Thomas; Cole, Elizabeth; Reed [Read?], Ralph; Pierce, Mary; Proctor, Robert; Hildreth, Jane; Wilson, John; James, Hannah;

Rich, Charles C., Jane Ann, and Minerva: Rich, William; Rich, Mrs. Elizabeth; Grubb, Henry, Jr.; Perkins, Mary; Coulson, Joseph; Evans, Margaret; Wiley, Allen; Adams, Sarah; Janney, Joseph; Biles, Rebeckah;

Rich, Joseph: Rich, William; Rich, Mrs. Alice; Grubb, Henry, Sr.; Wilmuth, Mrs.; Perkins, William; Perkins, Mrs. Mary; Coulson, Thomas; Borrow, Anna; Weilly, Henry; Weilly, Mrs. Martha; Adams, Mr.; Adams, Mrs. Mary; Janney, Thomas; Heath, Margery; Biles, William; Hellard, Joannah;

Richardson, Darwin Charles: Harnden, R.; Harnden, Mrs. Mary; Jaquith, Abraham; Adford, Mary; Jones, Hugh; Foster, Mary; Kidder, Ephraim; Crosby, Rachel; Frost, James; Foster, Elizabeth;

Riggs, Burr and Harpin: Riggs, Samuel; Baldwin, Sarah; Tomlinson, Agur; Johnson, Jeremiah; Johnson, Elizabeth; Chatfield, John; Harger, Anna; Hawkins, Joseph; Holbrook, Abigail; Gunn, Jobamah; Lane, Sarah;

Riggs, Nathaniel: Riggs, Edward, III; Riggs, Mrs. Mary;

Robbins, Lewis: Robbins, William; Gowing, Priscilla; Clark, Joseph; Wight, Marie; Winch, Samuel; Gibbs, Hannah; Simons, Robert; Walden, Thomasin; Jacobs, Joseph; Lynzey, Sarah; Kidder, James; Brown, Elizabeth; Abbott, Thomas; Stewart, Sarah; Royce, John; Perigo, Sarah; Ramsden, William; Ramsden, Mrs. Mary;

Roberts, Lucina: Roberts, John; Saxton, Patience; Wilcox, Edward; Stephens, Thomasine; Beach, Isaac; Birdseye, Hannah; Moses, John, Sr.; Thrall, Deborah; Beeman [Beaman?], Samuel; Chapman, Margaret; Willcockson, William; Wilson, Elizabeth; Saxton, Richard; Buell, Hannah; Durfee, Benjamin; Earle, Prudence; Buck, Jonathan; Andrews, Mary; Felt, Samuel; Felt, Mrs. Elizabeth; Newton, Moses; Howe, Sarah; Gearfield, Joseph; Gale, Sarah; Bellows, Nathaniel; Rose, Rorcas; Johnson, Joseph; Maynard, Sarah;

Rockwell, Caroline, Orrin P., and Peter: Witt, John; Baker, Elizabeth; Dane, Philemon; Thompson, Mary;

Rolfe, Samuel Jones: Rolfe, Henry; Rolfe, Mrs. Honor; Hale, Thomas; Dowsett, Thomasine; Toppan [Topham?], Abraham; Taylor, Susannah; Sewell, Henry; Drummer, Jane; Rolfe, Benjamin; Hale, Apphia; Nelson, Thomas; Lambert, Ann; Swett, Benjamin; Weare, Esther; Page, Thomas; Hussey, Mary; Flanders, Naomi; Page, Onesiphorus; Hauxworth, Mary; Elliot, Edmund; Haddon, Sarah; Tewkesbury, Henry; Copp, Martha; Carter, John; Brown, Martha; Martyn, Richard; Hoyt, Mary;

Roundy, Shadrach and Uriah: Roundy, Robert; Plumb, Deborah; Daland, Benjamin; Hodges, Catherine; Green, William; Kendall, Hannah; Torrey, Josiah; Wilson, Sarah; Needham, Daniel Danyell; Chadwell, Ruth; Hood, Richard; Newhall, Mary; Allen, Ephraim; Curtis, Philip; Holland, Obedience;

Rust, William Walker: Rust, Nathaniel; Wardell [Wardwell?], Mary; Potter, John; Kimball, Sarah; Wallis, Samuel; Watson, Sarah; Pickard, John; Tuttle, Johanna; Walker, Samuel, Jr.; Reed, Sarah; Bruce, George; Clark, Elizabeth; Peters, Andrew; Farnham, Elizabeth; Towle, Philip; Austin, Isabella; Garland, Jacob; Sears, Rebecca; Samborn, Josiah; Moulton, Hannah;

Sagers, Maria: Seager, John; Seager, Mrs. Elizabeth; Hull, Joseph; Harper, Experience; Taylor, Abraham; Whittaker, Mary; Harris, Thomas; Harris, Mrs. Thomas; Nott, John; Miller, Patience; Sweet, John; Jeffreys, [unknown]; Griffin, Benjamin; George, Sarah; Sweet, John; Jeffreys, [unknown]; Hamilton, William; Berry, Mercy; Whitford, Pasco; Bly, Mary; Matteson, Thomas; Shippe, Mary [Martha?]; Greene, John; Allen, Mary;

Sawyer, Meritable: Sawyer, Samuel; Emery, Mary; Lilly, George; Smith, Hannah; Nurse, Francis; Town, Rebecca; Richardson, Isaac; Fuller, Deborah; Goodale, Zachariah; Beauchamp, Elizabeth; Hutchinson, Edward; Bixby, Joseph; Wyatt, Sarah; Smith, William; Fuller, Thomas; Richardson, Ruth; Goodale, Zachariah; Beauchamp, Elizabeth; Newhall, John; Farrer, Susanna; Chadwell, Thomas; Smith, Hannah;

Schellenger, Elizabeth: Johnson, Isaac; Porter, Elizabeth; Harris, Daniel; Weld, Mary; Leek, Philip; Hedd, Johanna; Hitcheson, Mr.; Hitcheson, Mrs. Agnes;

Sherman, Lyman Royal: Sherman, Samuel; Mitchell, Mary Sarah; Knowles, Thomas; Newman, Elizabeth; Hurlbut [Hurlburt?], John; Deming, Mary; Savage, John; Ranney, Mary; Belden, Samuel; Hendy, Hannah; Seymour, Zachariah; Gritt, Mary; Arnold, Josiah; Wells, Mary; Tyler, Francis; Page, Sarah;

Shumway, Otis and Stephen Billings: Chamois, Pierre; Gould, Frances; Smith, Robert; French, Mary; Pratt, Thomas; Gleason, Susanah; Gale, John H.; Spring, Elizabeth; Whitney, John; Whitney, Mrs. Elinor [Ellen?]; Bridges, Edmund; Towne, Sarah; Hastings, Thomas; Hawkes, Anna; Field, John; Edwards, Mary; Crowfoot, Joseph; Hillier, Mary;

Simmons, Lucy: Simmons, Aaron; Woodworth, Mary; Kent, John; Griswold, Hannah; Curtiss, Thomas; Merriman, Mary; Collins, William; Morrell, Sarah; Clark, Ebenezer; Peck, Sarah; Hitchcock, John; Merriman, Abigail; Lewis, John; Lewis, Mrs. John; Babcock, James; Brown, Jane; Pittee, Joseph; Whitmarsh, Sarah; Card, Job; Acres, Martha; Greenman, Thomas; Weeden, Mary; Potter, Thomas; Tripp, Susanna Anthony; Fowler, Christopher; Fowler, Mrs. Christopher;

Simpson, Phoebe: Simpson, John; Simpson, Mrs. Mary; Wheeler, J. William; Drummond, Susannah; Neale, Daniel; Presley, Ursula; Sanford, Robert; Muse, Mary; Florence, William;

Slade, Aaron, Sr.: Hutchinson, Ralph; Bennett, Alice; Root, Joseph; Haynes, Hannah;

Slade, Aaron, Jr., Ann, Benjamin, and Clark: Hutchinson, John; Root, Hannah; Knight, John; Bridge, Mary; Chase, Isaac; Tilton, Mary; Eames, Thomas; Blanford, Mary; Patten, Nathaniel; Adams, Rebecca;

Slauson, Catharine: Slauson, Eleazer; Belden, Susanne; Ambler, Abraham; Bates, Mary; Howe, Nathaniel; Bowers, Miss; Waterbury, David; Newman, Sarah; Judson, James; Wells, Rebecca; Hawley, John; Pierson, Deborah; Hinkley, John; Lothrop, Bethiah; Lathrop [Lothrop?], John; Cole, Mary; Breed, Allen; Osborn, Mary Elizabeth; Palmer, Gershom; Denison, Ann; Wightman, George; Updyke, Elizabeth; Holmes, John; Sayles, Mary; Westcott, Robert; Westcott, Mrs. Katharine;

Smith, Asael, Jr., John, and Joseph, Sr.: Smith, Robert; French, Thomas; Scudamore, Mary; Curtis, Zacheus; Curtis, Mrs. Joanna; Look, Thomas; Look, Mrs. Sarah [Mary?]; Gould, Zaccheus; Deacon, Phebe; Baker, John; Baker, Mrs. Elizabeth; Curtis, Zacheus; Curtis, Mrs. Joanna; Look, Thomas; Look, Sarah [Mary?]; Hidden, Thomas; Hidden, Mrs. Thomas; Palmer, John; Northend, Margaret; Hunt, Samuel; Redding, Elizabeth; Stickney, William, Jr.; Dawson, Elizabeth; Brocklebank, Samuel; Brocklebank, Mrs. Hannah;

Smith, Catherine, Don Carlos, Hyrum, Joseph, Jr., Samuel Harrison, Sophronia, and William: Smith, Robert; French, Mary; Curtis, John; Looke, Mary; Gould, John; Baker, Sarah; Curtis, John; Looke, Mary; Hidden, Andrew; Hosetin, Sarah; Palmer, Francis; Hunt, Elizabeth; Stickney, John, Sr.; Brocklebank, Hannah; Bagley, Orlando; Colby, Sarah; Huntley, Aaron; Champion, Mary; de Wolf, Stephen; Jones, Hannah; Gates, George; Olmstead, Sarah; Dutton, Joseph; Merriam, Rebecca; Fuller, John; Rowley, Mehitable; Crocker, Jonathan; Howland, Hannah;

Smith, Francis: Smith, Thomas; Smith, Mrs. Abigail; Wheeler, Obadiah; White, Elizabeth; Rice, John; Stone, Tabitha; Cutler, Thomas; Dewey, Abigail; Rice, John; Stone, Tabitha; Wood, Abraham; Dakin, Sarah; Brown, Cornelius; Lamson, Sarah; Puffer, James; Ludden, Mary; Ellis, Joseph; Morse, Ruth; Cutler, Thomas; Dewey, Abigail; Rice, John; Stone, Tabitha;

Smith, John: Smith, James; Gunn, Azubah; June, Simeon; Smith, Azuba;

Smith, Julia Priscilla and Mary Jane: Smith, Robert; French, Mary; Curtis, John; Looke, Mary; Gould, John; Baker, Sarah; Curtis, John; Hidden, Andrew; Hosetin, Sarah; Palmer, Francis; Hunt, Elizabeth; Stickney, John; Brocklebank, Hannah; Johnson, Isaac; Harris, Mary; Leek, Thomas; Hitcheson, Sarah;

Smith, Lydia: Bean, Daniel MacBean; Fifield, Mary; Sanborn, Joseph; Gove, Mary;

Smith, Philomela: Smith, Ephraim; Briscoe, Abigail; Chesley, Thomas; Chesley, Mrs. Elizabeth; Witter, Josiah; Wheeler, Elizabeth; Morgan, Joseph; Parke, Dorothy; Tyler, Hopestill; Lovett, Mary; Safford, Joseph; Baker, Mary; Belcher, Sammel; Billings, Mary; Lyon, George; Tolman, Hannah; Loomis, Nathaniel; Moore, Elizabeth; Rockwell, Samuel; Norton, Mary; Warner, Andrew; Warner, Mrs. Mary; Boltwood, Robert; Gernor, Mary; Huntington, Chistopher; Rockwell, Ruth; Backus, William, Jr.; Pratt, Elizabeth; Bassett, Nathaniel; Joyce, Dorcas; Borden, John; Hough, Hannah;

Smith, Sylvester and Warren: Smith, Chileab; Hitchcock, Hannah; Golding, Mr.; Golding, Mrs.;

Snider, Mary: Fluger, Hans; Emich, Hans Valtin; Emich, Mrs. Hans Valtin; Mueller, Henrich; Mueller, Mrs. Henrich;

Snow, Lorenzo: Snow, Samuel; Jones, Abigail; Locke, Joseph; Locke, Mrs. Mary; Phillips, Caleb; Polly, Elizabeth; Lyon, Joseph; Bridge, Mary; Wadsworth, Ebenezer; Wadsworth, Mrs. Mary; Morey, Walter; Morey, Mrs. Mary; Davenport, John; Foster, Neomi; Holbrook, Daniel; Crafts, Abigail; Pettibone, John; Eggleston, Sarah; Bissell, Samuel; Holcomb, Abigail; Cornish, James; Browne, Phoebe; Hillyard, Andrew; Burr, Hannah; Barber, Thomas; Buell, Abigail; Case, Samuel; Westover, Mary; Phelps, Nathaniel; Phelps, Mrs. Eunice; Loomis, William; Morley, Martha;

Snow, Lucinia, Mary Minerva, Willard Trowbridge, William, and Zerubbabel: Snow, John; Greene, Mary; Cutler, James; Page, Phoebe; Brigham, Thomas; Rice, Mary; Warren, Joseph; Wheelock, Experience; Trowbridge, James; Jackson, Margaret; Ward, John; Spring, Mary; Park, Richard; King, Sarah; Fuller, John; Griggs, Hannah; Streeter, John; Whitcomb, Mary; Staples, Samuel; Lincoln, Hannah; Sheldon, John; Palmer, Deliverance; Rhodes, Zachariah; Randall, Mary; Mason, Pelatiah; Brooks, Hepsibeth; Hale, John; Tillinghast, Hannah; Mason, Benjamin; Round, Ruth; Millard, John; Horton, Sarah;

Soule, Cynthia Elizabeth: Soule, Nathaniel; Thorn, Rose; Slade, William; Holmes, Sarah; Sherman, Sampson; Tripp, Isabell;

Staker, Elizabeth: Schaeffer, Jacob; Mueck, Anna; Matthess, Peter; Matthess, Mrs. Anna; Schneider, Conrad; Harder, Anna M.; Schurtz, Michael; Schurtz, Mrs. Catharina;

Stanton, Daniel: Davis, Jabez; Linnell, Experience; Phinney, John; Phinney, Mrs. Joanna; Hall, Samuel; White, Elizabeth; Rising, John; Hall, Sarah;

Stevens, Jonathan: Stevens, Thomas; Rose, Robert; Rose, Mrs. Rebecca; Adams, Jeremy; Baseden, Rebecca; Meeker, Robert; Turberfield, Susan; Webb, Richard, I; Wilson, Grace; Weed, Jonas; Hoyt, Mary; Scofield, Daniel; Youngs, Sarah [Mary?]; Merwin, Miles; Baldwin, Elizabeth; Seeley, Obadiah; Stevens, Esther; Finch, Samuel; Finch, Mrs. Sarah; Bishop, John; Goodyear, Rebecca; Slawson, George;

Stevens, Lorain and Lyman: Stevens, Obadiah; Rose, Rebecca; Adams, Samuel; Meeker, Mary; Webb, Richard, II; Chamberlain, William; Chamberlain, Mrs. Joanna; Weed, Daniel; Weed, Mrs. Ruth; Scofield, Daniel; Merwin, Abigail; Seeley, Obadiah; Finch, Susanna; Bishop, Stephen; Slawson, Mercy, Hyatt, Thomas; Saint John, Mary; Smith, Samuel; Marvin, Rachel; Whitney, John; Smith, Elizabeth; Northrup, Daniel; Northrup, Mrs. Sarah;

Stilson, William B.: Stillson, Vincent; Stillson, Mrs. Mary;

Stockwell, Vilate: Stockwell, William; Stockwell, Mrs. Mary; Lambert, William; Lambert, Mrs. William; Singletery, Nathaniel; Belknap, Sarah; Greeley, Andrew; Brown, Sarah; Kinne, Thomas; Knight, Elizabeth; Richards, Joseph; Richards, Mrs. Susan; Stockwell, William; Lambert, Sarah; Shaw, William; Fraile, Elizabeth; Gale, Abraham; Fiske, Sarah; Kinne, Thomas; Knight, Elizabeth; Nurse, Samuel; Smith, Mary;

Streeter, Lucina: Streeter, Stephen; Smith, Deborah; Whitcomb, Jonathan; Whitcomb, Mrs. Hannah; Staples, Samuel; Boles, Mary; Lincoln, Thomas; Austin, Mary; Sheldon, Isaac; Woodford, Mary; Palmer, George; Mowry, Bethia; Rhodes, John; Waterman, Waite; Randall, William; Fowler, Rebecca; Mason, Sampson; Butterworth, Mary; Brooks, Timothy; Russell, Mary; Hale, Richard; Bullock, Mary; Tillinghast, Pardon E.; Taber, Lydia; Mason, Sampson; Butterworth, Mary; Round, John; Chase, Elizabeth; Millard, Robert; Thurber, Charity; Horton, John; Garnsey, Mehitabel;

Stringham, George, Julia, and William: Stringham, Peter; Stringham, Mrs. Ann; Barker, Samuel; Barker, Mrs. Naomi; Oakley, Thomas; Whitehead, Sarah; Albertis, Arthur; Way, Elizabeth; Hendrickson, Harmon; Sodder, Margaret; Jansen, William; Henrickson, Annetje; Willis, Henry; Pease, Mary; Titus, Edmond; Washburne, Martha; Powell, Thomas; Powell, Mrs. Priscilla; Townsend, John; Harcourt, Susanna;

Strong, Ezra: Strong, Jedediah; Woodward, Freedom; Ingersoll, John; Bascom, Abigail; Adams, John; Pinney, Abigail; Phelps, Timothy; Griswold, Mary; Bissell, Samuel; Holcomb, Abigail; Barber, Samuel; Drake, Ruth; Post, Stephen; Hosmer, Hannah; Gates, Stephen, Jr.; Woodward, Sarah; Geer, George; Allyn, Sarah;

Sumner, Josiah: Sumner, Hezekiah; Bidwell, Abigail; Clark, Daniel; Whitmore, Elizabeth; Lundy, Richard, I; Lyon, Jayne; Large, Joseph; Willson, Robert; Hoag, Anna; Overton, Samuel; Hall, Hannah; Collins, Nathaniel; Whiting, Mary; Adams, William; Bradford, Alice; Jones, Benjamin; Wildes, Elizabeth; Prior, John;

Sweat, John: Swett, Benjamin; Weare, Esther; Kent, John; Woodman, Sarah; Titcombe,

William; Bidfield, Elizabeth; Pierce, Daniel; Milward, Elizabeth; Frost, Charles; Bolles, Mary; Poor, John; Titcomb, Mary; Hale, John; Jacques, Sarah; Acres, Henry; Silver, Hannah; Worcester, Timothy; Cheney, Huldah; Pettengill, Samuel; Poore, Sarah; Buck, Ephraim; Brooks, Sarah; Clements, John; Ayer, Elizabeth; Merrill, Nathaniel; Merrill, Mrs. Sarah;

Tanner, John: Colgrove, Mr.; Colgrove, Mrs.; Sheldon, Isaac; Woodford, Mary; Palmer, George; Mowry, Bethia; Potter, Ichabod; Hazard, Martha; Tripp, John; Anthony, Susannah; Tefft, Samuel; Jenckes, Elizabeth; Sprague, Jonathan; Holbrook, Mehitable; Brownell, William; Smiton, Sarah; Taber, Philip; Cooke, Mary; Kenyon, James; Smith, Ester; Mumford, Thomas; Sherman, Sarah; Sanford, Samuel; Wodell, Sarah; Sisson, George; Lawton, Sarah;

Tanner, John Joshua, Matilda, Nathan, and Sidney: Tanner, Francis; Tanner, Mrs. Francis; Colgrove, Francis; Colgrove, Mrs. Anna; Sheldon, John; Palmer, Deliverance; Potter, Thomas; Tripp, Susanna Anthony; Tefft, John, Sr.; Sprague, Joanna; Brownell, Thomas; Taber, Esther; Kenyon, John; Mumford, Anna; Sanford, William; Sisson, Hope; Stewart, Charles;

Tanner, Louisa: Tanner, Francis; Tanner, Mrs. Francis; Badcock, John; Crandal, Jane;

Taylor, Julia Ann: Taylor, James; Thompson, Martha; Lea, John; Twin, Ann Taylor; Alexander, Anthony; Alexander, Mrs. Anthony; Patrick, John; Patrick, Mrs. Sarah; Kendrick, John; Jones, Mrs.; Jones, Robert; West, Rebecca; Fox, Henry; West, Anne; Williamson, John;

Tenney, William, Sr.: Tenney, Thomas; Mighill, Ann; Hardy, John; Jackman, Mary; Pearson, John; Pearson, Mrs. Dorcas; Thurston, Daniel; Pell, Ann; Hopkinson, Michael; Hopkinson, Mrs. Ann; Pearson, John; Pearson, Mrs. Dorcas; Johnson, William; Wiswell, Esther; Lovejoy, John; Osgood, Mary; Tenney, Thomas; Mighill, Ann; Hardy, John; Jackman, Mary; Pearson, John; Pearson, Mrs. Dorcas; Thurston, Daniel; Pell, Ann;

Tenney, William, Jr.: Tenney, Daniel; Hardy, Mary; Pearson, Benjamin; Thurston, Hannah; Jewett, John; Howe, Elizabeth; Hopkinson, John; Pearson, Elizabeth; Blanchard, Samuel; Daggett, Hannah; Johnson, William; Lovejoy, Sarah; Tenney, Daniel; Hardy, Mary; Pearson, Benjamin; Thurston, Hannah;

Thomas, Daniel Stillwell: Stillwell, Nicholas; Bayles, Rebecca; Hardin, Martin; du Sauchoy, Madeline; Hoge, William; Hume, Barbara;

Thompson, Achsa: Crossett, Anthony; Thompson, Laura;

Thompson, James Lewis, Mary L., and Samuel: Crossett, James; Rogers, Elizabeth; Lewis, John; Lewis, Mrs. John; Babcock, James; Brown, Jane; Pittee, Joseph; Whitmarsh, Sarah; Card, Job; Acres, Martha; Greenman, Thomas; Weeden, Mary; Potter, Thomas; Tripp, Susanna A.; Fowler, Christopher; Fowler, Mrs. Christopher;

Tippets, Alvah Lewis: Tippetts, Thomas; Dam, Judith; Hastings, Robert; Davis, Elizabeth; Austin, Thomas; Foster, Hannah; Gutterson, John; Buckmaster, Abigail; Austin, Thomas; Foster, Hannah; Lovejoy, Christopher; Russ, Sarah; Farnham, Ralph; Sterling, Sarah; Richardson, Joshuah; Richardson, Mrs. Hannah; Lewis, Isaac;

Davis, Mary; Baker, Thomas; Lewis, Mary; Rockwell, Joseph; Foster, Elizabeth; Foster, Edward; Hubbard, Sarah; Blake, John; Johnson, Elizabeth; Clark, Daniel; Whitmore, Elizabeth;

Tippets, John Harvey and William Plummer: Tippetts, Thomas; Dam, Judith; Hastings, Robert; Davis, Elizabeth; Austin, Thomas; Foster, Hannah; Gutterson, John; Buckmaster, Abigail; Austin, Thomas; Foster, Hannah; Lovejoy, Chistopher; Russ, Sarah; Farnham, Ralph; Sterling, Sarah; Richardson, Joshuah; Richardson, Mrs. Hannah; Pierce, Jacob; Whittaker, Mary; Harwood, Nathaniel; Barron, Mary; Gilson, Joseph; Gilson, Mrs. Hepsibah; Prescott, Jonas; Wheeler, Thankful; Farnworth, John; Farnworth, Hannah; Stevens, Richard; Heald, Hannah; Tibbetts, Thomas;

Towne, Elizabeth: Towne, William; Blessing, Joanna; Perkins, Thomas; Gould, Phebe; Stanley, Matthew; Fitts, Abraham; Thompson, Sarah; Choate, Mrs. Ann; Dike, Anthony; Dike, Mrs. Margery; Thompson, David;

Tracy, Moses: Tracy, Jonathon; Griswold, Mary; Parish, John; Wattell, Mary; Baker, John; Martin, Susannah; Backus, Stephen; Spencer, Sarah; Colvin, John; Allen, Dorothy; Barton, Andrew; Low, Rebecca; Burlingame, Thomas; Lippett, Martha; Ralph, Thomas; Ralph, Mrs. Eleanor;

van Alstyne, Phebe: van Alstyne, Jan Martense; Harmense, Dirckje; van Valkenburg, Jochem L.; Vrooman, Eva Hendrickse; van Valkenburg, Jochem L.; Vrooman, Eva Hendrickse; van Slyck, Jackques Cornelius; Ryckman, Grietje; LeRoy, Simeon; des Chalets, Claude; Zielle, Pierre; Damen, Cornelia; van Valkenburg, Jochem L.; Vrooman, Eva Hendirckse; van Slyck, Jackques Cornelius; Ryckman, Grietje;

van Benthuysen, Elizabeth and Jacobus: van Benthuysen, Paulus; van Kleeck, Cathalyntje; Dally, Jan; Obee, Elizabeth; van Wagenen, Gerret; Schepmoes, Dirck; Krom, Maria; van Hoesen, Volkert; Bensen, Marytje; van Hoesen, Volkert; Bensen, Marytje;

van Benthuysen, Keziah: van Benthuysen, Johannes; van Hoesen, Keziah;

van Leuven, Cornelius, Fredrick Matthew, John, Jr., and Ranson: van Leuven, Andries; Davidse, Mareitje; Wood, James; Heckleton, Anna; van Oosterhout, Jan; Jellis, Annetje; Schutt, William Jansen; Jacobs, Gritie; Knickerbocker, Harmen; Bogert, Elizabeth; Dyckman, Johannes, Jr.; Viele, Jannetje; Schoot, Patrick; Wilding, Margery; Booss, Martinus; Widergrien, Ursula; Dromm, Hans Adam; Dromm, Mrs. Anna Elizabeth;

Walker, Rhoda: Parris, Samuel; Parris, Mrs. Elizabeth; Coggeshall, John; Sturgie, Mary Hodge; Timberlake, Henry; Timberlake, Mrs. Mary; Round, John; Chase, Elizabeth; Bowen, Thomas; Brewster, Elizabeth; Salisbury, William; Salisbury, Mrs. Susannah; Eddy, Samuel; Savory, Elizabeth; Owen, William; Davies, Elizabeth;

Ward, Amy: Ward, William; Ward, Mrs. Elizabeth; Jones, Thomas; North, Richard; North, Mrs. Ursula; Wildes, William; Gould, Zaccheus; Deacon, Phebe;

Ward, Sally: Ward, John Turner; Jackson, Hannah; Trowbridge, James; Atherton, Margaret;

Warner, Salmon: Hutchins, Joseph; Corliss, Joanna; Page, John; Davis, Sarah; Stratton, Samuel; Fletcher, Elizabeth; Field, Zachariah; Stanley, Mary; Webb, John; Bassett, Anna; French, Thomas; Button, Mary; Mills, Simon; Buell, Mary; Pettibone, John; Eggleston, Sarah; Adams, Daniel; Phelps, Mary; Shepherd, Abraham; Filbrook, Judith;

Warren, Abigail: Warren, James; Warren, Mrs. James; Foss, John; Chadbourne, Mary;

Warren, Elizabeth: Warren, Thomas; Warren, Mrs. Susan; Sergent, William; Hackley, John;

Warriner, Nancy: Warriner, William; Scant, Joanna; Alvord, Alexander; Vore, Mary; Bartlett, Benjamin; Barnard, Deborah; Ferry, Charles; Harmon, Sarah; Willard, Simon; Sharp, Mary; Lakin, John; Bacon, Mary; Newton, John, Sr.; Larkin, Elizabeth; Ward, Increase; Wheelock, Record; Colton, George; Gardner, Doborah; Cooper, Thomas, Jr.; Slye, Mary; Pynchon, John; Hubbard, Margaret; Taylor, Edward; Fitch, Elizabeth; Burt, Nathaniel; Sikes, Rebecca; Heald, Thomas; Markham, Priscilla; Colton, Isaac; Cooper, Mary; Hitchcock, Luke; Burt, Sarah;

Webb, Chauncey Griswold, Edward Milo, and Edwin Densmore: Webb, John; Cunliff, Susanna; Graves, Benjamin; Hoar, Mary; Bates, John; Beckwith, Elizabeth; Markham, Daniel; Whitmore, Elizabeth; Griswold, John; North, Bathsheba; Stevens, Josiah; Hubbell, Sarah; Bushnell, John; Cole, Rebecca;

Webb, James, Jr.: Webb, John; Bassett, Anna; Cunliffe, Henry; Cunliffe, Mrs. Susanna; Graves, John; Graves, Mrs. John; Hoar, John; Hoar, Mrs. Mary; Bate, James; Withington, Ann; Beckwith, Matthew; Lynde, Elizabeth; Markham, Daniel; Markham, Mrs. Daniel; Whitmore, Francis; Whitmore, Mrs. Elizabeth;

Webber, Sarah: Martin, John; Esten, Joanna; Clark, Benjamin; Morse, Dorcas; Metcalf, Joseph; Bowers, Sarah; Leonard, Thomas; Watson, Mary; Tisdale, John, Jr.; Rogers, Hannah; Carpenter, Samuel; Readway, Sarah; Palmer, Jonah; Griswold, Elizabeth; Perrin, John; Polly, Mary;

Wells, Daniel Hanmer: Welles, John; Bourne, Elizabeth; Goodrich, William; Marvin, Sarah; Welles, Mary; Dickinson, Nathaniel; Gull, Mrs. Anne; Crow, John; Robbins, John; Goodwin, Elizabeth; Deming, John; Gilbert, Elizabeth; Williams, Thomas; Waterhouse, Rebecca;

Wells, Mehitable: Wells, William; Wells, Mrs. Mary; Tuthill, John; King, Deliverance; Brewster, Nathaniel; Ludlow, Sarah; Hawkins, Zachariah; Briggs, Mary Biggs; Reeve, Thomas; Purrier, Mary; Terry, Thomas; Terry, Mrs. Marie; Salmon, William; Curtis, Katherine; Barnes, William; Barnes, Mrs. Martha; Tuthill, John; King, Deliverance; Wells, William; Wells, Mrs. Mary; Reeves, James; Reeves, Mrs. Mary Terry; Satterly, William; Jenner, Mary; Wells, William; Wells, Mary Mrs; Tuthill, John; King, Deliverance; Brewster, Nathaniel; Ludlow, Sarah; Hawkins, Zachariah; Briggs, Mary Biggs;

Welton, Micah B.: Welton, John; Upson, Mary; Upson, Stephen; Lee, Mary; Bronson, John; Ventris, Sarah; Brooks, John; Warner, John; Howard, Margaret; Richason, Thomas; Richason, Mrs. Mary;

Whitney, Newell Kimball and Samuel Franklin: Whitney, Nathaniel; Hastings, John; Hammond, Abigail;

Whitney, Samuel: Whitney, John; Reynolds, Ruth; Hagar, William; Bemis, Mary;

Robinson, William; Adams, Ursula; Cutter, Richard; Williams, Elizabeth; Harrington, Robert; George, Susannah; Whitney, John; Reynolds, Ruth; Warren, John; Fowle, Margaret; Jennison, Robert; Jenison, Mrs. Grace;

Wight, Lyman: Wight, Thomas; Roundy, Alice; Morse, Daniel; Fisher, Lydia; Hinsdale, Robert; Woodward, Ann; Plimpton, John; Dammin, Jane; Howe, Abraham; Ward, Hannah; Martin, Thomas; Martin, Mrs. Joanna; Corbin, Clement; Buckminster, Dorcas; Morse, Anthony; Barnard, Mary; Peake, Jonathan; French, Sarah; Leavens, John; Wood, Hannah;

Wilder, Erepta and Levi: Wilder, Thomas; Wheeler, Mary; Gardner, Andrew; Mason, Sarah; Josselyn, Nathaniel; King, Sarah; Whitcomb, Josiah; Waters, Rebecca;

Willes, Eleazer: Lamson, Thomas; Skinner, John; Loomis, Mary; Filley, William; Filley, Mrs. Margaret; Cook, Mr.; Vore, Richard; Vore, Mrs. Ann; Brooks, Mr.; Wheeler, Thomas; Sayre, Rebecca; Turney, Robert;

Willes, Ira Jones and John: Welles, Joshua; Lamson [Lampson?], Asubah; Skinner, John; Filley, Mary; Cook, Nathaniel; Vore, Lydia; Brooks, John; Hanmore, Susanna; Wheeler, Ephraim; Turney, Ann; Grant, Peter; Grant, Mrs. Mary;

Willey, Jeremiah: Willey, Thomas; Willey, Mrs. Margaret; Pittman, William; Evans, Barbara; Peavey, Thomas;

Williams, Frederick Granger: Williams, John; Williams, Mrs. John; Fuller, Samuel; Lathrop, Jane; Knowlton, William; Welch, Elizabeth; Green, William; Carter, Hannah; Wheeler, Ephraim; Turney, Ann; Parke, Thomas; Thompson, Dorothy; Gallop, John; Lake, Hannah Anna; Prentice, John; Nichols, Esther; Granger, Lancelot; Adams, Joanna; Hanchett, John; Pritchard, Esther; Seymour, Richard; Woodruff, Hannah; Hollister, Stephen; Treat, Abigail; Cooley, Daniel; Walcott, Elizabeth; Gunn, Samuel; Wyatt, Elizabeth B.; Graves, John; Banks, Sarah; Parsons, Jonathon; Clark, Mary;

Wilson, George Deliverance: Wilson, Benjamin; Fuller, Ann; Beaman, Gamaliel; Clark, Sarah; Phelps, Edward; Adams, Elizabeth; Andrews, Robert; Melburn, Grace; Smith, Daniel; Grant, Mary; Fairchild, Samuel; Wheeler, Mary; Burwell, Samuel; Bunnell, Rebecca; Fairchild, Thomas; Preston, Sarah; Jackson, Moses; Hyatt, Deborah;

Winchester, Stephen: Winchester, Richard; Winchester, Mrs. Elizabeth; Sealis, Richard; Lea, Margery;

Winegar, Samuel Thomas: Schneider, Johannes;

Winegar, Alvin, Almira, and Elvira: Schneider, Johannes; Schneider, Mrs. Maria Magdelena;

Witt, Sarah: Witt, John; Witt, Mrs. Sarah; Baker, Edward; Baker, Mrs. Joan; Dane, John; Clark, Eleanor; Thompson, Joseph; Brackett, Mary;

Wixom, Solomon: Wixam, Robert; Wixam, Mrs. Alice; Remick, Christian; Remick, Mrs. Hannah; Chase, John; Baker, Elizabeth; Baker, William; Pierce, Mercy;

Wood, Daniel: Hacleton, Francis; Wakeman, Joanna; Schutt, William Jansen; Jacobs, Margaret; Hornbeck, Warnaar; de Hooges, Anneken; Vernooy, Cornelis C.; Cornelis, Annetje; de Mille, Isaac; Provoost, Benjamin; Alberts, Elsje;

Woodard, John: Woodard, John; Woodard, Mrs. John;

Woodruff, Azmon and Wilford: Woodruff, John; Winchell, Mary; Clark, John; Marvin, Rebecca; Woodford, Joseph; Newell, Rebecca; Smith, Joseph; Smith, Mrs. Lydia; Woodford, Joseph; Smith, Mrs. Lydia; North, Thomas; Royce, Martha; Hart, Thomas; Judd, Elizabeth; Thompson, Thomas; Woodruff, Abigail; Thompson, Joseph; Steele, Mary; Lathrop, John; Royce, Ruth; North, Samuel; Norton, Hannah; Bird, Joseph; Steele, Mary; Barnes, Ebenezer; Orvis, Deborah; Day, Thomas; Wilson, Hannah;

Woods, Charlotte: Woods, Samuel; Farwell, Hannah; Bigelow, James; Child, Elizabeth; Langley, William; Butterfield, Deborah; Foster, Nathaniel; Lovejoy, Frances;

Young, Brigham, Fanny, John, Jr., Joseph, Lorenzo Dow, Louisa, Nancy, Phineas Howe, Rhoda, and Susannah: Young, John; Young, Mrs. Sarah; Whitaker, John; Whitaker, Mrs. Margaret; Cotton, William; Ham, Elizabeth; Hearle, William; Hayden, Joseph; Ames, Hannah; Goodenow, John; Axtell, Mary; Maynard, Zachary; Goodrich, Hannah; Wheeler, John; Stearns, Sarah; Howe, Samuel; Bent, Martha; Mixer, Isaac, Jr.; Garfield, Rebecca; Howe, Samuel; Bent, Martha; Death, John; Peabody, Mary; Goddard, William; Miles, Elizabeth; Stone, Simon; Whipple, Mary; Brigham, Samuel; Howe, Elizabeth; Moore, Richard; Collins, Mary;

Young, Eunice Clark: Whitman, Valentine; Bartlett, Sarah; Sprague, Anthony; Tilden, Mary;

Young, John: Young, Rowland; Whitaker, Nicholas; Whitaker, Mrs. Martha; Ham, William; Stephens, Honor; Hayden, John; Pullen, Susannah; Ames, William; Ames, Mrs. Hannah; Goodenow, Edmund; Barry, Anne; Axtell, Thomas; Starr, Mary; Maynard, John; Axtell, Mary; Goodrich, John; Edwards, Elizabeth; Wheeler, Thomas; Meriam, Sarah; Beers, Sarah;

Zabriskie, Henry: Zabriskie, James; Danniloweczowac, Therfila; Vanderlinde, Joost; van Gelder, Fytje; Hopper, Andries; Hendricks, Gietje; van Blarcom, Jans; Thunis, Magdaleen; Haring, Jan Pieterse; Cozyns, Grietje; Bogert, Jan Laurens; Evarts, Cornelia; Bogert, Jan Cornelius; Strycker, Angenietje; Bertholf, Guilliam; Vermeulen, Martina;

Zabriskie, Sarah: Zaborowskij, Albrecht; Vanderlinde, Machitelt; Hopper, Henrick; van Blarcom, Marritje; Haring, Peter Janse; Bogert, Grietje; Bogert, Jan; Berholf, Maria.

Notes

Chapter 1: Early Mormons

1. The term comes from the western analogy of forest fires and the burning spirit that was evident in the district.

2. See Whitney Cross, *The Burned-Over District* (New York: Harper Torchbooks, 1950). Richard N. Ostling and Joan K. Ostling point out the Mormon church's American uniqueness and its internal contradictions in *Mormon America: The Power and the Promise* (San Francisco: Harper, 1999).

3. Martin Marty, foreword to *Mormonism and the American Experience*, by Klaus J. Hansen (Chicago: University of Chicago Press, 1981), xiii. Harold Bloom argues the Mormon church characterizes much of the American religion in *The American Religion: The Emergence of the Post-Christian Nation* (New York: Simon and Schuster, 1992).

4. Section 46 of *The Doctrine and Covenants of the Church of Jesus Christ of Latter-day Saints* (Salt Lake City: Church of Jesus Christ of Latter-day Saints, 1954), a collection of revelations given primarily to Joseph Smith Jr., outlines all the spiritual gifts available to believers.

5. Doctrine and Covenants 93:29.

6. The Book of Mormon is a collection of scriptures purportedly of ancient American prophets, one of whom, Nephi, testifies of the land of promise. See 2 Nephi 1:5–8.

7. Bloom, *American Religion*, 15–17, 31.

8. These terms were not contemporary with their own time; rather, they were inventions of later historians and have fallen from favor among some current scholars. However, they are useful for our purposes and will be used throughout the book. See, for example, Jon Butler, *Awash in a Sea of Faith: Christianizing the American People* (Cambridge, Mass.: Harvard University Press, 1990), 165.

9. This reform spirit is well reflected in the platform of Joseph Smith Jr., published in 1844, when he declared himself a candidate for the presidency of the United States. See Joseph Smith Jr., "General Smith's Views of the Powers and Policy of the Government of the United States," *Dialogue: A Journal of Mormon Thought* 3, no. 3 (1968): 28–36.

10. Nathan O. Hatch, *The Democratization of American Christianity* (New Haven: Yale University Press, 1989), 116.

11. Bloom, *American Religion,* 17.

12. Ibid., 16.

13. For a full discussion of the Mormon point of view on this topic see, for example, Ezra Taft Benson, *The American Heritage of Freedom: A Plan of God* (Salt Lake City: Deseret Book, 1961); J. Reuben Clark, *Our Constitution—Divinely Inspired* (Salt Lake City: Bookcraft, 1957); and Richard Vetterli, *The Constitution by a Thread* (Salt Lake City: Signature Books, 1967).

14. Joseph Fielding Smith, *The Progress of Man* (Salt Lake City: Deseret News, 1964), 196–237.

15. John L. Brooke, *The Refiner's Fire: The Making of Mormon Cosmology: 1644–1844* (New York: Cambridge University Press, 1994).

16. Ibid., 48–49.

17. Ibid., 38.

18. The six first members included three Smith brothers, Joseph, Jr., Hyrum, and Samuel H.; two Whitmer brothers, Peter, Jr., and David; and Oliver Cowdery. See Joseph Fielding Smith, *The Essentials of Church History* (Salt Lake City: Deseret News, 1950), 91, 113.

19. Larry E. Porter, "A Study of the Origins of the Church of Jesus Christ of Latter-Day Saints in the States of New York and Pennsylvania" (Ph.D. diss., Brigham Young University, 1971).

20. The Doctrine and Covenants records a revelation that these men traveled "into the wilderness among the Lamanites" (American Indians) to "declare my gospel" (Doctrine and Covenants 32:1).

21. Donna Hill, *Joseph Smith: The First Mormon* (Midvale, Utah: Signature Books, 1977), 116–25.

22. Parley P. Pratt claimed that the number of members "soon increased to one thousand," though no evidence exists to corroborate that claim. See Parley P. Pratt Jr., ed., *The Autobiography of Parley P. Pratt* (Salt Lake City: Deseret Book, 1964), 48.

23. Ben E. Rich, *Scrapbook of Mormon Literature* (Chicago: Henry C. Etten, 1910), 543–45.

24. It has been estimated that the number of Mormons in Kirtland in the summer of 1835 was between 1,500 and 2,000. See Leonard J. Arrington and Davis Bitton, *The Mormon Experience: A History of the Latter-Day Saints* (New York: Alfred A. Knopf, 1979), 21.

25. Doctrine and Covenants 107:22–33.

26. Marvin S. Hill, C. Keith Rooker, and Larry T. Wimmer, "The Kirtland Economy Revisited," *Dialogue: A Journal of Mormon Thought* 12, no. 1 (1979): 110–13.

27. Dean May, "A Demographic Portrait of the Mormons, 1830–1980," in *The New Mormon History,* ed. D. Michael Quinn (Salt Lake City: Signature Books, 1992), 122.

28. J. F. Smith, *Essentials of Church History,* 191–262.

29. W. H. G. Armytage, *Heavens Below: Utopian Experiments in England, 1560–1960* (Toronto: University of Toronto Press, 1961), 261.

30. May, "Demographic Portrait," 123.

31. These four great-great-grandparents were William Walker Rust (1807–94), Mary Thurston Rand (1806–39), Catharine Slauson (1806–95), and Parley Parker Pratt (1807–

57). My mother's family was not among the founding members of the church but joined in the 1850s in Europe.

32. The names of these early general authorities are available, for example, in D. Michael Quinn, *The Mormon Hierarchy: Origins of Power* (Salt Lake City: Signature Books, 1994); and J. F. Smith, *Essentials of Church History.*

33. The Web site for the *LDS Ancestral File* is <http://familysearch.org>. There are additional resources beyond the *LDS Ancestral File.* For example, the Family Tree Maker provides an excellent resource in its *Ancestral World Tree,* at <http://www.ancestry.com>. In addition, Rootsweb, at <http://www.rootsweb.com>, is a rich Internet resource, and the National Archives and Records Administration and the New York Public Library provide a number of resources for genealogical research. Individual families also provide a rich source of information on specific surnames. Such organizations are usually named after the first ancestor to arrive in America (for example, the George Denison family organization).

34. An exact count of the church membership during its first five years does not exist. Dean May points out that the first systematic reports on LDS membership were published in 1879, in "Demographic Portrait," 121. The relative percentage of my sample was determined in a variety of ways. For example, I extrapolated the sample size from the New York–Pennsylvania period. Larry Porter, in "Origins of the Church," has identified about 140 names of converts during this early period of the church, and 56 of them satisfied my criteria for inclusion in the study, representing 40 percent. This percentage suggests the church membership in the beginning of 1835 was approximately 1,500.

35. I have already identified additional names of early converts beyond the 583 who would qualify, but I decided that little additional information would be gained by continuing to recalculate the data. Because the Mormon church baptizes young people at eight years of age, only those family members who had reached the "age of accountability" were counted as members, because prior to that they were not yet born into the church.

36. Because there are no reliable estimates of church membership between 1831 and 1837, I engaged in an exercise to estimate its size each year up to 1837. The membership for 1830 is estimated to have been between 300 and 450 (Rich, *Scrapbook of Mormon Literature,* 543–45). Table 1 indicates the number of known baptisms each year until 1835, when I calculate it to have been about 40 percent of the church membership. I found the membership to have grown rather steadily except for 1834, so I projected this growth for the first half of the decade to be an extension of the line for the years 1835 and 1836. The best estimate of church membership for 1837, such as that by Dean May ("Demographic Portrait," 127), is approximately 2,500 members, which fits well with my projections through the first half of the decade.

37. In addition to those materials mentioned in the text, there are other valuable sources. For example, at the end of Lucy Mack Smith's family memoir, biographical accounts are given of the people she mentions. See Lavina Fielding Anderson, *Lucy's Book: A Critical Edition of Lucy Mack Smith's Family Memoir* (Salt Lake City: Signature Books, 2001). The journals of William E. McLellin also provide biographical information on the people McLellin mentions. See Jan Shipps and John W. Welch, *The Journals of William E. McLellin* (Urbana: University of Illinois Press, 1994).

38. This is now available on the Web, through MyFamily.com at <http://myfamily.com>,

or as part of a computer software package known as LDS Family History, Suite 2. See Susan Easton Black, "Membership of the Church of Jesus Christ of Latter-day Saints: 1830–1848," LDS Vital Records Library (Orem, Utah: Infobases, 1996). Or write to the LDS Family History Suite, 1875 S. State, Suite 3100, Orem, Utah, 84058.

39. May, "Demographic Portrait," 123.

40. Donald Q. Cannon and Lyndon W. Cook, *Far West Record: Minutes of the Church of Jesus Christ of Latter-Day Saints, 1830–1844* (Salt Lake City: Deseret Book, 1983).

41. Membership is indicated in the book by labels such as Sister Newel Knight, Brother David Whitmer, Bishop Edward Partridge, Elder Brigham Young, and so on. See B. H. Roberts, ed., *The History of the Church of Jesus Chirst of Latter-day Saints: Period I: History of Joseph Smith, by Himself,* 6 vols. (Salt Lake City: Deseret News, 1902–12).

42. On 24 February 1834, Joseph Smith received a revelation to send "five hundred of the strength of my house" to Missouri to defend the Saints in what was then identified as Zion (Doctrine and Covennts 103:30). The group, known as Zion's Camp, never came close to 500, and different names of these participants have been listed by various compilers. Backman has combined all major lists and has identified 207 men, 11 women, and 5 children. See Milton V. Backman Jr., *A Profile of Latter-Day Saints of Kirtland, Ohio and Members of Zion's Camp: 1830–1839* (Provo, Utah: Brigham Young University, 1983). The Danites were a paramilitary group that was organized to defend against those persecuting the Saints. See Quinn, *Mormon Hierarchy,* appendix 3.

43. Backman, *Profile of Latter-Day Saints.*

44. Among the more obvious secondary sources would be Arrington and Bitton, *Mormon Experience;* Richard L. Bushman, *Joseph Smith and the Beginnings of Mormonism* (Urbana: University of Illinois Press, 1984); D. Hill, *Joseph Smith;* Pratt, *Autobiography of Pratt;* Quinn, *Mormon Hierarchy;* Jan Shipps, *Mormonism: The Story of a New Religious Tradition* (Urbana: University of Illinois Press, 1985); J. F. Smith, *Essentials of Church History;* and Dan Vogel, *Religious Seekers and the Advent of Mormonism* (Salt Lake City: Signature Books, 1988).

45. See Backman, *Profile of Latter-Day Saints;* and Lyndon W. Cook, *Nauvoo Deaths and Marriages: 1839–1845* (Orem, Utah: Grandin Book, 1994).

46. Arrington and Bitton, *Mormon Experience,* 21.

47. The genealogical records in the *LDS Ancestral File* represent names submitted by ordinary LDS Church members, and inevitably there are mistakes in them. Further, records of families in colonial America are not always reliable. They were often constructed from scanty information, and errors in names and relationships are common.

48. Cross, *Burned-Over District,* 146.

49. My data indicate that 73 percent of all converts in the New York–Pennsylvania period (41 of the 56 saints from that group in this study) had been born in New England, while only 16 percent (9 in this study) were born in New York. Another 3 in this study were born in the Middle Atlantic region, 1 in the South, 1 in Canada, and 1 birthplace is unknown.

50. The more important connection comes through the Dwight Harding family, discussed in chapter 7. See Glen F. Harding, *A Record of the Ancestry, Family, and Descendents of Abraham Harding* (Ogden, Utah: Glen F. Harding, 1979).

51. For a history of the Zundel family, see Glen F. Harding, *A Record of the Ancestry and*

Descendents of John Jacob Zundel, Known as Jacob Zundel (Ogden, Utah: Glen F. Harding, 1973). For a full discussion of Rappist connections with the early LDS Church, see Karl J. Arndt, "The Harmonists and the Mormons," *American-German Review* 10 (1944): 6–9.

52. Karl J. Arndt, *George Rapp's Harmony Society, 1785–1847* (Rutherford, N.J.: Fairleigh Dickinson University Press, 1972), 541.

53. There is some dispute as to when John joined the church. Arndt claims John became disenchanted with the Harmonists in the early 1830s and traveled to Ohio, where he joined the LDS Church. See Arndt, "Harmonists and the Mormons," 7. However, LDS genealogical records show several of John Zundel's children to have been born in Pennsylvania: Philip in Phillipsburgh in 1832, John in Phillipsburgh in 1834, Thomas in Phillipsburgh in 1836, Gideon in Unity in 1838, and Margaret in Unity in 1840. See Black, "Membership of the Church."

54. Arrington and Bitton, *Mormon Experience,* 40–41.

55. Arndt, "Harmonists and the Mormons," 7.

56. F. Mark McKiernan, *The Voice of One Crying in the Wilderness: Sidney Rigdon, Religious Reformer, 1793–1876* (Lawrence, Kans.: Coronado, 1971), 19.

57. Of the 55 Ohio members in this study baptized in the fall and early winter of 1830, 75 percent (41) were born in New England, while 20 percent (11) were born in New York. Only 2 came from the Middle Atlantic region, and 1 came from the South.

58. McKiernan, *Voice of One Crying,* 29. Hampshire County is likely incorrect, since Montague is now in Franklin County, Massachusetts.

59. For a fuller account, see Newell G. Bringhurst, *Brigham Young and the Expanding American Frontier* (Boston: Little, Brown, 1986), 1–21.

60. A number of studies of Brigham Young are available, including Leonard J. Arrington, *Brigham Young: American Moses* (Urbana: University of Illinois Press, 1985).

61. Alan Taylor, "The Free Seekers: Religious Culture in Upstate New York, 1790–1835," *Journal of Mormon History* 27, no. 1 (2001): 42–66.

62. Ibid., 51.

63. Find the American Local History Network data at <http://scioto.org/OhioMigrations/> and <http://scioto.org/NewYorkMigrations/>.

64. Sydney E. Ahlstrom, *A Religious History of the American People* (New Haven: Yale University Press, 1972), 431.

65. Hatch, *Democratization of American Christianity,* 52.

66. Only a small percentage of these Wayne County and Geauga County residents were found in the *LDS Ancestral file,* which suggests that genealogical studies of church members are largely connected with their own direct-line ancestors, rather than with the population in general.

Chapter 2: Ancestors of Early LDS Converts

1. Rodney Stark and William Sims Bainbridge, *A Theory of Religion* (New Brunswick, N.J.: Rutgers University Press, 1996), 195–96.

2. Rodney Stark and Roger Finke, *Acts of Faith: Explaining the Human Side of Religion* (Berkeley: University of California Press, 2000), 120.

3. Ibid., 115.

4. Rodney Stark and William Sims Bainbridge, "Networks of Faith: Interpersonal Bonds and Recruitment to Cults and Sects," *American Journal of Sociology* 85 (1980): 1376–95.

5. Rodney Stark, "Extracting Social Scientific Models from Mormon History," *Journal of Mormon History* 25, no. 1 (1999), 185.

6. Bushman, *Joseph Smith,* 151.

7. George Bancroft is especially noted for this "myth." See George Bancroft, *History of the United States,* 10 vols. (Boston: Little, Brown, 1834–74), 1:1–3.

8. I took a random sample of 200 ancestors and found that their mean date of birth fell between 1646 and 1647. The birth dates were multimodal, but most fell between 1639 and 1657, with the median date of 1648. The range of birthdates was wide, ranging from 1615 to 1678, because some of the Saints joined the LDS Church at an advanced age while others were teenagers.

9. *World Almanac and Book of Facts,* 1997 ed., s.v. "United States Population."

10. In the remainder of this book, I will make specific reference mainly to unique names when comparing the number of ancestors of LDS converts with the general population of a town, county, or colony.

11. Sumner Chilton Powell, *Puritan Village: The Formation of a New England Town* (Hanover, N.H.: Wesleyan University Press, 1963), xviii.

12. Bruce C. Daniels, *Puritans at Play: Leisure and Recreation in Colonial New England* (New York: St. Martin's, 1995), 215–21.

13. Evarts B. Greene and Virginia D. Harrington, *American Population before the Federal Census of 1790* (New York: Columbia University Press, 1932), 21.

14. The following persons probably came with the Reverend Mr. Rogers: Thomas Barker, Constance Crosby, Thomas Elithorp Lambert, Francis Lambert, Edward Carleton, Humphrey Reyner, William Acy, Hugh Chaplin, Maximilian Jewett, Joseph Jewett, Robert Haseltine, John Haseltine, Ezekiel Northen, Jeremiah Northend, William Jackson, William Boynton, John Boynton, Jane Brocklebank, Thomas Nelson, John Spofford Tenney, and Thomas Tenney. See George Brainart Blodgette and Amos Everett Jewett, *Early Settlers of Rowley, Massachusetts* (Somersworth, N.H.: New England History, 1981), 1:ix–xiii.

15. Ibid., 1:323.

16. The *LDS Ancestral File* gives his baptism date as 1965, which means the original baptism records were lost, and the ordinance was done again via proxy. However, Abbott family records are explicit that he was baptized in 1830. See, for example, Lemuel Abijah Abbott, *Descendents of George Abbott, of Rowley, Mass.,* 2 vols. (Andover, Mass.: Lemuel Abijah Abbott, 1906), 1:555–56.

17. Blodgette and Jewett, *Rowley, Massachusetts,* 1:1.

18. Ibid., 1:24.

19. This is apparently characteristic of those settling in most of Massachusetts, as illustrated by Philip J. Greven's account of Andover, Essex County, in *Four Generations: Population, Land, and Family in Colonial Andover, Massachusetts* (Ithaca, N.Y.: Cornell University Press, 1970).

20. Book of Mormon, 2 Nephi 1:5–8.

21. Anthony Giddens, *Beyond Left and Right: The Future of Radical Politics* (Stanford, Calif.: Stanford University Press, 1994), 1.

22. This aspect of the Reformation was popularized by George Huntston Williams, *The Radical Reformation* (Philadelphia: Westminster, 1946).

23. Justin Winsor, *The Memorial History of Boston,* 4 vols. (Boston: James R. Osgood, 1881), 1:169.

24. Brooke, *Refiner's Fire,* 13–19.

25. G. H. Williams, *Radical Reformation,* 375.

26. John H. Bratt, ed., *The Heritage of John Calvin* (Grand Rapids, Mich.: William B. Erdmans, 1973); John Thomas McNeill, *The History and Character of Calvin* (New York: Oxford University Press, 1954).

27. Bratt, *John Calvin,* 210–11; McNeill, *History and Character of Calvin,* 20–21.

28. Brooke, *Refiner's Fire,* 11.

29. Henry Martyn Dexter, *Congregationalism: What Is It, How It Works, Why It Is Better than Any Other Form of Church Government, and Its Consequent Demand* (Boston: Moyes, Holmes, 1871), 72.

Chapter 3: The Pilgrims of Plymouth Colony

1. As George E. Ellis explains, "[Henry] was no heretic, but lived and died . . . a good Roman Catholic" (*Puritan Age and Rule in the Colony of the Massachusetts Bay, 1629–1685* [New York: Burt Franklin, 1970], 75).

2. M. Louise Greene, *The Development of Religious Liberty in Connecticut* (Boston: Houghton, Mifflin, 1905), 84.

3. John Foxe, *Foxe's Book of Martyrs* (New Kensington, Pa.: Whitaker, 1981), 1.

4. Ibid., 70.

5. Ibid., 51.

6. R. J. Acheson, *Radical Puritans in England, 1550–1660* (London: Longman, 1990), 19.

7. Ibid.

8. Ellis, *Puritan Age,* 63.

9. H. S. Stout, "Puritanism," in *Dictionary of Christianity in America,* ed. Daniel G. Reid (Downers Grove, Ill.: Intervarsity Press, 1990), 966.

10. Edward H. Bloomfield, *The Opposition to the English Separatists* (Washington, D.C.: University Press of America, 1981), x.

11. George F. Willison, *Saints and Strangers* (New York: Reynal and Hitchcock, 1945), 31–33.

12. Ibid., 31.

13. Acheson, *Radical Puritans in England,* 12.

14. Henry W. Clark, *History of English Nonconformity: From Wiclif to the Close of the Nineteenth Century* (London: Chapman and Hall, 1911), 184.

15. Smyth called his movement "Se-Baptism," suggesting the movement was for those without baptism. See James Robert Coggins, *John Smyth's Congregation: English Separatism, Mennonite Influence, and the Elect Nation* (Waterloo, Ont.: Herald, 1991).

16. Dorothy Brewster, *William Brewster of the Mayflower: Portrait of a Pilgrim* (New York: New York University Press, 1970).

17. Marion L. Starkey, *The Congregational Way: The Role of the Pilgrims and Their Heirs in Shaping America* (Garden City, N.Y.: Doubleday, 1966), 17–18.

18. Brewster, *William Brewster,* 68. See also Irvin Buckwalter Horst, *The Radical Brethren: Anabaptism and the English Reformation to 1558* (The Hague: Nieuwkoop-B. de Graaf, 1972).

19. William Bradford, *History of Plymouth Plantation: 1620–1647* (New York: Russell and Russell, 1968), 44–46.

20. M. L. Greene, *Religious Liberty in Connecticut,* 84.

21. Quoted in B. Roland Lewis, "The Pilgrims and the Utah Pioneers," *Improvement Era,* December 1920, 100.

22. Michael Watts, *The Dissenters* (Oxford, Eng.: Clarendon Press, 1978), 103.

23. Ahlstrom, *Religious History of the American People,* 144–46.

24. Francis J. Bremer, *The Purtan Experiment: New England Society from Bradford to Edwards* (New York: St. Martin's, 1976), 33–39.

25. M. L. Greene, *Religious Liberty in Connecticut,* 84.

26. Arnold Green, "New England's Gift to the Nation—The Township: An Oration Delivered in the City of Providence on July 5 [1875]," Making of America: University of Michigan Electronic Series, <http://www.hti.umich.edu/m/moagrp/>.

27. B. R. Lewis, "Pilgrims and Utah Pioneers," 95–103.

28. John Landis, *Mayflower Desendents and Their Marriages for Two Generations after the Landing* (Baltimore: Southern Book, 1956).

29. The fifteen heads of household (with early LDS convert descendants in parentheses) are as follows: John Alden (Elizabeth Hathaway; Lucy Simmons; Noah Packard; Joseph Coe; Mary Ann Kennedy; the John Young family, father of Brigham Young and his siblings; Joel Hills, Julia Ann, and Delcena Johnson; Cyril and Anson Call); Isaac Allerton (Mary Ann Kennedy); John Billington (Polly Chadwick; Rachel Marsh, Royal Marsh, Sr., Royal Marsh, Jr., Philania, and Edson Barney; Martin H. Peck); William Bradford (Josiah Sumner; Elizabeth Hathaway); William Brewster (Daniel Avery; Rhoda Walker; Sarah King); Peter Brown (Olive Farwell; Isaac Freeman); James Childon (Sophia Bundy); Francis Cooke (Soloman Chamberlain; Lydia and Ira Ames; John Tanner; Titus Billings; Stephen Chase; Noah Packard; Mary Ann Kennedy; Elijah Cheney); Edward Fuller (Lucy Mack and her children Hyrum, Sophronia, Joseph, Jr., Samuel Harrison, William, Catherine, and Don Carlos Smith; Frederick G. Williams); Stephen Hopkins (Stephen Chase; Titus Billings; Noah Packard); John Howland (Lucy Mack and her children Hyrum, Sophronia, Joseph, Jr., Samuel Harrison, William, Catherine, and Don Carlos Smith; Orson, Anson, Parley P., and William D. Pratt; Lyman Curtis; Emma Hale; Mary Ann Kennedy); Thomas Rogers (Alice, John, Jr., Luke, Samuel, Lyman E., and Nancy Miranda Johnson; Chauncy Calkins; Sarah Webber; Elizabeth Hathaway); Henry Sampson (Mayhew Hillman); George Soule (Lucy Simmons); Richard Warren (Mary Ann Kennedy; Olive Farwell; Isaac Freeman; Soloman Chamberlain).

30. Willison, *Saints and Strangers,* 125.

31. Of course, the ancestors of early LDS converts were not all born at midcentury, so comparisons must always be seen as approximate. Because the percentage contribution of Plymouth Colony to the fifth-generation ancestors of New England with *unique names* (14.4 percent) is very close to Plymouth's percentage among *all* fifth-generation ancestors of New England (15.3 percent), the number of unique names and the total number

of ancestors both show that these ancestors were highly overrepresented in the general population of Plymouth Colony.

32. G. D. Scull, "Historical Notes and Letters Relating to Early New England," *New England Historical and Genealogical Register* 38 (1884): 378–81.

33. Darrett B. Rutman, *Husbandmen of Plymouth: Farms and Villages in the Old Colony, 1620–1692* (Boston: Beacon, 1967), 23.

34. A total of 10,415 names of fifth-generation ancestors have been identified, but 5,083 names are unique. This means there is a general ratio of total to unique names of about 2:1.

35. This includes Mormon luminaries such as Lucy Mack (and Joseph Smith Jr.), Reynolds Cahoon, Oliver Cowdery, Luke Johnson, and Lyman Johnson.

36. William Howland, *John Howland: A Mayflower Pilgrim* (Detroit: The Pilgrim John Howland Society, 1926), 17–18.

37. Ahlstrom, *Religious History of the American People,* 138.

38. Albert E. Dunning, *Congregationalists in America* (Boston: Pilgrim Press, 1894), 153.

39. Bradford, *Plymouth Plantation,* 162.

40. Ibid.

41. Eugene Aubery Stratton, *Plymouth Colony: Its History and People, 1620–1691* (Salt Lake City: Ancestry, 1986), 62.

42. Arthur Howland was an ancestor of LDS convert David Crandall.

43. We recall that the ratio of total to unique names is 2:1, so the Barnstable ratio is about the same as the general ratio.

44. Archibald Bennett, "Orson Pratt as a Genealogist," *Deseret News,* 25 April 1936.

45. In addition to the names noted by Archibald Bennett, John Lathrop was the ancestor of John Coltrin Jr.; Fannie, Lavina, Phoebe, Zemira, William, Jr., and William Draper Sr.; Lois and Lydia Lathrop; George White Pitkin; Lovina S. Williams; Azmon Woodruff; John M. Chidester; Phebe L. and Warren Cowdery; Anson and William Dickinson Pratt; Catharine Slauson; and Mary Arey.

46. Clark, *English Nonconformity,* 187–91.

47. The dramatic episode leading up to his arrest and imprisonment is told in story form by Helene Holt in her novel *Exiled: The Story of John Lathrop, 1584–1653* (New York: Paramount Books, 1987), 66. See also Charles Henry Pope, *The Pioneers of Massachusetts* (Boston: Charles H. Pope, 1900), 292.

48. Holt, *Exiled,* 72.

49. Willison, *Saints and Strangers,* 316.

50. Stratton, *Plymouth Colony,* 61.

51. Ibid., 62.

52. Elijah Baldwin Huntington, *A Genealogical Memoire of the Lo-Lathrop Family* (Ridgefield, Conn.: T. H. Huntington, 1884), 28.

53. We noted above that the Reverend Charles Chauncey had arrived in Scituate in 1641 after leaving Plymouth because of conflicts over the proper mode of baptism. He carried his position into a settlement that continued that conflict.

54. Huntington, *Genealogical Memoire,* 33.

55. Pope, *Pioneers of Massachusetts,* 292.

56. Richard Lebaron Bowen, *Early Rehoboth,* 4 vols. (Rehoboth, Mass.: Rumford, 1945), 1:18.

57. Whereas the ratio of unique names to total ancestors in New England was about 1:2, in Rehoboth it was 102:324, or less than 1:3.

58. Ipswich and New Haven are the other two towns with more than 300 ancestors.

59. Rachel Marsh Barney's maiden name was also Barney.

60. Fifth-generation ancestors born in Rehoboth include Hannah Eddy, Ephraim and John Martin, Thankful and Samuel Bullock, Jathniall and John Peck, Sarah and Daniel Smith, Elizabeth Fuller, Aaron Clark, and Sarah Lange.

61. Bowen, *Rehoboth,* 1:25–35.

62. Ibid., 1:26.

63. In 1982, Jerome E. Anderson discovered a small volume described as the original records of the Baptist church in Swansea. These records suggest that the Swansea congregation was first formally established between 1663 and 1666, becoming either the first or the second Anabaptist congregation in Massachusetts. The Boston congregation was established in 1665. See Robert Charles Anderson, "Swansea, Massachusetts, Baptist Church Records," *New England Historical and Genealogical Register* 89 (1985): 21–49.

64. Bernie Bean, *The Life and Family of John Bean of Exeter and His Cousins* (N.p.: Bernie Bean, 1970), 1–5.

65. Bowen, *Rehoboth,* 1:26–27.

66. Bowen, *Rehoboth,* 3:131.

67. John Browne was an ancestor of early LDS convert John Anderson. He appears to be unrelated to Robert Browne, the source of Brownism. See Bowen, *Rehoboth,* 1:29.

68. Edwin S. Gaustad, *Liberty of Conscience: Roger Williams in America* (Grand Rapids, Mich.: William B. Erdmans, 1991), 116–17.

69. Bowen, *Rehoboth,* 1:29.

70. Stephen Marini, *Radical Sects of Revolutionary New England* (Cambridge, Mass.: Harvard University Press, 1982), 70.

71. Ibid., 68.

72. Bushman, *Joseph Smith,* 27–29.

Chapter 4: Puritan Ancestors in Massachusetts and Maine

1. See Charles Edward Banks, *The Winthrop Fleet of 1630* (Baltimore: Genealogical, 1968).

2. Many parallels are noted by the Mormon scholar James R. Christianson, ed., *Puritanism and Mormonism: Parallel Paths—A Parting of the Ways,* Regional Studies in Latter-Day Saint Church History (Provo, Utah: Brigham Young University Press, Department of Church History and Doctrine, 1988).

3. See Daniels, *Puritans at Play,* 4–9.

4. For example, John Cotton, Puritan minister and spokesperson for New England Congregationalism, was a direct-line ancestor of Edward Partridge Sr. and Olive Lowell.

5. This estimate was made by extrapolating from the number of conscripts in the militia in Boston compared with the number in the other towns. See Greene and Harrington, *American Population,* 19. This claim is supported by a survey of houses in various coastal

communities at the time, which indicated that 60 percent of Massachusetts houses were located in Boston. See Scull, "Historical Notes and Letters," 381.

6. These included the following LDS converts: Samuel Bent, Cyril Call, Jabez Carter, Polly Chadwick, Alpheus Cutler, James Holman, Clarissa and John Reed, Francis Smith, as well as Gardner, Mary Minerva, Willard Trowbridge, and Zerubbabel Snow.

7. Fortunately, there are a number of studies of Suffolk County towns. Of course, extensive studies of Boston are extant, but recent studies of small Massachusetts towns are now available, including those for Braintree, Dedham, and Hingham, that provide a good sense of life in these early communities. See Samuel A. Bates, ed., *Records of the Town of Braintree: 1640–1793* (Randolph, Mass.: Daniel H. Huxford, 1886); Samuel G. Drake, *History of Boston* (Boston: Luther Stevens, 1856); Ellis, *Puritan Age;* Greene and Harrington, *American Population;* Kenneth A. Lockridge, *A New England Town: The First Hundred Years* (New York: W. W. Norton, 1970); John J. Waters, "Hingham, Massachusetts: 1631–1661," in *Puritanism in Early America,* ed. George M. Waller, 143–54 (Lexington, Mass.: D. C. Heath, 1973); Walter Muir Whitehill, *Boston: A Topographical History* (Cambridge., Mass.: Harvard University Press, 1968); and Winsor, *Memorial History of Boston.*

8. Winsor, *Memorial History of Boston,* 1:157–58.

9. Lockridge, *New England Town.*

10. Ibid., 13.

11. This tension came in part because the church served as an ethical community, which David D. Hall sees as a supporter of the select, but it also served as a state-related church that attempted to provide instruction and moral discipline for everyone. See David D. Hall, "A World of Wonders: The Mentality of the Supernatural in Seventeenth-Century New England," in *Seventeenth-Century New England,* ed. David D. Hall and David Grayson Allen (Boston: Colonial Society of New England, 1984), 59.

12. Lockridge, *New England Town,* 31.

13. Quoted in ibid.

14. Ibid., 65.

15. Dedham LDS ancestors included the following (LDS converts are in parentheses): Gershom Wheelock (Charles Allen); John Houghton (John Badger); Esther Chickering (Rachel, Royal, Sr., Aramel, Edson, Philania, and Royal Barney Jr.); Sarah Crossman (Harrison Joseph Burgess); Dorothy Royle (Josiah Butterfield); Samuel Smith (Dominicus Carter); Ephraim Wight (Polly Chadwick; Ann and Thomas B. Marsh); Lydia Morse (Polly Chadwick); Ellis Wood and Mrs. Catherine Wood (Soloman Chamberlain); Benjamin Clark and Dorcas Morse (Sarah Webber); Jonas Houghton (Jonathan Crosby); Margaret Allright (Enos Curtis); Mary Fairbanks (Sheffield Daniels; Julia Hills); John Bacon, Rebecca Hall, and Joseph Morse (Ellis and Jullietty Eames); Hannah Plympton (Timothy Bradley Foote); Rebecca Paine (Isaac Farwell and Olive Hovey Freeman); Phillip Alcott (Algernon S. Gilbert); Dorothy Royle (Emma Hale); Samuel Morse (Elizabeth Haven); Michael Metcalf, Cornelius Fisher, Leah Heaton, Margaret Hunting, John Ellis Jr., Thomas Herring, Mrs. Mary Herring, Samuel Smith, Nathaniel Colburn, and Priscilla Clark (Julia Hills); John Houghton (James Sawyer and Joshua Sawyer Holman); Sarah Morse (Elias Hutchins); Eleazur Metcalf, Meletiah Fisher, Cornelius Fisher, Esther Ware, John Ellis II, Mary Herring, and Samuel Colburn (Almera Woodard, Julia Ann, Delcena D., Joel Hills,

Nancy Maria, Seth Garnzey, David, and Susan Ellen Johnson); Thomas Bayes (Mary Keeler); Alice Adams (Joseph C. Kingsbury); Thomas Eames (Anna, Esther, Hyruna, Joseph, Newell, and Polly Knight; Ann and Benjamin Slade); William Partridge and Sarah Colburn (Ann and Thomas B. Marsh); Samuel Mills and Frances Pimbrook (Daniel Sanborn Miles); Hannah Plympton (Clarissa Norton); Daniel Pond (Edward Partridge Sr.); Esther Chickering (Ann Eliza, Nancy F., and Sally Ann Peck); Mary Tilton (Clark Slade); Joseph Ellis and Ruth Morse (Francis Smith); Samuel Staples and Mary Boles (Lucina Streeter); Record Wheelock (Nancy Warriner); Thomas Wight, Lydia Fisher, Robert Hinsdale, and Ann Woodward (Lyman Wight); Thomas Wilder and Mary Wheeler (Levi and Erepta M. Wilder).

16. Lockridge, *New England Town,* 79–90.

17. Percentages for Essex County were calculated on the basis of Massachusetts's total LDS ancestors (4,395) and those with unique names (2,139), as shown in table 5.

18. Scull, "Historical Notes and Letters," 378–81.

19. Of course, New Hampshire was considered part of Massachusetts Bay Colony from 1641 until 1679, but the boundaries of the local units cut through the current border between the two states. See Victor C. Sanborn, "Stephen Bachiler: An Unforgiven Puritan," an address to the New Hampshire Historical Society in 1917, at <http://www.hampton.lib.nh.us/hampton/biog/bachilertoc.htm>.

20. Carla Gardina Pestana, "Sectarianism in Colonial Massachusetts" (Ph.D. diss., University of California, Los Angeles, 1987), 18–19.

21. Joshua Millet, *A History of the Baptists in Maine* (Portland, Maine: Charles Day, 1845), 24.

22. Ibid.

Chapter 5: Puritan Ancestors in Connecticut

1. New Haven was a separate colony until it joined Connecticut in 1665, but unless otherwise indicated it will be treated here as part of Connecticut.

2. Charles McLean Andrews, *Connecticut's Place in Colonial History* (New Haven: Yale University Press for the Connecticut Society of Colonial Wars, 1923), 9.

3. Frank D. Haines, "Roger Ludlow," in *Founders and Leaders of Connecticut, 1633–1783,* ed. Charles Edward Perry (Boston: D. C. Heath, 1934), 67.

4. Quoted in George Leon Walker, *Thomas Hooker: Preacher, Founder, Democrat* (New York: Dodd, Mead, 1891), 124–25.

5. Mary Jeanne Anderson Jones, *Congregational Commonwealth: Connecticut, 1636–1662* (Middletown, Conn.: Wesleyan University Press, 1968), 36.

6. Ibid., 42.

7. M. L. Greene, *Religious Liberty in Connecticut,* 37–39.

8. Quoted in Edward E. Atwater, *History of the Colony of New Haven to Its Absorption into Connecticut* (Meriden, Conn.: Journal Publishing, 1902), 228.

9. Quoted in Jones, *Congregational Commonwealth,* 38.

10. Paul R. Lucas, *Valley of Discord: Church and Society along the Connecticut River, 1636–1725* (Hanover, N.H.: University Press of New England, 1976).

11. Edwin Pond Parker, *History of the Second Church of Christ in Hartford* (Hartford, Conn.: Belknap and Warfield, 1892), appendix 1.

12. The figure 24 percent is actually a conservative estimate of Connecticut's percentage contribution among all of New England's fifth-generation LDS ancestors; its percentage among New England ancestors *with unique names* is actually 26.1 percent. See table 5.

13. Lewis G. Knapp, *In Pursuit of Paradise: History of the Town of Stratford, Connecticut* (West Kennewbunk, Maine: Phoenix, 1923), 12.

14. Louis B. Mason, *The Life and Times of Major John Mason of Connecticut, 1600–1672* (New York: G. P. Putnam's Sons, 1935), 83.

15. The Stratford heads of household (with LDS convert descendants in parentheses) are as follows: Joseph Judson (Joseph Coe; Heman Tilton and Orson Hyde; George White Pitkin; Catharine Slauson); Henry Gregory (Orson and Heman Tilton Hyde); John Welles (Joseph Coe; Daniel Hanmer Wells); Richard Harvey (Orson and Heman Tilton Hyde); Robert Coe (Joseph Coe); Joseph Hawley (Joseph Coe; John Gould; Catharine Slauson).

16. Thomas Hooker was a direct-line ancestor of LDS converts Shadrach Roundy and Uriah Roundy.

17. William C. Nichols, "A Biographical Sketch of the Life of Thomas Hooker" (International Outreach, 1994), <http://www.intoutreach.org/hooker.html> (Sept. 2003).

18. G. H. Hollister, *The History of Connecticut,* 2 vols. (New Haven: Durrie and Peck, 1855), 1:22.

19. Walker, *Thomas Hooker,* 71–93.

20. Clark, *History of English Nonconformity,* 11.

21. Quoted in Elias B. Sanford, *A History of Connecticut* (Hartford, Conn.: S. S. Scranton, 1888), 17.

22. These early LDS converts with Hartford ancestors included Joseph C. Kingsbury; Asa Lyman; Anson, Orson, Parley P., and William Dickinson Pratt; Philomela Smith; Edward Partridge Sr.; Algernon Gilbert; Hezekiah Peck; Lucy Simmons; Hyram Dayton; Eunice Dunning; Mary Lovisa Parker; Lorain, Jonathan, and Lyman Stevens; Salmon Warner; Chauncey Griswold, Edwin Densmore, James, Jr., and John Webb; and others.

23. Lucas, *Valley of Discord,* 29.

24. Ibid., xii–xiii.

25. William Goodwin was an ancestor not only of Edward Partridge Sr. but also of early LDS converts George White Pitkin and Daniel Hanmer Wells. Some of these connections take us to the sixth-generation ancestors.

26. E. B. Sanford, *History of Connecticut,* 17.

27. See Banks, *Winthrop Fleet of 1630.*

28. E. B. Sanford, *History of Connecticut,* 20. Ancestors of LDS converts in Warham's congregation (with their LDS descendants in parentheses) are as follows: Thomas Baskom (Peter Ingersol; Lydia Kellogg; Ezra Strong); Nicholas Denslow (Emma Hale); John Drake (Ezra Strong); Thomas Ford (Asa Lyman); William Gaylord (David Crandall); Giles Gibbs (Thaddeus Alvord; Jabez Brunson); Jonathan Gillett (Israel and Jonathan Watson Barlow; Aramel, Edson, Philania, and Royal Barney Sr.; Albert Brown; Chauncey Ira Calkins; Fannie, Lydia, Phoebe, Zemira, William, Jr., and William Draper Sr.; Mary Adalaine God-

dard; Lucy Gunn; Isaac, Diantha, and Horace Morley); William Hannum; John Hoskins (Amanda Egglestone; Lydia Kellogg); George Hull (Mary Parker; Daniel and Joseph Stewart Allen; Gideon and Gideon Hayden Carter); Roger Ludlow; John Moore (Lydia Kellogg; Albert Brown; George White Pitkin; Philomela Smith); George Phelps; William Phelps (Ezra Strong; Israel and Jonathan Watson Barlow); Humphrey Pinney (Lydia Kellogg; Ezra Strong); Eltweed Pomeroy (David Wyman Patten); William Rockwell (Asa Lyman; Philomela Smith); Brian Rossiter; Stephen Terry (Alpheus A. Harmon; Joseph C. Kingsbury); John Warham (Edward Partridge Sr.; Shadrach and Uriah Roundy; Salmon and George Washington Gee; Lucy Gunn; Nancy Lampson; John Gould; George White Pitkin); Roger Williams; Henry Wolcott (Frederick Granger Williams).

29. Jones, *Congregational Commonwealth,* 12.

30. Lucas, *Valley of Discord,* 38.

31. Hollister, *History of Connecticut,* 113.

32. For information on Saybrook see Gilman C. Gates, *Saybrook at the Mouth of the Connecticut: The First One Hundred Years* (Orange, Conn.: Wilson H. Lee, 1935).

33. Ibid., 50.

34. Because there was so much migration in and out of Saybrook, it is impossible to indicate all of the relationships. However, among the LDS associations, in addition to Clarke, Parker, Post, and Pratt are the following (LDS convert descendants are in parentheses): Lieutenant Thomas Leffingwell (Erastus Bingham; Vinson Knight); Matthew Griswold (William Martin Ford); Captain John Mason (Alvah Beman); Christopher Huntington (Lois Huntington Cutler); Thomas Bliss (Daniel Avery); Thomas Bliss (Fannie, Zemira, William, Jr., and William Draper Sr.).

35. Atwater, *Colony of New Haven,* 28–30.

36. Rollin G. Osterweis, *Three Centuries of New Haven, 1638–1938* (New Haven: Yale University Press, 1953), 18.

37. Quoted in Atwater, *Colony of New Haven,* 59.

38. Francis J. Degnan, *A New Look at Old New Haven* (New Haven: Yale–New Haven Teachers Institute, 1992), 5.

39. Atwater, *Colony of New Haven,* 230.

40. A. T. Atwood, *Hermetic Philosophy and Alchemy* (New York: Julian, 1960), 232–33.

41. Atwater, *Colony of New Haven,* 37–39.

42. Ibid., 92–102.

43. These converts included Mary Parker; Philo Dibble Sr.; Joseph, Phebe, and Chandler Holbrook; Justus Morse; Phebe Ann Morton; Parley P., Orson, Anson, and William Dickinson Pratt; Solomon and Truman Angell; Nathan Bennett Baldwin Sr.; Laura and Timothy Baldwin Clark; John, Jr., and Zebedee Coltrin; William Draper Sr.; Algernon Gilbert; Charles Nelson Baldwin; Rebecca Bearce; Hezekiah Peck; Mary Lovisa Parker; Lucy Simmons; James, Martha, Reuben, and Samuel McBride; Abigail and Betsy Mead; Lyman, Jonathan, and Lorain Stevens; Amanda Egglestone; Emma Hale; and David Bunnell.

44. There were a number of small hamlets in the colony, and Edward Atwater gives detailed information about the inhabitants of the various towns. Great migration took place between New Haven, Stamford, Guilford, Long Island, Branford, and so on, and it would not be fruitful to attempt to sort out the ancestors in the individual towns. The

town of New Haven remained the center of the colony, and most of the population lived there. See Atwater, *Colony of New Haven.*

Chapter 6: Schismatic New England

1. Lucas, *Valley of Discord,* ix.
2. Ibid.
3. Philip F. Gura, *A Glimpse of Sion's Glory: Puritan Radicalism in New England, 1620–1660* (Middletown, Conn.: Wesleyan University Press, 1984), 7.
4. Alexander Young, *Chronicles of the Pilgrim Fathers of the Colony of Plymouth, 1602–1625* (New York: Da Capo, 1971), chap. 4.
5. Jay W. Palmer, "The Roots of Our Search Committee: A Four Hundred Year Tradition" (Unitarian Universalist Church, 1997), <http://members.aol.com/cwood64801/search.html> (summer 2000).
6. John M. Mecklin, *The Story of American Dissent* (New York: Harcourt, Brace, 1934), 68.
7. Pope, *Pioneers of Massachusetts,* 321.
8. Ibid., 378.
9. Quoted in Charles E. Batchelder, "Rev. Stephen Bachiler, Puritan Emigrant," in *Descendants of Rev. Stephen Bachiler, of England, a Leading Non-Conformist, Who Settled the Town of New Hampton, N.H. and Joseph, Henry, Joshua and John Batcheller of Essex Co., Massachusetts,* ed. Frederick Clifton Pierce (Chicago, Ill.: W. B. Conkey, 1968), 25. Skelton was an ancestor of LDS convert Lydia Chamberlain.
10. Pynchon was a direct-line ancestor of LDS convert Nancy Warriner.
11. Their names were William Blake, Thomas Woodford, Thomas Ufford, Henry Smith, Jehu Burr, John Cable, John Reader, Matthew Mitchell, Samuel Butterfield, Edmund Wood, and Jonas Wood.
12. Gura, *Glimpse of Sion's Glory,* chap. 11.
13. It would be counterproductive to list all the ancestors and their connections with individual LDS converts. The LDS converts having Springfield ancestors included Charles Allen; Benjamin Andrews; Israel and Jonathan Watson Barlow; Aramel, Edson, Philania, Royal, Jr., Rachel, and Royal Barney, Sr.; Mary Adeline Beman; Jane Bicknell; Titus Billings; Electa Chamberlain; Lydia Dibble; Wealthy Eddy; Elisha Hurd Groves; Benjamin Kimball Hall; Malinda Hanson; Alpheus A. and Oliver Harmon; Sarah Sawyer Hastings; Chandler, Joseph, and Phebe Holbrook; Lydia Kellogg; Celia Kent; Joseph and Nancy Kingsbury; Nancy Lampson; Amanda Morgan; Lucy Morley; Justus Morse; Phebe Ann Morton; Ezekiel and Ann Eliza Peck; David Pettigrew; Caroline, Orrin P., and Peter Rockwell; Elizabeth Schellenger; Ann, Benjamin, and Clark Slade; William, Jr., and William Tenney Sr.; Nancy Warriner; Lyman Wight; Frederick G. Williams; Fanny, John, Jr., Susannah, Louisa, Brigham, Nancy, Joseph, Lorenzo Dow, Phineas Howe, and Rhoda Young.
14. See Butler, *Awash in a Sea of Faith;* and John Callender, *Discourse on the Civil and Religious Affairs of the Colony of Rhode Island* (New York: Books for Libraries, 1843).
15. Williams was a direct-line ancestor of early LDS converts Eleazer Miller, Lucina Streeter, and Catharine Slauson. For information on Williams, see Samuel Hugh Brockuner, *The Irrepressible Democrat: Roger Williams* (New York: Ronald, 1940); Raymond L.

Camp, *Roger Williams, God's Apostle of Advocacy: Biography and Rhetoric,* vol. 36 of *Studies in American Religion* (Lewiston, N.Y.: Edwin Mellen, 1989); Cyclone Covey, *The Gentle Radical: A Biography of Roger Williams* (New York: Macmillan, 1966); Gaustad, *Liberty of Conscience;* W. Clark Gilpin, *The Millenarian Piety of Roger Williams* (Chicago: University of Chicago Press, 1979); Ola Winslow, *Master Roger Williams: A Biography* (New York: Macmillan, 1957).

16. Covey, *Gentle Radical,* 8.

17. Quoted in Martin E. Marty, *Pilgrims in Their Own Land* (Boston: Little, Brown, 1984), 76.

18. Ellis, *Puritan Age,* 268.

19. Covey, *Gentle Radical,* 4.

20. Quoted in Gaustad, *Liberty of Conscience,* 38.

21. Ibid., 38–44.

22. Quoted in ibid., 39–40.

23. Quoted in ibid., 40.

24. Quoted in ibid., 42.

25. John N. McClintock, *History of New Hampshire* (Boston: B. B. Russell, Cornhill, 1888), 49.

26. See Thomas A. Jacobson, *The Robertses of Northern New England* (New York: Heritage Books, 1994).

27. Everett S. Stackpole, *History of New Hampshire,* 4 vols. (New York: American Historical Society, 1945), 1:11; Hamilton Hurd, *History of Rockingham and Strafford Counties, New Hampshire, with Biographical Sketches of Many of Its Pioneers and Prominent Men* (Philadelphia: J. W. Lewis, 1882), 759.

28. Stackpole, *History of New Hampshire,* 1:11.

29. John Scales, *History of Dover, New Hampshire* (Manchester, N.H.: John B. Clarke, 1923), 5.

30. Jacobson, *Robertses,* 5–6. It is not clear who the parents of Rebecca were, but she must have been the daughter of either William or Edward Hilton. They were the ancestors of early LDS converts David Cluff, Heber C. Kimball, Daniel Sanborn Miles, and Mary Thurston Rand.

31. B. R. White, *Hanserd Knollys and Radical Dissent in the 17th Century* (London: Dr. William's Trust, 1977), 41.

32. Scales, *History of Dover,* 303.

33. McClintock, *History of New Hampshire,* 33.

34. Quoted in Scales, *History of Dover,* 36. Edward Starbuck was an ancestor to Mary Thurston Rand and through marriage is related to early converts Aaron, Amasa F., Olive M., Selah, Nathan Calhoon, and Elijah Cheney as well as Andrew Lee Allen.

35. Ibid., 1.

36. Ibid., 74.

37. Bachiler's name was also spelled Batchelder and Batcheller.

38. Gura, *Glimpse of Sion's Glory,* 3–4.

39. Pope, *Pioneers of Massachusetts,* 26.

40. Alastair Hamilton, *The Family of Love* (Cambridge, Eng.: J. Clarke, 1981), 34.

41. Ibid., 36.

42. Ibid., 34–39.

43. Ibid., 128–35.

44. Quoted in ibid., 130.

45. A number of additional churches were found in England at that time. For example, Montanism, which had died in the fifth century, experienced a brief resurrection. It was based on the belief that the Holy Spirit would manifest itself to the pure and faithful. Montanus had taught that people were like musical instruments on which the Holy Spirit plays: "Behold, the man is a lyre, and I sweep over him as a plectrum" (quoted in Henry Chadwick, *The Early Church* [London: Pelican Books, 1967], 52).

46. See Philip Mason Marston, *The Reverend Stephen Bachiler: Saint or Sinner?* (Concord, N.H.: Society of Colonial Wars in the State of New Hampshire, 1961); and Sanborn, "Stephen Bachiler."

47. Marston, *Reverend Stephen Bachiler,* 160.

48. John Winthrop, *The Journal of John Winthrop,* ed. Richard Dunn and Laetitia Yeandle (Cambridge, Mass.: Harvard University Press, 1996), 1:65.

49. Bachiler was an ancestor of Heber C. Kimball, Thomas Jefferson Butterfield, Josiah Butterfield, and Mary Thurston Rand.

50. Marston, *Reverend Stephen Bachiler,* 3.

51. Ibid., 1.

52. Joseph Dow, *History of the Town of Hampton: From Its First Settlement in 1638 to the Autumn of 1892* (Hampton, N.H.: Peter E. Randall, 1988), 8; Hurd, *History of Rockingham and Strafford Counties,* 318.

53. Dow, *Town of Hampton.* I found 42 heads of household, among them the following (with their LDS convert descendants in parentheses): Henry Ambrose (Julia Foster; Abigail Glidden); Stephen Bachiler (Heber C. Kimball; Thomas Jefferson and Josiah Butterfield; Mary Thurston Rand; Heman Tilton Hyde; Samuel Jones Rolfe); Thomas Chase (Anna, Esther, Hyruna, Joseph, Jr., Joseph, Sr., Newell, and Polly Knight; Ann and Clark Slade); William Cole (Aaron Cheney, Amasa Cheney, Olive M. Cheney, Selah Cheney); Moses Cox (Mary Thurston Rand, Andrew Lee Allen, Daniel Sanborn Hyde); John Cross (Benjamin Andrews); James, Sr., and James Davis Jr. (Alva Lewis, John Harvey, and William Plumber Tippets; Salmon Warner; Aramel, Edson, Philania, Royal, Jr., Rachel Marsh, and Royal Barney Sr.); William Godfrey (Andrew Lee Allen); Daniel Hendrick (Heber C. Kimball); Christopher Hussey (Samuel Jones Rolfe); Edmund Johnson (Aaron, Amasa, Olive M., and Selah Cheney); John Marston (Laban Morrill); William Marston (Mary Thurston Rand); William Moulton (Daniel Sanborn Miles; Mary Thurston Rand; Samuel Brown; Clarissa, John F., and Olive Boynton); John Moulton (William Walker Rust; Aaron and Amasa Cheney); Robert Page (Samuel Brown; Samuel Jones Rolfe; Heman Tilton Hyde); Isaac Perkins (Mary Thurston Rand; Daniel Sanborn Miles); John Philbrick (Daniel Sanborn Miles; Mary Thurston Rand); Thomas Philbrick (Joseph, Sr., Joseph, Jr., Hyruna, Esther, Newell, Anna, and Polly Knight; Mary Thurston Rand; William Walker Rust); John Sanborn and Robert Tucke (Mary Thurston Rand; Lydia Smith; Daniel Sanborn Miles); William Sanborn (Heman Tilton Hyde); William Sergeant (John F. Boynton); Richard Swain (Samuel Brown; Mary Thurston Rand; Lydia Chamberlain).

54. Ibid., 87.

55. Ibid.

56. Hurd, *History of Rockingham and Strafford Counties,* 363. The name is attached to the museum (Tuck Museum), which houses the Hampton Historical Society and its genealogical holdings.

57. Ibid., 199–200.

58. Marston, *Reverend Stephen Bachiler,* 7.

59. Emery Battis, *Saints and Sectaries: Anne Hutchinson and the Antinomian Controversy in the Massachusetts Bay Colony* (Chapel Hill, N.C.: University of North Carolina Press, 1962), 342.

60. George Barstow, *The History of New Hampshire* (Concord, N.H.: I. S. Boyd, 1842), 50–52.

61. Dow, *Town of Hampton,* 7.

Chapter 7: The Antinomian Crisis

1. Sydney V. James, *Colonial Rhode Island: A History* (New York: Charles Scribner's Sons, 1975), 21.

2. Gertrude Huehns, *Antinomianism in English History* (London: Cresset, 1951), 38, 90.

3. Battis, *Saints and Sectaries,* appendixes 2 and 3.

4. Thomas W. Bicknell, *Story of Dr. John Clarke* (Providence, R.I.: T. W. Bicknell, 1915), 59.

5. Selma R. Williams, *Divine Rebel: The Life of Anne Marbury Hutchinson* (New York: Holt, Rinehart and Winston, 1981), 14–15.

6. Ibid., 52.

7. Ibid.

8. See Hamilton, *Family of Love.*

9. Battis, *Saints and Sectaries,* 11.

10. Ibid., 83.

11. Ibid., 85.

12. Marty, *Pilgrims in Their Own Land,* 29.

13. See Charles Francis Adams, *Antinomianism in the Colony of Massachusetts Bay, 1636–1638* (New York: Burt Franklin, 1967); and Battis, *Saints and Sectaries.*

14. The document is reprinted in Adams, *Antinomianism in the Colony,* 67–233.

15. Drake, *History of Boston,* 148. There is ample evidence that John Winthrop, the first governor of Massachusetts, "had a principal hand in it."

16. Quoted in Adams, *Antinomianism in the Colony,* 71.

17. William Dyer was the husband of Mary Dyer, who was hanged in 1660 for Quakerism, and he was the ancestor of William Wines Phelps. One of the best refutations of Welde's work came from John Wheelwright, in a book he called *Mercurius Americanus,* reprinted in John Wheelwright, *John Wheelwright: His Writings* (Boston: Prince Society, 1876), 181–228.

18. Lowell Bennion gives more weight to grace than most Mormons, though he also recognizes that the Mormon faith stresses "individual agency and responsibility, struggle and conquest, works and achievement" ("For by Grace Are Ye Saved," *Dialogue: A Journal of Mormon Thought* 1, no. 4 [1966]: 101).

19. Thomas Welde's *Short Story* was published in 1644 and reprinted in Adams, *Antinomianism in the Colony,* 72–233.

20. Battis, *Saints and Sectaries,* 177–79.

21. Adams, *Antinomianism in the Colony,* 188.

22. Richard Godbeer, *The Devil's Dominion: Magic and Religion in Early New England* (Cambridge, Eng.: Cambridge University Press, 1992), 9.

23. Battis, *Saints and Sectaries,* 50.

24. Ibid., 57.

25. Francis J. Bremer, *Anne Hutchinson: Troubler of the Puritan Zion* (Huntington, N.Y.: Robert E. Krieger, 1981), 1–3.

26. Quoted in Edwin S. Gaustad, ed., *A Documentary History of Religion in America to the Civil War* (Grand Rapids, Mich.: Christian University Press, 1993), 133.

27. Those traveling to Rhode Island, having been banished because of their Antinomian activities, as well as later followers, included: William Hutchinson (husband of Anne), William Aspinwall, Samuel Cole, William Dyer (husband of Mary), Edward Rainsford, John Batton, John Sanford, Richard Cooke, Richard Fairbanks, Oliver Mellows, Samuel Wilbour, John Oliver, Richard Gridley, Zachariah Bosworth, William Townsend, William Pell, Richard Hutchinson, James Johnson, Thomas Savage, John Odlin, Gamalial Wayte, Edward Hutchinson, Isaac Gross, Richard Carder, Robert Harding, Richard Wayte, John Porter, Jacob Elliott, Thomas Wardell, William Wardell, William Baulston, William Freeborn, Henry Bull, William Salter, Dr. John Clarke, John Coggeshall, Mr. Easton of Newbury, Richard Bulgar, and Philip Sherman of Roxbury. Bicknell, *Dr. John Clarke,* 69.

28. Harding, *Abraham Harding,* 39–42.

29. Pope, *Pioneers of Massachusetts,* 212.

30. See Harding, *Abraham Harding.*

31. Winsor, *Memorial History of Boston,* 1:173.

32. Battis, *Saints and Sectaries,* 57.

33. Ibid., 114.

34. Winthrop, *Journal of John Winthrop,* 132.

35. The eight Exeter companions were Richard Merrys, Richard Bulgar, Philemon Purmot, Isaac Grosse, Chistopher Marshall, George Baytes, Thomas Wardell, and William Wardell. See Drake, *History of Boston,* 224.

36. Quoted in Stackpole, *History of New Hampshire,* 1:44.

37. Wayne Clark Gilman, *The Hingham Founding Fathers of "Old Colony" New Hampshire* (Boston: Heritage Books, 1955).

38. Stackpole, *History of New Hampshire,* 1:44.

39. The ancestors were as follows (with LDS convert descendants in parentheses): Thomas Wight (Newell, Hyruna, Esther, Anna, Joseph, Sr., Joseph, Jr., Polly, and Vinson Knight; Thomas B. and Ann Marsh; Esther, Ezekiel, and Hezekiah Peck); William Wentworth (Andrew Lee Allen; Huldah Chapman; Elezer Freeman, Caroline Eliza, Freeman, Levi Stillman, Uriel Chittendon, and Moses Chapman Nickerson); Samuell Walker (Amanda Melissa Barnes; William Walker Rust); Darby Field or Fifield (Mary Thurston Rand; Lydia Smith); Edmund Littlefield (Aaron, Elijah, Amasa F., Olive M., and Selah Cheney; Lydia Clisbee; Waldo Littlefield); John Cram (Lydia Chamberlain); William

Wardell (William Walker Rust; Edmond and James Durfee); Robert Smith (Andrew Lee Allen); Nicholas Needham (Uriah and Shadrach Roundy); William E. Coole (Aaron, Elijah, Amasa F., Nathan Calhoon, Olive M., and Selah Cheney).

40. Stackpole, *History of New Hampshire,* 1:44.

41. Albert D. Rust, *Record of the Rust Family* (Waco, Tex.: Albert D. Rust, 1891), 21. The term "servant" at that time signaled simply that he was employed by Quincy.

42. Battis, *Saints and Sectaries,* 307.

43. Pope, *Pioneers of Massachusetts,* 479.

44. John Bean's LDS descendants were Mary Thurston Rand and Lydia Smith; Alexander Gordon's were Andrew Lee Allen and Mary Thurston Rand through Mary Gordon; and John Sinclair's was Julia Foster through Sarah Sinclair.

45. Edward J. Cowan, "Prophecy and Prophylaxis: A Paradigm for the Scotch-Irish?" in *Ulster and North America: Transatlantic Perspectives on the Scotch-Irish,* ed. H. Tyler Blethen and W. Wood Curtis Jr., 15–23 (Tuscaloosa: University of Alabama Press, 1997).

46. Bean, *Life and Family of John Bean,* 3.

Chapter 8: Anabaptists, Quakers, and Gortonists

1. George Washington Greene, *A Short History of Rhode Island* (Providence, R.I.: J. A. and R. A. Reid, 1877), 140.

2. See Hans J. Hillerbrand, *Radical Tendencies in the Reformation: Divergent Perspectives* (Kirksville, Mo.: Sixteenth Century, 1988).

3. See Horst, *Radical Brethren.*

4. E. Belfort Bax, *The Rise and Fall of the Anabaptists* (1903; reprint, New York: A. M. Kelley, 1970), 388.

5. Ibid. See also Hillerbrand, *Radical Tendencies.*

6. Isaac Backus, *A History of New England with Particular Reference to the Baptists,* 3 vols. (1871; reprint, New York: Arno and New York Times, 1969), 1:87.

7. We previously noted Williams's descendants, Eleazer Miller, Lucina Streeter, and Catharine Slauson. Other ancestors (with their Mormon convert descendants in parentheses) are as follows: Stukeley Westcott (Catharine Slauson); William Arnold (Lydia and Celinda Ackermann); John Greene Sr. (Anna Pixley Johnson; Orson, Parley P., Anson, and William Dickinson Pratt; Maria Sagers; Reynolds and William Farrington Cahoon; Evan Melbourne and John P. Greene); William Harris (Lydia and Celinda Ackermann); William Carpenter (Horace, Diantha, Isaac, and Lucy Diantha Morley; Laban Morrill; Martin Horton, Ann Eliza, Nancy F., and Sally Ann Peck); Thomas Olney (James William, Solomon, and Truman Osborn Angell).

8. Gilpin, *Millenarian Piety,* 31.

9. John 3:4; Ephesians 2:10.

10. Gilpin, *Millenarian Piety,* 53–54.

11. Sidney Perley, *The History of Salem Massachusetts,* 2 vols., (Salem, Mass.: Sidney Perley, 1924), 1:272–73.

12. Callender, *Discourse on Rhode Island,* 34.

13. Gilpin, *Millenarian Piety,* 59.

14. Ibid., 148.

15. Quoted in Gaustad, *Liberty of Conscience,* 93.

16. Gilpin, *Millenarian Piety,* 171.

17. Dan Vogel describes Roger Williams as a prime example of the Seeker beliefs that parallel those of Mormonism in *Religious Seekers,* 58, 61, 81, 85, 99, 141–42, 184.

18. "Anabaptize" means to rebaptize.

19. Quoted in Bicknell, *Dr. John Clarke,* 152.

20. John Clarke, "Ill-Newes from New England: Or a Narrative of New-Englands Persecution," in *Colonial Baptists: Massachusetts and Rhode Island,* ed. Edwin S. Gaustad, 1–113 (New York: Arno, 1980), 21, 23.

21. Backus, *History of New England,* 1:126; Edwin S. Gaustad, *Baptist Piety: The Last Will and Testimony of Obadiah Holmes* (Grand Rapids, Mich.: Christian University Press, 1978), 140.

22. O. K. Armstrong and Marjorie M. Armstrong, *The Indomitable Baptists: A Narrative of Their Role in Shaping American History* (Garden City, N.Y.: Doubledaay, 1967), 59.

23. Leon H. McBeth, *The Baptist Heritage* (Nashville, Tenn.: Broadman, 1987), 7–8.

24. Gaustad, *Baptist Piety,* 44.

25. Ibid., 45.

26. See Don A. Sanford, *A Choosing People: A History of the Seventh Day Baptists* (Nashville, Tenn.: Broadman, 1992).

27. Robert G. Gardner, *Baptists of Early America: A Statistical History, 1639–1790* (Atlanta: Georgia Baptist Historical Society, 1983), 44.

28. Henry E. Turner, *The Greenes of Warwick in Colonial History* (Newport, R.I.: Davis and Pitman, 1877), 8.

29. The Clarke brothers (with their LDS convert descendants in parentheses) were as follows: William Clarke (Emer, Martin, and Preserved Harris); Thomas Clarke (Anson, Orson, Parley P., and William Dickinson Pratt); Joseph Clarke (Rebecca and Thomas Burdick); Thomas Hazard Clarke (John Tanner; Jesse Baker).

30. See R. C. Anderson, "Swansea, Massachusetts."

31. Ibid.

32. Gaustad, *Liberty of Conscience,* 116–17.

33. Bowen, *Early Rehoboth,* 1:29.

34. H. L. Peter Rounds, "Lists of Baptists in Rehoboth, Massachusetts in the 1700s," *New England Historical and Genealogical Register* 88 (1984): 21–34.

35. Gaustad, *Baptist Piety,* 22.

36. The early LDS convert descendants of John Crandall included Celinda and Lydia Ackermann; Lebbeus T. Coons, Sr.; David Crandall; Sanford Porter; and Louisa Tanner. Those of Obadiah Holmes included Rhonda, Ira, Alfred, Huldah, Russell W., and Sterry Fisk; Martin Horton, Hezekiah, Ann Eliza, Nancy, and Sally Ann Peck; Catharine Slauson; Cynthia Elizabeth Soule; Erastus Wightman; Benjamin Freeman Bird; Alpheus Gifford; and Keziah Pearce.

37. Gaustad, *Baptist Piety,* 128–33.

38. Ibid., 10–11.

39. Quoted in ibid., 18.

40. Gardner, *Baptists of Early America,* 44.

41. Pestana, "Sectarianism," 77.

42. Backus, *History of New England,* 1:288.

43. Anna B. Williams, *The Rogerines* (Boston: Stanhope, 1904), 126.

44. Quoted in Richard L. Bushman, *From Puritan to Yankee* (Cambridge, Mass.: Harvard University Press, 1967), 165.

45. Frances M. Caulkins, *History of New London* (New London, Conn.: H. D. Utley, 1905), 201–10.

46. John R. Bolles and Anna B. Williams, *The Rogerenes* (Boston: F. H. Gilson, 1904), chap. 2; Caulkins, *History of New London,* 203–4. Curiously, the Griswold family has a large number of contact points with early LDS converts. Elizabeth was the daughter of Matthew Griswold, who had settled in Saybrook. Matthew's brother Edward was the ancestor of LDS converts Lucy Simmons; Hannah Griswold; Chauncey Griswold Webb; George Washington Gee; Alvah and Mary Adeline Beman; William, Sr., William, Jr., Fannie, Lydia, Phoebe, and Zemira Draper; Daniel Kent; Ezra Strong; Vinson Knight; William Wines Phelps; Moses Tracy; and Lydia Kellogg. Another brother of Matthew was Michael Griswold, who was the ancestor of Vilate and Roswell Murray.

47. McBeth, *Baptist Heritage,* 123.

48. Brooke, *Refiner's Fire,* 85.

49. We recall from chapter 7 that Wheelwright was Anne Marbury Hutchinson's brother-in-law, and he was implicated in the Massachusetts Antinomian crisis.

50. McClintock, *History of New Hampshire,* 41; Knollys quoted in B. R. White, *The English Baptists of the Seventeenth Century* (London: Baptist Historical Society, 1983), 5–7.

51. Scales, *History of Dover,* 91. Thomas Roberts was an ancestor of early LDS converts David Cluff, Heber C. Kimball, and Mary Thurston Rand.

52. Quoted in ibid., 165. Starbuck was the ancestor of Mary Thurston Rand; Aaron, Amasa F., Olive M., and Selah Cheney; and Andrew Lee Allen.

53. Millet, *History of the Baptists,* 24–27.

54. Ibid., 27.

55. Bicknell, *Dr. John Clarke,* 153. We have outlined the LDS connections of Coddington and the Clarkes, so we note here only that Caleb Carr was the ancestor of Lavina Draper and John Portineus Greene.

56. Pestana, "Sectarianism."

57. The ancestors (with their LDS convert descendants in parentheses) are as follows: Joseph Boyce (Polly Chubuck; Cassandra Buffum; Elias Hutchins; Lyman Curtis); William King and Agnes Elwill (Mehitable Wells); John Marston (Laban Morrill); William Marston (Mary Thurston Rand); Samuel Shattuck (Josiah and Thomas Jefferson Butterfield; David Nelson; David Wyman Patten); John Smith (Betsy Taylor Putnam; Vilate Stockwell); Lawrence Southwick, Daniel Southwick, and John Southwick (Polly Chubuck); Lawrence Southwick (Elias Hutchins; Lyman Curtis); Henry Trask (Lyman Curtis).

58. George Selleck, *Quakers in Boston, 1656–1964* (Cambridge, Mass.: Thomas Todd, 1976), 7.

59. Jonathan M. Chu, *Neighbors, Friends, or Madmen: The Puritan Adjustment of Quakerism in Seventeenth Century Massachusetts Bay* (Westport, Conn.: Greenwood, 1985), 59–77.

60. Alexander Starbuck, *The History of Nantucket* (Boston: C. E. Goodspeed, 1924), 15–16. Richard Swaine was an ancestor of LDS converts Samuel Brown, Lydia Chamberlain,

Mary Thurston Rand, and Abigail Glidden. John Heard was an ancestor of Aaron, Amasa F., Olive M., and Selah Cheney; Mary Thurston Rand; and Andrew Lee Allen.

61. Selleck, *Quakers in Boston,* 1.

62. William Marsten was an ancestor of Mary Thurston Rand.

63. James Bowden, *The History of the Society of Friends in America,* 2 vols. (New York: Arno, 1972), 1:153.

64. Thomas Harris was an ancestor of LDS converts Martin, Emer, and Preserved Harris.

65. Selleck, *Quakers in Boston,* 11.

66. Christopher Holder was an ancestor of LDS converts Caroline, Freeman, Moses Chapman, Elezer Freeman, Uriel Chittendon Hatch, and Levi Stillman Nickerson; Huldah Chapman; Darwin, Eli, and Stephen Chase. John Copeland had ties to Mormon converts through his brother, Lawrence, who was an ancestor of LDS convert Marshall Moore Hubbard. John Rouse was an ancestor of Rachel Marsh Barney.

67. Arthur J. Worrall, *Quakers in the Colonial Northeast* (Hanover, N.H.: University Press of New England, 1980), 10.

68. We note that Mary Dyer, the mother of the so-called monster child that Anne Hutchinson helped deliver in 1637, was a direct-line ancestor of LDS convert William Wines Phelps.

69. See Carla Gardina Pestana, *Quakers and Baptists in Colonial Massachusetts* (Cambridge, Eng.: Cambridge University Press, 1991).

70. Lawrence and Cassandra Southwick were ancestors of LDS converts Polly Chubuck, Elias Hutchins, and Lyman Curtis.

71. Samuel Shattuck was an ancestor of LDS converts Josiah and Thomas Jefferson Butterfield, David Nelson, and David Wyman Patten.

72. Selleck, *Quakers in Boston,* 9–10.

73. Quoted in Horatio Rogers, *Mary Dyer of Rhode Island: The Quaker Martyr* (Providence, R.I.: Preston and Rounds, 1896), 38.

74. Quoted in ibid., 59.

75. Bowden, *Society of Friends,* 1:29–30.

76. Quoted in Melvin B. Endy, *William Fowler, the Magistrate, and One Line of His Descendants* (Boston: N.p., 1973), 55.

77. William J. Frost, *The Quaker Family in Colonial America: A Portrait of the Society of Friends* (New York: Edwin Mellen, 1973), 53–54.

78. Worrall, *Quakers,* 71.

79. Chu, *Neighbors, Friends, or Madmen,* appendix 1.

80. Worrall, *Quakers,* 28.

81. Scales, *History of Dover,* 39.

82. Coleman was likely an ancestor of LDS convert Nancy Fowler. See Hurd, *History of Rockingham and Strafford Counties,* 807–9; and Worrall, *Quakers,* 27.

83. Hurd, *History of Rockingham and Strafford Counties,* 809.

84. Starbuck, *History of Nantucket,* 18.

85. Quoted in Lewis G. Janes, *Samuell Gorton: A Forgotten Founder of Our Liberties, First Settler of Warwick, R. I.* (Providence, R.I.: Preston and Rounds, 1896), 83.

86. Ibid., 28.

87. Kenneth W. Porter, "Samuell Gorton: New England Firebrand," *New England Quarterly* 7 (1934): 405–44.

88. Quoted in ibid., 411.

89. Gura, *Glimpse of Sion's Glory,* 276.

90. Noted in K. W. Porter, "Samuell Gorton," 427.

91. Brooke, *Refiner's Fire,* 46.

92. Ibid.

93. Turner, *Greenes of Warwick.* John Greene Sr. was a direct-line ancestor of early LDS converts John P. Greene; Anson, Parley P., Orson, and William Dickinson Pratt; Maria Sagers; Reynolds and William Farrington Cahoon; Anson and Cyril Call.

94. Brooke, *Refiner's Fire,* 46.

95. Quoted in ibid.

96. James, *Colonial Rhode Island,* 31.

97. Randall Holden was an ancestor of LDS converts Anna, Esther, Hyruna, Joseph, Jr., Newell, Polly, and Vinson Knight; Ezekiel, Hezekiah, Berthena, Nicholas, Polly, Sally Ann, Nancy F., Ann Eliza, and Martin Horton Peck; Clarissa and John Reed.

98. The descendants of Richard Waterman and John Warner are listed among the early residents of Providence.

Chapter 9: LDS Ancestors Engaged in Alchemy and Astrology

1. D. Michael Quinn, *Early Mormonism and the Magic World View* (Salt Lake City: Signature Books, 1987), 225–27.

2. See Brooke, *Refiner's Fire.*

3. Jan Shipps has provided an extensive review of the responses of Mormon scholars to Brooke's book in *Mormonism,* particularly chapter 10, "Thoughts about the Academic Community's Response to John Brooke's *Refiner's Fire.*"

4. Quinn, *Mormon Hierarchy,* 563–64.

5. Jan Shipps, "Another Side of Early Mormonism," in *Journals of McLellin,* ed. Shipps and Welch, 3.

6. John W. Welch, "The Acts of the Apostle William E. McLellin," in *Journals of McLellin,* ed. Shipps and Welch, 16.

7. Ibid.

8. Godbeer, *Devil's Dominion,* 5–23.

9. Butler, *Awash in a Sea of Faith,* 3.

10. Hall, "World of Wonders," 273.

11. Butler, *Awash in a Sea of Faith,* 3

12. See Cowan, "Prophecy and Prophylaxis."

13. Ahlstrom, *Religious History of the American People,* 198.

14. Hall, "World of Wonders," 202.

15. Arthur Edward Waite, *The Brotherhood of the Rosy Cross* (New York: University Books, 1961), 72.

16. Jakob Böhme, *Mysterium Magnum; Or, an Exposition of the First Book of Moses Called Genesis,* trans. John Sparrow, vol. 2 (London: J. M. Watkins, 1965), 2nd epistle, verse 6.

17. Waite, *Brotherhood,* 182.

18. Christopher McIntosh, *The Rosicrucians: The History and Mythology of an Occult Order* (Wellingborough, Eng.: Crucible, 1987), 19.

19. Godbeer, *Devil's Dominion,* 27–30. It is because of the Puritans' dedicated efforts that Keith Thomas is able to claim that by the end of the seventeenth century magic had been rooted out of the mainstream institutional religious life of people. See Keith Thomas, *Religion and the Decline of Magic* (New York: Scribner, 1971), 643–47.

20. Butler, *Awash in a Sea of Faith,* 68.

21. Brooke, *Refiner's Fire,* chap. 1.

22. Ibid., xiii.

23. See Henry W. Rugg, *History of Freemasonry in Rhode Island* (Providence, R.I.: E. L. Freeman and Son, 1895).

24. See R. Swinburne Clymer, *The Rosicrucians: Their Teachings* (Quakertown, Pa.: Philosophical, 1941); McIntosh, *Rosicrucians;* Waite, *Brotherhood.*

25. Atwood, *Hermetic Philosophy and Alchemy,* 26.

26. Quoted in Ronald Sterne Wilkinson, "The Alchemical Library of John Winthrop, Jr. (1606–1675) and His Descendants in Colonial America," *Ambix* 11 (1963): 33.

27. Butler, *Awash in a Sea of Faith,* 75–76; Wilkinson, "Alchemical Library of John Winthrop," 33–51.

28. Susan Crawford, ed., *The Hartlib Papers* (Ann Arbor, Mich.: UMI Research Publications, 1995), CD disk 1.

29. Brooke, *Refiner's Fire,* 36.

30. Wilkinson, "George Starkey, Physician and Alchemist," *Ambix* 11 (1963): 121–52.

31. Ibid., 128.

32. Mark Stavish, "The History of Alchemy in America" (1996), *Hermetic Library,* <hermetic.com/stavish/alchemy/history.html) (2003). Wilkinson, for example, points out that Robert Child is often seen as the author of these works, while Mark Stavish, for one, thinks it was George Starkey. See Wilkinson, "George Starkey," 40.

33. Butler, *Awash in a Sea of Faith,* 75–76.

34. Stavish, "History of Alchemy."

35. Ronald Sterne Wilkinson, "New England's Last Alchemists," *Ambix* 20 (1973): 129–38.

36. Jonathan Brewster was an ancestor of LDS converts Daniel Avery, Rhoda Walker, and Sarah King.

37. See Brewster, *William Brewster.*

38. Brooke, *Refiner's Fire,* 58.

39. Leon Clark Hills, *History and Genealogy of the Mayflower Planters and First Comers to Ye Olde Colonie* (Washington, D.C.: Hills, 1941), 46.

40. Wilkinson, "Alchemical Library of John Winthrop," 46.

41. Brooke, *Refiner's Fire,* 8, 37.

42. Quoted in David S. Lovejoy, *Religious Enthusiasm in the New World: Heresy to Revolution* (Cambridge, Mass.: Harvard University Press, 1985), 84–85.

43. Quinn, *Early Mormonism,* 28–31.

44. Godbeer, *Devil's Dominion,* 132.

45. Ibid., 138.

46. Simon Bradstreet was an ancestor of Edward Partridge Sr.

47. Marion Barber Stowell, *Early American Almanacs: The Colonial Weekday Bible* (New York: B. Franklin, 1977), 13.

48. Samuel Danforth's brother Jonathan was a direct-line ancestor of converts Ebenezer and John Edward Page.

49. Quoted in Godbeer, *Devil's Dominion,* 139.

50. Since 1687 the Tulley almanacs in Boston and the Leeds almanacs in Philadelphia had dominated the market, until Benjamin Franklin's almanacs, authored by Richard Saunders, came into existence in 1733. See ibid., 144–49.

51. Hall, "World of Wonders," 7.

52. The Julian calendar was 11 minutes and 14 seconds too long, and the error accumulated such that every 128 years the calendar had moved one day out of correspondence with the movements of the sun and moon. In 1582 Pope Gregory XIII decreed that the day following 4 October 1582 would be designated 15 October, so that a closer correspondence could be achieved. He adjusted the calendar so that every third year ending in 00 (1600, 1700, 1800, etc.) remained common years rather than leap years, so that the calendar would correspond closely with the revolutions of the moon.

53. Quinn, *Early Mormonism,* 59–66.

Chapter 10: Witchcraft among LDS Ancestors

1. Gamioni Salgado, *The Elizabethan Underworld* (New York: St. Martin's, 1992), chap. 4.

2. Barbara Ehrenreich and Deirdre English, *Witches, Midwives, and Nurses,* 2nd ed. (Old Westbury, N.Y.: Feminist, 1973), 5–6.

3. Barry Reay, *Popular Cultures in England, 1550–1750* (London: Longman, 1998), 104.

4. Quoted in Butler, *Awash in a Sea of Faith,* 72.

5. Godbeer, *Devil's Dominion,* 7–8.

6. Ibid., 33.

7. Ibid., 34.

8. Paul Boyer and Stephen Nissenbaum, *Salem Possessed: The Social Origins of Witchcraft* (Cambridge, Mass.: Harvard University Press, 1974), 1.

9. Winthrop, *Journal of John Winthrop,* 325.

10. Quoted in Marilynne K. Roach, *The Salem Witch Trials: A Day-by-Day Chronicle of a Cummunity under Siege* (New York: Cooper Square, 2002), xxiii. See also Robert J. Taylor, *Colonial Connecticut: A History* (Millwood, N.Y.: Kraus-Thompson, 1979), 23–24.

11. Godbeer is a bit more conservative in his figures, claiming that 61 accusations of witchcrafts were made during this time in 28 different communities that resulted in 16 convictions and at least 14 executions. See Godbeer, *Devil's Dominion,* 237.

12. John Putnam Demos, *Entertaining Satan: Witchcraft and the Culture of Early New England* (Oxford, Eng.: Oxford University Press, 1982), 112.

13. Quoted in ibid., 100.

14. Boyer and Nissenbaum, *Salem Possessed,* 12–13.

15. Demos, *Entertaining Satan,* 403.

16. Quoted in ibid., 332. Peter Johnson, a drowning victim of Cole's, was also an an-

cestor of LDS converts Aaron, Amasa F., Olive, and Selah Cheney. James Philbrick was an ancestor of Joseph, Jr., Joseph, Sr., Newell, Vinson, Hyruna, Anna, and Polly Knight; Daniel Sanborn Miles; and William Walker Rust.

17. Hurd, *History of Rockingham and Strafford Counties,* 322.

18. Isabel Austin was born in England, and after arriving in America she married Philip Towle, who was a seaman from Ireland. The Rust line runs through their son, Benjamin Towle, who was born in Rockingham, New Hampshire, in 1669.

19. Rebecca and Rachel Brabrooke were daughters of John Brabrooke (Brabrook) of Massachusetts, an ancestor of Daniel, Elias, and Maria Pulsipher.

20. Demos, *Entertaining Satan,* 331–32.

21. See Lucas, *Valley of Discord.*

22. Carolyn S. Langdon, "Connecticut Witchcraft: What Was It?" *Connecticut Historical Society Bulletin* 38, no. 1 (1973): 23–29.

23. Quoted in R. J. Taylor, *Colonial Connecticut,* 36.

24. Godbeer, *Devil's Dominion,* 66.

25. Ibid., 236.

26. Wells was an ancestor of Lucy Gunn, Catharine Slauson, and a number of Johnson brothers and sisters: Almera Woodard, Delcena D., Emily, Joel Hills, and Nancy Maria.

27. R. J. Taylor, *Colonial Connecticut,* 38.

28. Langdon, "Connecticut Witchcraft," 27.

29. R. J. Taylor, *Colonial Connecticut,* 47–61.

30. Ibid., 62–78. Disborough was an ancestor of Hanna and Zina Redfield.

31. Drake, *History of Boston,* 495–97.

32. The Parsons were ancestors of LDS converts Titus Billings, Oliver Harmon, Amanda Morgan, and Charles Morris Phelps.

33. Mason Arnold Green, *Springfield, 1636–1886: History of Town and City* (Springfield, Mass.: A. S. Nichols, 1888), 101–9.

34. Godbeer, *Devil's Dominion,* 66.

35. Ibid., 242.

36. Perley, *History of Salem,* 1:177.

37. Godbeer, *Devil's Dominion,* 191.

38. Jonathan Walcott and Nathaniel Ingersoll were ancestors of LDS converts Asahel, Hiram, Isaac, and William Chadwick Perry. Walcott was also an ancestor of Mary Mott.

39. A formal complaint was the legal document used when the accusers took steps to have someone arrested and then examined by the magistrates. Those Walcott accused included the following: Sarah Cloyce, Elizabeth Proctor, Philip English, Lydia Dustin, Susannah Martin, Dorcas Hoar, Sarah Morrell, George Burroughts, John Alden, John Floyd, Elizabeth Fosdick, Wilmot Redd, Sarah Rice, William Proctor, Elizabeth Howe, Arthur Abbot, Martha Carrier, Mary Toothaker, and Margaret Toothaker. Those Ingersoll accused included the following: Sarah Cloyce, Elizabeth Proctor, Daniel Andrew, George Jacobs Jr., Rebecca Jacobs, Sarah Buckley, Mary Whittredge, Elizabeth Hart, Thomas Farrar, Elizabeth Colson, Benjamin Proctor, Mary de Rich, and Sarah Pease. For a list of accusers and accused see Enders A. Robinson, *The Devil Discovered: Salem Witchcraft, 1692* (New York: Hippocrene Books, 1991), 104–8.

40. Putnam descendants included Isaac, Asahel, Hiram, and William Chadwick Perry, as well as Betsy Taylor Putnam.

41. Those the Putnams accused included the following: Martha Cory, Sarah Good, Sarah Osbourne, Tituba, Rebecca Nurse, Dorcas Good, Corey Giles, Bridget Bishop, Abigail Hobbs, Mary Warren, William Hobbs, Deliverance Hobbs, Nehemiah Abbot Jr., Mary Easty, Sarah Wildes, Edward Bishop Jr., Sarah Bishop, Mary Black, Mary English, Philip English, Lydia Dustin, Susannah Martin, Dorcas Hoar, Sarah Morrell, George Burroughts, Sarah Dustin, Bethia Carter, Bethia Carter Jr., Ann Sears, George Jacobs Sr., Margaret Jacobs, Daniel Andrew, George Jacobs Jr., Rebecca Jacobs, Sarah Buckley, Mary Whittredge, Elizabeth Hart, Thomas Farrar, Elizabeth Colson, Sarah Proctor, Sarah Bassett, Susannah Roots, Elizabeth Cary, Elizabeth Paine, Elizabeth Fosdick, Mary Ireson, Margaret Hawkes, and Candy. See Robinson, *Devil Discovered*, 104–8.

42. LDS descendants of Rebecca Nurse included Meritable Sawyer, Vilate Stockwell, Betsy Taylor Putnam, and Harrison Joseph Burgess.

43. Robinson, *Devil Discovered*, 150–52.

44. Quoted in Sally Smith Booth, *The Witches of Early America* (New York: Hastings House, 1975), 164.

45. The Proctors were ancestors of Lydia and Electa Chamberlain.

46. Quoted in Boyer and Nissenbaum, *Salem Possessed*, 102.

47. Godbeer, *Devil's Dominion*, 217.

48. Quoted in ibid., 206.

49. Henry Rust was also an ancestor of Nancy Kingsbury. His life is outlined in Rust, *Record of the Rust Family*, 1–13.

50. There was a 1669 incident in Andover involving a Goodman or Goody Rust in connection with one John Godfrey, who was accused of appearing in two places simultaneously. He was said to have been both in Ipswich and in the home of Goody Rust in Andover at the same time. See Demos, *Entertaining Satan*, 48–49.

51. Quoted in ibid., 20.

52. Rust Genealogical Data File, 2003.

53. William Nelson Gemmill, *The Salem Witch Trials* (Chicago: A. C. McClurg, 1924), 185–88.

54. His confession (ibid., 186) reads as follows:

> I used, when any creature came into my field, to bid the devil take it; and when I was a young man I could make all my cattell come round about and follow me.
>
> Once I saw some catts together with the appearance of a man who called himself "A Prince of the Air," and he promised me I should be a captain if I would honor him, which I promised to do. The reason I was discontented was because I was in love with a maid named Barker who slighted my love. The first appearance of the catt was behind Captain Bradstreet's house. The next week a black man appeared in the day time in the same place and called himself, "Prince and Lord," and told me I must worship him, and said I should never want for anything. And whenever after that I went to prayer in my family the devil was angry. I signed his book buy making a mark like a square with a black pen which the devil brought to me.
>
> I told the devil I would serve him until I was fifty years old. The first person that I afflicted was Martha Sprague, and the devil put me up to it. I did it by pinching my

coat and buttons when I was angry. I was baptized by the black man in Shaw's River alone, and was dypt all over.

55. Puritans did not dip but sprinkled.

56. Mary Walcott was an ancestor of Mary Mott, Hiram Perry, and William Chadwick Perry, while Mary Warren's father was a direct-line ancestor of LDS convert Lewis Abbott.

57. Dorothy Eames was an ancestor of LDS convert Mary Bailey.

58. Gemmill, *Salem Witch Trials,* 185.

59. Quoted in Robinson, *Devil Discovered,* 226.

60. Godbeer, *Devil's Dominion,* 242.

61. Robinson, *Devil Discovered,* 265–66. Mercy Beamsley was the second wife of Andrew Peters and through him a direct-line ancestor of William Walker Rust. Andrew's sister, Elizabeth Peters, was the wife of John Sadie, the father of John Sadie Jr.

62. Abraham Perkins was the brother of Isaac Perkins, ancestor of Mary Thurston Rand (the wife of William Walker Rust) and Daniel Sanborn Miles.

63. Mary Perkins Bradbury was an ancestor of Abigail Glidden.

64. Robinson, *Devil Discovered,* 266.

65. Most geneological accounts list his wife as Hannah Rust, but this is a mistake. For an account of Mary's relationship with Daniel Ringe Jr. see Rust, *Record of the Rust Family,* 18–19.

66. William Walker Rust's direct line does not run through Mary but through her brother, John Rust.

67. The Perkins family were ancestors of Daniel Sanborn Miles; Mary Thurston Rand; Elizabeth Towne; Alvah Lewis, John Harvey, and William Plumber Tippets. Thomas Perkins married Phoebe Gould; they were forbears of Elizabeth Towne. Phoebe's sister, Priscilla, married John Wildes, and they were direct-line ancestors of LDS converts Clarrisa, Levi Ward, Sr., Soloman, and Thomas Hancock Jr.; as well as Amy Ward.

68. Boyer and Nissenbaum, *Salem Possessed,* 12.

69. Robinson, *Devil Discovered,* 296.

70. Many ancestors of Joseph Smith Jr. were actively involved in these aspects of the witchcraft hysteria, both as accusers and accused. John Gould was Joseph Smith Sr.'s great-grandfather.

71. Boyer and Nissenbaum, *Salem Possessed,* 203–6; Godbeer, *Devil's Dominion,* 191.

72. Boyer and Nissenbaum, *Salem Possessed,* 5.

Chapter 11: Generational Connections

1. See Jon Butler, *Becoming America: The Revolution before 1776* (Cambridge, Mass.: Harvard University Press, 2000); and *Awash in a Sea of Faith.*

2. Pestana, "Sectarianism," 230–79.

3. Ethel R. Jensen, *Beneath the Casing Rock: The George Smith Rust Family* (Provo, Utah: Stevenson's Genealogical Center, 1981), 1–3.

4. They were John Howland, his wife, Elizabeth Tillie (Tilley), and her parents, John Tillie and Joan Hurst, as well as Samuel Fuller and his parents, Edward Fuller and his wife.

5. John Mack married the niece of Rogerenes Samuel and Bathsheba Fox. Lucy Mack's

uncle, Elisha Mack, also married into a family connected to the Rogerenes. His son Ebenezer, through whom Lucy's line runs, belonged to the Open-Communion Baptist Church in Lyme. See Brooke, *Refiner's Fire,* 85.

6. Jonathan Parsons, "Account of the Revival at Lyme," in *The Great Awakening: Documents Illustrating the Crisis and Its Consequences,* ed. Alan Heimert and Perry Miller (Indianapolis: Bobbs-Merrill, 1967), 190.

7. Captain Samuel Brocklebank and Sargeant John Palmer were LDS ancestors who distinguished themselves in the militia. Brocklebank was a selectman and held other civic offices, and he was a deacon of the Rowley Church. William Stickney Jr. was a strong member of the church in both Boston and Rowley, while Andrew Hidden would leave a large Rowley progeny. For accounts of these people see Blodgette and Jewett, *Rowley, Massachusetts.*

8. According to Byron Marchant, the LDS ancestral records are incorrect because Robert Smith actually married Rebecka Keas rather than Mary French. See Byron Marchant, *Mormon Roots* (Salt Lake City: Metamorphosis, 1994), 5.

9. Brooke, *Refiner's Fire,* 74; Hall, "World of Wonders," 15–16.

10. Brooke, *Refiner's Fire,* 65; D. Hill, *Joseph Smith,* 16.

11. In a 1668 court-mandated survey, Topsfield recorded no illiterates. See Hall, "World of Wonders," 34.

12. Paul Boyer and Stephen Nissenbaum, eds., *The Salem Witchcraft Papers: Verbatim Transcripts of the Legal Documents of the Salem Witchcraft Outbreak of 1692* (New York: De Capo, 1977), 3:301–2.

13. Robinson, *Devil Discovered,* 295.

14. Ibid., 296.

15. Hall, "World of Wonders," 159.

16. Brooke, *Refiner's Fire,* 107.

17. Ibid., 71, 76.

18. H. S. Stout, "Great Awakening," in *Dictionary of Christianity in America,* ed. Daniel G. Reid (Downers Grove, Ill.: Intervarsity Press, 1990), 495.

19. Marini, *Radical Sects,* 13.

20. Jonathan Edwards restricted his "harvest of souls" mainly to the Northampton, Massachusetts, area, though his writings penetrated every corner of Puritan New England. James Davenport and Benjamin Pomeroy conducted their evangelistic travels in southern New England and never ventured north of Boston.

21. Annetta Gertrude Dresser, *The Philosophy of P. P. Quimby* (Boston: Builders Press, Church of the Truth, 1895), 6–8.

22. Brooke, *Refiner's Fire,* 67.

23. D. Hill, *Joseph Smith,* 16.

24. Reprinted in Mary Audentia Smith Anderson, *Ancestry and Posterity of Joseph Smith and Emma Hale, with Little Sketches of Their Immigrant Ancestors, All of Whom Came to America between the Years 1620 and 1685, and Settled in the States of Massachusetts and Connecticut* (Independence, Mo.: Privately printed, 1929).

25. D. Hill, *Joseph Smith,* 21.

26. Marini, *Radical Sects,* 12.

27. Ibid., 68–69.

28. At least 45 fifth-generation ancestors of LDS converts were born in the village of Gloucester, including William Sargent Jr., an ancestor of LDS converts John Farnum, Abram, Clarissa, and Olive Boynton. He was also an ancestor of Universalist Winthrop Sargent. Universalists Isaac Elwell, Abraham Sawyer, Hannah Tucker, and John Somes were descendants of early colonialists who were also ancestors of LDS converts.

29. Bushman, *Joseph Smith,* 27–28.

30. D. Hill, *Joseph Smith,* 22.

31. These sentiments are found in a letter Asael wrote to his friend, the town clerk in Topsfield, in 1796. See ibid., 21–22.

32. For a fuller account of the family, see Bushman, *Joseph Smith.*

33. Quoted in Lucy Smith, "Joseph Smith, the Prophet and His Progenitors for Many Generations," chap. 14, p. 1, <http://www.centerplace.org/history/misc/jsp.htm> (2003).

34. A lone early Massachusetts ancestor was Alan Breed, who was one of the earliest settlers of Lynn. Breed's Hill in Charleston, where the battle of Bunker Hill was fought, took its name from him. See Alonzo Lewis and James R. Newhall, *History of Lynn, Essex County, Massachusetts* (Boston: John L. Shorey, 1865), 115.

35. Mary Lou Madsen Nichols, "History of the Ezekiel Brown Family," unpublished book obtained from a great-great-granddaughter, Mary Lou Madsen Nichols, who lives in Molalla, Oregon.

36. Ibid.

37. Adams, *Antinomianism in the Colony,* 339–40; Keith Thomas, *Religion and the Decline of Magic* (New York: Scribner, 1971), 135.

38. Backus, *History of New England,* 1:322; for the order see Wade C. Wightman, *The Wightman Heritage* (Baltimore: Gateway, 1990), 11.

39. Quoted in Wightman, *Wightman Heritage,* 11.

40. John Wightman was a direct-line ancestor of early LDS converts Nancy Case, Catharine Slauson, and Lillis Ballou.

41. David Benedict, *A General History of the Baptist Denomination in America,* 2 vols. (Freeport, N.Y.: Books for Libraries, 1813), 1:522.

42. The Williams, Holmes, and Westcott connections have been outlined above. John Sayles was an ancestor of early LDS convert Catharine Slauson and an 1836 convert, Erastus Wightman.

43. Backus, *History of New England,* 2:516.

44. Brooke, *Refiner's Fire,* 79–81.

45. Marini, *Radical Sects,* 18.

46. Mary Hewitt Mitchell, "The Great Awakening and Other Revivals in the Religious Life of Connectucut," in *Tercentenary Commission of the State of Connecticut: Committee on Historical Publications* (New Haven: Yale University Press, 1934), 28.

47. Ibid.

48. Stanley Grenz, *Isaac Backus: Puritan and Baptist,* NABPR Dissertation Series, no. 4 (Macon, Ga.: Mercer University Press, 1983), 1–2.

49. C. C. Goen, *Revivalism and Separatism in New England: 1740–1800* (New Haven: Yale University Press, 1962), 84–85.

50. The original baptism date is not found in the LDS Church records, some of which were lost, though Charles Billings notes that they were baptized in 1834 along with his wife

Mary Ann Dixon and Jane Elizabeth's husband, Christopher Flintoff Dixon, who was Mary Ann's brother. See "The Utah Wightman's and Their Origins," at <http://www.concentric.net/ssbray/wightman.htm> (summer, 2000).

51. See A. Taylor, "Free Seekers."

Chapter 12: Ancestors of the American Religions

1. Butler, *Becoming America,* 1–7.
2. Brooke, *Refiner's Fire,* 38.
3. Butler, *Awash in a Sea of Faith,* 2.
4. See for example Bushman, *From Puritan to Yankee.*
5. See Lucas, *Valley of Discord;* and Bushman, *From Puritan to Yankee.*
6. Lovejoy, *Religious Enthusiasm,* 114–15.
7. Dresser, *Philosophy of Quimby,* 13.
8. Ahlstrom, *Religious History of the American People,* 1021–23.
9. Mary Baker Eddy, *Science and Health with Key to the Scriptures* (Boston: First Church of Christ Scientist, 1875), 135.
10. Kenneth L. Cannon II, "Brigham Bicknell Young, Musical Christian Scientist," *Utah Historical Quarterly* 50, no. 2 (1982): 124–38. No historical LDS connection with Edward A. Kimball has been found, even though the same name is associated with prominent Mormons.
11. While the LDS Web site FamilySearch, <http://familysearch.org>, was usually sufficient to trace Mormon ancestry, it was also necessary to rely on other genealogical sources, such as Ancestry.com, <http://www.ancestry.com>, to identify and trace the ancestors of non-Mormons.
12. A total of 47 birth- and death places of fifth-generation ancestors of Christian Science founders have been identified so far. Only two birthplaces and one death place were not recorded as New England, because they are unknown. In other words, almost all of the fifth generation were born and died in New England. Among the 73 members of the sixth generation, a total of 16 birthplaces were England or Scotland, while 52 were New England, and 5 are unknown. A dramatic shift occurs in the death places, in that 64 of them were in New England, while only 3 were in England and 4 remain unknown.
13. In comparing the sixth-generation Christian Science ancestors with the fifth-generation Mormon ancestors, we find the following common ancestors (with LDS descendants in parentheses): Augusta Simmons (William Pabodie, Elizabeth Alden); Mary Baker Eddy (John Lovejoy, Mary Osgood, Ralph Farnham, Elizabeth Holt, Elizabeth Short, George Abbott); Julius Alphonso Dresser (William Wentworth, Elizabeth Kenney, Duncan Stewart); Annette Seabury Dresser (David Alden); Brigham Bicknell Young (John and Sarah Young, John and Margaret Whitaker, Elizabeth Ham, William Hearle, Joseph Hayden, Hannah Ames, John Goodenow, Mary Axtell, Zachary Maynard, Hannah Goodrich, John Wheeler, Sarah Stearns, Samuel Howe, Martha Bent, Isaac Mixer Jr., Rebecca Garfield, John Death, Mary Peabody, William Goddard, Elizabeth Miles, Simon Stone, Mary Whipple, Samuel Brigham, Elizabeth Howe, Richard Moore, Mary Collins).
14. See Gary Land, ed., *Adventism in America: A History* (Grand Rapids, Mich.: William B. Erdmans, 1986).

15. Godfred T. Anderson, "Sectarianism and Organization: 1846–1864," in *Adventism in America,* ed. Land, 47.

16. Everett N. Dick, "The Millerite Movement: 1830–1845," in *Adventism in America,* ed. Land, 1.

17. Roy G. Graham, *Ellen G. White: Co-Founder of the Seventh-Day Adventist Church* (New York: Peter Lang, 1985), 23.

18. The vision has been described in the following way: "Ellen Harmon saw a company—a people, a church—on the march. And the pathway to be traversed was pictured as a lighted way, lifted high above the world, with a radiant, penetrating light set up at its beginning, whose beams pierced the enveloping darkness clear through to the City of God at the end of the illuminating pathway. This amazing light was declared to be the autumnal true Midnight Cry—of the Seventh-Month Movement—in which all had rejoiced, as they awaited the expected coming of the Lord" (LeRoy Edwin Froom, *Movement of Destiny* [Washington, D.C.: Review and Herald, 1971], 82).

19. Of the 90 sixth-generation birth- and death places that have been identified, a total of 59 birthplaces were in England or Wales, while 14 were in New England, and 17 are unknown. A dramatic shift occurs in the death places, in that 59 were in New England, while only 5 were in England, and 26 remain unknown. Of the 71 members of the fifth generation for whom records have been found, only 16 were born in England, while 41 were born in New England, and 12 are unknown. Only 1 of the fifth-generation ancestors died in England, while 44 died in New England, and the death places of 26 are unknown.

20. William Miller's ancestors included John Leonard, Sarah Heath, Matthew and Elizabeth Beckwith, Henry Burt, Eulalia March, Nathaniel Phelps, Elizabeth Copley, John Stebbins, Abigail Bartlett, Alexander Edwards, Sarah Baldwin, Isaac Sheldon, Mary Woodford, John Warner, Priscilla Symonds, Richard Montague, and Abigail Downing. Joseph Bates's ancestors included Thomas Nye, Agnes Rye, Thomas Tupper, and Katharine Gator. Ellen Gould Harmon's ancestors included William Roberts, Christian Remick, and Hannah Foster. John Harvey Kellogg's ancestors included Robert Boltwood, Mary Gernor, William Lewis, Mary Hopkins, Samuel Moody, and Sarah Deming.

21. B. W. Ball, *The English Connection: The Puritan Roots of Seventh-Day Adventist Belief* (Cambridge, Eng.: James Clarke, 1981).

22. M. James Penton, *Apocalypse Delayed: The Story of Jehovah's Witnesses,* 2d ed. (Toronto: University of Toronto Press, 1997), 15.

23. Ibid., 62–64.

24. See Billy Kennedy, *Faith and Freedom: The Scots-Irish in America* (Greenville, N.C.: Ambassador, 1999).

25. Armstrong and Armstrong, *Indomitable Baptists,* 165.

26. Ronald Knox, *Enthusiasm: A Chapter in the History of Religion* (New York: Oxford University Press, 1950).

27. See Millet, *History of the Baptists.*

28. Roger Finke and Rodney Stark, *The Churching of America, 1776–1990* (New Brunswick, N.J.: Rutgers University Press, 2000), 174–75.

29. Bloom, *American Religion,* 15–17, 31.

30. Ibid., 127.

Index

VAL D. RUST is a professor of education at the University of California at Los Angeles and the author of *Toward Education for the Twenty-first Century* (1997) and other works.

The University of Illinois Press
is a founding member of the
Association of American University Presses.

University of Illinois Press
1325 South Oak Street
Champaign, IL 61820-6903
www.press.uillinois.edu